COMPLETE RESOURCE BOOK

Searchlights

The all-age resource for

Common Worship

Year B

David Adam

kevin mayhew

First published in 2005 by

KEVIN MAYHEW LTD
Buxhall, Stowmarket, Suffolk, IP14 3BW
E-mail: info@kevinmayhewltd.com
Web: www.kevinmayhew.com

9 8 7 6 5 4 3 2 1 0

ISBN 1 84417 427 1
Catalogue No 1500816

Cover design by Angela Selfe
Edited and typeset by Katherine Laidler

Printed in Great Britain

Contents

Introduction

Searchlights is as much as about God's search for us as our search for God. God seeks to meet us through his creation, through each other, through our experiences, as well as through Scripture and tradition. *Searchlights* seeks to share in the exciting discovery that God actually looks for us and wants contact with us. God, like the shepherd in the parable, seeks after that which is lost until he finds it (Luke 15:3-7). It is wonderful to discover that if we turn towards God – what the Bible calls repentance – we find he runs almost with an indecent haste to meet us in love and forgiveness (see Luke 15:11-32). In using *Searchlights* we must let this seeking God find us and give himself to us.

Searchlights is also about our probing the darkness and uncertainty of our lives to discover the light and the sureness of God. We are to seek God through the regular reading of the Scriptures, through worship in church, through meeting together and through our day-to-day experiences of life. We may be mature in years and yet a child in our faith. Sometimes a new awareness will come as fresh to us as it would to an infant. Sometimes the lesson for the children may speak stronger than thoughts set out for the adults. If so, let us use that and let it speak to us. The light we search for is the Light of God.

Each Sunday is based on Common Worship and the readings set for the day. Year A will mainly use St Matthew's Gospel, Year B will use St Mark, and Year C will use St Luke. St John's Gospel is used throughout the three years to enrich the season or the passages being used. I have focused mainly on the Gospel readings, trying to draw out various aspects to meet the needs of different stages of life. My overall aim is to show that God seeks each of us and desires to speak to us and through us. The difficult task for all who lead worship is to keep a freshness and a liveliness that can be so easily lost; along with this is a need for the Gospel to relate to our present situation. Remember, God is never boring – by his very nature God cannot be boring; we should not present or preach dullness in his name! Though my overall aim is to come before God and to bring others into the awareness of his presence and love, I have tried to keep these other aims within my sights.

Different age groups need a different approach and things that relate to their experience and ability. Yet I have, as far as possible, kept all groups within the setting of the lectionary readings and season. There are separate lessons for children and young people of each age group to help them to grow in the faith. Their age-related teaching and worship aim to bring them gradually into the fuller worship of the whole church. On major festivals it is good that the whole church worships together and shares with each other. The aim is not just to give children or adults facts about what we believe but rather to introduce them to the living and loving Lord.

Let all the material be seen as flexible. If you are inspired by a children's lesson or the thought for the week, use that. Let the heart be touched by God; use all your senses in proclaiming his presence and his power.

Draw near to God, and he will draw near to you.
James 4:8

David Adam

How to use this book

What you are to use on the Sunday should be prayed over and pondered from the Monday to the Saturday. Use the set readings for your Bible study and meditation time throughout the week leading to the Sunday. All who are called to teach, preach or lead study groups need to know that their aim is to introduce people to the God whom they know and not to provide a Sunday lecture or lesson. We need to take time to discern what God wants us to say and how we are to do it. Pray, prepare, ponder the words before you seek to present them to others.

Each week is set out as follows:

Aim

It is important to make sure that you focus on what is to be taught. Above all, be sure that your focus is on the Presence and love. You may like to print the aim of the week in any handout or magazine that your church has. If you carry the aim around with you during the week, it often draws other events into focus which you can then relate to others.

Preparation

This is over and above your personal preparation and relates to what the aim is seeking to convey. It also involves seeing that you have the necessary material before the Sunday arrives.

Opening activity

This is an opportunity to show that worship is not just within formal settings and services. It also seeks to attract attention to the issues of the week. The more people who are involved in the activities, the better. Sometimes, if the whole church cannot do the activity, it can be transferred to one of the groups of young people.

Opening prayer

Though this is to focus the mind on the issues of the Sunday, it obviously also helps us to turn our hearts and minds to the ever-present God.

Opening song

This ought to relate to the theme of the day. Sometimes it is good for it to be sung by an individual and for the congregation to sit quietly. If it is a new song, let the musicians play it over two or three times before worship begins.

Readings

It is good to have these printed in the monthly magazine or pew leaflet saying what is to come next week. On the day, if you have a handout, try and include the readings in full. It is important that all who read are audible; if necessary, rehearse the readers. Encourage everyone to read the Scriptures and think about them at home and before coming to church, as this enriches the whole church. Where possible, it is good to use more than one voice for the readings and to include a dramatic presentation. Let there be silences after each reading.

I have used the New Revised Standard Version of the Bible.

As far as the children are concerned, separate and illustrated Bible stories, such as those published by Lion, are a good starting point. Once children can read, the International Children's Bible (New Century Version) is suitable for young readers. There is a helpful dictionary, pictures and maps to go with this version. New Century also produce The Youth Bible for the older ones.

Thought for the day

This is meant to touch the heart and the will as well as the mind. If you are using the thought for the day, do spend a good deal of time with it the week before. This can also be used as preparation for those who are teaching the young people. The thought is meant to lead to some sort of action or reaction.

Question time

The questions are useful for a study group or those who are seeking to teach and preach. Beware of over-analysis and much talk. Make sure you speak to God more than you talk about him.

Illustration

The illustration is meant to go with the thought for the day but can often be used in one of the groups. Find illustrations from your locality that relate to what is going on and which throw a light on the Scripture passages or are enlightened by these passages. Remember visual aids often speak more directly than words, as does your own way of life.

Intercessions

It is good to start by telling the congregation the response for the prayers and then keep a short silence before the prayers begin. After each section keep a short silence. I have started the intercessions with an act of praise or thanksgiving to God rather than plunging straight in. It helps to give people time to focus their thoughts and their attention on the ever-present God. Sometimes a piece of music playing gently in the background during the intercessions or someone playing a single instrument can create the right feeling. A variety of voices, people, and places around the church for the intercessions are good. Again, make sure they are audible.

Memory verse

For many people learning verses is out of fashion. I find that learning by heart (not just the mind) helps us to store up a treasure we can use in times of dryness or doubt. The verse is used to strengthen our faith and often it is an affirmation of what we believe.

Suggested music

Do not be afraid to use recorded music. Have a variety of instruments and allow children to take part in simple playing. The organ is not always the ideal instrument for setting the scene or leading the people. Remember music is important to people and often helps to set the atmosphere and get into the right frame of mind. Music can be used to set a feeling of calm and to give people a space to express themselves. Involve as many people in the musical presentation as is possible or practical. Remember, young children love making and playing instruments.

The main sources of music I have used are:

Hymns and Songs for Assembly (Kevin Mayhew, 2002)

Hymns Old and New: One Church, One Faith, One Lord (Kevin Mayhew, 2004)

Kidsource (Kevin Mayhew, 2002)

New Hymns and Worship Songs (Kevin Mayhew, 2000)

The Children's Hymn Book (Kevin Mayhew, 1997)

The Source (Kevin Mayhew, 2002)

Candles, Lamps and Torches each have their own aims, teaching, activities and songs. The names for these groups imply the receiving of light and the giving out and handing on of light.

CANDLES – 3-5 year olds

This group especially needs to be made to feel at home in church, to be welcomed and accepted. There is need for much play and song and a lot of adult attention. It is good to involve young parents with this group as helpers; they often learn as much as the children. It is important that the feeling given to the children is that they are loved and cared for by God who is ever with them. Parents should be encouraged to see what their child is doing and to pray with them each week.

LAMPS – 6-10 year olds

This is an age range of greatly varying abilities, so it may be necessary to split the group into two and use the teaching and activities according to their ability. This age group is very ready to adventure and stretch themselves. Let what they do help to extend their awareness and vision of each other, of what is around them and of their God. Some at least will enjoy reading out aloud and many will like a little drama; seek to use this potential as much as possible.

TORCHES – 11 plus

This is the group that the church finds hardest to keep. There is a feeling they have heard it all and know it all! Help them to discover that church can be fun and yet at the same time bring before them the depths of life and faith that are to be discovered, adventured and enjoyed. These young people are journeying towards adult life and cannot be treated just as children. Respect their growing pains and their problems: if possible, allow any of them to talk freely to you. It is important to have more than one adult present in our dealings with these young people. An additional helper is always useful. Encourage this group to become part of the church congregation as often as possible. It is best if they have specific tasks that are theirs to do within the main body of the church. Readers, intercessors, musicians and singers, future teachers and priests can come from this group. Remember you are dealing with the Church of today and tomorrow in these young people. Strengthen their faith and support them in their searching.

ADVENT
First Sunday of Advent

Aim
To make people more aware that Christ comes to them today.

Preparation
Make an Advent wreath with four candles in a circle and a central candle for Jesus.

Opening activity
Explain the reason for an Advent wreath. Ask a relay team to pass on the light from the back of the church to the Advent candle. Let one of the younger members light the Advent candle.

Opening prayer
When we close our eyes in prayer,
come, Lord Jesus.
When we give our hearts to you,
come, Lord Jesus.
When we call upon your name,
come, Lord Jesus.
When we seek to work for you,
come, Lord Jesus.
When we are afraid of the dark,
come, Lord Jesus.

Opening song
Let him find us waiting when he comes.
Let him find us waiting when he comes.
Let him find us ready,
with a heart that's steady.
Let him find us waiting when he comes.

(To the tune of 'She'll be coming round the mountain')

Readings
Isaiah 64:1-9
Psalm 80:1-7,17-19
1 Corinthians 1:3-9
Mark 13:24-37

Thought for the day
Happy New Year! This is the first Sunday in the Church Year. We celebrate the Church's New Year by lighting a candle. It is called an Advent candle. Advent is about the coming of God into the world.

Isaiah sees God's coming as something that is frightening, because we have not been looking for our God; in fact, we have been ignoring him. God has been coming to us and we have not let him into our lives. But because God has made us and loves us, he will have mercy upon us. We may annoy our parents, we may ignore them, but they still continue to love us and care for us. We are not alone in the world; if we seek God he comes to us.

Psalm 80 has the refrain 'Show us the light of your countenance and we shall be saved.' We ask the hide-and-seek God to reveal himself to us. Let us learn to look for God in our everyday life.

God has shown himself to us in the face of Jesus Christ. In Jesus we have a new hope, for God's grace – that is the free gift of himself – has been given to us in Christ Jesus. This is a gift to each of us. Will we unwrap this gift and make it ours, that he may enrich us?

The Gospel tells us not to put off, or be put off, for the Son of Man comes. The times may be full of trouble and distress, yet he still comes to us. We should look for signs of his coming and of his presence in our lives.

We have been left in charge of this world, each with our own responsibility, each with our own work. We are accountable to God. He comes to see how we are dealing with his world. We need to keep alert, that we may be aware of his coming: to be awake and not go around with our eyes closed.

Question time
What does the word Advent mean?

There are three different comings of God: he has come, is come, will come. These relate to the past, the present and the future. Which is the most important to us?

Illustration
It was near Christmas and in the Advent season, and Peter waited for God to come. He prayed every day, 'God, show me your face and I shall be saved.' Peter had tried to live a good life; he was now old and looked forward to the coming of God. He continued to work in his paper shop, where he had worked most of his life. Here he heard all sorts of conversations and met many people. A single mum was telling a friend how she did not have enough money to buy presents for her child. When everyone else had gone, Peter said to her, 'I heard what you said. I have a few toys on the shelves; they are not selling very well, go and pick anything you would like.' She could hardly believe it for there were some wonderful things on the shelves. As she went away with her arms full, Peter was delighted. His reward was her smile.

Later that day, he caught a young lad stealing a magazine from the shelves. He was on the way out with the magazine up his jumper when Peter stopped him. He could have called the police or told the boy's parents. He saw the boy was poor and afraid, and he felt sorry for him. 'If you want a magazine, and have no money, talk with me,' he said. 'Magazines are soon out of date; I can always find one to give you. You must not just help yourself. Take the magazine for free and ask me another time.' The boy's face changed from a look of fear to a beaming smile. He thanked Peter and ran from the shop.

An old man came into the shop and was saying how lonely he was since his wife died. This would be his first Christmas on his own – he was not looking forward to it. Peter said, 'We were expecting a friend to come for

Christmas, and he has said he cannot make it. We have prepared for his coming. Would you come to us instead? We would love to share Christmas with you.' The old man's face lit up in a beautiful smile and he said, 'You have made me feel so wanted, and I would love to come.'

That night Peter prayed his Advent prayer, 'Show me your face and I shall be saved.' In a dream God spoke to him and said, 'Peter, today I came to you, and three times you made me smile. Grace and peace be upon you.'

(Apologies to Tolstoy!)

Intercessions

As we begin another Church Year
let us give thanks to God that he has made us,
that he loves us
and that he comes to us.

O God, you are our Maker:
you give us life, you give us love,
your give us yourself.
Help us to give our lives, our love
and ourselves to you.
Keep us alert and aware of your presence,
that we may meet you each day
and know that you come to us in grace and in love.

Lord, as you come to your Church,
help us to reveal your glory.
Grant that we may show your grace
and your goodness in our lives.
We thank you for the grace and goodness
revealed in Jesus Christ
and that we are enriched in him.

We remember churches that are struggling
against the darkness of evil, of opposition, of apathy.
We remember especially
Christians who are being persecuted for their faith.

Silence

Come, Lord Jesus;
come, our Saviour and our God.

As we pray for your world,
we remember those who are seeking
to bring peace and goodwill among all.
We pray for those involved in war or the threat of war.
We think of those caught up in earthquakes,
famine or flood.

Silence

Come, Lord Jesus;
come, our Saviour and our God.

Lord, let your presence be known
in our homes and our actions.
May people be thankful for us
and our care of all that is around us.
We pray that you will show yourself to us
through our loved ones and friends.

Silence

Come, Lord Jesus;
come, our Saviour and our God.

We remember all whose lives are darkened
by pain and distress;
all who are struggling with doubt and despair;
all whose faith is shaken
by what is happening around them.
We pray for members of our community and friends
who are ill at this time.

Silence

Come, Lord Jesus;
come, our Saviour and our God.

God our Father, your grace has been given to us,
in the gift of eternal life and in your abiding presence.
We pray for all who are departed from us,
for friends and loved ones
in the fullness of your eternal kingdom.
We rejoice with them in the gift of life and your love.

Silence

Merciful Father,
accept these prayers
for the sake of your Son,
our Saviour Jesus Christ.
Amen.

Memory verse

Keep awake – for you do not know when the master of the house will come.
Mark 13:35

Suggested music

Thou didst leave thy throne
O come, O come, Emmanuel
Maranatha

CANDLES

Aim

To prepare for the coming of Jesus.

Teaching

This is Advent Sunday and it tells us someone is coming soon. Who is coming? When do we remember that Jesus is coming? Do you know how many Sundays there are in Advent? (Show the Advent Candles or hold up four fingers.) What happens after four Sundays?

When Jesus came, the night was dark. There were stars shining in the sky. If you looked out on the hills you could see shepherds guarding their sheep in case there were wolves or robbers. One young shepherd had to keep the light burning to scare away the darkness and the dangers. He liked to keep a great big fire burning. What do you think he put on the fire?

He put on a big piece of wood, a log – and he threw it on to the fire. He did not get too close because fire burns. Now he watched the sparks fly upwards like bright lights in the dark. They flew higher and higher right up into the sky. Joel – that is his name – watched the sparks rise into the night. He thought that they would go up higher and then go out, but he saw that they were getting brighter. The sky was being filled with light. It wasn't sparks he was watching; it was God's angels of light coming down from heaven. He began to hear them singing. The shepherds were nearly all asleep, they would miss the angels and their song – so Joel woke them up. Wake up! Wake up! The shepherds jumped up for they thought a wolf was coming. But they got a big surprise. Joel pointed upwards and they heard and saw angels in the sky. The angels were singing a beautiful song: 'Glory be to God in the highest and peace on earth.' Then the angels told them Jesus is coming and he is coming to Bethlehem. The shepherds were very excited and all of them wanted to go to Bethlehem and see Jesus.

Activities

We are going to make some shepherds to take into church, and later they will go and see Jesus. (Next week the children will make an angel; the third week, Mary and Joseph; and the fourth week, the baby Jesus and a star.) The figures can be coloured in and stuck to a piece of kitchen roll tube to make them stand. Each child should end up with a nativity group.

We will also colour in one candle to remind us that Jesus is coming and he comes to us.

Prayer

O God, you are always with us, even in the dark.
You come to us because you love us.
As you told the shepherds about Jesus,
help us to learn about his coming and his love for us.
Amen.

Song

Jesus bids us shine

LAMPS

Aim

To show that God looks for us and comes to us.

Activities

I like playing hide and seek. Shall we have a game of hide and seek?

(*After the game*) Now let us look for hidden faces on the sheet. How many can you find? Tick where they are. There should at least be 12. Now add your own face somewhere on the drawing. There is also one candle to be found. Colour it in and make its flame bright.

Teaching

Have you been hiding from God?

We hide from God when we do not speak to him, when we do not say our prayers. God looks for us. He waits for us to speak to him but we keep hidden if we do not speak to him. Sometimes we hide from him because we have done something we know God would not like.

Read Genesis 3:1-9.

In the story of Adam and Eve in the garden, Adam and Eve did what God asked them not to do. He told them they could do lots of things, they could eat lots of things, but they should not eat from the tree in the middle of the garden. Eve was encouraged to look at the fruit from the tree in the middle of the garden by the snake. She saw it was good to look at. It smelt nice and she was sure it would taste nice. So what do you think she did? Yes, she took a bite and she liked it. Then she gave some to Adam. He wasn't sure he should eat it but when she said it tasted good he also ate some. As soon as they had both eaten some they knew they had done something wrong. They knew they had done what God asked them not to do. So they hid from God in the bushes of the garden. God knew they were hiding from him and he called out, 'Where are you?' For a while they still hid from God but they knew he would seek them until he found them, so they came to him. God was sad that they had done what he did not want them to do. He could not let them loose in his garden any more. But he still loved them and promised he would look after them.

Prayer

As the clouds hide the sun,
so often you are hidden from us, O God.
Let us know that you are always there,
you are always with us.
You love us and never leave us.
Amen.

Song

God is love: his the care

TORCHES

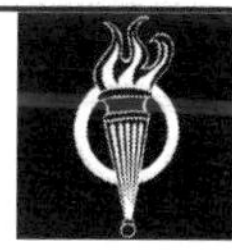

Aim

To show we have to be aware of the coming of God.

Teaching

Get the young people to enjoy this short sketch about getting up and being awake.

Mother Y'up?
Child M'up.

Pause

Mother Y'up?
Child M'up.

Pause

Mother Y'up?
Child M'up.

Pause

Mother Y'up yet?
Child M'up now.

Pause as mother and child come together

Mother You have missed the school bus. Now I will have to take you and I will be late for work. You need to wake up in the morning.

How often do we miss things because we lie in or are asleep?

Sometimes it would seem we are still asleep on our way to school or at school because we are not aware of what is going on around us. What are the lovely things we would miss if we did not open our eyes and ears?

Do you notice the sunshine or the birdsong? Are you in such a rush that you are not aware of anything except that you are late?

If a driver is unaware of what is around him, he becomes a danger to other drivers on the road. He has to be aware of other drivers, of cyclists and pedestrians. What else must he be aware of?

When we are awake we have to keep our senses well-tuned. Which sense do we need to use most in a classroom? Which senses do we use when we are with friends at a mealtime?

How do we know that God comes to us?

Activity

Here are illustrations of people unaware of what they are doing. Mark what is wrong. Colour in the quotation from Mark 13:37.

Prayer

Awaken us, O God, to your coming.
Open our eyes that we may see you.
Open our ears that we may hear you.
Open our lips that we may talk about you.
Touch our hearts that we may love you.
Come, Lord, come among us.
Amen.

Song

Be still and know that I am God

Second Sunday of Advent

Aim

To show we need to prepare for the coming of our Lord.

Preparation

Before most people come in get the children to lay sheets of black card randomly on the floor, but not blocking the whole of the way to the seats. Put up a notice at the door: PLEASE DO NOT STAND ON THE BLACK HOLES.

Opening activity

Explain that in our world black holes are dangerous – they can gobble people up. Blindfold one or two children and have others lead them past the black holes but avoiding them. Then let one child say, 'I know a better way', and let him remove all the black holes. Then the child could say, 'Now your journey is easier.'

Let us renew the promises made for us in baptism.

Opening prayer

Lord Jesus, help us to prepare for your coming to us.
Let us make room in our lives
and not put any obstacles in your path,
that we may know your love and your glory.
Amen.

Opening song

Jesus, come among us
with your glorious light.
Jesus, come among us;
help us do what's right.

Jesus, come among us,
come now and every day.
Jesus, come among us;
hear us as we pray.

(Tune: *Caswall*, 'Glory be to Jesus')

Readings

Isaiah 40:1-11
Psalm 85:1-2, 8-13.
2 Peter 3:8-15a
Mark 1:1-8

Thought for the day

Isaiah is sure that our God is coming to us and that we need to prepare. He tells us of the messenger that will go before his coming to see all is ready. In the olden days, when travel was difficult and dangerous, if a king was on a journey someone was sent ahead to see if the road was fit for a king. The aim was to remove obstacles in the road, to fill in holes and to level off bumps: rough places were made smooth. Then they had to make sure the king would get a good reception, that accommodation was prepared, making sure there was room for the king and he would be welcome. Once everything was ready the king would come in all his glory.

Today's psalm asks, 'Show us your steadfast love, O Lord, and grant us your salvation . . . that his glory may dwell in our land.'

St Peter is also sure that the Lord will come, and asks what sort of person you will be when he comes. Will you be a holy and a godly person? Do not put things off, for you do not know when the Lord will come. Strive to be found at peace.

St Mark is sure that Jesus is the Promised One and that John the Baptist is the messenger to prepare his way. John says to the people, 'Turn around; you are going the wrong way. You will not be ready for God if you go on like this. Repent and be cleansed. Say sorry for the wrong you have done and turn to God.'

Question time

The count down to Christmas has begun. This is the Second Sunday in Advent. How many more Sundays before Christmas? How many more days?

Are you prepared for Christmas, for the coming of Jesus?

Illustration

The Sunday before the beginning of Advent used to be called 'Stir up Sunday' for two reasons. The prayer for the Sunday begins, 'Stir up, O Lord, the wills of your faithful people'; a wonderful prayer that wants us to 'bring forth the fruits of good works'. It is by what we do that we will be known, so it is important that our works are good, important that we do something.

Traditionally 'Stir up Sunday' was also the time when the Christmas cake was made. Mother would get all the ingredients – the flour, the fruit, the eggs – and mix them together. Everyone in the house had a stir of the cake before it went into the oven. All this was part of the preparations before Christmas.

We now often spend weeks preparing for this one day. How much time do we spend preparing for the coming of God to us?

If someone is coming to stay, we will make sure there is room for them, that we have time for them, that we will give them some attention. Our God comes and seeks room in our lives; he wants us to be aware of him, for us to give him some of our time and attention.

Are you prepared for this?

Intercessions

We pray that we and your whole Church
may be prepared for your coming to us.
When you come
may you find us a holy and a godly people;
may you find us striving for peace
and looking forward to your glory.

Silence

Lord, change us:
and we shall be changed.

We remember today all who are being baptised.
We pray for the parents and the Godparents.

We come with all who are sorry for their sins
and want to lead a new life;
with all who seek forgiveness and cleansing.

Silence

Lord, change us:
and we shall be changed.

We remember all who are striving for peace.
Bless the leaders of nations and peacekeeping forces.
Guide the United Nations and the work of relief agencies.
May we strive for justice and freedom for all peoples.

Silence

Lord, change us:
and we shall be changed.

Lord, we ask that our homes
may be places of welcome, love and harmony.
May we make room for you in our lives and our work.

Silence

Lord, change us:
and we shall be changed.

We come before you with all who are struggling:
those who are ill at home or in hospital;
the world poor, the oppressed
and all who suffer from violence or rejection.
We ask that we may know your healing presence.

Silence

Lord, change us:
and we shall be changed.

And we remember before you all who have died,
our friends and loved ones departed
and all your saints.

Silence

Merciful Father,
accept these prayers
for the sake of your Son,
our Saviour Jesus Christ.
Amen.

Memory verse

Prepare the way of the Lord, make his paths straight.
Mark 1:3

Suggested music

On Jordan's bank the Baptist's cry
Make me a channel of your peace
Come and praise the Lord our King

CANDLES

Aim

To prepare for the coming of Jesus.

Teaching

Have you ever been sent with a message or been asked to go somewhere and get something? It is important that messengers carry the right message and don't get it wrong. If you were sent to the kitchen for a biscuit and brought back some soap, it would be wrong.

God has often sent messages to people and he makes sure they get the right message. God calls his messengers 'angels'.

Once, long ago, God sent a messenger – one of his angels – to a little town called Nazareth, to the house of a young woman called Mary. The angel knew exactly which house to go to. Mary had been outside in the garden working, looking after plants. Now she was having a quiet time in the house, waiting until her mother came home. Suddenly she saw God's messenger in the room. The door was open and she did not hear the messenger knock or come in, but suddenly he was there. Mary was frightened and hid her eyes. But the angel said to her, 'Do not be afraid, Mary. I come from God and God is very pleased with you. God knows that you love him and try to do what he wants. He now wants you to do something special; he wants you to have a baby that you will call Jesus.'

Mary was not really sure what the angel meant and asked him. Meanwhile, God and the messenger waited for her answer. (If possible, show a picture of Mary with the angel.) The angel told Mary that God would make it happen and that she would be the mother of Jesus.

Mary said, 'I will do what God wants.' The angel was very happy and went back to God to say he had delivered the message. And all the angels rejoiced.

Activity

We are going to pass on a message from one to another. I will whisper it and pass it on. 'God loves you.' See if we get it right.

We will colour in an angel for our Christmas crib – let it be gold and silver, if possible. Do you remember whom the angel came to last week?

How many candles are there to colour in?

Prayer

God, we thank you
that you sent the angel messenger to Mary
and that she let Jesus be born into the world.
We will try to do what you want us to do
because we know that you love us.
Amen.

Song

Jesus bids us shine

LAMPS

Aim

To show it does matter what you do.

Teaching

Fred was always naughty. He never listened to what he was told and he was always doing wrong things. He often got lost because he wandered away and had no one to help him. Once he had to be brought home by the police and this made his parents very sad.

Once he was in a special place and he was asked to make a cake. He was told what to put in it but he did not listen. He did not use flour, or fruit or icing. He thought he would use gunpowder and fireworks. He found it very hard to mix them together but he did it. Then he went to the oven and when it was hot enough he put in his cake. He waited and then there was great big BANG. It blew the oven to pieces and brought the house down; all his toys and things were destroyed. Fred flew into the air and landed with a BANG. At that moment he fell out of bed and woke up. It had been a terrible dream. When his mother asked him later that day to help her make a cake, he was ever so careful and did exactly what she asked him to do. From now on he would really try to do as he was told.

John the Baptist told people to repent – to be sorry for doing wrong. They were going the wrong way and had to turn around.

How can we learn to do what is right? Listen. Obey. Do what we are asked.

Activity

Act out the story of the Prodigal Son (Luke 15:11-24). Make them see how the son went the wrong way and how he had to turn around.

Look at the pictures on the sheet and see how many people are doing wrong things.

Prayer

God, we thank you that you love us always.
When we are sorry
you forgive us what we have done wrong
and you welcome us with love.
God, help us to do what you would like us to do
and to be the children you would like us to be.
Amen.

Song

Father, we adore you

TORCHES

Aim

To explore the meaning of Baptism.

Teaching

If you are going on a long journey where you have never been before, what do you need to have and know? You need to know where you are going. You need maps and guides, and you need to look at signposts.

Let us look at a map of where we live and work out how to get to somewhere about 40 miles away. (Help the children to understand a map.) It is easier if you can go with someone who has been there before, or if someone goes in front of you showing you the way.

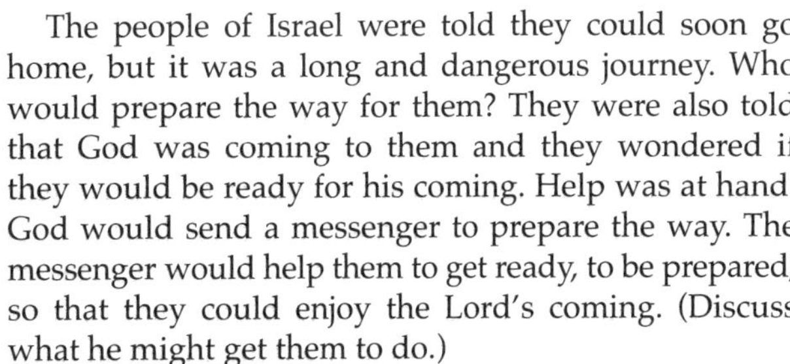

The people of Israel were told they could soon go home, but it was a long and dangerous journey. Who would prepare the way for them? They were also told that God was coming to them and they wondered if they would be ready for his coming. Help was at hand: God would send a messenger to prepare the way. The messenger would help them to get ready, to be prepared, so that they could enjoy the Lord's coming. (Discuss what he might get them to do.)

John lived in the desert by himself for a long time. He often spoke to God and God sent him to tell the people that Jesus was coming. John was God's messenger. John wore clothes made of camel hair and had a leather belt around his waist – just like one of God's messengers of a long time ago.

He started saying to the people, 'Get ready, be prepared, for the Lord is coming soon.' He saw a lot of people were doing wrong things and going down wrong roads, so he said, 'Turn around, repent, you are going the wrong way.' Tell the children that 'repent' means turn around and stop doing bad things. John asked people to come and say sorry for what they had done wrong. He said he would make them clean and ready for the coming of the Lord. To make them clean he had them come and be dipped in the river Jordan until the water went over their heads. This dipping in the river was called baptising. And everyone called John 'the Baptist'.

We were not baptised in the river. Where were we baptised? We were not dipped right under the water. Do you know what happened to you? Three drops of water were poured on to your head: one to tell you God made you and loves you; one to tell you that Jesus comes to you and loves you; one to tell you that the Holy Spirit is with you and loves you.

Activity

At the command, run to a corner marked North, South, East or West. If I say, 'Stop, you are going the wrong way', stop and do not run again until I say the word 'run'. If I say anything without the word 'run', and you run, you will be out. The last person to reach a corner will also be out. If I say, 'Repent', and you are running, you have to turn and go in the opposite direction. For example, if you are going to North, you need turn to the South.

Prayer

God, help us to do what is good
and to walk in the right ways.
When we do wrong
may we turn again to what you want us to do.
Guide us by your presence and protect us with your love,
that we may walk in the way that leads us to you.
Amen.

Song

God is so good

Third Sunday of Advent

Aim

To encourage people to see that Jesus comes in acts of kindness and righteousness.

Preparation

Cut out newspaper headlines of saving acts, rescue missions, healings.

Opening activity

Have a few people read the headlines and after each one let them end with the words:

In every act of healing and love,
the Lord comes.

Opening prayer

O Lord God, you have asked us to share
in your saving acts;
to care for those in need and those who are ill,
to help people come to freedom.
Make us worthy of this calling
and to know that as much as we do it to the least
we do it to you.
Amen.

Opening song

Let him find us caring when he comes.
Let him find us caring when he comes.
Let him find us sharing
and our love declaring.
Let him find us caring when he comes.

(To the tune of 'She'll be coming round the mountain')

Readings

Isaiah 61:1-4, 8-11
Psalm 126 or the Magnificat
1 Thessalonians 5:16-24
John 1:6-8, 19-28

Thought for the day

Jesus chose to speak on this passage from Isaiah and relate it to his ministry. He was the 'anointed one', the Messiah. In his baptism the Spirit of the Lord was seen to descend upon him.

The Lord wants us to share in his mission. We are asked to bring the Good News to the poor – surely everyone who has not heard and received the Good News is poor! We are called to bind up the broken-hearted, to proclaim liberty for captives, and to comfort all who mourn. We must remember the Lord loves justice and hates wrongdoing.

In both the psalm and the Magnificat there is a feeling of the new order beginning, when God's people are freed to do righteous acts.

The writer to the Thessalonians asks us to 'hold fast to that which is good: abstain from every evil'.

Question time

John came to testify to the light of Christ, which has come into the world. Do we see that we are called also to testify to the light of Christ?

Can we be Christ to others and see Christ in others without mistaking ourselves for the Christ?

Illustration

Once upon a time there was a man who went out to sea in a little boat. It was a lovely day and he was enjoying himself. Then the mist suddenly came down. Now he did not know which direction he was going in. He rowed around until he was very tired, then he let himself drift. He did not know that he was drifting towards the rocks. Suddenly he heard a crunch and a scraping. His boat was torn on the rocks and it began to sink. Fortunately he managed to escape on to the rocks. He was now very cold and hungry and he prayed to God to come and rescue him.

Soon a motorboat came by and invited him aboard – but he refused, saying, 'I have help coming.' A little later a fishing boat saw him and tried to persuade him to come off the rock but again he said, 'There is no need to worry I have help on the way.'

That night the man died alone in the cold. He went to heaven and complained to God that he had not come to help. God said, 'I came in a motorboat and you refused my help. I came again in a fishing boat and you still refused my help. You are here today because you did not recognise my help when it came – yet still you are loved.'

Intercessions

Eternal light shine in our hearts,
that our days may be bright with your presence.
May we be aware
of the great things that you have done for us
and rejoice in your salvation.

We remember all who walk in darkness
and do not know the love of God.
We remember those who have never heard the Good News.
We pray that the whole Church may reach out
in mission, in service and in love.
We pray especially for the Church
where it has lost vision or sense of outreach.

Silence

Eternal light,
shine in our hearts.

Remember our world where people are oppressed;
where there is hunger and poverty.
We ask you to strengthen all who work for peace
and to relieve the poor.
At this time we pray especially for . . .
May we do all that we can to help.

Silence

Eternal light,
shine in our hearts.

We give you thanks for our homes and our loved ones,
for the freedom and the peace that is ours.
May we be sensitive to the needs of those around us
and be of help when we can.

Silence

Eternal light,
shine in our hearts.

God give strength and courage to all who are ill,
to those involved in accidents or acts of violence.
We remember those who have lost their freedom
or their homes.
We pray especially for . . .
We give thanks for all who work in hospitals
and for our own doctors.

Silence

Eternal light,
shine in our hearts.

We rejoice that you have freed us
from the slavery of sin and death
and brought us to the glorious liberty
of the children of God.
We rejoice in the gift of eternal life,
and pray for friends and loved ones departed.

Silence

Merciful Father,
accept these prayers
for the sake of your Son,
our Saviour Jesus Christ.
Amen.

Memory verse

My spirit rejoices in God my Saviour.
Luke 1:47

Suggested music

Tell out, my soul
Give me joy in my heart
I, the Lord of sea and sky

CANDLES

Aim

To continue with the Christmas story.

Teaching

Who can remember what we call God's messengers? The messengers were sent to the shepherds and to Mary. (If there is no reply, get them to look at the angels they have made.)

Mary told Joseph how the angel came to her and said that she would have a baby. Joseph wished the angel would come and speak to him. He looked for it all day but it did not come. Then at night, when it was dark and he was asleep, the angel came and spoke to him in a dream. The angel had a message for Joseph: 'Joseph, son of David, I want you to look after Mary and the baby she is going to have. You must call the baby Jesus because he will save his people.' When Joseph woke up he thought about his strange dream. He would look after Mary and call the baby Jesus.

Now Joseph had to get ready to go on a long journey and take Mary with him. They were going to go from Nazareth, where they lived, right down to Bethlehem to have their names written in a book. It was about 76 miles. If we had to go that far we would go by car or by train. Joseph would walk and Mary would walk with him or ride on their donkey. They would have to walk every day for a whole week. They would be very tired. Mary would be especially tired because her baby was soon to be born.

Near the end of the week they went past Jerusalem. There were lots of other people walking and riding camels, horses or donkeys. They had six miles to go and they were very slow because Mary could not go any faster. Joseph looked after her and helped her. At last they could see Bethlehem and they could see the fires in the hillsides where the shepherds were looking after their sheep.

It was now quite dark. Joseph looked up at the stars and said thank you to God that Mary had got safely to Bethlehem; it would be good if her baby was born there.

Activity

We are going to colour in Joseph and Mary and then we will colour in three candles for three Sundays in Advent. Do you know how many more Sundays there are in Advent?

Prayer

God, we thank you for the message of the angels
and for Mary and Joseph.
As we look forward to Christmas
help us to know that Jesus comes to us.
Amen.

Song

Jesus' love is very wonderful

LAMPS

Aim

To discover that Jesus is the Messiah.

Teaching

Show the hallmarks on a piece of silver or gold and explain why they are there. It is to stop people pretending something is silver or gold when it is not. You may like to have three or four pieces that the children can look at, including at least one which has no hallmarks but looks like silver or gold.

When people looked forward to the Messiah – Jesus – coming into the world, they wanted to be sure they had got the right person. They were told certain things:

- He would be born in Bethlehem.
- He would descend from David.
- He would bring the Good News – the Gospel.
- He would mend broken hearts.
- He would set free those who were prisoners.
- He would tell of God's goodness.
- He would comfort the sad.

These are some of the hallmarks of the Messiah and that is how people were to recognise him when he came.

Let us check and see if Jesus could be the Messiah. Does Jesus have all the hallmarks? You may have to show how Jesus frees people from the prison of their illness, like the man from Gadara.

Activity

Look at a map of the Holy Land and draw a line from Nazareth to Bethlehem. See how close it comes to Jerusalem. They would have to go through or past the big city, and six miles further south is Bethlehem. It is 76 miles. How long would it take to walk? What would they take with them? They would take food, water and maybe a tent. Why would they be slower than most travellers?

Prayer

God, we thank you that you sent Jesus
to be our Saviour,
to heal the ill
and to bring joy to the world.
We pray we may be ready to celebrate
his coming into the world.
Amen.

Song

Who's the King of the jungle?

TORCHES

Aim

To share in the joy of the Magnificat.

Teaching

When the angel Gabriel came to Mary and told her she would give birth to Jesus she was very happy. She was going to be the mother of the Son of God. God cared so much for the world. Mary wanted to sing a song of joy. She knew there was a song that Hannah had sung when she left the child Samuel with Eli. (Let the group read 1 Samuel 2:1-5 with a different reader for each verse.)

Now let us look at Mary's song. It is very like Hannah's. Mary was giving thanks because God keeps his promises and he comes to help his people. She knew that she would be remembered for being the mother of the Saviour and that people would call her blessed. Do you know what the initials BVM stand for? The Blessed Virgin Mary. You may like to explore what 'Magnificat' means.

Activity

We have a picture of Mary to colour in. She is giving thanks to God for keeping his promise.

Colour in the words underneath and see if you can learn them. You can tell me what it means for your spirit to rejoice – and why you rejoice in God your Saviour.

Do the wordsearch.

Prayer

God, we rejoice in your greatness
for you are wonderful.
We give thanks that you sent your Son
to be our Saviour.
May we be prepared for his coming to us.
Amen.

Song

Magnificat

Fourth Sunday of Advent

Aim

To show God's kingdom comes when his will is done.

Preparation

Have an Advent candle in each corner of the church, and something to light them.

On a piece of paper have the words:

The Lord is my light and my salvation.
The Lord is here.
His Spirit is with us.

Opening activity

Get groups of children to gather in the corners of the church. Let an adult be with them to light the candle. Starting in the north-east corner, let the adult light the candle and give it to a child. The child will say, 'The Lord is my light and my salvation.' Another child in the group will shout, 'The Lord is here.' Everyone will respond, 'His Spirit is with us.'

Let this be repeated in each corner, followed by the opening prayer.

Opening prayer

Lord Jesus, you come to us as the Light of the World.
Take away from us the darkness
and help us to walk in your light and come to your love.
Amen.

Opening song

We are marching in the light of God

(This is sung as the children walk to their places and the four candles are placed in the Advent wreath.)

Readings

2 Samuel 7:1-11, 16
Magnificat or Psalm 89:1-4, 19-26
Romans 16:25-27
Luke 1:26-38

Thought for the day

David is aware that he lives in a good house and that God's dwelling is only a tent. He wants to build a splendid house for God. It is a wonderful idea but the danger is that we may feel we can only find God in his house. At least with a tent God was travelling with the Israelites: when they moved, God moved with them. God also says to David, 'I have been with you wherever you went.'

God promises David that he will make him a house and a kingdom that will last for ever. God will be ever-present within it.

The love that God showed to David is celebrated in Psalm 89. In the same way Mary praises God for the great things he has done and shall do for ever.

St Paul tells us that this same God is able to strengthen us through Jesus Christ, to whom all glory belongs.

God will not force himself upon us. If we lock him out, he will not break down the doors. If we ignore him, he will still care for us and love us. If we do not obey him, his kingdom cannot come in us. But once we say, 'Here am I; let it be to me according to your word', then the kingdom is come in us. Notice how God and the angel wait upon Mary's response. Without Mary, or someone like her, the Son of God cannot come into the world. When Mary says 'Yes' a new age begins. Let us learn to pray, 'Your kingdom come in us. Your will be done in us.' When we obey the king, his kingdom comes in us.

Question time

Are we aware that God is not restricted to the church but goes with us in all that we do?

Do we seek to allow God's kingdom to come in us by doing his will?

Illustration

Are you ready for Christmas? Have you sent all your cards? Bought presents? Got the food ready? What will you do on Christmas Day? Will you make room for Jesus: make sure Christ is in Christ-mas?

It was Jessie's birthday and she looked forward to it. She lived in an old people's home and had friends around her – but she was invited to her daughter's for her birthday. She would be with the family, including the three children. They made sure there was a nice room ready for her and the house was warm. Her daughter had bought the food she liked. All was ready.

On the first night her daughter had an evening class, the children were out with friends, and her son-in-law decided to go to the pub. On her birthday the children had other things to do and so would be out all day – football, swimming and netball are important. Jessie's son-in-law spent the day in the garage tinkering with his car, and her daughter decided to do some last-minute shopping on her own. Again Jessie was left alone. They had a meal together in the evening, then the children went on the computer and the others watched television. Jessie was glad to go back to the home where people had time to talk to her and give their attention to her.

Will we make time for Jesus on his birthday, or will we be too busy doing other things?

Intercessions

O God, as we prepare for Christmas
may we be ready for your coming to us.
As we make space for friends and relatives
may we make room in our lives for you.
In our daily living let us seek to do your will
and help to bring in your kingdom.

Through the working of the Church,
through obedience to you,
through reaching out in mission,
through the proclaiming of the Gospel,
your kingdom come:
your will be done.

Through our striving for peace,
through our caring for the poor,
through our desire for justice,
through the ways we seek to improve your world,
your kingdom come:
your will be done.

Through our love in our homes,
through our honesty and sensitivity,
through our relationships and friends,
through our hopes and our ambitions,
your kingdom come:
your will be done.

Through the healing of the ill,
through looking after the lonely,
through our compassion and care,
your kingdom come:
your will be done.

We remember especially today
any who have asked for our prayers
or who are in trouble or danger.
We ask that we may share with them
in the fullness of your kingdom.

Silence

Merciful Father,
accept these prayers
for the sake of your Son,
our Saviour Jesus Christ.
Amen.

Memory verse

Here am I, the servant of the Lord; let it be with me according to your word.
Luke 1:38

Suggested music

Thy kingdom come, O God
Come, thou long-expected Jesus
Thou didst leave thy throne

CANDLES

Aim

To enter into the joy of the coming of Jesus.

Teaching

Can you remember last week when Joseph and Mary set off to walk to Bethlehem? Well, they have walked all week except Saturday, the Sabbath, when they worshipped in the synagogue (church). Every day, Monday to Friday, they walked miles. When Mary was tired she sat on the donkey but she walked a good bit of the time. Now she was very tired – and the donkey was tired. They were walking more slowly than most other people, and it would be getting dark when they arrived in Bethlehem. The stars were coming out in the sky and they could see the fires the shepherds had lit in the hills to frighten away wild beasts. Joseph wished Mary would go a little faster but knew she could not for she was soon to have her baby. When they got to Bethlehem all the inns were full of people. At the last place they tried, Mary could hear the noise and the singing, the place was crowded; she prayed that she could have somewhere quiet.

Joseph brought the innkeeper to see Mary. He explained that there was no room, but he had a quiet cave behind the inn. If Mary did not mind sharing it with the cow and the hens, she could make herself comfortable there. How pleased Mary was: this was better than a noisy inn. Now she could settle down.

As she rested she listened to the cow munching hay and the hens quietly clucking.

She knew the time had come: the baby Jesus was to be born in the stable. She was so happy. There in the quiet, with Joseph looking after her, the baby Jesus came, and Mary and Joseph gave him their love. Mary hugged the baby and said, 'Hello, Jesus.'

Activity

We know that Jesus was born on Christmas Day. Let us colour in the picture of Jesus lying in the cradle of hay. Then we will put all our nativity figures together so that we can take them into church (or take them home). Some of the figures could be used on Christmas Day. If there is time, let the children talk about the crib figures.

Prayer

God, we thank you
for the coming of Jesus into the world
and for loving us.
Amen.

Song

Away in a manger

LAMPS

Aim

To help the children prepare for Christmas.

Teaching

How many Advent candles are lit this week? That means that Christmas is now very near. How many days to Christmas? Have you got everything ready? What do you still have to do?

A whole week before Jesus was born, Joseph and Mary had walked towards Jerusalem. Every day they walked about ten miles. Before they left home they had to get things ready for the journey. What sort of things would they need? They were taking a donkey for Mary to ride on when she was tired. What would they need for the donkey? Perhaps they needed money for food and for shelter.

Eight days after leaving their home in Nazareth, they came to Bethlehem late in the evening. They had arrived long after the other travellers because Mary could only travel very slowly as her baby was soon to be born. Mary wanted somewhere quiet, but every inn was busy and full. She needed to stop soon. An innkeeper felt sorry for her and offered Mary and Joseph shelter in a cave in the hillside. It was just what Mary wanted and she could rest. Now she made Joseph check that they had brought the things needed for the baby. What do you think he brought? There was water where they were for washing. He brought swaddling bands and salt! After the baby was born Joseph helped to wash him and dry him. He did it so carefully because he loved him. He gently rubbed salt all over the baby's body to protect him from infection (explain). Then he wrapped him up in the swaddling bands (explain) and gave him to Mary. His mother said to him, 'Jesus, welcome into the world.' Joseph smiled and he too said, 'Jesus, welcome into the world.'

Let us say what Joseph and Mary said: 'Jesus, welcome into the world.'

Activity

Colour the picture of Jesus in the manger and the words 'Jesus, welcome into the world.' This is to take home and put it up where it can be seen.

Prayer

Lord Jesus, may we make room for you
in our home and in our lives.
We welcome you into the world
and are glad that you come to us.
Amen.

Song

Jesus' love is very wonderful

TORCHES

Aim

To prepare for Christmas by getting the young people to understand the names of Jesus.

Teaching

When the angel came to Mary at Nazareth he told her of the baby she would have and the baby's name. Let us read Luke 1:26-38. Let this be done by three readers:

- Narrator to read verses 26-28a
- Gabriel to read 28b
- Narrator to read 29-30a
- Gabriel to read 30b-33
- Narrator to read 34a
- Mary to read 34b
- Narrator to read 35a
- Gabriel to read 35b-37
- Narrator to read 38a
- Mary to read 38b

What name did the angel Gabriel say Mary was to give the baby?

Gabriel also said that Jesus 'will be called the Son of the Most High' (verse 32) and 'the Son of God' (verse 35).

What are the other names for Jesus?

- Jesus = Joshua = Saviour
- Christ = the Anointed One = the Messiah
- Redeemer
- Lord (of lords)
- King (of kings)

Activity

We will colour in and put up some of the names of Jesus.

Prayer

Jesus, you came into the world
to be our Saviour.
We thank you that you became a child of earth
so that we may become children of God.
Amen.

Song

Jesus, Name above all names

CHRISTMAS
Christmas Day

Aim
To rejoice that Jesus Christ has come into the world.

Preparation
Have some of the titles of Jesus around the church, and also some of the crib figures that the children have made. If possible, there should also be a central crib with figures. Invite the children to come to church dressed as shepherds or angels. Choose someone to come as Mary and someone as Joseph. A mother may like to bring her baby as the baby Jesus.

You may like to prepare a present of a candle for each person or each family.

Opening activity
Let the Advent candles be lit by children coming from the four corners of the church. Then let the central candle be lit by a mother with her baby. As each lit candle is placed in its holder, let someone else say, 'Jesus is here' and everyone replies, '*He is come among us.*'

Opening prayer
Lord Jesus, you have come among us,
to share in our lives and to let us share in yours.
As you give yourself to us today,
help us to give ourselves to you.
Amen.

Opening song
Any Christmas carol

Readings
Isaiah 52:7-10
Psalm 98
Hebrews 1:1-4 (5-12)
John 1:1-14

Thought for the day
God came down to us so that we might come with our love to him. He became human so that we might share in the Divine. This is a great mystery and full of riches for us to explore.

Isaiah invites us to sing for joy because our God 'reigns'. God is in control; he acts and the whole earth shall see 'the salvation of our God'. The Psalm repeats this, saying, 'All the ends of the earth have seen the victory of our God.'

The writer to the Hebrews tells us that what the prophets and the psalmists had looked forward to has happened. The hopes and promises of the Old Testament have happened in the coming of a Son.

John starts like Genesis – 'In the beginning' – for a new world has dawned for us. All the words of promise have become a reality in the Word made flesh. The Word, which was from the beginning, is made flesh: He comes as the light and the life of us all. And to all who receive him, who believe in his name, he gives the power to become children of God.

Activities
This story of our salvation is packaged in many words. It is important that we get behind all the words and come before our Saviour this day. Concentrate on the events. Tell the story. Get the children to carry the crib figures to the crib. Let Mary and Joseph walk up to the crib. Let a mother bring her baby and stand between Mary and Joseph. Get the angels to stand around the crib and the shepherds to visit it. When all are beside the crib, you may like to bless the crib and ask that it will be a blessing to all who see it.

Look at the names of Jesus. Have them read out by the children, and sing 'Jesus, we adore you' (verse 2 of 'Father, we adore you') after each of the names.

At the end of the service you could give everyone a candle to take home. Let it be wrapped up as a present. Have the words 'Jesus is the Light of the World' written inside or on the wrapping paper. Do not forget to wish everyone a very blessed and joyful Christmas.

Question time
The Christmas story raises many questions, but this is not a day for questions; it is a day for rejoicing.

Illustration
Mother and Father had wrapped up the present in beautiful paper with tinsel and bows. The present was in a big box. For a long time it remained unopened as if their child was frightened of it. Then the paper was taken off and folded up carefully, the present was taken out of the box, and the child played the whole day with the box. The child enjoyed having the box and playing with it. Mother and Father hoped that their child would soon realise what a wonderful present had been given to her . . .

I knew an old lady who was uninterested in presents. Whenever she was given a present, she was very grateful. She always remembered to say, 'Thank you'. But she did not open the gift. In her house I saw a pile of unopened gifts and I felt it was rather strange and sad.

Today I would like to give you all a present of a cheque for one million pounds. But you can only have it on one condition: you are to frame it, to show how generous I am, but not cash it.

Let us get behind the tinsel and the wrappings today and discover God's greatest gift. He gives himself to us. Let us come and give ourselves to him.

Intercessions
Father, we rejoice and sing,
for you love us with a great love.
We give thanks to you
for the coming of our Lord Jesus Christ into our world
and into our lives.

Let us enjoy your presence with us,
and the love you offer to us in Jesus our Lord.

We give thanks for all who celebrate Christmas,
all who are worshipping in churches and in their homes,
all who acknowledge Jesus in their midst.

Bless the outreach and the mission of your Church.
Give all your people the courage to tell the Gospel story
and proclaim your presence and love.

We remember all whose lives are darkened by fear,
those who have no faith,
those who doubt God and themselves.

Silence

Jesus, Light of the World,
come scatter the darkness.

We ask for peace on the earth
and good will among all peoples,
that we may learn to accept your peace,
share your peace
and live your peace.
We remember before you
all who suffer from war or violence at this time,
especially . . .

Silence

Jesus, Light of the World,
come scatter the darkness.

We give thanks for our homes
and the friends with whom we will celebrate
this Christmas.
We remember absent friends and loved ones.
We remember all who are lonely
or feel rejected at this time.

Silence

Jesus, Light of the World,
come scatter the darkness.

We remember in your presence
all who are ill at home or in hospital,
all who are struggling in any way.
We pray for doctors and nurses
and everyone who will have to be at work today.

Silence

Jesus, Light of the World,
come scatter the darkness.

We give thanks that Jesus came down to lift us up,
that he lived that we might not die.
We remember loved ones departed
in the fullness of your kingdom.

Silence

Merciful Father,
accept these prayers
for the sake of your Son,
our Saviour Jesus Christ.
Amen.

Memory verse

God so loved the world that he gave his only Son, so that everyone who believes in him may not perish but may have eternal life.
John 3:16

Suggested music

Carols to fit each piece of the story as it is enacted. You may like to try 'See him lying on a bed of straw' after the blessing of the crib, and you may like to end the service with 'Go, tell it on the mountain'.

The following list of Carols may be useful:

Away in a manger
Born in the night, Mary's child
Child in the manger
Come, come to the manger
Ding, dong, merrily
Infant holy, infant lowly
Joy to the world
Silent night
The Virgin Mary had a baby boy
What child is this?
While shepherds watched
Once in royal David's city

CANDLES, LAMPS and TORCHES

There are times when it is important for the whole congregation to worship together and Christmas is one of them. There are no worksheets for Christmas Day as there is plenty of activity within the service. Let the children be as involved as possible. Let them sing a carol on their own: 'Away in a manger' is possibly the simplest but they may like to attempt something like 'Come, they told me, pah-rum-pum-pum-pum!'

If you want to let others tell the story of Christmas, you could use the Candles lessons for Advent. If you do this, the lesson for the First Sunday of Advent is best to be kept until after the other three.

If an activity is needed, let the children make a Christmas card for Jesus and place it at the crib.

First Sunday of Christmas

Aim

To show that the people involved in the birth of Jesus were ordinary people involved in an extraordinary event.

Preparation

Bring some negatives of photographs, and a good clear print.

Opening activity

Light the Advent and Christmas candles with children coming from the corners of the church. If possible, let the Jesus candle be lit from a hidden area of the church.

Opening prayer

Lord Jesus, we thank you
for coming into the world and living among us.
When the days are dark
may we know that you are with us
and that you are the Light of the World.
Amen.

Opening song

Mary had a baby, yes, Lord

Readings

Isaiah 61:10–62:3
Psalm 148
Galatians 4:4-7
Luke 2:15-21

Thought for the day

Isaiah invites us to rejoice in the Lord and in his salvation. Likewise the psalm asks us to praise the name of the Lord; to join in with all creation and give him praise. This should be our aim throughout our worship.

God's promised time has come and his Son is born of the Blessed Virgin Mary. Like the shepherds, we are invited to glorify and praise God.

The shepherds were very ordinary men who worked on the hillsides tending sheep. By the nature of their job they rarely went to church – but that did not prevent God from knowing them and them from knowing God. They saw the angels, not because they were good but because God is good and comes to ordinary people in ordinary places. Shepherds on a hillside, Mary and Joseph travelling on a road, stars in the sky and a stable for a birth are all ordinary and familiar. We know these things and we can experience them, but it is only half the picture.

Show a negative and explain what it is. A negative is not a black and white photograph or a photograph without colour. If you look at a negative it is sometimes hard to see what the picture is, but it has the potential of making a picture. The negative is important but it is only half the picture. A print is necessary for us to see and understand the whole picture.

We all know about the shepherds and sheep but the other part of the picture makes the whole picture – angels and God are to be discovered. Our world is full of mystery, wonder and a presence. Our minds cannot wholly grasp the mystery but our hearts can. Let us spend some time today thinking upon God and his love.

There are not two separate worlds: heaven and earth are one. God is with us. It is our own lack of vision that prevents us from seeing this.

Question time

The Bible tells of God through his messengers, the angels. How do we tell of God's presence?

Does our vision of the world include the mystery of God?

Illustration

Sally was naughty at school. She did not pay attention to what was written on the board, nor was she all that keen on being out in the country because she was not really interested in the flowers or the birds. A beautiful scene did not move her with joy. Starry nights did not fill her with awe. Then it was discovered that Sally was very short-sighted and needed glasses. She had not been able to see what was around her, so her world and her life were restricted by her vision. Once she had glasses the world became a place full of wonder and beauty. She loved going out into the country to enjoy the scenery, to watch the birds and see the flowers. Once Sally saw more clearly, her whole world changed.

Intercessions

Lord God, we thank you for the gift of sight
and for the deeper sight
that lets us see you at work in your world.
We pray that our vision may not be impaired
but that we may see you more clearly
and love you more dearly day by day.

We give thanks for the Church throughout the world
and the telling of the Good News.
We pray for all evangelists and preachers,
for pastors and ministers,
for all who have the care of your people.
Teach us to ponder on their words
and treasure them in our hearts.

Silence

May we see you more clearly
and love you more dearly.

We remember all who work to provide us
with food and shelter.
We pray for shepherds and farmers,
for all food producers.
We remember all who work in shops and factories.

Silence

May we see you more clearly
and love you more dearly.

We thank you for our homes and our loved ones.
We remember those who taught us the faith.
We pray for our teachers
and all who have been an example to us.

Silence

May we see you more clearly
and love you more dearly.

We remember today all whose sight is impaired.
We pray for all who have lost vision
or hope in the world,
all who feel lonely,
all who have lost a sense of wonder.
We pray especially for those who are ill
at home or in hospital.

Silence

May we see you more clearly
And love you more dearly.

We ask that we may have a vision of your presence
and of your eternal kingdom.
We pray for our loved ones
who have passed from our sight.

Silence

Merciful Father,
accept these prayers
for the sake of your Son,
our Saviour Jesus Christ.
Amen.

Memory verse

God has sent the Spirit of his Son into our hearts, crying, 'Abba! Father!'
Galatians 4:6

Suggested music

Abba, Father
Joy to the world!
Once in royal David's city

CANDLES

Aim

To share in the wonder of Christmas.

Teaching

Go over the Christmas story of the angels appearing to shepherds. Tell of the angels singing, 'Glory to God in the highest', and of the shepherds deciding to go and see the baby. Then tell of the visit to Mary, Joseph and the baby Jesus.

Then let the children act out the story. Have a few tea towels for head-dresses for the shepherds. Maybe dress the angels in white (choir surplices are ideal). Joseph and Mary could be in their ordinary clothes, and Mary could have a doll for Jesus.

Ask the children, 'Who would like to be an angel?' Who would like to be a shepherd? Who would like to be Mary and Joseph?

Set the scene by telling them the shepherds were sitting and sleeping around the fire, and some were watching the sheep. Give the shepherds time to do this. 'Then an angel appeared and said . . .' Let the children use their own words. If they get stuck for words encourage them: 'A new baby has been born in Bethlehem. He is called Jesus. Go and see him.' Let the shepherds travel across the room to Mary and Joseph. As they travel, all could sing 'Here we go to Bethlehem'.

Allow the shepherds to comment on the baby, and encourage Joseph and Mary to welcome them. If there are too many children for all to take part, the play could be repeated with other children whilst the first actors watch.

Activity

Draw an angel using children's hands to draw around for the wings. Colour the angel in gold and use glitter to make it shine. If the angels are not to be taken home, they could be mounted on black paper to show them off. A few stars could be added to the paper.

Prayer

God, we thank you for the song of the angels
and for the shepherds seeing Jesus.
We come this day to give Jesus our love.
Amen.

Song

Here we go up to Bethlehem

LAMPS

Aim

To encourage the children to look deeper into the story of Christmas.

Teaching

Begin by seeing how much the children already know about the story. Let them tell it in their own words. Did they know that Bethlehem was where David was born and that he looked after sheep in the hills?

Being a shepherd is a dangerous job, especially at night. In the darkness they had to look out for bears, for wolves – David once had to tackle a lion. So you had to be brave to be a shepherd. Sometimes it was robbers who came to steal the sheep. Do you know another name for sheep robbers? (Rustlers.)

There was always at least one shepherd awake – you cannot see wild beasts or rustlers if your eyes are closed. It was because they were awake and watching that the angels were able to come to them. (It is important for the children to recognise angels as God's special messengers and not just large fairies! Spend some time talking about the angels and their message.)

Let the children say what the reaction of the shepherds must have been. Let them discuss what the shepherds would do and what they felt like at the stable. Could they see that this was more than an ordinary baby? Maybe not with their eyes, but what did their minds and hearts tell them?

Activity

Have Christmas cards of the shepherds, of angels, and of Joseph and Mary. Cut each card into three at random angles. Now turn the cards face downwards. Get the children to pick one piece only and see if they can find someone with a matching piece. When the pieces are matched let them collect more until they make a card or cards. Once one card is made, or after a few minutes, they should be allowed to pick up another piece until all pieces are matched and the pictures displayed.

Wouldn't it have been easier if the cards were face upwards to start with? Seeing the picture makes it easier.

Prayer

Father, we thank you
that Jesus was born in the city of David
and that he came to be our Saviour.
As the shepherds came to see the baby Jesus
may we rejoice in his birth.
Amen.

Song

There's a star in the east on Christmas morn

TORCHES

Aim

To encourage those who feel they know the story to look at it more deeply.

Teaching

God and his angels are never far away; it is just that we cannot see them. They are part of our world but remain hidden most of the time. Think of other words for hidden – 'unseen', 'invisible'. Just sometimes, someone is able to tell us of their presence. Can you think of any Bible stories about angels?

- Jacob and his ladder
- Mary at the Annunciation
- Joseph before Jesus was born
- The shepherds on the hillside

There are lots of things we cannot see but we can know: the air we breathe, sound, radio waves and so on. We would see even less if we closed our eyes or refused to look. The angels could only appear to people who would be aware of them.

The shepherds were not looking for the angels but they were alert, awake and watching – if anything moved, they would be aware of it. They were looking into the darkness of the night. Most people would have said, 'There is nothing to see in the dark', and turn away from it. In the emptiness of the night they were open to the coming of God, to the song of the angels. We often miss the coming of God because we are too noisy or too busy. How can we change this?

For the rest of the session let the young people talk about what the shepherds had seen and heard and their reaction to it.

Activity

Colour in the worksheet and learn the text.

Prayer

God, we thank you for you are ever with us.
We give you praise for the song of the angels
and we pray that we may know
your love and your presence
in our homes and in our lives.
Amen.

Song

Once in royal David's city

Second Sunday of Christmas

Aim

To encourage people to wonder at the mystery of Christmas.

Preparation

A globe of the world, a picture of a dinosaur, a picture of early humans and a photograph of yourself.

Opening activity

Continue to light the Advent ring with children carrying lights from the corners of the building and someone from a hidden place carrying the light for Christ. They may like to sing as they go 'Walk, walk in the light' or the chorus of 'Lord, the light of your love' (Shine, Jesus, shine).

Show the globe and say you would have liked to show a speck of dust for that is how tiny the world is in comparison to the universe. Let a child hold up a picture of the dinosaur and say, 'The dinosaurs are gone – but they prepared the way for us.' Another child can show the early humans and say, 'Without such people we would not be here today.' Let a child hold up its own photograph or yours and say, 'Without all that has gone before us, we would not be here today.' Then let the children say together, 'All were part of God's plan.'

Opening prayer

Blessed are you, Lord, God of all creation,
you have called us into your marvellous light,
you have given us life
and chosen us to know your love
through Christ our Lord.
Amen.

Opening song

Praise to the Lord

Readings

Jeremiah 31:7-14 and Psalm 147:12-20
or Ecclesiasticus 24:1-12 and Wisdom 10:15-21
Ephesians 1:3-14
John 1: (1-9) 10-18

Thought for the day

It may be hard to realise from the readings that we are still giving thanks for Christmas. Yet all the readings are about God caring for his chosen people and coming to them as their Redeemer. They tell of the Word of God, or the Wisdom of God, taking flesh and dwelling among us. All of today's readings can be seen as songs of praise.

The reading from Ephesians is amazing in that it is all one sentence in the Greek. Here St Paul is pouring out his praise to God for caring for us and calling us. Notice how it starts, like many Jewish prayers of praise, saying, 'Blessed be God.'

It starts in a surprising way by telling us how God chose us before the world began. No, we did not choose God; he chose us (see John 15:16). He wants us to be part of his team! He wants us to be holy – that is, to belong to him – and he wants us to be blameless – without sin – before him in love (Ephesians 1, verses 3-4).

Out of his goodness and grace – for we do not deserve it – God wants us to be part of his family and to enjoy all the privileges of belonging with him as our Father, through Jesus Christ (verses 5-6).

In Jesus we have redemption; he has bought our freedom through his own death. He has ransomed us from death. Through him our sins are forgiven – not because we deserve this but through the riches of his grace that he has lavished upon us (verses 7-8).

God has made known to us the mystery of his will, to gather up all things in Christ. Divisions disappear and all are one in him, not absorbed but fulfilled in him (verses 9-10).

In Christ, because we are made part of God's family, we obtain an inheritance. In him we have heard the word, the Good News of salvation, and as an assurance of this we have received the Holy Spirit. As God's people let us live to praise his glory.

Wow! What a lot Paul packs into a sentence!

You could say John summarises this and says, 'And the Word became flesh and lived among us, and we have seen his glory, the glory as of a Father's only Son, full of grace and truth' (John 1:14).

Question time

Did you understand that? I am not sure I did – but I can feel it. Jesus came to earth so that we might belong to heaven. Jesus shared in our humanity so that we might share in his divinity. Do you see this as a problem to solve (with God's help) or a mystery to be enjoyed?

Illustration

I get tired of letters through the door that say you have been especially chosen – I know that everyone is getting such a letter. Then it tells me I have won £10,000 – whoopee! But the small print says, 'if my number comes up', and the real chances of that are more than a million to one.

God is not like that. God's offer is not gifts (though he does offer us them); he offers himself to us in Jesus Christ our Lord. We do not deserve this; we cannot win it. God has chosen to give himself to us. All we have to do is accept his presence and his love.

Intercessions

Blessed are you, Lord, God of all creation.
The whole universe belongs to you
and yet you care for each one of us.
You come to us in love to be our Saviour and our friend.
You have chosen us to be your people
and given us of your Holy Spirit
We give you thanks and praise.

We share with all who continue to give thanks
for the coming of Jesus into the world.

We remember before you those who proclaim the Gospel
by living lives of holiness and goodness.
We pray for those preparing for Confirmation
and all who are seeking to know you better.

Silence

Let us praise the name of the Lord.
His name only is exalted.

We bring before you rulers of people,
politicians and leaders of nations.
We remember all who are striving
to bring peace and unity to humankind.
We think especially today of rescue workers,
of ambulance workers and firefighters.

Silence

Let us praise the name of the Lord.
His name only is exalted.

We give thanks that you care for us as our Father
and that we all belong to your family.
We pray for our own parents, families and friends.
May we know that you are with us and love us.

Silence

Let us praise the name of the Lord.
His name only is exalted.

You are our Redeemer and are with us in our troubles.
We remember all whose lives are endangered at this time,
all who are fearful and anxious.
We pray to you for those who are ill at home or in hospital.
We trust in your love and power.

Silence

Let us praise the name of the Lord.
His name only is exalted.

You save us from destruction
and have chosen us to be one with you in your kingdom.
We ask you to bless our loved ones departed
with your love and grace.

Silence

Merciful Father,
accept these prayers
for the sake of your Son,
our Saviour Jesus Christ.
Amen.

Memory verse

The Word became flesh and lived among us, and we have seen his glory.
John 1:14

Suggested music

It is a thing most wonderful
What a friend we have in Jesus
A great and mighty wonder
We have a gospel to proclaim

CANDLES

Aim

To let the children know that they are loved by God.

Teaching

This is the story of a little boy who had lots of toys but he was very sad. He had enough food, nice clothes and lived in a big house but he was not happy. He thought that his mummy and daddy did not love him and he felt very lonely – all by himself. One night Mummy heard him crying because he was frightened of the dark. She came into the room put a light on and hugged him and kissed him. She told him how much she loved him and she stayed with him until he was asleep.

The next night his daddy came upstairs with him and told him a story. He also gave him a big hug and told him that he loved him. Then he told him how Mummy and Daddy would always love him and look after him. The little boy smiled because he was very happy. Everyone noticed the change. He was not afraid of the dark because he knew he was loved and that Mummy or Daddy would come if he needed someone.

God saw that lots of people were afraid of the dark and were sad and lonely, so he sent Jesus into the world to show that he loved them all. Jesus showed that God loves children and cares for people who are ill. God wants us to be happy.

Where was Jesus born? (Get the children to reply.) Who looked after him? (Mary and Joseph.) He loved them and they loved him. When he grew up, he would tell everyone that God loves them.

Let us sing 'Jesus' love is very wonderful'. We will stretch as tall as we can when we sing, 'So high you can't get over it'. Then we'll go down as low as we can when we sing, 'So low you can't get under it'. Then we will stretch our arms out wide when we sing, 'So wide you can't get round it'. Then we will hug ourselves when we sing, 'Oh wonderful love'.

Activity

We will colour in the words 'Jesus loves me' and the picture.

Prayer

God our Father, we thank you for your love.
Jesus loves us and we are happy.
We would like to give our love to you.
Amen.

Song

Jesus' love is very wonderful

LAMPS

Aim

To show God loves us and cares for us.

Teaching

There was a Nativity play at school. (Have you been in a Nativity play? What is it about?) When it was over the weather was very stormy and the teacher was worried about one little lad who had a mile to walk in the dark. She asked, 'Are you not afraid? Would you like me to drive you home?'

'No, Miss,' he replied.

After they all had some tea and cakes, the teacher asked again, 'Are you sure you don't want me to take you home?'

'Yes, Miss, I am sure.'

Yet she was still worried, so when the lad got his coat on she asked him again, saying, 'It will only take me a little while, I would be happy to get you home.'

'There's no need, Miss, I have a good coat and a big torch.' He produced a great big torch and waved it. 'I am not afraid of the dark. Anyway, my father is coming for me with the car.'

Why did this boy feel so safe and secure? Because his parents cared for him and would protect him at all times. (If possible, talk about being loved and cared for.)

God our Father cares for all the people in the world, and his Son Jesus Christ came to show us that love. Talk about how Jesus shows the love of the Father.

Activity

Write a letter home, saying, 'Thank you for loving me.' Colour in the worksheet.

Prayer

God our Father, we thank you for Jesus
who is the Light of the World
and we thank you that he shows your love for us.
May we learn to love you more and more every day.
Amen.

Songs

Jesus loves me, this I know
Wide, wide as the ocean

TORCHES

Aim

To explore the idea of 'The Word made flesh'.

Teaching

Sophie wanted a bike but she knew her parents couldn't afford to buy her one. Her father promised that she would have one some day. Sophie thought, 'Promises, promises.' At Christmas she liked opening her presents and she left Uncle Simon's until the last. It was a big box, nicely decorated. Inside was another box, which had 'China: breakable' written on it, then another box and another. The last box was small and it had 'mobile phone' written on it, but it felt very light. Sophie opened the box and found a piece of paper and a small key. Written on the paper was: EES DNA DEHS EHT OT OG.

Let us try and read it. Can anyone understand it?

Sophie tried three times and then realised it was a secret code. Her uncle Simon loved sending her secret messages. This one was easy and she was soon able to read the words. Read it backwards and it says: GO TO THE SHED AND SEE.

Sophie now knew this was the key to their garden shed. She hurried out with her mother and father watching. She opened the shed and there she found a beautiful shining . . . Can you guess? Yes, Uncle Simon had sent her a bicycle.

I like codes and secret signs.

INRI: This is whom the wise men sought: It is a code where J and I are the same. It means '**J**esus of **N**azareth **R**ex **I**udaeorum (which means King of the Jews).

IHS: This is whom the shepherds came to see. This time the secret code is harder for it is written in Greek; in English it would be written JES. So what do you think it would stand for?

For hundreds of years it was promised that the Christ would come, but it felt like 'Promises, promises'. Then in Bethlehem the promise became true. The Christ came as a little baby or, as St John says, 'The Word became flesh'. Jesus, who had been present when the world was made, was now seen on earth as Mary's child, but only those who can read the code can understand it.

Activity

Let the young people decipher the various codes on the worksheet. Then let them write a message of their own to say, 'Thank you for the birth of Jesus.'

Prayer

We thank you, Lord God,
that what was secret for many ages
has been made known to us.
We give you thanks for the Word made flesh,
that Jesus has been born in Bethlehem
and told us of your love.
Amen.

Song

Come on, let's celebrate

EPIPHANY
The Epiphany

Aim
To show how the Christ was revealed to all nations.

Preparation
Have a star on a pole, and figures of the three wise men at the back of the church. If possible, also have three children dressed as wise men carrying the gifts, and five children carrying the Advent and Jesus candles.

Opening activity
The star will lead the procession as the opening hymn is sung. It is then placed over the stable. The star is followed by the bearers of the lit candles that will be placed during verse one.

During verse two the gold-bearing wise man will be placed at the crib. The child dressed as the gold-bearer will place her gift and stand near the crib.

During verse three the same will happen with the figure bearing frankincense and the child bearing the gift of frankincense.

At the fourth verse the last figure is placed at the crib and the child comes forward with the myrrh.

The children around the crib kneel for verse five and then go to their seats during the chorus.

Opening prayer
O God, who by the shining of a star
brought the wise men to see the Christ and to offer gifts,
may we know his presence today
and offer him our love and our lives.
Amen.

Opening song
We three kings of Orient are

Readings
Isaiah 60:1-6
Psalm 72:(1-9) 10-15
Ephesians 3:1-12
Matthew 2:1-12

Thought for the day
Many of the Jews believed that the Christ would only be for their own nation: they were the chosen people and no other. Yet throughout the Scriptures there are suggestions that the Christ was for all peoples. Today's readings are chosen to show this. Isaiah asks the Jews to arise and shine because their light has come and the glory of the Lord is risen upon them. Isaiah goes on to say that nations and kings will come to that light. He even says they will bring gifts of gold and frankincense (Isaiah 60:1, 3, 6). Psalm 72 also declares, 'All kings shall bow before him and all nations do him service'.

St Paul declares how he was given a revelation to perceive that the Gentiles had become sharers in the promise of Christ through the Gospel (Ephesians 3:4). So, we, who are among the Gentiles, have access to God in boldness and confidence through Christ.

The fulfilment of the prophecy is seen in the coming of the wise men, who are Gentiles, to the Christ – they are the first of the rest of the world.

Question time
Do you realise we are Gentiles (that is, non-Jews)?

What gift would you bring as a symbol of your life?

Illustration
The wise men were not all that wise because they went to the wrong place and the wrong person. They went to the capital, Jerusalem, and to King Herod. Fancy asking him, 'Where is he who is to be born king of the Jews?' Herod hadn't a clue but he knew who would know about the Messiah, about the Christ. He asked the chief priests and scribes. They told him, 'In Bethlehem in the land of Judah.' Lucky for the wise men it was only about seven miles away. Herod sent them off and told them to search diligently for the child and to tell him when they had found him. Fortunately, the wise men did not trust Herod or his interest in the Christ child.

We assume there were three because we are told of three gifts. We know that they were rich, foreign and wise, but we do not know that they were kings. The shepherds were ordinary Jews smelling of sheep and probably not able to read or write. These men were different indeed, almost in total contrast. It helps us to see God calls all peoples to come to him – rich and poor, the known and the stranger, simple and wise; all are invited to come to God.

Intercessions
God, we give thanks to you
for your love towards all peoples of the world.
You have chosen to give yourself to us all
and invite us to give ourselves to you.
Blessed are you, Lord God, for all things come from you
and of your own do we give you.
We come in our poverty to your riches,
in our foolishness to your wisdom,
in our sorrows to your healing and joy.

Silence

Light of Christ,
shine in our lives.

As we remember the wise men,
we pray for the rich and the comfortable,
all who have plenty of this world's good things.
May they know that all things come from you
and their lives are a gift from you.
May the riches of the world be put to good use.
We remember the world's poor,
the homeless and the hungry.

Silence

Light of Christ,
shine in our lives.

We pray for all who are seekers,
who search for the truth,
who look for meaning
and who desire to know you.
We pray for pilgrim peoples,
especially those on their way to Bethlehem
or Jerusalem.
We pray for those who are new to our church
or community.

Silence

Light of Christ,
shine in our lives.

We give thanks for all who come to you in worship,
all who are aware of awe or mystery in their lives.
We pray for leaders of worship, choirs and organists,
for all who give us a sense of wonder and beauty.

Silence

Light of Christ,
shine in our lives.

We come with all who are in pain or sorrow.
We remember those whose sickness finds no cure,
those who are permanently ill
and those with a short time to live.
We pray for doctors and nurses
and all who are involved in healing.

Silence

Light of Christ,
shine in our lives.

Lord, we worship and adore you.
We offer you our joys and sorrows,
our sickness and health,
our riches and our poverty.
We remember all who have enriched our lives
by their goodness.
We pray for loved ones who are now in the fullness
of your kingdom.

Silence

Merciful Father,
accept these prayers
for the sake of your Son,
our Saviour Jesus Christ.
Amen.

Memory verse

We have access to God in boldness and confidence through faith in him.
Ephesians 3:12

Suggested music

The first Nowell
From the ends of the earth
As with gladness men of old

CANDLES

Aim

To encourage the children to offer themselves to God.

Teaching

Show a star. Do the children ever see stars? Do they know the names of any stars?

The wise men liked looking at the stars. One night they saw a very bright star – it looked bigger than all the others. They knew it was shining because someone important had been born into the world – a special baby – and they must go and see him. The wise men set off at night. (Why?) They travelled across the desert and for many miles until they came to Jerusalem. Here they were a little lost, so they asked someone the way. They asked the king but he was a wicked king and he did not know. The church people knew and said they would have to go to Bethlehem. It was only seven miles away, so they were lucky. (Compare distances to places near home.)

At last they came to where Jesus was. They each brought him a gift. Do you know what they were?

Activity

Have some gifts wrapped for the children to unwrap. Explain these are not gifts to keep but for them to look at. You could have many wrappings on the gifts and the children can pass around one gift at a time and unwrap a layer when the music stops. Each gift could be contained in a box. The gold could be a brooch or a ring. The frankincense could be some incense grains or an incense stick, which could be lit for them to smell. You may be able to get some myrrh from the chemists; if not, use a small medicine bottle filled with bits of silver paper. When all the gifts are unwrapped talk about them and why they were given to Jesus.

Colour the picture of the wise men bringing their gifts. Cut them out and stick each to a piece of kitchen roll tube so they stand up. The star could be stuck on to a longer piece of tube (black, if possible).

Prayer

Father, we thank you that the wise men found Jesus
and that the wicked king did not.
We would like to give Jesus our love this day.
Amen.

Song

Guide us, guide us little star,
we have travelled very far.
We have seen your lovely light
as we journey through the night.
Now we come to Christ our King
and our love to him we bring.

Let the leader sing a line (to the tune of 'Twinkle, twinkle, little star') and then the children echo it.

LAMPS

Aim

To encourage the children to offer a gift to Jesus.

Teaching

Talk about stars, planets and shooting stars. Do they know the names of any stars? Let us draw a star – a five-pointed star. It is actually quite hard to draw a five-pointed star. The star of King David is easier to draw or to make; it can be done by using two triangles (demonstrate).

The wise men decided to follow a bright star because they believed it would bring them to a very special baby, and they decided to bring special gifts with them. What were these special gifts? Produce each of the gifts and talk about them. Gold and frankincense are easy to understand; myrrh is more difficult. See if you can get ideas from the children, using the carol 'We three kings' as an aid. You could ask, 'What sort of people would have such gifts to offer?' If you could offer the most precious thing you have, what would it be? Talk about the offering of our self.

Activity

Give children gifts of gold, frankincense and myrrh to offer to Jesus. Let each of them say why they have brought this gift. Give others a piece of paper on which they write the gift they would like to bring to Jesus.

Prayer

God, we thank you
for the gift of Jesus to the whole world.
He shows us your love and care.
We offer you our lives and our love today.
Amen.

Song

The wise may bring their learning

TORCHES

Aim

To let the young people discover that Jesus has come for the whole world.

Teaching

Begin by showing a Japanese, an African or an Indian Christmas card – if at all possible, all three. Any cards that show a different Christ and Virgin will do. Get them to notice that Jesus is not 'English'. You can also show them some cards of the wise men that depict them of differing nationalities.

For a long time the Jewish people called themselves the 'chosen people' and believed that God was only concerned with them. We know that God loves the whole world and wants to give himself to all peoples.

In their Temple (church) at Jerusalem the Jews did not allow anyone who was not a Jew to go into the inner part of the Temple. There was a notice forbidding Gentiles. They believed the Christ was only for them. The Good News, the Gospel, tells us that the Christ came for us all, for every nation at all times and in all places. The shepherds were Jewish but the wise men were not; they were Gentiles like us. Epiphany celebrates the coming of the world to the God who came into the world.

Activity

Have lots of Epiphany cards – Christmas cards with the wise men on them. Explain why they are Epiphany cards: because they are about the coming of the Gentiles – the whole world – to Jesus. They show Jesus being revealed to the world.

Let the young people cut these cards into three in any shape. Mix them all up and place them face downwards. Now ask everyone to collect a whole card. It will mean them helping each other and exchanging.

Prayer

God, we thank you
that you have revealed your love for all people,
in all places and at all times.
We can find you wherever we are
and know that you are with us
and that you care for us.

Song

He's got the whole world in his hands

First Sunday of Epiphany
The Baptism of Christ

Aim

To encourage people to think about the Holy Trinity.

Preparation

Get a group to decorate the font with flowers and with symbols of Father, Son and Holy Spirit and of the Holy Trinity.

Opening activity

Divide the congregation into three groups. Get them to repeat sentences after you.

Leader: In the power of God
Group 1: In the power of the Father
Group 2: In the power of the Son
Group 3: In the power of the Spirit

Get the groups to respond in the same way with the following sentences:

In the peace of God . . .
In the love of God . . .
In the presence of God . . .

They could also renew their baptismal vows.

Opening prayer

Blessed are you, Father, Son and Holy Spirit.
You reveal your love to us
as our Creator, Redeemer and Guide.
You are three Persons and yet only one God.
We worship and adore you.
Amen.

Opening song

Father, we love you

Readings

Genesis 1:1-5
Psalm 29
Acts 19:1-7
Mark 1:4-11

Thought for the day

At the beginning of Creation we hear of the Creator, the word of God and the wind (Spirit) of God.

St Paul asked the disciples at Ephesus if they had received the Holy Spirit. They replied they were baptised by John the Baptist and had not heard of the Holy Spirit. Water baptism and repentance was not enough; they needed to be baptised in the name of the Lord Jesus and to receive the gift of the Holy Spirit.

Today many people are baptised in water but they are hardly aware that they are immersed in the presence of Father, Son and Holy Spirit. Such people are like the people Paul met at Ephesus. We need to see that our baptism in water is an outward and visible sign of our immersion in the presence of Father, Son and Holy Spirit. Each day we should rejoice that we are in the presence and power of Father, Son and Holy Spirit.

Jesus came to John to be baptised. He did not need to come to repent; he came to commit himself to the next stage of his life and mission. Jesus shared in our humanity and his baptism was part of his identification with us. Furthermore, it was a sign of approval and his anointing; he was now equipped for the task for which he came. The Spirit comes upon him and the voice of the Father is heard. Here we have a brief glimpse of the Holy Trinity. There is also a feeling that it is like the beginning of creation – a new world is about to begin. In the same way, the dove comes as it came to Noah after the flood destroyed the old world. Something new is about to happen.

Question time

Are you aware that every day you are in the presence of Father, Son and Holy Spirit?

Is there one person in the Trinity that you neglect? If there is, how can you correct this?

Illustration

Have a nice mug, which is empty. Get people to admire it, tell them how beautiful it is – but it is useless unless it has something in it – it is no use empty! Only when it has something in it does it fulfil its purpose. People and their minds are the same: we are no use if we are empty.

Borrow a jacket or a fleece, lay it before you and admire it. How good it is for keeping out the cold. Now command it to raise an arm or to sit up straight. When it fails to act, say you know a secret way of getting it to do things. Now get the owner to put it on and raise an arm. The jacket is of no use unless it is occupied.

Nature abhors a vacuum – something will always fill an empty space. Let us be filled and immersed in Father, Son and Holy Spirit.

Intercessions

We rejoice in your presence and your love,
Father, Son and Holy Spirit.
You have made us, you have redeemed us,
and you guide us.
We remember in your presence
all who are being prepared for baptism or confirmation:
all who are seeking to know the gifts of the Spirit.
We pray for our own clergy
and for all who are being prepared
for ordination and ministry.

Silence

God ever with us:
hear us, Father, Son and Holy Spirit.

We pray for all who are starting new work or new studies,
for the newly married and the newly engaged,
for all who are testing their vocations.
We pray for all who seek to bring peace to our world.

Silence

God ever with us:
hear us, Father, Son and Holy Spirit.

We give thanks for our homes and our loved ones,
for our godparents and our godchildren.
We ask your blessing upon them.
We remember all who come from broken homes
or who are suffering from broken relationships.

Silence

God ever with us:
hear us, Father, Son and Holy Spirit.

We pray for all who feel they have lost their way,
who are troubled and distressed,
that they may know your love and care.
We remember also those who are ill at home or in hospital,
all who are struggling at this time.

Silence

God ever with us:
hear us, Father, Son and Holy Spirit.

We praise you for giving us life and life eternal.
We remember especially today
friends and loved ones who have enriched our lives
but who are now departed from this world.
We commend all to you, Father, Son and Holy Spirit.

Silence

Merciful Father,
accept these prayers
for the sake of your Son,
our Saviour Jesus Christ.
Amen.

Memory verse

A voice came from heaven, 'You are my Son, the Beloved; with you I am well pleased.'
Mark 1:11

Suggested music

Have you heard the raindrops
O let the Son of God enfold you
Breathe on me, Breath of God

CANDLES

Aim

To let the children enter into the wonder of the baptism of Jesus.

Teaching

What do we use water for? Drinking and watering the garden, and many other things. Water gives life and refreshes us.

Did you know that water can destroy life? Floods and drowning – maybe someone knows the story of Noah.

Water washes, makes things clean. We should always wash our hands before meals.

Jesus had lived at his home in Nazareth until he was ready for the special work only he could do. At the beginning of his work he went to the river Jordan to be baptised in the water by John. This was a very special time for Jesus. John, in his rough clothes, led him into the river and dipped Jesus right under the water. This was to be a new start for Jesus, a new sort of life. As he was coming out of the water there seemed to be a hole in the sky and out of it came the Spirit of God, like a dove descending. He knew then that his special work was to begin. Then there came a voice from heaven – it was God the Father and he was speaking to Jesus. He said, 'You are my Son, the Beloved; with you I am well pleased.' What was God the Father saying to Jesus?

At the baptism of Jesus, the Father was heard to speak and the Spirit was seen coming upon him. What do we call the Father, Son and Holy Spirit?

Activity

In and out the Jordan
Make a circle with one person in the middle to give the commands – this may need to be the teacher for the first time. Children have to react to the words of the one in the middle. Tell them the Jordan is a river.

In the Jordan (everyone jumps in)
On the bank (everyone jumps out backwards)
On the Jordan (no one moves)
In the bank (no one moves)

Vary the order of these words. Anyone who makes a wrong move or wobbles is out. The last person left is the winner.

Prayer

Father, we thank you that you made us
and that you love us.
Jesus, we thank you that you came to earth for us
and that you love us.
Spirit, we thank you that you are ever with us
and that you love us.

Song

Father, we adore you

LAMPS

Aim

To get the children to think about the Trinity.

Teaching

When Jesus was ready to begin his special work he went to see John the Baptist at the river Jordan. Do you know what 'Baptist' means? It describes what John did to people. He immersed them in the river until the water flowed over their heads. It was to wash away their sins (talk about what this means) and give them a new start.

When a farmer dips his sheep, it is to get rid of anything that would harm the sheep and to protect them for the future. The farmer has to make sure the sheep go right under the water. Water is used to refresh and renew as well as to destroy what would harm.

When Jesus came to John it was to be the start of his ministry; his baptism was special for him. Let us imagine the scene. Jesus has travelled almost to Jerusalem and is now on the bank of the river Jordan. John knows Jesus because they are cousins. He knows how good and special Jesus is and feels that Jesus should really baptise him. Jesus tells him he wants to be baptised. John and Jesus go into the river Jordan and Jesus is immersed right under the water. When he comes out he is ready for his ministry. He walks on to the river bank and the Spirit of God comes upon him like a dove. He is anointed with the Spirit – Christ means 'the Anointed One'. At the same time a voice is heard from heaven: 'You are my Son, the Beloved; with you I am well pleased.'

At the baptism of Jesus we have one of the few signs of the Trinity in the New Testament. What do we mean by Trinity? Three in One. Who are the Three in One? The One is God, for there is only one God. The Father is God, the Son is God and the Holy Spirit is God. Three persons, one God.

When you were baptised, you were baptised in water but, far more important, you were immersed in the presence of Father, Son and Holy Spirit. You are in God's presence and in his love.

Activity

Divide into two groups with you as the leader. Get the first group to make statements about Jesus and the second group to make statements about the Holy Spirit.

Leader: The Father is here.
Group 1: Jesus is here.
Group 2: The Holy Spirit is here.

The Father is with me . . .

Try to get a rhythm to this and for the children to enjoy making statements. Once they get used to it, let someone else be the leader.

Prayer

God, we give thanks to you for our baptism
and that we are always in your presence
and in your power,
Father, Son and Holy Spirit.
Amen.

Song

Glory to God, glory to God

TORCHES

Aim

To discover the meaning of baptism.

Teaching

Jesus and his disciples liked nicknames. They called Simon 'Peter', which means 'Rocky', because Jesus said he would be firm like a rock. They called Thomas 'Didymus', which means 'twin'; no doubt he had a twin brother or sister. They called James and John 'Boanerges', which means 'the Sons of Thunder', because they were quick to get angry. John, who was immersing people in the Jordan to wash away their sins, was called 'The Baptist'. What do you think it means? Dip, dunk, immerse.

Do you know where you were baptised (christened)? Jesus was baptised by John in the river Jordan. When Jesus came out of the water, the Spirit of God descended like a dove upon him and the Father from heaven said, 'You are my Son, the Beloved; with you I am well pleased.' Together at the baptism of Jesus are Father, Son and Holy Spirit.

When you were baptised it was probably not in a river but in a font. Do you know what a font is? Where is it in our church? Water was poured over your head three times: once for the Father, once for the Son and once for the Holy Spirit. Maybe you were not dipped right under the water but the priest said you were immersed in God – Father, Son and Holy Spirit. We should remember this every day of our life. We should say, 'I am in your presence, Father. I am in your presence, Son. I am in your presence, Spirit.' We should enjoy being in the peace, in the power and in the presence of God every day. We can do this by talking to Father, Son and Holy Spirit each day.

Activity

Draw the baptism of Jesus, showing the presence of Father, Son and Holy Spirit. Use symbols for the Father and the Holy Spirit. Because it is hard to draw the 'voice of God', the Father is often depicted as a hand in the sky or an eye in the sky. See if they would like to suggest any other symbols. The Spirit is usually depicted as the dove.

Prayer

We give you thanks, Father, Son and Holy Spirit,
for we are immersed in your presence.
You never leave us.
You always love us.
Help us to love you every day
and to enjoy your presence in our prayers.
Amen.

Song

The King is among us

Second Sunday of Epiphany

Aim
To learn the value of listening.

Preparation
Have various sounds on a tape recorder or CD player: the sound of a car horn, a doorbell, church bell, police car, owl, curlew, or whatever you think people might recognise.

Opening activity
Play the sounds and ask people to recognise them.

Opening prayer
O God, you speak often with a quiet voice
waiting for us to listen.
Help us to keep alert to your call,
to keep our ears and our hearts open
to what is happening around us
for in such events you speak.
Amen.

Opening song
In the morning early

Readings
1 Samuel 3:1-10 (11-20)
Psalm 139:1-6, 13-18
Revelation 5:1-10
John 1:43-51

Thought for the day
The story of Samuel at Shiloh illustrates how the Church must often appear. Eli represents the Church; he is old and losing his vision. The light in the church has almost gone out. The sons of the 'vicarage', Hophni and Phineas, are not interested in following in their father's footsteps. Into this situation is introduced a youngster and, as ever, he disturbs the church. Eli is trying to sleep. Samuel lies on his mattress listening to the sounds of the night. A voice calls. Samuel, who is about 12 years old, jumps up and wakes the old man Eli and says, 'You called.' Tired, Eli says, 'I did not call. Go back to bed, my son.' The Lord calls again, 'Samuel!' Once more Samuel jumps up and runs to Eli because he doesn't know it was the Lord who was calling. Again Eli says, 'I did not call. Go back to bed, my son.' It is not long before the Lord calls a third time. For a third time Samuel disturbs Eli. This old priest, his vision fading, is able to guide the young man and send him back to his room, saying, 'If he calls, you shall say, "Speak, Lord, for your servant is listening."'

The Church might be very old and find the young disturbing, but God speaks through new voices. At the same time the young will be lost without the guidance of the old.

Samuel heard the voice and said, 'Speak, Lord, for your servant is listening.' In this way God was able to speak to Samuel and *through* Samuel.

The reading from Revelation suggests that through Christ we will learn of the deep secrets of God.

In the Gospel, Philip heard Jesus say, 'Follow me.' He responded immediately by going and telling Nathaniel that he had found the one who fulfilled the law and the prophets – that is, the Christ. Nathaniel nearly did not listen to Philip because of prejudice, saying, 'Nothing good can come out of Nazareth!' Philip invited him to come and see.

Question time
How often do we fail to hear because we are unwilling to listen? We are often too busy or too prejudiced to hear the voice of God.

How can we make room in our lives to hear the still small voice of God?

Illustration
Hello!
Are you receiving me?
Hello!
Are you receiving me?
Hello!
Are you receiving me?

This was a conversation, if you can call it that, on a mobile phone. The person was in a bad reception area. There was too much interference from hills and trees. They would have to go to a better reception area.

It is amazing how many people and nations are good at speaking but find it very hard to hear anyone. Our speakers (mouths) seem to be far more active than our receivers (ears). A proverb from the East says, 'God gave us two ears and one mouth so that we should listen twice as much as we speak.'

Intercessions
Blessed are you, Lord God, Creator of all life.
We thank you because we are wonderfully made.
You have given us the gift of communication,
eyes to see, ears to hear and lips to speak.
Teach us not only to speak to you but to listen,
to be quiet in your presence
and know that you are God.

Silence

Lord, hear us:
graciously hear us.

We pray for all who listen to you in prayer
that they may speak to us of your word.
We ask your blessing upon the leaders of our churches,
upon pastors and counsellors,
upon all who are called to listen
to the needs and troubles of others.

Silence

Lord, hear us:
graciously hear us.

Guide the leaders of the nations
in the ways of justice and peace.
Keep our ears open
to the cry of the poor and the oppressed;
let us always be sensitive to the needs of others.
We pray for relief agencies
and all who are working to relieve suffering.

Silence

Lord, hear us:
graciously hear us.

Lord, in our homes help us to listen to each other
with undivided attention.
Teach us to be sensitive to the various calls for us
to share and to care for each other.
We ask you to protect our homes and loved ones.

Silence

Lord, hear us:
graciously hear us.

We remember before you all whose voices are unheard,
people who feel neglected or unwanted.
We pray for the lonely and those who have no helpers.
We remember also all who are ill at this time
at home or in hospital.

Silence

Lord, hear us:
graciously hear us.

We rejoice that you hear us and offer us eternal life.
We pray for our loved ones departed
and for all who have served you faithfully on earth.

Silence

Merciful Father,
accept these prayers
for the sake of your Son,
our Saviour Jesus Christ.
Amen.

Memory verse

Speak, Lord, for your servant is listening.
1 Samuel 3:9

Suggested music

Will you come and follow me
Be still and know that I am God
Be thou my vision

CANDLES

Aim

To show that God cares for even the smallest of his children.

Teaching

Who has helped Mummy or Daddy at home? (Let the children talk about how they are helpful.)

Have you ever helped to clean the church? Some people do it every week. Wouldn't it be good if you could sweep the floors and hoover the carpets? If you were careful, you might be allowed to polish the pews or the brass. What we can all do in church is be very quiet and say our prayers. God likes to hear every one of us . . .

There was once a boy who lived in a church. He helped an old man called Eli to look after things. The boy's name was Samuel. (Show the children pictures of Samuel and Eli.)

'I like helping you,' Samuel said to Eli. 'Do you think God is happy with what I am doing?' Eli smiled because Samuel worked carefully. 'God is happy with the way you sweep the floor and keep the place tidy. God is happy that you help me and that you say your prayers. God loves you.'

Samuel was very glad that God loved him and it made him enjoy helping. What do you think Samuel did when it got dark? Yes, like you, he would go to bed. Here is a little mat that he used for a bed. It is not as nice as your bed but he found it very cosy.

One night Samuel went and lay down on his mat. (Let a child lie on Samuel's mat.) Eli went to bed in a different place at the other end of the church. Let us put Eli in his bed. Soon both were fast asleep.

Suddenly in the dark Samuel heard a voice calling his name. Let us say his name two times. 'Samuel, Samuel.' Who do you think was calling? Samuel thought it could only be Eli so he ran to the old man and woke him up and asked him what he wanted. 'You called me and here I am.' Eli said, '*I* did not call you. Go back to bed.'

Samuel went back to bed and was nearly asleep when the voice called again. Let us say it together: 'Samuel, Samuel.'

He ran to Eli woke him up and said, 'You *did* call me.' But Eli said, 'I *did* not. Go back to bed.'

Samuel went back to bed but before long do you know what happened? Yes. The voice called again – let us say the words: 'Samuel, Samuel.' Samuel again woke Eli. This time the wise old man knew that something special was happening. Who do you think was speaking to Samuel? Eli told Samuel to lie down again and if God called to say, 'Speak, Lord, for your servant is listening.'

Samuel lay down and was very quiet. He hoped God would call him again. He had never thought that God would bother with a little lad like him. But God cares for all his children – he cares for you. Samuel waited for a while (pause). Then God called again (let us say it together): 'Samuel, Samuel.' This time Samuel sat up and said, 'Yes, God, I am listening to you.' God told him some very special things that no one knew.

In the morning Samuel said to Eli, 'Isn't it wonderful? God has spoken to me even though I am still small. I know God loves me and I love him.'

Activity

Act out the following:

This is the way we sweep the floor,
sweep the floor, sweep the floor,
this is the way we sweep the floor
early in the morning.

Repeat with the following sentences:

This is the way we polish the pews . . .
This is the way we say our prayers . . .
This is the way we listen to God . . .

Prayer

Dear God, we thank you that you love all children,
that you hear our prayers and speak to us.
Amen.

Song

Two little eyes to look for God

LAMPS

Aim

To encourage the children to listen.

Teaching

What sounds do you like to hear? Are there some nice sounds that it is hard to hear? Some bird sounds are really beautiful but you have to be very quiet to hear the birds. You have to be quiet and still. If you make a noise or run about you will frighten them away. If you want to watch birds or wild animals you have to practise being still and quiet. Let us see how still and quiet we can be.

When Samuel had finished helping the old priest, Eli, it was dark. He went to his room and lay down on his bed. Eli did the same in his room and soon both were asleep. In the stillness and quietness a voice called Samuel by name. Let us say his name quietly together: 'Samuel, Samuel.' (Encourage the children to whisper.) Samuel ran, and woke up Eli, and said, 'You called.' But Eli was tired and did not call. He sent Samuel back to bed. (Repeat this two more times, getting the children to whisper the call of God.)

Eli suddenly realised that in the quiet God had called Samuel. He told him to go back to his room and if the voice called again to say, 'Speak, Lord, for your servant is listening.'

Samuel went back to his room and was very still. Let us be very still (*pause*). Now let us call Samuel again: 'Samuel, Samuel.' There in the quietness Samuel knew it was God calling to him and he said. 'Speak, Lord, for your servant is listening.' Let us repeat those words.

Because Samuel listened, God was able to speak to him.

If you had covered your ears or made a lot of noise you would not have heard this story. You heard because you were quiet and good at using your ears.

Activity

Play 'Musical statues'. Run about and shout while the music plays. When the music stops everyone has to be still and quiet. Anyone who makes a sound or moves is out. The last one in is the winner.

Prayer

God, we thank you for the sounds of birds
and that we are able to hear.
Help us to listen carefully
and to be quiet in our prayers.
Amen.

Song

I love to be with you, Jesus

TORCHES

Aim

To encourage stillness and alertness.

Teaching

Get the young people to act out the story of Samuel and Eli.

Narrator The young boy Samuel lived in the Temple church at Shiloh. He was there to learn from the old priest, Eli, and to help in looking after the church. Some days they were very busy and became tired.

Samuel I am so tired, I am going to my room to sleep.

Eli So am I. Have a peaceful night and God bless you.

Samuel God bless you too. Goodnight.

Narrator Soon both were asleep. Then in Samuel's room a voice was heard.

God Samuel, Samuel.

Narrator Samuel jumped out of bed and ran to Eli's room.

Samuel What do you want? You called me.

Narrator This woke Eli up from a nice sleep.

Eli I was asleep. I did not call. Go back to bed.

Narrator Samuel went back to bed but lay awake listening. He was sure he had heard someone call his name.

God Samuel, Samuel.

Narrator Samuel was sure Eli was calling, for who else could it be? And he ran to Eli.

Samuel You called?

Eli I did not call. Go back to bed and let me sleep.

Narrator Samuel had not been in bed for long when the voice called again.

God Samuel, Samuel.

Narrator Again, for a third time, Samuel went and woke Eli. This time the old priest was wide wake. Eli knew it must be God calling Samuel.

Eli It was not I but God calling you. Go back to your room and if he calls again say, 'Speak, Lord, for your servant is listening.'

Narrator Samuel went back to his room and waited quietly, listening for any sound.

God Samuel, Samuel.

Narrator This time Samuel did not run away but stayed in his room.

Samuel Speak, Lord, for your servant is listening.

Narrator There in the quiet God spoke to Samuel and told him things that no one else knew.

Activity

Talk about using a mobile phone and how some areas are bad reception areas. Get the children to write text messages to God.

Prayer

God, you often speak with a still, small voice.
Teach us to be still and quiet in our prayers.
Help us to listen carefully to all who would talk to us and teach us.
Amen.

Song

Speak, Lord, I am your servant

Third Sunday of Epiphany

Aim

To show that miracles are mysteries and signs of the kingdom.

Preparation

Have some road signs and a wedding photograph.

Opening activity

Get people to look at the road signs and say what they mean. Show them the wedding photographs, and ask how they know what it is. You could do the same with other photographs or posters that show signs of what they are about.

Get someone to do a charade of a well-known television programme and see who can interpret the actions.

Opening prayer

God, you reveal your presence to us
through your creation;
you speak to us through signs and symbols.
Make us aware of you and your love
through Jesus Christ our Lord.
Amen.

Opening song

Songs of thankfulness and praise

Readings

Genesis 14:17-20
Psalm 128
Revelation 19:6-10
John 2:1-11

Thought for the day

All of today's readings are full of mystery. There is King Melchizedek who meets Abram and brings him bread and wine; Revelation invites us to the marriage supper of the Lamb.

We will concentrate on the Gospel and, according to St John, the first miracle of Jesus.

Miracles are wonderful events that we cannot fully explain – if we could, they would not be miracles. We are to see each miracle as a sign of the kingdom of heaven and the kingship of Christ.

The first miracle is a joyful occasion for it is a wedding. For the people who lived in Cana, weddings were usually held on a Wednesday evening. The couple would wear wedding robes and crowns on their heads. They would be treated like a king and a queen. This might be the greatest celebration of their life. They would be led home by torchbearers filling the street with light. A canopy would be carried over their heads, just like royalty. They would not go away for a honeymoon but would have 'open house' and a party, which would last for a week! That would take a lot of planning. There would be lots of guests and they would all wash their hands and their feet when they came to the house. There were large water jars outside for this purpose.

Jesus, his mother and disciples were at the party. It is thought that the bride or groom might have been a relative of Jesus. Cana was near Nazareth where Jesus lived.

There was singing and dancing and all were enjoying themselves. Suddenly Mary said to Jesus, 'They have no wine.' The party was not meant to end but soon it would be over. The wine had run out. The bride and groom would be embarrassed for they had run out of resources.

Jesus looked at the six big water jars that had been used for washing. Each jar held between 20 and 30 gallons. Jesus said to the servants, 'Fill the water pots.' They filled them right to the top. 'Now,' said Jesus, 'take some to the steward who is in charge.' They obeyed Jesus again. When the steward tasted the water it had become wine. He called the bridegroom and said, 'Everyone serves good wine first. But you have kept the best until now.' He did not know of the miracle; only the servants knew. You can imagine the surprise of the groom. The party could go on and people could enjoy themselves.

Question time

What is more important in this story: that Jesus can turn water into wine or that he can meet our failing resources?

Can you name a person whose life has been changed by Jesus?

Illustration

Have you ever heard of Dracula? Dracula is supposed to come when you are asleep and drain away your life. When you wake up in the morning you are at least half dead. It is not a true story but sometimes we can wake exhausted; we can feel we have no energy. Human resources do run out. Our batteries need recharging; we need to be refreshed and renewed.

When we feel we have reached the bottom of the barrel we need outside help. There are times when we are unable to help ourselves but Jesus is able to help us. In John 10:10, Jesus says, 'I came that they may have life, and have it abundantly.' You can trace this giving of abundant life, and how Jesus meets various needs and losses of well-being, in John's Gospel:

Need more wine – 2:1-11
Loss of well-being – 4:46-54
Lack strength – 5:2-9
Lack energy (food) – 6:1-14
Lack of security and safety – 6:16-21
Lack of vision and light – 9:1-7
Loss of life – 11:1-44

Jesus meets our drained resources with his generosity and power.

Intercessions

You, O Lord, are almighty, endless in power and in love.
When we have no power to help ourselves
help us to know we can trust in you,
in your presence and in your power.

We pray for the Church
that it may know its true resources and power
are from you;
that it may be enabled
to proclaim your saving power and your love.
Give your Church the ability
to be a healing instrument in the world,
to bring peace,
and to proclaim your presence.

Silence

Almighty God,
we know all power comes from you.

We remember all who struggle for survival,
the poor and the oppressed,
the hungry and the homeless,
all who feel powerless.
We ask you to bless all
who strive to bring justice and peace to our world.

Silence

Almighty God,
we know all power comes from you.

We give thanks for all who have enriched our lives
by their love and goodness.
We ask that your love may be experienced in our homes
and among our loved ones and friends.
We pray for homes where there is conflict,
violence or abuse,
especially for any who live in fear
or feel unable to change.

Silence

Almighty God,
we know all power comes from you.

Give strength to the weak,
refresh the weary,
encourage the fearful
and protect all who are endangered.
We remember friends and loved ones
who are ill or in need of comfort and refreshment.

Silence

Almighty God,
we know all power comes from you.

We rejoice that you give us life in all its abundance
and life eternal.
We pray for all our loved ones departed
that they may have the fullness of life in your kingdom.

Silence

Merciful Father,
accept these prayers
for the sake of your Son,
our Saviour Jesus Christ.
Amen.

Memory verse

Hallelujah! For the Lord our God the Almighty reigns.
Revelation 19:6

Suggested music

How sweet the name of Jesus sounds
Give me joy in my heart
Life for the poor was hard and tough

CANDLES

Aim

To show that the presence of Jesus brings joy.

Teaching

Show a picture of a wedding. Who has been to a wedding? Maybe someone has been a bridesmaid or a pageboy? Weddings often begin in church when the bride and groom ask God to bless them and keep them happy together. After the church service there is a wedding party. There will be lots of nice things to eat and drink and everyone is happy. Who has been to a party?

Jesus went to a wedding at Cana. Jesus' mother was there (can you remember her name?) and so were some of the disciples. When they went to the house there were six great big pots of water near the door. (Count your six big water pots.) The water was used for washing hands and feet and lots of people had used it.

It was a lovely party. The bride and groom had crowns on their heads and were just like a king and queen. They were very happy (show bride and groom happy faces) and enjoying themselves. Jesus and the disciples were enjoying themselves too.

At the party, Mary told Jesus that they had run out of wine. There were no shops where they could buy more wine so the party would have to stop. This would make the bride and groom very sad (show bride and groom sad faces).

When Jesus heard this he asked that the water pots be filled up to the top with water. The servants obeyed Jesus and did what he asked. 'Now,' he said, 'give some to the man who is helping to organise the wedding.' Again, they obeyed Jesus. 'This is wonderful wine: the very best wine. It is better wine than we had at the beginning,' said the man. He did not know that Jesus had turned water into wine. The helpers who had obeyed Jesus knew and they smiled. The bride and groom also smiled (show the faces) because the party could keep going. Jesus had made everyone happy.

Let us smile because Jesus loves us and wants us to be happy.

Activity

Make happy and sad faces using paper plates. Colour in six large water pots, blue on one side and red on the other.

Let us pretend we are at the wedding and we are helping to wash people's hands and feet. Now let us obey Jesus.

'Fill the water pots with water.' (Show blue side or at this point colour them blue.)

'Take them to the man who is organising the wedding.' (Let another child be the man.)

When he tasted the water it had become wine. (Colour other side of pots.)

He said, 'This is lovely, give some to everyone.' (Pretend to pour out wine for all.)

To practise listening and obedience they could play 'Simon says'.

Prayer

Jesus, we thank you
for all the lovely things you do for us
and that you look after us.
Help us to look after others.
Amen.

Song

Jesus' love is very wonderful

LAMPS

Aim

To show that our resources are limited but God's are not.

Teaching

Our planet earth is like a spaceship travelling though space. It has lots of wonderful things on board but all are in limited supply – some things could run out if we are not careful. If we go out in a car and drive and drive, it will suddenly come to a stop. Why? Yes, it would run out of fuel. You would have to fill it up again or you would go nowhere. Can you think of some of the resources we might run out of on earth? (Oil, gas, coal, petrol.) In some areas of the world people run out of drinking water and have to walk for miles just to get some water. Without water no living thing can survive. (If possible show posters of Water Relief or of people in the desert drawing water.)

Even strong people run out of energy and strength. Only God does not run out and only God can supply all our needs.

When Jesus was at the wedding in Cana the party ran out of wine. Mary told Jesus. Then Jesus asked the servants to fill the water pots with water. Do you know how many water pots there were? How many litres did each one hold? (6 pots x 20 gallons = 120 gallons = 120 x 4.546 = 545 litres or about 819 bottles!). That is a lot of water. It took more than one person to carry each pot. The person in charge was surprised when he was presented with the water pots and asked to drink. When they gave him some he was amazed for it was the best wine. Every water pot was full of wine. This was a very generous amount of wine and there would be plenty left even after the party.

The person in charge went to the groom and said, 'What wonderful wine, the very best.' The groom was a little puzzled but very pleased. The servants who knew what Jesus had done were all smiling.

Jesus is able to do this not because he is a magician but because he is God. This is one of the signs of God's kingdom. It points us to the power of Jesus and shows us how generous God always is. This is a miracle. Can you tell me of any other miracle that Jesus did?

Activity

Play charades and get the children to mime filling the car with petrol, switching on a light switch, sleeping to restore energy, eating to do the same. Let someone mime a starving person. Someone can mime drawing water from a well. Once someone guesses correctly, let them come to you for the next subject.

Prayer

God, you are all-powerful and a generous God,
always ready to help us
and give us of your goodness.
We thank you for our lives and all we are able to do.
Amen.

Song

I've got that joy, joy, joy

TORCHES

Aim

To show that Jesus changes people as well as water.

Teaching

Let us look at the wedding feast at Cana. Tell me what you know.

Now let us act it out, showing how Jesus took ordinary water and turned it into wine. (Give them various parts and let them be inventive – but do not allow them to make Jesus like a magician. Talk about miracles and signs.)

Jesus has the power to change the common and the ordinary into something special. Jesus has the power to change lives if we will let him.

Here is the story of a man who wrote a beautiful hymn. He lived a very wild and wicked life. He captured people and made them slaves. Once, because he gambled his money, he became the slave of a slave. He did not know where he was going nor did he see the wrong he was doing.

His name was John Newton and on 10 March 1748 he was in a sailing ship at sea. There was the most terrible storm and big waves broke over the boat. The cabin where John Newton slept was filling with water. He and another man struggled to the deck. The other man was immediately swept overboard and lost.

The ship was called the *Greyhound*. The sea had ripped away the upper timbers on one side and the boat was filling with water. The pumps were being manned but they could not keep the water level from rising. Fortunately a lot of the cargo was beeswax and dyewood and this kept the ship afloat. They filled leaks with bedding and clothes and nailed wood over them. Soon the crew were saying, 'It is too late, we cannot save ourselves.'

John Newton went to the captain and said, 'If this will not do, the Lord have mercy on us.' He later promised if they were saved from drowning he would change his way of life. As he went back to the pumps, he asked again and again for God to have mercy on people as wicked as himself.

For nearly four weeks the ship drifted and when they had almost given up hope the wind blew the sails in the direction they wanted. The *Greyhound* sailed safely into Donegal. Two hours later there was such a storm that the ship would have been lost at sea.

John Newton gave his life to Jesus and became a changed man. He discovered that Jesus changes lives. He became a priest in London and wrote many hymns. This is one of them. What do you think he means when he says:

> Amazing grace! How sweet the sound
> that saved a wretch like me.
> I once was lost, but now am found,
> was blind but now I see.

(See how verse two can relate to his sea journey in the *Greyhound*.)

Jesus is our Saviour and can change lives.

Activity

Get two groups to do extempore plays about Jesus' first miracle and about John Newton on the *Greyhound*.

Prayer

Jesus, you are able to change emptiness into fullness
and to turn lives from wickedness and wastefulness
to goodness and usefulness.
We ask you to bless our lives
with your presence and power.
Amen.

Song

Amazing grace

Fourth Sunday of Epiphany

Aim

To continue to show signs of the Christ.

Preparation

Collect signs of power, such as national and local power suppliers. Also have signs that express danger – for example, danger of electricity, signs at the petrol station to switch off mobile phones, a sign about radiation. Place a sign near the sanctuary which says, 'Enter with caution.'

Opening activity

Show the signs and see if all are recognised. Talk about the dangers of misusing power and how it can be lethal.

Opening prayer

Lord of all power and might,
you are able to do all things.
Help us to approach you with reverence and awe.
Yet because you are a God of love
let us come with joy and hope into your presence.
Amen.

Opening song

Praise, my soul, the King of heaven

Readings

Deuteronomy 18:15-20
Psalm 111
Revelation 12:1-5a
Mark 1:21-28

Thought for the day

The people of Israel recognised the dangers of approaching such a powerful person as God. Being too close made them aware of their sinfulness and their mortality. They feared both the voice of God and the fire. They asked that someone stood between them and God. As light reveals darkness, so the presence of God can reveal our weakness and sinfulness.

If there is any evil in the world, and I am sure there is, we should expect it to cry out against or oppose goodness. Evil and God cannot exist side by side.

In Mark's Gospel we are shown Jesus at the beginning of his campaign. Jesus has received the Father's approval at his baptism. He has been tested by the devil and chosen the way he will take. Disciples have been selected. Now he must begin his campaign. As you might expect, we hear of his beginning in a church. People recognised a personal authority. But there was also opposition. The Church is made up of humans; it is not perfect, and it needs salvation. The man with the unclean spirit shouts out, 'What have you to do with us, Jesus of Nazareth? Have you come to destroy us? I know who you are, the Holy One of God.' Whatever you make of 'unclean spirits', for Jesus here is opposition. It is worth noting that the unclean spirits recognise Jesus; they know him. Knowing of Jesus is not enough. We are called to love him and obey him.

Here was confrontation, a testing time for Jesus. Talk is all right, but can Jesus produce the action to go with his words? There was even more at stake, for most believed that demons were so powerful that only God could cast them out. Did Jesus have the power? Jesus showed that even his words were powerful enough. It was not the man but the evil spirit Jesus addressed: 'Be silent and come out of him.' This was not a request but a command, and the spirit came howling out of the man.

The people were amazed. This was a new teaching with authority ('Whose authority?' we must ask). He commands even evil spirits and they obey him. (Surely only God can do that!)

We may find it hard to believe in evil spirits, yet there are many people who struggle against evil and disease, and have the feeling they are not dealing with something passive but with a cunning and resourceful enemy.

Jesus began his ministry in the synagogue at Capernaum and immediately his fame spread throughout all Galilee. But only some will see the signs pointing to Jesus as the Son of God.

Question time

In a world where evil exists, if we seek to do good and be good, should we not expect opposition?

Can you think of other signs in the ministry and life of Jesus?

Illustration

Show an array of lights.

An ordinary lamp is useful when the sun goes down for it helps us to see around the house in the dark. A torch is useful for it is the sort of light you can carry around with you and use whenever you need it. Laser light is used in hospitals for surgery and it is also used as a military weapon – laser always has to be used with great care. A security light is good to welcome you home and also to show up any intruders. People who like to sneak about in the dark do not like security lights – especially if linked with a burglar alarm.

The greatest light we have is the sun. Without the sun all life on earth would perish. We need the sun to survive. We also need it to see where we are going. Yet we cannot look directly at the sun and sometimes we cannot even stay in the sunshine without some protection.

In the same way, we cannot behold the full glory of God but Jesus reveals God to us.

Intercessions

Gracious God,
you give us a glimpse of your glory
in the face of Jesus Christ.
Through him we are able to come before your presence
and to rejoice in your love.
Through him alone
we are counted worthy to approach you.

We give you thanks and praise
for the coming of Jesus into our world.

Silence

Lord of all power and might,
hear our prayer.

We remember in your presence
all who have not heard the Good News.
We pray for those
who do not know anything of being healed or forgiven.
Grant that the Church may proclaim
your love and saving power.
We pray for all who administer the sacraments
and who preach the word.

Silence

Lord of all power and might,
hear our prayer.

We pray for areas of our world
where darkness seems to triumph over light.
We remember people who are possessed by drug addiction.
We remember also those
who feel that they are possessed by evil.
May they all come to know the glorious liberty
of the children of God.

Silence

Lord of all power and might,
hear our prayer.

We give you thanks and praise
for those who have shared their faith with us,
for all who have encouraged us in the way of goodness.
We ask your blessing upon them
and upon our loved ones and friends.

Silence

Lord of all power and might,
hear our prayer.

We pray for all who have been ill for a long time,
for those whose illness finds no cure.
We pray for all
who feel they are losing their faculties or mobility,
all who cannot cope on their own.
We remember those who are in hospices.

Silence

Lord of all power and might,
hear our prayer.

We rejoice in the fellowship of the saints.
We remember loved ones who are departed from us.
We commend the whole of creation and ourselves
to your unfailing love.

Silence

Merciful Father,
accept these prayers
for the sake of your Son,
our Saviour Jesus Christ.
Amen.

Memory verse

Alleluia! I will give thanks to the Lord with my whole heart.
Psalm 111:1

Suggested music

I am the God that healeth thee
Give thanks with a grateful heart
Jesus shall reign

CANDLES

Aim

To show the love of Jesus as revealed in healing.

Teaching

Jesus went to the synagogue (explain) on the Sabbath to teach people about the love of God. There were a lot of people there and some of them would be fishermen because Capernaum was beside the sea. All of them were dressed up in their best clothes for going to church. Jesus stood up to teach them and they all listened very carefully. They thought that he was a wonderful teacher and they would have been happy to listen to him all morning – all except for one man. He was a strange man and a bit of a wild man. No one was ever sure about what he would say or do. He suddenly shouted out in church, 'What have you to do with us, Jesus of Nazareth? Have you come to destroy us? I know who you are, the Holy One of God.'

Everybody was horrified at the noise the man made and wanted him to be quiet. Some wanted to get him to leave the church because he was being a nuisance. I wonder how many listened to his words. (Repeat the words.) He asked two questions and both were very wise. He asked, 'What have you come here for?' Well, Jesus had come to teach and to tell them about the love of God. Jesus had come because God loves everyone and he wanted these people to know it.

The other question was a bit strange: 'Have you come to destroy us?' Well, Jesus did not come to destroy anyone; rather, he came to set them free and help them lead a full life. Yet the man was right for Jesus came to fight against evil and sickness and anything that hurt people. This man was ill and needed healing. Jesus would seek to make him better.

There was something in this man that recognised Jesus as the Holy One of God. He knew who Jesus was and wanted to shout about it. A lot of people in church did not know who Jesus was. Jesus asked him to be quiet. And then he did something wonderful: he commanded the evil to come out of the man. Jesus' words were very powerful and the evil left the man and the man was made well.

Everyone in church was amazed. Jesus not only spoke about God but he acted like God. At once all over the area people were talking about Jesus. What do you think they were saying?

Activity

Let everyone run around until the music stops. Then they must be absolutely still. The next time the music starts only those touched by the leader can move. Leave only a few to be still each time. When the music stops all are still. Repeat this process. Only those touched by the leader are to move. Let them see that the leader brings freedom of movement.

Prayer

Jesus, we thank you for the stories you told
and all that you taught us.
We thank you that you healed people
and wanted them to enjoy living.
Amen.

Song

Jesus' hands were kind hands

LAMPS

Aim

To show how Jesus speaks with authority.

Teaching

When soldiers are in the army, they have to obey their leaders. Leaders are people with authority. Sometimes to get authority you need to train, to get a certificate, to be put in charge. Can you think of some people who have authority?

Police have authority. Doctors have a different kind of authority. Some people are given the authority to run for their country or to play football. Sometimes you need authority (a ticket) to enter a building, for example.

Jesus went to the synagogue in Capernaum by the Sea of Galilee. No doubt Andrew and Peter and some more of the fishermen were also there. The church was full of people and Jesus stood up to teach. He spoke wonderful words that he didn't get from any book, and the people were amazed at his teaching. Suddenly it was stopped by another man who stood up and asked Jesus what he thought he had come to do. What do you think Jesus came to do? The man said, 'What have you to do with us, Jesus of Nazareth? Have you come to destroy us? I know who you are, the Holy One of God.' It sounds as if the man wanted to be rid of Jesus and that he was frightened of Jesus. Somehow he recognised the power and the authority that Jesus had. He knew where Jesus came from but, more than that, he was the first person to call Jesus 'the Holy One of God'.

This was a man who was troubled in spirit – some said troubled by evil spirits – yet he recognised Jesus. Jesus spoke with authority and commanded the man to be quiet and the evil that was bothering him to leave him. Because Jesus had power, this is exactly what happened. The people had been frightened of this man but Jesus was able to control him, just with a few words; not only control him but make his life better. The people were amazed. They were amazed at the teaching of Jesus and at his power of command. Some began to wonder about what the man had shouted, for he called Jesus 'the Holy One of God'. Soon all over Galilee people were talking about Jesus, his authority and power.

Activity

Play 'Simon says'. Point out how Simon speaks with authority and anyone who disobeys is out. Jesus uses his authority to bring people in.

Prayer

Lord of power and authority,
we thank you for your miracles of healing.
You show us God wants us to be well and healthy
and to enjoy living.
Amen.

Song

Kum ba yah

TORCHES

Aim

To show that miracles are signs.

Teaching

What are the signs of a good footballer or a boxer? How are they different? Next year one of our class may play football for England. Well, not yet but maybe one day. Why not yet? How do you get the power? Some of it comes through practice and hard work, but some of it is a gift or a talent. This is also true for musicians. Who plays a musical instrument or sings in a choir? It takes learning and talent. Some people are very gifted. (Let the children name gifted players and musicians; let them tell you about some of their heroes.)

When Jesus went to Capernaum the people in the Synagogue recognised he was gifted. They saw that Jesus was a very good teacher and that he knew a lot about God and people. They would have been glad to sit all day and listen. But one man had other ideas. He would rather Jesus left. Just by being present Jesus disturbed this man. The people in church knew this man and whispered that he had a wicked spirit inside him. Something that was evil had this man under control and wanted to stop Jesus. The man shouted out, 'What have you to do with us, Jesus of Nazareth? Have you come to destroy us? I know who you are, the Holy One of God.' (Look at this sentence by sentence.)

The man was obviously disturbed and troubled. He was also frightened for he could see how full of power and authority Jesus was. He knew that Jesus would fight evil and seek to destroy wickedness. What he did not know was that Jesus loves people even when he does not love their wickedness. (Help the young people to understand this by comparing it to the love of parents; Jesus hates the sin but loves the sinner.) The man knew where Jesus had come from. Can you remember where? He also knew where Jesus got his power and authority because he recognised him as the Holy One of God.

You would think that Jesus wanted everyone to know but he told the man to be quiet. Jesus wanted people to recognise him themselves and not just be told. But then he revealed his power by making this disturbed and frightened man well just with a few words. In Mark's Gospel this is the first miracle, and it shows the power of Jesus and points to where his authority came from.

Activity

Let the children do charades of their favourite powerful person. Get them to understand this includes musicians, pop singers and actors. After a while ask them to think of a sign of the power of Jesus (miracle) and see if they can mime that. Let them work in pairs to do this so that one can be the person needing healing if required.

Prayer

Jesus, you just need speak the word
and people are healed.
We thank you for the words of the Bible,
especially the Gospels.
More than anything, we thank you
that you are the Word made flesh.
Amen.

Song

Jesus is the name we worship

The Presentation of Christ

(To be used on the Sunday nearest to 2 February, if not on the day. There is no separate teaching for the children and young people as the service has action for all. If the groups need to go out they can use the illustration section and colour candle templates.)

Aim

To rejoice in the Light of Christ.

Preparation

Have a large candle to represent the Light of Christ and candles for everyone to light during the service. If this is not possible, let at least the younger members of the church have candles to carry (under careful supervision).

Opening activity

Once everyone is in church, put out all lights and sit in the darkness for a moment. If it is not dark, ask everyone to close their eyes. Tell them the darkness represents our lives and our world without Christ. Ask them to let Jesus bring light into their lives. Tell them to open their eyes when they hear the word 'eyes' mentioned.

Opening prayer

Let Jesus bring light to your lives.
The Lord Jesus give light to your eyes,
give light to your mind,
give light to your heart,
give light to your hands,
give light to your whole life
today and for ever.
Amen.

Opening song

Lord, the light of your love (Shine, Jesus, shine)

Readings

Malachi 3:1-5
Psalm 24:(1-6) 7-10
Hebrews 2:14-18
Luke 2:22-40

Thought for the day

Forty days after the birth of Jesus, Joseph and Mary went to Jerusalem to give thanks in the Temple for the birth of Jesus. By Jewish law, Mary could not enter a holy place or touch anything holy until she had given thanks to God for her child. They brought the traditional offering of a pair of doves.

In the Temple there was a man called Simeon. He was a righteous and devout man. It had been revealed to him by the Holy Spirit that he would not die before he had seen the Lord's Messiah – that is, the Christ. It was no coincidence that he was in the Temple. The Holy Spirit guided him. He came into the Temple exactly when Mary and Joseph brought in Jesus.

Archbishop William Temple said, 'When I pray coincidences happen; when I do not pray they do not happen.' Obviously prayer opened his eyes and enlightened him.

Simeon took Jesus in his arms and said the words we call the 'Nunc Dimittis', which is the beginning of his prayer in Latin. Simeon would now be happy to die, for he had seen the salvation of God in the child Jesus. He saw Jesus as a light that would lighten the nations of the world and someone who would bring glory to Israel. It is this image of Jesus as the Light of the World that we celebrate today with lighted candles. By tradition this is the fortieth and last day of the Christmas season, as we turn towards Lent. Some churches have lit a Christmas candle at every service until today. As this is the last day, everyone lights a candle from the Christmas candle and processes around the church. This is to rejoice in Christ as the Light of the World.

Simeon blessed the family and warned them that there would be opposition to Jesus. They had hardly time to be amazed at all of this when Anna, an 84-year-old widow, came and gave thanks to God for Jesus. She was a prophet and told how Jesus was the Redeemer. Here, in the holiest place of Israel, Jesus was welcomed as the Light and the Redeemer by these two people.

Question time

Mary and Joseph returned to Nazareth and Jesus grew in wisdom and strength. What do you think his parents felt after the episode in the Temple?

Do we recognise Jesus as the Light of the World, and how do we let that light shine in our lives?

Illustration

The illustration today is one of action. We will look to the candle that represents Christ in our midst and we will ask the light of Christ to shine in our lives. Then we will come forward during the singing of a hymn and receive a light. (If this is difficult, there are templates of candles on the worksheets in the Candles, Lamps and Torches books that can be photocopied, and people can come forward and receive one of these candles.)

Have a short silence, then pray:

Blessed are you, Lord our God,
for you have called us out of darkness
into your bright light.
You have called us to be children of light.
May the brightness of your presence
scatter all the darkness that is within us and about us.
Grant that the lights that we receive
may remind us of your light
and of your love towards us,
Jesus Christ our Lord.
Amen.

Let everyone come the shortest way to the Christ candle and walk back by going right around the inside of the church.

Sing the hymn 'Walk in the light'.

Let the leader say, 'Receive this light and shine as lights in the world.'

Let the candles remain lit as long as is practical. You can say, 'The Christmas season is ended. We now turn towards Lent and Easter.'

Intercessions

Blessed are you Lord our God, Creator of light and life.
We rejoice in your presence
and seek to live fully in your light.

By the word that created light out of darkness,
grant that your light may shine in your Church.
Let our lives be filled with your light
that others may be drawn to your light.
Let the Church throughout the world
be radiant with your light and love.

Silence

Light of Christ,
shine upon us.

By the light that has come into the world,
reveal your peace and justice to the nations.
Lord, guide our rulers and thinkers
that we may live in harmony and generosity,
that none may hunger or suffer from want.

Silence

Light of Christ,
shine upon us.

By the light that shines in the face of Jesus Christ,
fill our homes with your love and joy.
Bless our families and friends and all whom we meet.

Silence

Light of Christ,
shine upon us.

By the light that destroys darkness,
bring hope and comfort to all who suffer,
all who are ill at home or in hospital.
We remember all whose lives are darkened
by fear or their past.

Silence

Light of Christ,
shine upon us.

By the light that conquers death,
give to your saints and all the faithful departed
the fullness of life and joy in your eternal kingdom.

Silence

Merciful Father,
accept these prayers
for the sake of your Son,
our Saviour Jesus Christ.
Amen.

Memory verse

The Lord is my light and my salvation.
Psalm 27:1

Suggested music

Christ is the world's Light
Faithful vigil ended
Christ, whose glory fills the skies
Colours of day (Light up the fire)
This little light of mine

ORDINARY TIME
Proper 1

Sunday between 3 and 9 February inclusive
(if earlier than the Second Sunday before Lent)

Aim

To show the need for prayer.

Preparation

Have a large notice at the door to say the service will begin with the opening words and then a two-minute silence. In large letters put 'PRAY SILENCE' on the door.

Opening activity

Tell everyone that after the opening words there will be a two-minute silence. Help them to relax by telling them if little ones make a noise to walk about with them rather than restrict them too much. Our communication with God is more important than perfect silence.

Opening prayer

Lord God, still our hearts and minds
from their busyness.
In the quiet let our thoughts and our love
be directed to you.
Make us alert to your presence and your power in our lives
and aware that you love us.
Amen.

Opening song

What a friend we have in Jesus

Readings

Isaiah 40:21-31
Psalm 147:1-12, 20c
1 Corinthians 9:16-23
Mark 1:29-39

Thought for the day

Isaiah tells us that God is Almighty; that he gives power to the faint and strengthens the weary. There is no doubt of God's power and that he knows all that he has made. Then we are told 'those who wait for the Lord shall renew their strength'. We should all take these words to heart.

The psalm tells us though the Lord knows all the stars he is still concerned for us and heals the broken-hearted, and has pleasure in those who await his gracious favour. It would be good if we knew this in our lives.

In Mark's first chapter we get a glimpse of how busy Jesus was. On the day of rest he went to the synagogue. He taught with authority and healed the man who had an unclean spirit. At midday he went home with Simon Peter. Here Simon's mother-in-law had taken ill and was lying down with a burning fever. Jesus went to her and took her by the hand and raised her up. How many people does Jesus, the risen Lord, still take by the hand and help them to rise? Peter's mother-in-law immediately feels well and looks after her guests. There are two things to notice here. First, Peter is obviously married. The second is that the ministry of Jesus often depended on the care of such noble women as Peter's mother-in-law.

As it was the Sabbath, movement was restricted. When the sun went down a new day began. Because there were no clocks, it was said to be evening when three stars could be seen in the sky or when the last rays of sunlight had gone. The people waited patiently but were anxious not to miss Jesus. As soon as it was dark the streets were full of people coming to see Jesus and bringing the sick and indisposed with them. Often, in history, people come out of the darkness to him who is the Light of the World. It looked as if the whole of Capernaum had come out. Jesus must have looked after people well into the night and was probably exhausted.

Like any sensible person, Jesus knew he could not go on pouring out his energies without being renewed and refreshed. He needed new power. So, we are told, 'while it was still dark he got up and went out to a deserted place and prayed'. His ministry could only continue if he maintained a constant link with the Father. We often lack power and energy because we seek to go in our own strength. Remember the words of Isaiah: 'Those who wait for the Lord shall renew their strength.'

Jesus put himself out to get up extra early. Then he sought a place where he would have a time of quiet, and there he prayed. If Jesus felt the need to do this, there must be something wrong in our lives if we do not make time to pray.

Question time

Are we aware that our resources are limited and that only God is Almighty?

Do we make time and space in our day for prayer? If we are too busy to pray, our lives are on the wrong track.

Illustration

It is not often you see one of these in church – a battery charger. Sometimes, even when there is fuel in the tank, the engine will not start. This is because there is no spark, no electricity to fire the engine. Then you need the battery charger. It will slowly revive the flat battery and give it new life. Then we will be able to get going again. Also a car cannot run for long without being refuelled. You need to fill it up regularly with petrol. The more miles you do, the more petrol you need.

Some of you may have battery chargers at home to charge up batteries for CD players or other things that need electricity to keep them going. Many modern torches come with a charger so that the battery can produce a bright light.

Sometimes people are a bit like a beautiful car with a full tank of petrol but a flat battery. They should be able to do all sorts but they are flat and dull or feeling run down. So many seem to lack a bright spark in their lives. When this is so, we need power from outside ourselves. Listen again to Isaiah: 'Those who wait for the Lord shall renew their strength.'

Intercessions

Blessed are you, Lord God Almighty.
You are the giver of life and power;
all energy, all strength comes from you.
We come to you for renewal and refreshment.
We come to rest in your presence
that we may find strength and hope in you.

We pray for all who preach the word
and administer the sacraments,
that they may find great strength from your presence.
May the Church be a place of stillness and refreshment.
May your people show
that you give joy and peace to their lives.

Silence

Lord God, we wait before you.
Renew our strength.

We pray for all who are responsible
for the limited resources of our world,
that we may use them with respect and care.
We ask your blessing
on all who provide our homes with power and light:
those who work in the oil, gas and electric industries.
We remember all who are in emerging nations
and are looking to new sources of power.

Silence

Lord God, we wait before you.
Renew our strength.

We pray for all who expend their energies
in caring for us and loving us.
We ask you to bless our homes and our loved ones.
We pray for those who have taught us
and all who have provided for our needs.

Silence

Lord God, we wait before you.
Renew our strength.

Father, all-powerful,
we remember the needs of the weary,
the powerless, the ill.
We ask your blessing on all who feel
that they cannot cope with life
or who are drained of their resources.
We pray especially for those who are terminally ill.

Silence

Lord God, we wait before you.
Renew our strength.

Father, you are the giver of life and life eternal.
We remember in your presence
the holy ones who have served you.
We pray for our loved ones departed,
that all may be renewed by your power.

Silence

Merciful Father,
accept these prayers
for the sake of your Son,
our Saviour Jesus Christ.
Amen.

Memory verse

Those who wait for the Lord shall renew their strength.
Isaiah 40:31

Suggested music

Be still, for the presence of the Lord
I lift my eyes to the quiet hills
O, how good is the Lord
Give thanks with a grateful heart

CANDLES

Aim

To show how Jesus loves and heals.

Teaching

Do you remember when Jesus was in the church and someone shouted out because he was poorly? What did Jesus do?

Jesus also spoke to all the people in church and told them about God's love. Jesus had been busy all morning. Now it was nearly 12 o'clock. It was time to go and have something to eat. Jesus was staying at Capernaum with a fisherman – do you know his name? Yes, it is Simon Peter. Peter said it was now time to go home and have some food. With Peter were his brother Andrew and his friends, James and John. They were all disciples of Jesus and they were going to Simon Peter's house to eat. It was not very far to go and they were soon in the house. It was nice and cool inside but there was no food set out for them. Nothing was ready because someone in the house was poorly. Peter's mother-in-law (explain) was not very well. She was lying on a bed and had a fever that made her feel very hot. She was too ill to stand up and look after them. Perhaps they would have to go somewhere else.

Jesus was more bothered about the womann who was poorly than about eating. He could see she was not at all well and wanted to help her. He went over to her where she was lying and took hold of her hands. The hands of Jesus felt so strong and cool around her hot hands. Jesus looked at her and, still holding her hands, helped her to get up and stand on her feet. She felt better as soon as he had touched her. She was made well and wanted to do something for Jesus. She did what she was best at. She told them to sit down and she brought the food she had prepared earlier to them for to eat. Everyone in the house was amazed that Jesus had made her better just by taking her by the hand. It was a miracle.

Activity

Play 'Sleeping lions'. Pretend that you are in a deep dark jungle. You are very sleepy. While I count to ten you are to lie down and sleep. No one must move. If you move or make a noise you are out and must come and sit with me. When there is one left, go over to them, take them by the hand and say, 'Arise, for you have done well.'

Prayer

Jesus, you love people and do not want them to be ill.
We thank you for our lives and all you give to us.
Amen.

Song

Jesus' hands were kind hands

LAMPS

Aim

To show the power of Jesus in healing.

Teaching

Can you remember what happened when Jesus was in the synagogue? He did two things: he taught and he healed a troubled man. He had been busy all morning so he must have been tired and hungry. Now it was midday and he was looking forward to having something to eat. He was in Capernaum, which is beside the Sea of Galilee, and he was staying with Simon. Do you know Simon's other name, which Jesus gave to him? (Peter). Can you tell me the name of Simon's brother and those of his other two fisherman friends? (Andrew, James and John). With Jesus, how many does that make? Say their names and count them on your fingers. There were five people going to the house for a meal. When they got there they found the meal was not quite ready and the house was in darkness. For a moment they wondered what was wrong. Then they saw Simon's mother-in-law was lying on a bed in the dark corner. She was poorly. She could not stand up because she had a burning fever. She was very hot and shaky.

Jesus was sorry that she was not well and went over to her. He bent down and touched her hands, gripping them with his own. His hands were so strong and cool. Her hands were hot and shaky. It was as if Jesus gave his strength and coolness to her. Still holding her hands, he raised her to her feet and immediately she was better and began to look after her guests. (Let two children act this out.)

At about 6 o'clock that evening Jesus was thinking of having a rest when there was a noise outside. When they looked out, the street was full of people. Some had come themselves, others were brought by friends. They were ill and troubled people, and they wanted Jesus to heal them. He spent a long time helping and healing people and many went home very happy.

Activity

Let children act various illnesses and infirmities. They could mime being lame, blind or deaf. Let other children bring them to Jesus. All should express their joy and thanksgiving at the healing power of Jesus.

Prayer

Lord Jesus, your hands are full of power.
You heal and you bring comfort to people.
When we are troubled
let us learn to put our hands in yours
and to trust in you.
Amen.

Song

God is love: his the care

TORCHES

Aim

To encourage the group to make time and space for prayer.

Teaching

If you had to train for a match in the morning, play a tough game in the afternoon, come home and help out, then have homework to do, how would you feel? I am sure you would feel tired. If you pour out your strength and energies all day, you need space and time to recover. What do you do when you want to relax and be restored to strength?

In Mark chapter 1 we can see how busy Jesus is each day. On the day of rest, the Sabbath, he was teaching in the synagogue and there he healed a man tormented by evil. When he went to the house of Simon for a meal, he found Simon's mother-in-law ill with a burning fever. He took her by the hand and healed her. As soon as the Sabbath was over, at about 6 o'clock in the evening, crowds came to the door of the house to be healed. Jesus was busy well into the night, listening, touching and healing. By the time he finished he must have been very tired.

Jesus rested and slept but, we are told, 'In the morning, while it was still very dark, he got up and went out to a deserted place, and there prayed.' Jesus knew he had been using up a lot of energy. He would need to be recharged and strengthened. The only way his power could be restored was to keep in contact with his Father. He would do this often by finding a quiet place and praying. To do this he had to get up very early – before 6am – so that he could get some time alone with the Father. He did not lie in but got out and went to a quiet place. Jesus did this before he started his ministry and whenever he was busy. He always made time for prayer. In Mark 6:31 Jesus encouraged the disciples to find a quiet place. Then later, in Mark 6:46, after a busy day Jesus went up a mountain to be alone and to pray. Prayer is important if we are to live full and energetic lives.

A famous church leader at the time of the Reformation wrote, 'I am so busy that I find I cannot do with less than four hours a day in the presence of God.'

We must learn to be people of prayer. Our prayers are important to us so we must not put them off or miss them. Let us promise that we will pray every day, that we will spend some time rejoicing in the presence of God.

Activity

Play 'Musical bumps'. Tell them to run around as fast as they can. When the music stops, flop down and rest. There must be no movement: they must be absolutely still. Any one who moves is out. Tell them to thank God for his presence and for rest each time they are still.

Prayer

God, you are always with us,
you never leave us.
Help us to come before you in quietness and stillness,
that we may know your power and your peace.
Amen.

Song

Be still and know that I am God

Proper 2

Sunday between 10 and 16 February inclusive
(if earlier than the Second Sunday before Lent)

Aim

To show that Jesus cares for the lonely, rejected and outcast.

Preparation

Contact the Leprosy Mission, Goldhay Way, Orton Goldhay, Peterborough PE2 5GZ. Get some posters to show lepers, a pew leaflet and some prayers.

Opening activity

Give someone a bell, put a bandage around their head and place a poster over their head saying, 'Please do not touch.' Let them stand near the door. If anyone comes too close they are to ring the bell and call out. 'Unclean!'

Before the service begins let the 'leper' remove the bandage and notice, put down the bell and say:

Jesus, Jesus, wonderful Lord,
the moment you touched me
you made my life whole.

Opening Prayer

Lord Jesus, reach out and touch us who stand afar off.
Cleanse us from our sin,
heal us from our wickedness
and make us whole and healthy to serve you.
Amen.

Opening song

Jesus, Jesus, wonderful Lord

Readings

2 Kings 5:1-14
Psalm 30
1 Corinthians 9:24-27
Mark 1:40-45

Thought for the day

Leprosy was the most terrible of diseases and still can be. It was often wrongly diagnosed and people were sent into exile when they could have stayed at home. At its worst, parts of the body would drop off. You could lose fingers or toes, even whole hands and feet.

Almost as bad as the illness was the isolation. If you became a leper you were forced to leave your home and loved ones. You had to go and live in wild and lonely places. Lepers were not allowed into towns or cities. If a leper popped his head through a door, the house became unclean. No one was allowed to touch a leper. The leper had to keep at least two metres away and shout, 'Unclean'. If the wind was blowing towards you, the leper had to keep over 50 metres away. If a leper disobeyed this rule, the leper could be put to death. Being a leper was a lonely and sad life. The only people you could meet up with were other lepers.

The leper in today's Gospel was desperate. He came close to Jesus. It would seem he trusted Jesus and was confident that Jesus could heal him. The disciples probably held their noses and pulled away. In faith, the leper said to Jesus, 'If you choose, you can make me clean.' Jesus had the power of life or death over this man. As ever, Jesus came to give life. Jesus touched him and said, 'I do choose. Be made clean.' No doubt the touch was as important as the words; Jesus often made actual physical contact with people. Jesus was more concerned for the man than the law. He wanted the man to know he was touchable and lovable.

Question time

Are there times when we stand afar off and count people as untouchable or repugnant?

Do we isolate certain people?

How can we make ourselves and our community more accepting?

Illustration

There was a lady who lived off the west coast of Scotland on one of the islands, the island of Harris, and she had leprosy. She was forced to live alone on the seashore, where she lived off plants and shellfish. She bathed in the liquid off the shellfish and plants. All her flesh became healed and without leprosy. She praised Jesus in these words:

There is no plant in the ground
but is full of his virtue.
There is no form in the strand
but is full of his blessing.
Jesu! Jesu! Jesu!
Jesu! meet it were to praise him.

There is no life in the sea,
there is no creature in the river,
there is naught in the firmament,
but proclaims his goodness.
Jesu! Jesu! Jesu!
Jesu! meet it were to praise him.

There is no bird on the wing,
there is no star in the sky,
there is nothing beneath the sun,
but proclaims his goodness.
Jesu! Jesu! Jesu!
Jesu! meet it were to praise him.

Intercessions

Blessed are you, Lord our God.
You love every one of us and reach out to help us.
We are ever in your care and under your protection.

We come as a divided Church,
often full of mistrust and rejection.
We do not find it easy to accept the sinful
or to forgive our hurts.

We often carry a history of hurts and resentment.
Wholesome God, we come for healing and guidance.

Silence

Let your presence
bring us wholeness and hope.

We come as part of a world
where there is much violence and hatred.
People live in fear of each other
or are at war with each other.
There are many homeless and rejected people.
We pray especially for those with leprosy or AIDS.

Silence

Let your presence
bring us wholeness and hope.

We rejoice in your love and the love of our families.
We remember all lonely people,
all who feel rejected,
all who cannot cope on their own.
Lord, make our community
a loving and caring community.

Silence

Let your presence
bring us wholeness and hope.

We remember all who are isolated through illness.
We pray for those who are in hospital or in a home
and who have no visitors.
We remember those from our own community
who are ill at home or in hospital.

Silence

Let your presence
bring us wholeness and hope.

We rejoice that in you all ills come to an end
and all pain is taken away.
We give thanks for the gift of eternal life.
We give thanks for all the saints
and we remember loved ones who are departed from us.

Silence

Merciful Father,
accept these prayers
for the sake of your Son,
our Saviour Jesus Christ.
Amen.

Memory verse

O Lord my God, I cried out to you, and you restored me to health.
Psalm 30:2

Suggested music

Empty, broken, here I stand
When I feel the touch
What a friend we have in Jesus

CANDLES

Aim

To show God likes us to be well and happy.

Teaching

Has anyone ever been away from home in hospital? Did it make you sad that you could not be at home? At least you knew that you would get better soon and go home. A little girl was far away from her home in another country. She missed her mother and father but she was kept very busy helping in the big house. One day she noticed that the lady of the house was crying and wondered if she could help. She was told the lady's husband, Naaman, was ill and that he would not get better. He would have to leave his home and his family because he was getting worse. The little girl was sorry for Naaman and his family. All day long she wondered how she might help. Then all of a sudden she remembered a special man of God who lived in her own land. He was called Elisha and he did wonderful things with God's help. She knew what she should do: she should tell the family all about Elisha. She went to them and said, 'In my country there is a man of God called Elisha and I think he might be able to make my master Naaman better.'

They decided to go to Elisha. They had to pack bags, food, clothes, money and some gifts for God's holy man. It was a long journey but at last they arrived. Elisha had seen Naaman coming and knew why. Elisha sent a message to Naaman and this is what it said: 'Go and wash seven times in the river Jordan and you will get better.'

When Naaman heard this he was very angry. He thought Elisha would get him to do something wonderful or say some magic words. All Elisha did was tell Naaman to go and wash. Naaman said, 'There are better and cleaner rivers at home; why could he not let me go to one of them?' He was not going to do what he was asked. But his servants persuaded him by saying, 'You are lucky. The man of God has asked you to do something easy. Why not try it?'

So Naaman went down to the Jordan and dipped his feet in. Then he washed once. Was that enough? Two times, three times, let us count on our fingers, right up to seven times. He was not better after the first time, not even after six times. But after seven times God made Naaman well. Isn't God wonderful!

I am sure Naaman said a big 'thank-you' to Elisha's God and 'thank you' to Elisha. There was someone else he would have to say 'thank you' to; who was it?

Activity

Let the children play 'In the river'. Let the children make a circle around you. When you shout, 'In the river', everyone has to jump in the river. When you shout, 'On the bank', everyone has to jump backwards. This is easy. But if you shout, 'On the river' or 'In the bank', everyone must stand still. See how many can survive to jump in the river seven times.

Prayer

Father God, we thank you
for making us strong and healthy.
Keep us safe from all illness
and protect us from evil.
Amen.

Song

Thank you, Lord, for this new day

You may like to add a verse:

'Thank you, Lord, for healing us.'

LAMPS

Aim

To show how Jesus touched people and made them well.

Teaching

There are some things that are dangerous to touch. At the zoo there are notices saying, 'Please do not touch.' Where do you think you would see such a notice? Why is it there? Electricity is dangerous and we cannot touch it. Fire is dangerous and we cannot touch it. Can you think of anything else that is dangerous to touch?

When Jesus was in the Holy Land it was believed to be dangerous to touch a leper. Why do you think that is? Yes, if you touch a leper you might catch his disease. This is why we have to wash our hands if we touch anything that might have germs.

No one was allowed to touch a leper. He was not allowed to touch anyone or to eat in the same house or even live in the same house as anyone who did not have the disease. (Discuss what this would mean.) Lepers had to keep their distance from other people, far enough away so that they could not touch each other. So all lepers were very lonely as well as being ill.

When Jesus was in the countryside a leper came near to him – but probably kept the right distance away. He said to Jesus, 'If you choose, you can make me well.' That was a wonderful belief because it was thought that no one could heal a leper. The disciples were probably frightened even to be near this man. Jesus went right over to him and touched him. Jesus actually touched the man's body and said, 'I do choose. You are made well.' It was at that very moment, when Jesus touched him and said the words, that the man was made well.

Let us think of other people who were touched by Jesus and made well. (Ask the children if they can remember any examples.)

Listen to these words that you heard in church:

Jesus, Jesus, wonderful Lord,
gently you touched me
and made my life whole;
how can I thank you except that I see
your way of life is truly for me.

Activity

Choose one person to be the 'leper'. This person is to seek to touch others. They then become lepers. When there is one person left, let that person be Jesus. Let Jesus go around each person and touch him or her. When they are touched they have to say, 'Thank you, Jesus', and return to their seat.

Prayer

Lord Jesus, we thank you for healing people
and making them well.
Help us to keep in touch with you through our prayers.
Amen.

Song

Jesus' hands were kind hands

TORCHES

Aim

To show how Jesus loves and reaches out to everyone.

Teaching

Imagine you are on a bus or a train and a smelly tramp comes and sits beside you. He is dirty and covered in sores. What would you most likely do? You would move. Yes, I think I would too. Why? Maybe he had something that was catching. Do you know the difference between infectious and contagious? (Explain)

When Jesus was in the Holy Land the worst disease was leprosy. It made people not very nice to look at and frightening to be with. It was believed to be quite contagious. So a leper was not allowed to touch anyone, not even loved ones or friends. He was not allowed to sit in the same house or eat at the same table. All healthy human contact was forbidden. The nearest a leper could come was over two metres – so that you could not even stretch to touch each other. Leprosy was also believed to be infectious. So if a leper just looked round the door into your house, the whole house was made unclean. Leprosy made for very sad and lonely people. If they came too close to you, you were allowed to throw stones at them, even kill them.

Imagine how horrified the disciples were when a leper came close to Jesus. Maybe some were tempted to pick up stones. They were amazed that Jesus stopped and listened to the man. They were about two metres apart and the man was saying, 'You can make me well if you want to.' Of course Jesus would like the man to be made well – but this was leprosy. The man was untouchable. Imagine the disciples' horror. Jesus went over to the man and touched him. He actually put his arms around this foul-smelling man and said, 'I do choose for you to be well.' At that very moment the man lost his illness and his spots, and he was made well. No one went around touching lepers, but then no one healed them either. Here again we see a miracle, a sign of the power and love of God as revealed in Jesus. To Jesus no one is untouchable or beyond help.

Activity

Let the children look at literature from the Leprosy Mission and decide if there are ways in which they can help. (They might like to make an offering of some sort.) Talk about untouchables and how Jesus loves everyone.

Prayer

Lord Jesus, you bring healing to the ill,
strength to the weak
and love to the lonely.
Help us to care for all who are in need
and be grateful for all that we have.
Amen.

Song

Oh! Oh! Oh! How good is the Lord

Proper 3

Sunday between 17 and 23 February inclusive (if earlier than the Second Sunday before Lent)

Aim

To show our God is a healing and forgiving God.

Preparation

Make sure there is a printed copy of Psalm 41 for everyone.

Opening activity

Use Psalm 41 with its response. Let sections be read by different people (verses1-2, 3-4, 5-6, 7-9, 10-13). After the last response let everyone say verse 13 twice. At the end ask everyone to keep a short silence and give thanks to God for his healing and forgiveness.

Opening prayer

O God,we thank you
for the newness of this day and the newness of life.
Our past is behind us
and you give us new opportunities
to live fuller and more faithful lives.
We rejoice in your forgiveness and healing powers,
loving Lord.
Amen.

Opening song

New every morning is the love

Readings

Isaiah 43:18-25
Psalm 41
2 Corinthians 1:18-22
Mark 2:1-12

Thought for the day

In the mind of the Jews at the time of Jesus there was a definite link between illness and sinfulness. If you were ill it was because God was punishing you for your sins. God was a stern God who often punished his people. Jesus came to show that God has always been a loving and forgiving God. A parent may not like what a child is doing but the parent will still love the child. God hates sin but it does not stop him loving the sinner. This love is a free gift; it is the grace and goodness of God towards us. We cannot earn this gift but we need to learn to accept it.

In the reading from Isaiah, God tells the people to realise he is active now and is doing new things. There will be rivers flowing in what was a desert. Though his people had forgotten him and sinned against him, God will forgive them and not hold their past sins against them.

The Psalmist asks God for forgiveness and healing; the two go together.

We are told Jesus was 'at home' in Capernaum, but at whose home? Was it Peter's or even the home of the writer of this Gospel? We are not told, but Jesus is at home. Are you sure Jesus is at home in your house?

Here in Capernaum Jesus healed the man in the synagogue, Simon's mother-in-law, and all those who came to him once the Sabbath was over. It is not surprising that crowds came again for teaching and healing. This time there were some scribes keeping an eye on Jesus and making sure he did the right thing.

Four men brought a paralysed friend to Jesus. When their way was barred by the crowds, they struggled on to the roof and broke through the plaster and brush wood. (Remember, the houses had flat roofs and outside stairs up to them.) Then they lowered the man. It is a wonderful action to bring people to Jesus.

Jesus looked at the man and said, 'Son, your sins are forgiven.' I am sure the man hoped for more but perhaps this had to be said first. The Scribes were annoyed because only God can forgive sins. Who did this Jesus think he was? Jesus could see what they were thinking and turned to the paralysed man and said, 'I say to you, stand up, take your mat and go to your home.' With those few words Jesus healed the paralysed man. If sin is portrayed as illness, surely if the man was healed he was also forgiven. This is another sign, a pointer to who Jesus really is. The people glorified God and said, 'We have never seen anything like this.' Let us be sure we have come before Jesus and found forgiveness and healing.

Question time

Do you accept forgiveness as a healing with the ability to help you to live in the now?

The man being carried by four and lowered into the dark room is very like a funeral! Do you recognise Jesus has the power to say to you, 'Rise, get up and go home'?

Illustration

What a wonderful hymn our opening song was; we need to take it to heart. Read verse 1. We are here awake and alive due to the love of God. During the night we have been refreshed and restored in our powers.

Read verse 2. This verse can change our lives if we take it to heart. 'New perils past': some of the things we feared yesterday did not happen or were not half as bad as we thought. 'New sins forgiven': you need to accept this. What wrongs you did before today are forgiven as long as you intend to lead a new life. You need not carry a great load of guilt around with you; guilt does not change the past but forgiveness changes the future. In the grace and goodness of God you are given a new day – learn to live it. Do not drag old sins and guilt around with you, for they will hamper your life. Start the day anew. Give thanks for the love and the healing power of God in your life. Know you are 'ransomed, healed, forgiven'. Start each day in the presence of God and with new hope in your heart: 'new thoughts of God, new hopes of heaven'.

Intercessions

Blessed are you, Lord our God.
You forgive us our sins and cleanse us from all iniquity.
You give us the chance to start every day anew.

Lord, may your Church be an accepting and loving Church.
May it help to free those who are paralysed
by fear and doubt.
May it reach out to those who do not know of your love
and bring them to you.
We remember we are part of your mission
and we pray for all who are involved in outreach.

Silence

Holy and strong one,
let us rejoice in your saving power.

We remember in your presence
all who are struggling to survive.
We pray for those suffering from drought or flood,
all who are underfed or homeless.
Bless all who work for the relief of the poor and troubled.
We remember the work of Christian Aid, the Red Cross
and all who are good neighbours.

Silence

Holy and strong one,
let us rejoice in your saving power.

We give you thanks for our friends and family,
especially for those who brought us to know you.
We pray for all who teach in our church
and all who set an example of care and love
in our community.

Silence

Holy and strong one,
let us rejoice in your saving power.

Lord, let your presence bring comfort to the suffering;
may they know your love and care.
We remember all who are paralysed
or suffering from strokes,
all who are unable to move about freely
and all who are housebound.

Silence

Holy and strong one,
let us rejoice in your saving power.

We give thanks for the power of the Resurrection,
and that you offer us life eternal.
We remember all who have lost loved ones this week
and we pray for our loved ones departed.

Silence

Merciful Father,
accept these prayers
for the sake of your Son,
our Saviour Jesus Christ.
Amen.

Memory verse

Lord, be merciful to me: heal me for I have sinned against you.
Psalm 41:4

Suggested music

Praise, my soul, the King of heaven
What a healing, Jesus
Give thanks with a grateful heart

CANDLES

Aim

To show Jesus has the power to forgive and to heal.

Teaching

Have you ever done anything that was naughty? Was Mummy or Daddy cross with you? When you do naughty things it makes them sad but they still love you. Jesus loves us all and wants us to be happy.

We are going to look at a house like the one Jesus was in. It has a flat roof and stairs on the outside of the house. It is a sunny country so they do not need sloping roofs. Often people would sleep on the roof or rest up there.

Look: this is the house. It is really made of wood and clay. See the steps. It would be easy to climb up them – but not if you were helping to carry someone. (Show the sequence of pictures and the roof being taken to bits. Take the lid off your house and show the hole prepared earlier.)

Look at the picture of the men lowering the paralysed man. (Be sure the children understand the man could not walk.) He needed friends to bring him to Jesus. When Jesus saw the man he was sorry for him. He said, 'Son, your sins are forgiven.' Jesus probably knew the man wanted something else. What do you think he wanted? Yes, he wanted to be made well. He wanted to walk like other people. Jesus then said to the man, 'Stand up, take your mat and go to your home.' Only Jesus could do this and he did it to make this man well again.

Activity

You will need to prepare the house before the session. Let the children make men to carry a stretcher and a man to lie on the stretcher. The stretcher could be made by one of the children. Groups of six could do a little each. Then each group could make the event happen.

Prayer

Lord Jesus, you are strong and lovely.
You want us to be healthy and happy.
Thank you for healing the man who could not walk.
Amen.

Song

These hands

LAMPS

Aim

To show the power of Jesus and to encourage the children to tell of this power.

Teaching

When Andrew met Jesus, he brought his brother Simon to know him. Andrew brought a boy to Jesus with five loaves and two fish – do you know what happened next?

Sometimes people cannot get to Jesus because they are poorly. Some people do not even know anything about Jesus. If you have a friend who does not know about Jesus, maybe you could see if your friend would come with you next week.

Four men had a friend who could not go and see Jesus. In fact their friend couldn't go anywhere because he was paralysed. He could not move his feet and maybe he could not move his hands. Let us imagine how difficult this must be. He had seen doctors but no one could make him better. He was often alone at home and very sad. One day the friends came to see him and they were very excited. Jesus was back in Capernaum where they lived. The last time he was here he had made lots of poorly people better.

'How can I go and see him? I cannot walk.' 'We will take you. We will carry you,' said the friends. They set off carrying the man on a mat but he was very heavy and it took a long time. When they got there they could not get into the house. They nearly went back home again. One of them said, 'Let us take our friend on to the roof and maybe we can get to Jesus that way.' It was a great struggle to get on to the roof, even though there were stairs. Why?

When they got on the roof they started to break the plaster and make an opening. Now they lowered their friend right to the feet of Jesus. They had kept their promise and they brought him to Jesus.

Jesus was very sorry for this man for he looked so sad. Jesus said, 'Son, your sins are forgiven you.'

Some people said, 'Who does Jesus think he is? Only God can forgive sins.' Who do *you* think Jesus is? Then Jesus did something wonderful to show his power, he said to the man, 'Get up and walk.' And the man did just that. Imagine how happy the man was. He would thank Jesus and his friends. His friends were also happy because they would not have to carry him back home! Jesus is so powerful; it is good to know him.

Activity

Let us make a house like the one Jesus was in. We can even make a hole in the roof. We can also make a mat like the man was carried on and put some 'ropes' on each corner. Now let us act this story out.

Prayer

Jesus, we know you love us;
help us to love you.
Let us tell our friends about your love and power
that they may know you.
Amen.

Song

Give me joy in my heart

TORCHES

Aim

To see signs of God in the work of Jesus.

Teaching

The Jews believed that all suffering and pain was caused by sin – not simply your own wrongdoing but the wrongdoing of others. Pain and sickness came into the world because of the freedom that God gave to the whole world – the human body as well as the human being can go astray; genetics can go wrong as well as right.

The Jews were sure that a loving God did not want his people to suffer – but if they sinned it was their own fault. But this is not always true – life is not so simple. You cannot say if a person suffers it is the fault of their sin. In fact, some very wicked people do not seem to suffer much.

When the man who was paralysed was brought to Jesus there is no doubt he hoped for healing. Jesus looked at the man and said to him, 'Son, your sins are forgiven.' This angered the scribes for they believed that no one could forgive sins; only God could forgive. And they started to complain. Jesus knew he had the power to forgive and the power to heal. If the man was forgiven, then the scribes would surely expect him also to be made well. Jesus turned to the man and said, 'Stand up, take your mat and walk.' This was a paralysed man who hadn't walked for years. It would not be possible for him just to get up – but Jesus made it possible. The man was healed and forgiven. It is no wonder the people were amazed and glorified God. They were saying, 'We have never seen anything like this.' Jesus had shown power in forgiving and in healing – yet only God can do this. Who do *you* think Jesus is?

Activity

Let us act out the healing of the paralysed man. Choose someone light in weight for the paralysed man and place him/her on a mat or large bath-towel. Let four carry him/her around the room and pretend to go on to the roof. Let them gently lower the paralysed man before Jesus. First, Jesus forgives the man. Three or four scribes object, saying. 'He cannot do this. Only God can do this. Who does Jesus think he is? Only God can forgive sins.' Maybe a disciple can whisper, 'Oh yes, he can, for he is the Son of God.'

Jesus can ask, 'Which is easier, to say "Your sins are forgiven", or to heal the man?' Jesus can go to the man and help him to stand, saying, 'Stand up, take your mat and go home.' Someone can say, 'This is a sign of great power. We are all amazed. Who can Jesus be?' Let the man get up and go out shouting 'Praise God, Alleluia.' Let someone whisper, 'Do you think Jesus can mend roofs?'

Prayer

Lord Jesus, we thank you that you have shown us
the love and the forgiveness of the Father.
We think you are great and do wonderful things.
Amen.

Song

Jesus wants all of me

Second Sunday before Lent

Aim

To show that Jesus Christ was with the Father before the foundation of the world.

Preparation

Have some paper bags ready for the younger children. Also have a picture of the earth from space.

Opening activity

Look at the earth and describe its beauty and balance. What makes the earth a habitable place is its water, warmth and air. Ask the children with bags to go outside the church and get the bags filled with air. Have someone outside to keep an eye on them and to help them if they look lost. Are the bags empty? Where did the air come from? Where was it before that? We cannot see the air but it is around us and in us. Thank God for the gift of air.

Opening prayer

O God, in you we live and move and have our being.
Nothing can separate us from you,
only our own turning away.
Help us to know and to rejoice in your presence
today and always.
Amen.

Opening song

Thou, whose almighty word

Readings

Proverbs 8:1, 22-31
Psalm 104:25-35
Colossians 1:15-20
John 1:1-14

Thought for the day

Today's readings are telling us that Jesus was there before the creation of the world and working with the Father. John's Gospel starts with the same words as Genesis: 'In the beginning'. Genesis says, 'In the beginning God . . .' and John says, 'In the beginning was the Word, and the Word was with God, and the Word was God.' Not only was Jesus present but Jesus shared in the creation: 'all things came into being through him . . . in him was life and the life was the light of men' (John 1:3-4).

Not only was Christ there, but we are actually in him. All creation is in him, as it is in the Father and the Holy Spirit. Paul in Colossians says of Christ, 'In him all things in heaven and on earth were created.' This is a great mystery, which we will never fully understand with our minds, but we can know it with our hearts. We need to rejoice in God and need to know in our hearts that we are never outside of him.

Question time

How do we show that we live in God and in his love?

Illustration

There is a fountain in India with fish around it. On the fountain are words by the Indian poet Kabir: 'I laugh if I hear the fish in the sea are thirsty. I laugh if I hear man goes in search of God.'

Just think of a little fish living in a mighty ocean being told its whole life depends on water. One morning it sets out to find water. It leaves its home and travels to cold seas but it cannot find water there. It then travels south to warmer climes, still seeking, but it cannot see water there. It searches all of the seas and all this time it is restless and weary, spending much of its energy. At last it meets an old fish on the seabed and asks, 'Where is the water for I would like some?' 'Do you not know you live in the water, you move in the water, you only exist because of the water? There is no need to look for it, you are in it. If you did not have it you would die. Enjoy being in it; know that it is all around you.' This was wonderful news; there was no need to seek but there was a chance to enjoy the element in which it lived.

St Paul, when he was speaking about God to the Greeks on the Areopagus, says, 'In him we live and move and have our being' (Acts 17:28). This is a wonderful reality to discover: we need not seek God for we are in God, in his presence and in his love. Let us enjoy this reality.

Intercessions

Blessed are you Father, Son and Holy Spirit.
You have made us
and in you we live and move and have our being.
In you we rejoice.
In you is the fullness of life.

We give thanks
for the wonders and the beauty of Creation.
May we delight in your world
as you delight in it.
May your Church show a great love and care for the world
– as you love and care for it.
We pray for all who do not know
of your love or your presence.
We ask you to bless all who preach the Word.

Silence

Lord of love,
in you we live and move and have our being.

We pray for all who teach us
to respect and love your world.
Bless all who work in conservation
and in protecting the resources of the earth.
Help us to enjoy the world and delight in it
with artists and musicians and all craftspeople.

Silence

Lord of love,
in you we live and move and have our being.

God, we thank you for your presence
in our homes and communities,
in our schools and in our work.

Bless our loved ones
and all who have enriched our lives by their goodness.

Silence

Lord of love,
in you we live and move and have our being.

God, we ask your presence to bring comfort and hope
to all who are struggling at this time.
We remember those injured in accidents or acts of violence,
those who are ill
and all who are in hospital.

Silence

Lord of love,
in you we live and move and have our being.

You give life and light;
in you life and light are eternal.
May all our loved ones departed and all the saints
rejoice in the fullness of eternal light and love.

Silence

Merciful Father,
accept these prayers
for the sake of your Son,
our Saviour Jesus Christ.
Amen.

Memory verse

In Christ all things in heaven and on earth were created.
Colossians 1:16

Suggested music

Christ be with me
Christ is the world's Light
Christ's is the world in which we move

CANDLES

Aim

To help the children to know that God loves us and made the word in which we live.

Teaching

Look at this modelling clay. I can make things with it. Watch, I will make a cat. Now I will make something else (a human) – what is it? Yes it is a boy or a girl. Who would like to make something? (Let the children make things and say what they are.) Now I am going to take the clay away. If you do not have the clay you cannot make anything.

Once God did something very wonderful and he made it out of nothing. He had nothing to start with. He made the whole world in which we live. God the Father, Son and Holy Spirit decided to make a beautiful world. This is how it all began.

First, God made the sun, the moon and the stars. He made the sun to shine at day and the stars to shine at night. Then God made water. He made rain and rivers. He made streams and seas. What do you call a large sea? Yes, it is an ocean. Then God made the land – or we would all have had to be fish! He made hills and mountains, valleys and beaches and he made them all out of his love. He thought, 'How lovely.'

Then he made grass, trees and flowers and all growing things. Tell me some of the things that God made. He made all these out of his love. He saw that they were lovely.

Then in the waters God made fish; in the air he made birds, large ones and small ones; on the land he made animals. Tell me the names of some. God loved all that he made and thought they were lovely.

After he made the world, God decided it was now time to make people. God wanted someone who would love him because he loved everything. He wanted someone who would love the world like he loved the world. So he made the first man and called him Adam. Then, because God knew Adam would like someone to share the world with, he made a woman and called her Eve. They would love each other as God loved them. They would learn to love the world like God loved the world. And God made all of this out of his own love.

Activity

Have pictures of beautiful things for the children to stick on a frieze. Let them also draw something they love and add it to the frieze and write their name against it. Have in big letters underneath: GOD MADE ALL OF THESE.

Prayer

God, Father, Son and Holy Spirit,
thank you for the lovely world, which you made.
As we look at the world and at ourselves
help us to know you made us out of your love.
Amen.

Song

God who made the earth

LAMPS

Aim

To show that God is always present.

Teaching

There was a man with a wonderful telescope and he looked for all the planets. He counted them off as he saw them but there was always one missing. He looked again and again but there was one he could not find in the sky. Which one was that? It was the earth. He could not see it in space because he was actually on it.

The absent-minded professor set out to look for his glasses when they were actually on his head. He searched his laboratory for them until someone pointed out that he was wearing them.

Think about the fish that looked for water when it lived in the sea. It would be like us going in search of air or in search of God. God is always with us even though we cannot see him. God the Father, Son and Holy Spirit is always there.

Before the Universe was made,
before the earth was created,
before there was life
God is there, always there.

At the beginning of the Universe,
at the Big Bang,
at all the stages of evolution,
God is there, always there.

At the beginning of our galaxy,
at the making of sun and moon,
at the beginning of the stars
God is there, always there.

Activity

Get the children to work through each day of Creation in Genesis adding after each day:

God is there, always there.

Then let them look at a day dawning, at the beginning of school lessons, at the start of playtime, and let them add: **God is there, always there.** See how creative they can be with beginnings.

Prayer

God, you were there at the beginning of the world
and the beginning of life.
We thank you that you are always with us.
You never leave us.
You are always ready to help us.
Amen.

Song

If I were a butterfly

TORCHES

Aim

To encourage the young people to be aware of the presence of God.

Teaching

St Patrick was born on the west coast of Britain around the year 390. When Patrick was only 16 he was captured by raiders and taken away as a slave to Ireland. He was made to look after sheep in the mountains. It could be very lonely but other Christians taught Patrick that God was always there. Because he trusted in God he spoke to God in prayer. He said, 'I often prayed in the daytime . . . up to a hundred prayers and at night nearly as many.' Patrick was happy to know that God was with him and cared for him. Every day he used to remind himself of God's presence by saying, as he tightened the laces on his tunic:

I bind unto myself today,
the strong name of the Trinity,
by invocation of the same,
the Three-in-One and One-in-Three.

After six years he escaped from being a slave but later returned to Ireland to teach about God. When he met two Irish princesses he told them about God. He said, 'Our God is the God of all, the God of heaven and earth, sea and river and all that are therein. He inspires all things; he gives life to all things.'

Patrick was sure of the presence and power of God. These are some of his words about Christ:

Christ with me, Christ before me,
Christ behind me, Christ in me,
Christ beneath me, Christ above me,
Christ on my right and on my left.

Patrick was sure of the presence of God because he spoke to God every day. His praying kept him in touch with God. It is easy to forget friends and relatives if we do not keep in touch with them. Let us make sure we keep in touch with God every day.

Activity

Look at St Patrick's affirmation of the presence of Christ. It is often called the 'prayer of seven directions'. Can you find each direction? Notice there are six directions to show God is all about us, and one to show he is in us. God is greater than us always. See if you can write a prayer of seven directions.

Send a text message to God, expressing your love for him.

Prayer

Christ is with me, Christ is before me,
Christ is behind me, Christ is within me,
Christ is beneath me, Christ is above me,
Christ on my right and on my left.
Christ all around me and within.

(Let this prayer be prayed visualising the reality or even acting out the directions.)

Song

Think of a world without any flowers

Sunday before Lent

Aim

To show that Jesus is the Son of God and fulfils the longings of the law and the prophets.

Preparation

If it is a sunny day, have a mirror to reflect the sunlight; a strong torch to shine will be more practical on a dull day.

Opening activity

Make the light dance around the church and especially around the sanctuary by using the mirror. If this is not possible, and it is not in many churches, use the torch, letting it pick out points of architecture. Never shine the light directly at people. Tell the people you do not shine the light at them because you fear you might dazzle them and hurt their eyes.

Opening prayer

Father, most holy,
whose Son Jesus Christ was transformed on the mountain,
shine upon us in your goodness
until our lives reflect your glory:
through the same Jesus Christ our Lord.
Amen.

Opening Song

Lord, the light of your love (Shine, Jesus, shine)

Readings

2 Kings 2:1-12
Psalm 50:1-6
2 Corinthians 4:3-6
Mark 9:2-9

Thought for the day

A week before the events in today's Gospel the disciples were at Caesarea Philippi. It was there that Peter had confessed Jesus as the 'Christ' and there that Jesus told them of the suffering ahead. Perhaps there was a need for some of the disciples at least to see some brightness behind the dark clouds that threatened.

Jesus took Peter, James and John up a mountainside for them to be alone. Tradition says this was Mount Tabor but this is a good way from Caesarea Philippi and it has a fortress on the top. It is more likely to have been Mount Hermon. Maybe they even went up to the snow line.

What happened on the mountain was an experience the disciples could not put into words. They became aware of the radiance of Jesus and of the presence of Moses and Elijah. In Jesus they were aware that all that Moses and Elijah had hoped for was fulfilled. Like Moses, Jesus would bring his people to the freedom of the Promised Land. He would give them a new way of life and free them from slavery. Elijah was said to be the greatest of the prophets. Now, in Jesus, all the hopes of the prophets were to be fulfilled. In the Christ is the second Moses and the second Elijah whom the people of God longed for. Such a vision would carry the disciples a long way, but there was more: the cloud that overshadowed them was hiding the presence of the Father. God was there in his fullness but for their sake his glory had to be hidden. As God had appeared to Moses in the cloud, now he was present on this mountain. Then there was the voice from the cloud saying, 'This is my Son, the Beloved, listen to him!'

Then the vision faded and they descended the mountain and made their way to Jerusalem. But they had been there; they had a glimpse of the glory of God as revealed in Jesus Christ.

We are offered a glimpse of this glory as we turn towards Lent and the events of Holy Week. We are also asked to 'Listen to him!' Listening also means obeying.

Listen again to the words of St Paul:

> For it is the God who said,
> 'Let light shine out of darkness',
> who has shone in our hearts
> to give the light of the knowledge of the glory of God
> in the face of Jesus Christ.
> *2 Corinthians 4:6*

Even when the vision faded the disciples had their eyes fixed on looking at Jesus. We seek in the days ahead to look at Jesus and to get a glimpse of the glory of God.

Question time

How do you think the transfiguration of Jesus on the mountain helped the disciples in the troubles ahead?

Do you try to get a glimpse of glory in your life by discovering the hidden glory of God?

Illustration

The day before the civil rights campaigner Martin Luther King was killed by a sniper's bullet he said words of encouragement to a large crowd:

> We've got difficult days ahead. But it does not matter to me now. Because I have been to the mountain top, I won't mind. Like anyone else I would like to live a long life . . . but I am not concerned about that now. I just want to do God's will. And he's allowed me to go up the mountain. And I have looked over and seen the Promised Land. So I am happy tonight, I am not fearing any man. Mine eyes have seen the glory of the coming of the Lord

Like Martin Luther King, if we are to survive dark days, we need to have a vision of the glory of our God.

Intercessions

Blessed are you Lord God our Father.
You have revealed your hidden glory
in the face of our Lord Jesus Christ;
in Christ you have given us the hope of life eternal.

Bless your Church, O Lord,
with the radiance of your presence.
In each place of worship may we bow before your glory.
We ask you to transform with your brightness
all those places where worship
appears to be dull or lifeless.
Fill all preachers and teachers
with a vision of your glory.

Silence

Glorious God,
give us a glimpse of your glory.

Lord of light, transform the dark places of the world
by your presence.
We remember all who live in slums
and shanty towns,
all who live among war and dereliction.
Let the radiance of your presence
bring hope to their lives.

Silence

Glorious God,
give us a glimpse of your glory.

Glorious God, fill our homes with your love
and our lives with your glory.
Be with us and all our loved ones
and deliver us from darkness.

Silence

Glorious God,
give us a glimpse of your glory.

We remember all who suffer,
all who are in hospital,
all who are lonely and feel rejected,
all whose lives are in a dark cloud.
We think of those who are fearful of the future
and those whose lives are full of sadness.
Lord, may the light of your love transform their lives.

Silence

Glorious God,
give us a glimpse of your glory.

Give us a glimpse of your glory
and awareness of your gift of eternal life.
As we rejoice in the fellowship of all your saints,
grant to our loved ones departed
the joy and glory of your kingdom.

Silence

Merciful Father,
accept these prayers
for the sake of your Son,
our Saviour Jesus Christ.
Amen.

Memory verse

It is the God who said, 'Let light shine out of darkness',
who has shone in our hearts.
2 Corinthians 4:6

Suggested music

God of mercy, God of grace
Hail to the Lord's anointed.
Father of heaven, whose love profound

CANDLES

Aim

To show that Jesus brings light to our lives.

Teaching

When it gets dark what do you do? Yes, you put on a light and the darkness disappears. Streetlights make our towns and villages safer. If we have to go down a dark street, we take a torch with us so that we can see more clearly in the dark. Perhaps at home you have a light that is left on all night or a light that comes on when it is dark. (Let the children talk about different lights.)

What is the brightest light we have ever seen? Yes, it is the sun. But no one can look at the sun because it is too bright. It can hurt our eyes by its brightness and can even make us go blind. We should never look directly at the sun. The sun gives the world light and life but we cannot look directly at it.

When Jesus went up a mountain with Peter, James and John it was to show them who he really is, to let them see he is the Light of the World. High up in the mountain, when they were away from everyone else and very quiet, Jesus said his prayers. While he was praying the three disciples saw his clothes glowing bright and white. They were amazed at the brightness. Then from a cloud they heard a voice – it was the voice of God. God actually spoke to them and said to them, 'This is my Son, my loved one; listen to him.' The disciples looked around to see who spoke but they could see no one, only Jesus. God was behind the cloud because he was too wonderful for the disciples to look at; he protected them from his brightness by the cloud. When they were going down the mountain they thought they would like to tell everybody what had happened, but Jesus said, 'Do not tell anyone just now; keep it a secret.' We are lucky because we know that secret. We know Jesus is God's Son and he is the Light of the World.

Activity

Play musical statues. Every time the music stops shine a light around, aiming at the feet of the children. Anyone who moves or cannot be quiet is out. This is more effective if it can be done in a semi-dark room.

Prayer

Jesus, we know you are the Light of the World.
Shine in our lives
and make them bright and beautiful.
Amen.

Song

God who made the earth.

LAMPS

Aim
To help the children to be aware of the glory of Jesus.

Teaching
Have you ever climbed a very high hill? What was the view like from the top? Yes, from the top you can see a lot further. Now, what are the highest hills called? Mountains. Maybe someone knows the name of the highest mountain in the world? On the top of very high mountains, what is there all the year around? Yes, snow, because the higher you get on mountains, the colder it is. Let us pretend we are climbing a high mountain and suddenly we see snow, blinding white, too bright to look at. What could we do? Yes, we could put sunglasses on or cover our eyes or look away. Let us pretend we are covering our eyes with our fingers and looking at the brightness. High above us is the sun. We must not look directly at the sun. Even some lights are too bright to look at and need to be covered to protect us from their brightness. Can you think of any such lights?

Once Jesus went up a high mountain with three of his disciples, Peter, James and John. The disciples were sad because Jesus told them what would happen to him when he went to Jerusalem. Do you know what was going to happen to Jesus? But he did not want them to worry too much because something else would happen to him three days later. What was that? Well, we know all of the story, but the disciples did not. Jesus took them up a mountain to show them they need not be so worried.

On the mountain with no one else around the disciples watched Jesus praying. Suddenly his clothes became shining bright, so bright they could hardly look at him. They were looking at the hidden glory of Jesus, and it was a very special moment. Then from a cloud they heard a voice saying, 'This is my son, my loved one, listen to him!' The disciples knew this was the voice of God. Do you remember at the baptism of Jesus the voice of God was heard from a cloud? The Father was reminding the disciples of what Jesus had come to do and he asked them to listen carefully to Jesus. God's glory was too bright to look at, just as you cannot look directly at the sun, so it was hidden behind the cloud. Now when they looked at Jesus he looked quite ordinary again. Wouldn't it be wonderful to tell everyone of what they had seen and heard? Jesus wanted them to keep what they had experienced a secret for a while. It seemed to be a day for sharing and keeping secrets. Jesus did not want anyone to be told of his hidden glory until after the resurrection.

Activity
Let us sing just one word over and over to the tune 'Amazing grace'. The word we will sing is 'Glory'.

Here are some words. Can you make a sentence out of them?

> HAS GLORY OF REVEALED FACE IN JESUS HIS GOD THE CHRIST

If possible, have these words separately on large cards and let the group put them in order.

Prayer
God, we give thanks to you for your glory
and that you show your love and care to us
through Jesus Christ, your Son, our Lord.
Amen.

Song
God is love: his the care

TORCHES

Aim
To explore the hidden glory of God.

Teaching
St John tells us that no one has seen God at any time (John 1:18). God cannot be looked upon by any one. We cannot even look at the sun in its brightness. So the Bible often spoke of the hidden glory of God. God is always present but keeps his glory hidden to protect us. As a symbol of the hidden glory of God we have a cloud, sometimes a cloud with a silver lining.

When Moses met God he met him in a cloud; he never saw God but could communicate with him. It was in a cloud that God came to the Tabernacle where the Jewish people prayed. It was the cloud of the presence of God that filled the Temple when it was dedicated after Solomon built it. It was a cloud of smoke that filled the Temple when Isaiah had his vision of God and he heard the angels singing, 'Holy, holy, holy! The Lord Almighty is holy! His glory fills the world.'

One of the symbols of the glory of God is a cloud with the sun above it. From below we would not see the sun because of the cloud.

When the disciples were troubled about the future, Jesus took Peter, James and John up a mountainside to be alone with him. There in the quiet they would see the hidden glory of God.

After a steep climb, high on the mountain, Jesus prayed. As he was praying the disciples saw a change come over him. There was a dazzling brightness that they could hardly look at. Just as Moses had met God on the mountain, God was being revealed to them. There was also a cloud and from the cloud the voice of God saying, 'This is my Son, my loved one, listen to him.' The disciples did not know what to do but they were sure they would tell everyone what they had seen and heard.

When the vision had faded and they were coming down the mountain Jesus asked them to keep it all a secret until after all the things that were to happen to him in Jerusalem. We know this secret because those things did happen. St John would write of Jesus, 'We beheld his glory, the glory of the only Son of the Father.'

Activity
Make a collage of clouds with hidden words behind them; words like GOD, GLORY, JESUS, FATHER, CHRIST, SON OF GOD. Let the clouds be dark and the

colour behind them be white, gold or silver. Let the colour show a little around the edges of the cloud. Have three disciples looking up at the clouds and a radiant Jesus at prayer.

Prayer

Glory to you, Father, Son and Holy Spirit.
The whole earth is full of your glory.
Open our hearts to know your hidden presence
and your deep love for us.
Amen.

Song

Be still, for the presence of the Lord

LENT
First Sunday of Lent

Aim
To encourage a positive approach to Lent.

Preparation
Have a dartboard with Velcro darts. Alternatively, have a large drawing of a donkey for 'Pin the tail on the donkey'.

Opening activity
Let as many as possible aim for the target or pin the tail on the donkey. If people miss totally give them another chance. Have pictures around of goal scorers and other achievers, including musicians and scientists. What do you do if you miss the mark or fail to get a goal or hit the wrong note? Yes, you try again, and you practise to improve your aim.

Opening prayer
Lord, on the way of goodness,
when we go astray lead us back to you.
When we stumble lift us up.
Help us to do what you would have us do
and to become the people you would have us be.
Amen.

Opening song
Forty days and forty nights

Readings
Genesis 9:8-17
Psalm 25:1-10
1 Peter 3:18-22
Mark 1:9-15

Thought for the day
You may have noticed a colour change in some of the things in church. We have changed to purple or Lent array for this new season, which began on Ash Wednesday. There are forty days in Lent to remind us of the forty days Jesus spend in the wilderness. Lent is a time when we look at our priorities and make sure we are on the right track: it is about trying to truly be the people of God. Lent is not so much a negative time as a positive time when we check that we are not going astray. It can partly be summed up in today's Psalm: 'Show me your ways, O Lord, and teach me your paths'(Psalm 25:4).

In the Gospel we hear of the baptism of Jesus, the descent of the Spirit and the voice of God. It would seem all is wonderful but immediately the same Spirit drives him into the wilderness. It is his own abilities and talents that will tempt Jesus. Remember temptation is not wicked: temptation is about choice and decision. Wickedness only gets the upper hand if we take the lower road and miss our target. Being lazy or a couch potato when we have so much ability is wicked.

Temptation helps us to strengthen in our purpose and choose a better way of living. Sin is when we lower our aims, choose a way without God and when we live below our potential.

In the wilderness Satan tempted Jesus. Satan means the adversary, the one who is against us. At this stage the temptations of Jesus come from within. Another word for Satan is 'Diabolos' which means 'that which throws apart' or 'that which is divisive'. Quite often it is when we do not make up our mind or commit our heart that we are defeated. For Jesus the time for decision and commitment had come. In the wilderness Jesus would ask of himself, 'Who am I? What am I called to do? How will I do it?'

Mark tells us that Jesus was with wild beasts: this could be leopards, lions, bears, jackals or snakes. All these creatures are signs of danger but perhaps Mark was thinking of the prophecy of Isaiah 11:6-9, which said that in the times of the Messiah all animals will live in harmony and peace.

Mark also mentions the ministration of angels. Whenever we are tempted, troubled or distressed we are not alone, divine help is at hand: our God is with us.

Question time
Would you consider making some Lent affirmations to help you be loyal to God?

Give everyone a copy of the following on a piece of paper:

> I will learn to give away and so make room for the new. (Almsgiving and more)
> I will get rid of things that hinder my life, like bad habits. (Fasting, pruning and more)
> I will make sure my lines of communication with God are kept open. (Prayer)

Do you check your way of life every so often? If not, why not?

Illustration
Some people say they like doing what comes naturally. A man let his garden grow naturally and when asked why it was a mess he said, 'I was leaving it to God.' God will not do for us what he has given us the ability to do. If you want a good garden or a good life, you have to work at it. With the garden, if you want flowers it is no use filling the beds with vegetables. You will get out what you put in. You will get more, for you will also get weeds. If you leave your life to run itself, it will also produce weeds. Gardens and life need regular tender loving care.

Lent is a time for looking at what you have and making improvements.

In the garden some plants need splitting to give them more room to grow. You can often give away the extra to someone else. If you do not divide some plants, they will choke themselves. If we do not learn to give, we will do the same. Make room for the new in your life.

There is a constant need to weed and also to prune. Get rid of what hampers growth. Cut back on what has become rank and is taking over.

Learn to work in relationship with the soil and the climate. Learn to work in relationship with God.

Nothing is achieved without effort, without practice, without learning. If you want a good garden you have to give it priority over other things and the same is true of life.

Intercessions

Blessed are you, Lord God, creator of the universe.
You have given us this world to enjoy
and so that we may work in harmony with you.
You have given us talents and abilities
that we may enrich each other.
Blessed are you, Lord God.

Lord, you bless your Church with great riches,
with people of talent,
with a variety of gifts.
Help us to use them aright to your glory
and for the benefit of all.
We remember especially all who lead us in worship
and who teach us the faith.

Silence

Show us your ways, O Lord,
and teach us your paths.

Gracious God,
what a wonderful world you have given us.
We ask your blessing upon all who work the land
and who provide food for us.
We remember all who are working in conservation
and in caring for people in desolate or spoiled areas.

Silence

Show us your ways, O Lord,
and teach us your paths.

We thank you for the comfort of our homes
and the gifts you have given
to each member of our families and loved ones.
Help us to be aware of each other's needs
and the needs of those who are not as well off as we are.

Silence

Show us your ways, O Lord,
and teach us your paths.

Lord, you are always ready to help us in our troubles.
We bring before you
the sorrows and sighing of our world.
We remember all who are ill,
all injured in accidents or acts of violence,
all who are hungry or homeless.
We ask your blessing upon each one
and on all who care for them.

Show us your ways, O Lord,
and teach us your paths.

We praise you for the gift of eternal life.
We pray for all our loved ones who are departed from us
and are now rejoicing in the fullness of your kingdom.

Silence

Merciful Father,
accept these prayers
for the sake of your Son,
our Saviour Jesus Christ.
Amen.

Memory verse

Show me your ways, O Lord, and teach me your paths.
Psalm 25:4

Suggested music

Lead us, heavenly Father, lead us
O Jesus, I have promised
O let the Son of God enfold you

CANDLES

Aim

To show God's love for the world.

Teaching

Show the children a wooden Noah's Ark or a picture. Tell them about Noah and the animals going into the Ark and how God was sending rain on the world because the people were doing bad things. The rains came down and the floods came up (make sure the children know what a flood is). Repeat 'The rains came down' and make actions with your hands. 'The floods came up', make actions with your hands. The floods covered the streets, the houses, the trees, the hills, the mountains and the whole earth. As you list these (and anything else the children can think of that would be covered by the floods), say and act out, 'The rains came down and the floods came up' after each suggestion.

Water covered all the earth but Noah, his family and all the animals were safe. Why? Because, they were in the ark. When the rain stopped they could not leave the ark for there was very deep water everywhere. After a long time, Noah sent out a big black bird called a raven to see if there was dry land and it did not come back. It flew round and round until it could find dry land in the mountains. Noah then sent out another bird, a dove, but it came back because there was still too much water. After a week he sent it out again. When it came back it had a branch in its beak. Noah knew the waters had gone down. After another week he sent out the dove again and it did not come back – the floods had gone away. The first thing Noah did was to get out of the ark and say 'Thank you' to God for keeping them safe. God told Noah to look up at the sky. Noah looked up and the sky was full of beautiful colours. It was a rainbow. Has anyone seen a rainbow? (Show a picture of a rainbow.)

God promised that such a big flood would not cover the earth again. God put the rainbow in the sky to remind us that God loves the world and God loves you and me.

Activity

Use a wooden model of Noah's Ark for the story. Give each pair of children a piece of coloured wool (about 50 centimetres), making sure they know the name of the colour. Have all the colours of the rainbow. When you call out a colour the children with that colour form an arch and the rest then pass underneath the arch. Sometimes call out three or four colours to make arches and let the rest pass through. Finally call out all the colours and let the rainbow be made. You could try to pass under it. (A reminder of the colours: red, orange, yellow, green, blue, indigo and violet.)

Give each child strands from all the colours and ask them to make a rainbow by sticking them on the template provided.

Prayer

God, we thank you for the colours of the rainbow
and for showing your love for the world
in the sun and the rain.
Amen.

Song

Read or sing verses of 'Mister Noah built an ark'. Teach the children the two refrains.

LAMPS

Aim

To encourage the children to enter into the adventure of Lent.

Teaching

Here is a sad story about a donkey. When the donkey's master was going away for a long time he left the donkey with plenty of water to drink and two great big piles of food. There was beautiful hay to the right and left of the donkey. The donkey looked at both piles and saw it was great food but it could not make its mind up which to eat first. Should it eat the right pile or the left? Should it start on one pile and eat it down or nibble at both? The donkey could not make up its mind and its head swayed from left to right. Just as it was about to eat, it thought it heard a voice saying, 'Try the other pile of hay.' Poor old donkey could not make up its mind. When the master returned the donkey had died of starvation. All the food was still there but it had been unable to make up its mind what to eat first.

Lent is a time to make up our minds and be sure we are making good decisions. Lent lasts for 40 days, right up until Easter. During those 40 days we will try to give our love to God every day. How do you think we can do that? Yes, by deciding to say our prayers every day and to care for others.

As soon as Jesus was baptised he was ready to go and do what God the Father wanted him to do. But he wanted to make sure that what he did was right. He did not rush into doing things. He spent forty days praying and sorting himself out in the wilderness. He would seek to know not only what God wanted him to do but how to do it. Jesus spent time making sure he made the right decisions. He did not want anything to stop him from showing his love for God and God's world.

Let us see how we can decide to love God more.

Activity

This session could begin with more attempts at pinning the tail on the donkey.

Make simple Lent decisions (see worksheet). Talk about each of the decisions in turn and how the children will try to keep their promises. They need to know that to do good things they must try not to do bad things. In caring for all of God's people, maybe the group could do something each week of Lent to help some deprived children in our world. It is important that the decisions are positive and the children feel it is a sense of adventure and joy to go out and accomplish them. Make a collage of temptations, of things that might stop us keeping our Lent affirmations.

Prayer

God, help us to be good and kind to everyone
and to remember you are with us every day.
Amen.

Song

Two little fishes, five loaves of bread

TORCHES

Aim

To encourage the young people to make Lent affirmations.

Teaching

Once upon a time there was a poor woodsman who wished he was rich. He thought he would make his family a lot happier if he had more money and was able to buy lots of things.

He did not seem to notice his family was already a happy family. In the forest he met a wicked spirit who promised to make the woodsman rich on one condition: he would give the wicked spirit his heart and in exchange have a heart of stone. The woodsman did not think this was too bad and agreed. Now when he cut down beautiful trees and made money, he did not care if it made a big hole in the forest. He brought presents home – expensive presents – but he did not stay because he was too busy making money. He did not have time to show his love for his wife or his children, which made them very sad. The children had lots of presents but rarely saw their father. He became rich but was a very lonely man. Because he had a heart of stone he could not love anyone. One day he said in a loud voice, 'What a wrong decision I have made. I do not want a heart of stone. My family is more important than riches.' Fortunately for him, a good spirit was waiting for him to make his own mind up and make the right decision. 'If you truly love your family more than money, you can be given your heart back today. Are you sure this is what you want?' The man was so sure he wept for joy. He never saw the good spirit but he went home and kissed his wife and hugged his children. He was rich not because of money but because he was loved by his family. This is an old story about deciding what is important in life and what really matters to us.

When Jesus was over 30 years old he was baptised by John the Baptist in the river Jordan. It was time for Jesus to do the work the Father had sent him to do. Jesus had to be sure he made the right decisions. To do this he went into the wilderness, a very lonely place, so that he could spend a lot of time with the Father. He would give his love to the Father and know the Father loved him. He would decide how to do what God the Father wanted him to do. He was in the wilderness for 40 days and nights deciding what to do and how to do it.

Last Wednesday – do you know its name? – Lent began. There are 40 days in Lent, just as Jesus had 40 days in the wilderness. (Work it out, Ash Wednesday to Easter is six weeks and four days. Does that make 40 days? No, it does not, it makes 46 days. The Sundays are not counted, so if you take them away how many days in Lent? Yes, 40.) We are given 40 days to say how we will best serve God and do what he wants us to do. What sort of things can we promise to do? Encourage the group to make their own suggestions. If necessary give them headings:

Show our love for God
Show our love for others
Do what God wants us to do

Activity

Encourage the young people to make affirmations of what they would like to achieve. Get them to stretch themselves but not beyond what is sensible. Introduce to them the traditional ideas of:

Prayer (All need to promise to pray daily.)

Fasting (Show it as giving up time or things so that we can do something better; sometimes it is making room for God.)

Almsgiving (Let it be seen as a reflection of God's love and generosity to us. It can be as a result of fasting that we have something we can give away.)

Prayer

God our Father, we thank you for your love
and for the love in our homes.
Help us to show your love and kindness to others
and to remember you are with us every day.
Amen.

Song

When a knight won his spurs

Second Sunday of Lent

Aim

To encourage people to be faithful to their Lord.

Preparation

Bring a spring fastened tight in a box. There are many children's toys like this. It is best if the spring will jump right out when opened. Failing this, you could use a jack-in-the-box.

Opening activity

Ask one of the children to open the box in front of everyone, making sure the lid is pointed in a safe direction. After the laughter show them how you press the spring back down. The harder it is pressed down, the better it will jump.

Tell them, in science it is understood that to every action there is a reaction. If you pull back an elastic band and fire it from your finger, the further back you pull it, the further it will go. To every action there is a reaction.

Opening prayer

O God, as you have called us to follow you,
let nothing stop us or lead us astray.
In all our life be our Guide and our Friend.
Amen.

Opening song

Will you come and follow me

Readings

Genesis 17:1-7, 15-16
Psalm 22:23-31
Romans 4:13-25
Mark 8:31-38

Thought for the day

Have you ever played 'Follow the leader'? It is fun when the leader is doing nice things and safe things, but you have to think twice if the leader starts to do things that are dangerous.

Jesus called the disciples to follow him. They left their homes and their work and went around the country with Jesus. It was a wonderful time of miracles and crowds following him. Life was a great adventure. When they were sitting around a campfire one evening, Jesus asked them if they knew who he really was. After a while Peter said, 'We know that you are the Anointed One of God. You are the Christ.' Peter was very excited about this because he believed Jesus was very popular and powerful. But Jesus warned them of the troubles ahead. He told them the elders, the chief priests and the scribes would reject him and that he would be killed. Jesus did not want to be killed but he knew if he did God's work he would face opposition. He knew that evil is always against goodness. Peter would not believe it. He took Jesus aside and told him it could not be so. Jesus wished it was not so but he knew trouble lay ahead. Peter was trying to persuade him to run away or hide or go somewhere else. Peter did this because he loved Jesus. Jesus saw that Satan was using Peter's love to tempt him. He spoke very strongly to his friend and said, 'Get behind me, Satan! For you are setting your mind not on divine things but on human.' We have to be careful that our friends do not lead us astray from what God wants us to do. Sometimes they cannot understand that we need to be willing to give up all to follow our Lord.

Jesus did not promise that following him would be easy. He said there would be times when we would have to deny even our own desires. If we are following the crucified one, we too have to take up our cross. Jesus knew that some things are lost by being kept to ourselves. We lose the ability to play the piano or to do well at sport if we do not practise. Practice means denying ourselves the time to go out whenever we feel like it. To follow Jesus means discipline. There can be no discipling without discipline.

Question time

Do we understand that Jesus did not promise us safety, comfort or well being, but that he did promise us his presence at all times?

How are our Lent Affirmations faring? Do we need to have another look at them?

Illustration

When Columbanus wanted to go and serve God as a monk his mother was not pleased. She loved him dearly and was afraid that he was wasting his life. He had lots of talent and ability. He could be someone very important in Ireland. She talked to him and tried to dissuade him, but he knew God was calling him to leave home and serve him in a monastery. His mother tried all sorts of ways to stop him. Though she loved him dearly, she was acting for Satan. Columbanus got ready to go. His mother went to the door of the house and lay down in the doorway to stop him. Columbanus was very sorry to see his mother do this, but he carefully stepped over her and went to serve God wherever God called him. In time, Columbanus did wonderful work for God in France and Italy. For a moment it would have been easy to give in and stay at home.

Intercessions

Blessed are you, Lord God.
You have called us into life,
to love and serve you.
You have promised that you are with us always
and that you are our Helper and our Guide.

We give thanks for all who hear and obey your call:
for men and women who willingly sacrifice
and deprive themselves
for the good of others.
We remember all who have spent their lives
in your service.
We ask you to give strength to all who are quietly seeking
to give you their love and their lives.

We remember today all who suffer rejection,
pain or distress
for following you.

Silence

Lord, as you have called us,
hear us when we call upon you.

We remember with gratitude
all who have given their lives in research and exploration
for the good of others.
We ask you to bless all scientists, technicians
and leaders of people.
We pray for those working among the poor
and the deprived of our world.

Silence

Lord, as you have called us,
hear us when we call upon you.

We give thanks for all our parents and loved ones do for us,
for their love, their sacrifice and their care.
We seek your blessing upon our homes and our families.
We remember all who have no one to care for them.

Silence

Lord, as you have called us,
hear us when we call upon you.

We give thanks for the dedication of doctors
and nurses and hospital staff.
We ask your blessing on all who are in hospital
or who are ill at this time
and upon all who look after them.
We remember all who feel that no one cares about them.

Silence

Lord, as you have called us,
hear us when we call upon you.

We rejoice that you have called us to eternal life
and that you have invited us
to enjoy your presence for ever.
We pray for all who have given their lives
in the service of others,
and for our loved ones departed.
May they now rejoice in the fullness of your kingdom.

Silence

Merciful Father,
accept these prayers
for the sake of your Son,
our Saviour Jesus Christ.
Amen.

Memory verse

If any want to become my followers, let them deny themselves and take up their cross and follow me.
Mark 8:34

Suggested music

Take up thy cross
Jesus calls us: o'er the tumult
Take my life, and let it be

CANDLES

Aim

To encourage the children to be generous.

Teaching

Once upon a time there was a beggar who sat by the roadside. He was near the market and begged for food. Most of the farmers who came to the market gave him a few of their seeds. The beggar put these in a sack behind his back, so that no one could see it. Then he could beg for some more. One day a prince came along and the beggar shouted for help. He had a lot in his sack but he thought the prince would give him something special. The prince came to him and said, 'You give me something first.' The beggar put his hand around the back and took a handful of grain. But he let it trickle through his fingers and brought out one single tiny grain. For a moment the prince took the grain in his hand and then gave it back to the beggar. The grain was changed into a tiny piece of gold. Now the beggar was sad that he had been so greedy. If he had given the whole sack to the prince, just think what the prince might have done with it.

Jesus wants us to give him some of our time in prayer. He wants us to give him our love and our friendship. How can we do that? We can say our prayers every day. We can try and be good and kind. We can be generous and not greedy. Listen to this story of someone who gave all that she had to God (Mark 12:41-44).

There was a poor woman who had very little of anything but she wanted to give something to God. She wanted to go to the Temple church and give God something that was special to her. She looked around the house but she did not have anything that she could give. All that she had was two tiny coins – it was all the money she had. She could not really spare it but she wanted to be generous and to give it to God. Off she went to the Temple to put it in the big money box at the church. As she went she saw rich men carrying purses full of money. They dropped their money into the box bit by bit, making as much noise with it as they could. She waited until she thought no one was watching and she came forward and dropped her two tiny coins in the box. They did not make a sound. Then she went away thinking no one would have noticed but it did not matter because God knew she had given a gift. What she did not know was that Jesus also saw her and he said to his disciples, 'This poor woman has given more than the others. For the others had put in what they had to spare but she has given all that she had.'

Activity

Get the children to act out the two stories. Let some be generous farmers who give grain. You could use rice or any other grain, giving them a small handful each. Let the beggar hide it all in a bag. Make sure all see the beggar give only one tiny grain and then go off sadly with a bagful.

Have a box or tin for the children to drop coins in, making a noise. Let the poor woman's coins be tiny. Make sure they all understand how generous she is.

Prayer

God, we love you
for you have given us life and many good things.
Help us to be kind and willing to share with others.
Amen.

Song

Two little fishes, five loaves of bread

LAMPS

Aim

To encourage the children to trust God at all times.

Teaching

The disciples had left their homes to follow Jesus. It was an exciting time because wonderful things were happening. What do you call the wonderful things Jesus did? Miracles. Can you tell me of any of the miracles that Jesus did? Because of the miracles, crowds came to see Jesus. Do you remember how one sick man being carried could not get to Jesus because of the crowds? What did his friends do?

Jesus was very popular and lots of people came to hear him speak. It was good to be with Jesus and to see how the crowds loved him. It would be nice for anyone to follow him. But Jesus knew that hard times were coming. Jesus understood that if you try to be good, evil will try to stop you. Did you know that? If you want to be good and follow Jesus, all sorts of things will try and stop you – even friends. Some may tell you not to bother going to church or saying your prayers. But we know that if we do what they say, we are giving in to sin.

When Jesus was alone with his disciples he warned that he would not always be popular. Some of the elders, the chief priests and the scribes were already against him. Jesus warned his disciples that he would be killed but that he would rise again. Peter could not believe it. If Jesus was God's anointed Son, how could people go against him? Peter loved Jesus and did not want anything awful to happen to him. So Peter tried to tell him it would not happen, or if it was going to happen in Jerusalem, Jesus should not go there. Peter wanted Jesus to be safe. But Jesus knew that he had to do this for God and not be afraid to go to Jerusalem or to die. He did not want to die, but if he didn't, how would the world know of his love? Peter was trying to stop him doing what God wanted him to do, to make a different choice. Jesus saw that the Satan was using his friend to see if he could stop him working for God the Father. So Jesus spoke very strongly to his friend Peter and said, 'Get behind me, Satan! For you are setting your mind not on divine things but on human.' This must have come as a shock to Peter – fancy Jesus saying that to him. Jesus did not fall out with Peter, and Peter did not fall out with him. Jesus was pointing out to Peter that the way ahead was dangerous and there was going to be suffering and pain. Being a disciple is not always easy; sometimes it is costly and painful. (Get the children to talk about this openly – including their having to be in church.) Jesus was telling the disciples about the awful things that were going to happen, and asking them to trust him in the days that were ahead. Jesus does not promise it will be easy for us to follow him. He asks us to trust him even in the dark days and to know he is there and loves us.

Activity

Play 'Blind man's buff'. When the blind man is about to catch someone, let someone else lead him astray by tugging him from behind. After this, let the person with their eyes covered be led around the room by a friend they can trust. Get the children to talk about whom we can trust and who might lead us astray. If there is still time talk about their Lent Affirmations. Has anyone been led astray?

Prayer

God, you have called us to be your disciples.
You want us to trust you and obey you,
whatever is happening.
Teach us to know you are with us,
even when the days are dark and life is hard.
Amen.

Song

When we walk with the Lord (Trust and obey)

TORCHES

Aim

To encourage the young people in their faithfulness and to give them a sense of adventure.

Teaching

Let us look at our Lent Affirmations and see who found them hard and who has not kept them. (Talk about why they do not keep them. Were they too hard or were the young people too weak? What were the distractions?) We must remember that temptation is a testing and the alternatives it offers us are nice; if they were not, we would not be tempted. Temptation is testing us to see if we really want to give our love and our lives to God. It is easy to follow someone if they offer us rewards. We will do jobs for people if they pay us. But Jesus does not promise us an easy time if we follow him. He tells us the truth. His followers should expect persecution and rejection. If your leader is crucified for saying and doing what he did, how can you hope to escape? Being a Christian is not for wimps; it demands courage and dedication. But this is true of many things in life if we want to achieve anything. Sportsmen and women have to give up much free time to develop their abilities. If you want to play an instrument well, it takes hours of practice. Anyone who wants to do well in exams has to give much time to study. Once you choose to give yourself to something you are likely to come up against resistance.

The more you want to give yourself to something, the more things seem to come in your way. (Get them to talk about this.)

Jesus knew what he was called to do. He had come to show God's love to us all. To do this did not mean giving us things; he had to give himself. He could not let anything stop him from giving himself fully for us.

Peter loved being with Jesus – there was so much power and popularity, and thousands followed Jesus. Peter thought that with all the power that Jesus had he could do almost anything. Peter was right: Jesus could have used force to win over people, but God's way was not force but love. When Jesus talked about dying, Peter reacted strongly. He did not want Jesus to die. So he tried to persuade Jesus to avoid such conflict, perhaps not go to Jerusalem. Maybe Jesus could give in a little. It was now the turn of Jesus to react. He saw that Satan was using his friend to lead him astray and he spoke strongly to Peter: 'Get behind me, Satan! For you are setting your mind not on divine things but on human.' Jesus had to do this to show Peter they were here to do the Father's will and not their own. Jesus had to go to Jerusalem.

Then Jesus told them that if anyone wanted truly to be a disciple, they would have to be willing to deny themselves, to take up their cross and follow him. (Get the group to discuss what this means to them and their discipleship.)

Activity

Use elastic bands and let them fire them across the room – not at each other. See who can send theirs the furthest. Note that it is the one who stretches it most. If you can obtain some small boxes, they can then make a propeller with an elastic band. Again, see whose propeller does well. Talk about action and reaction. If you throw something very high, it will come down harder. If you push hard on a gate with a spring, it will come hard back at you. As would a punch ball! If you try to do God's will the evil and the worldly are likely to oppose you. (See if they can begin to understand this.)

Prayer

God, you have called us to work with you
and to do good for the world.
Protect us from all evil
and keep us in the right way
today and always.
Amen.

Song

Give me oil in my lamp

Third Sunday of Lent

Aim

To show we are accountable for our actions.

Preparation

Have a copy of the Ten Commandments for everyone. After each commandment have the words.

Lord, have mercy on us:
take away our sin.
Lord, have mercy on us:
grant us peace within.
(Tune: 'Glory be to Jesus')

Opening activity

Let ten different people read out the commandments. Try and vary the age of the readers. Let one half of the congregation sing the first two lines of the above Kyrie and let the other half of the congregation sing the other two lines. Repeat this after every commandment.

Opening prayer

Blessed are you, Lord God,
giver of order and harmony to our world.
Help us to understand what you would have us do
and give us the will-power to do it.
Amen.

Opening song

A man there lived in Galilee

Readings

Exodus 20:1-17
Psalm 19
1 Corinthians 1:18-25
John 2:13-22

Thought for the day

It was about mid-April. Jesus went to the holiest place in the Holy City: the Temple in Jerusalem. It was a very special place where God promised to be present. It was the time of the Passover when the people celebrated God delivering them from slavery and the beginning of the journey to the Promised Land. Every Jewish male who lived within 15 miles of Jerusalem was obliged to attend the feast. The aim of every Jew is to spend at least one Passover in Jerusalem. It is thought there could be anything from a quarter of a million to two million Jews attending the Temple over eight days.

Every Jew over the age of 19, including Jesus, would have to pay the Temple tax, so that the services and the sacrifices could continue. Each had to pay half a shekel, which was about two days' pay. This had to be paid in Temple shekels or Jewish shekels; other currencies were seen as unclean. As pilgrims came from all over the known world, in the Temple Courts there were moneychangers. If trade had been straightforward, there would have been no objection. But this is what Jesus saw: the exchange rate was extortionate. For the exchange to the shekel people were being charged a whole day's wage or 50 per cent profit. Outside, doves could be bought for about a day's wage; inside they were being sold for almost twenty times as much. In the name of religion people were being cheated; this was extortion. It seemed no one spoke against this injustice. It made Jesus really angry that the Church was being used like a robbers' den. Jesus made a whip and drove the sheep and the oxen out of the Temple, overthrew the tables and poured the money out.

There are times when it is right and necessary to be angry. Jesus was angry against the evil being done in the name of the Church. Evil often triumphs because good people are afraid to speak out. When we hear of people being driven out of their homes, or the great rain forests being destroyed, we should be angry and we should act. When we hear of the loss of animal species through greed and carelessness, we should act. It was because he was angry with the slave trade that William Wilberforce acted and brought about its abolition.

Question time

Can you think of something that we should be angry about? Perhaps you feel that some group or government is ignoring God's commandments.

Is there something within our own church or community that needs cleansing?

Illustration

There was a farmer who planned to go to France for his holidays. As he would be driving on the Continent he decided to get some practice in. He started to drive on the right-hand side of the road and to go around roundabouts anticlockwise. To say the least, he caused all sorts of trouble and had one or two close accidents. He was finally stopped by the police and charged with dangerous driving. He had broken dozens of rules in the Highway Code, and that mattered because it is written for the well-being and safety of us all. We need rules to protect us and to help us to get the best out of life. Rules are not to restrict us as much as to give us the greatest freedom within certain parameters.

What if there were no rules in a game of football? You could have as many people as you like on your team. You could pick up the ball and run or even take it home! You could make the goalposts narrower than the football so that no one could score. But you would not have a game; you would have chaos. We need rules and standards to enjoy living together in community.

Jesus was angry with the moneychangers because they were being unjust. They were using their privileged position to make unfair demands. They were robbing people in the name of God. Jesus could not turn a blind eye. He had to act. He had to show that what was being done was not right and needed to be changed. Perhaps on a larger scene Jesus was already hinting that the time for animal sacrifices had come to an end and that a great sacrifice was about to be made in his own crucifixion.

Intercessions

Blessed are you, Lord our God, Creator of the world,
bringing all out of chaos.
We thank you for the guidance of the Scriptures
and for the Commandments.
We remember all who influence the lives of others
through their example or through the media.
We pray that young people
may be given good guidance as they grow,
that they may move with confidence and freedom.
In its rules may the Church show love and compassion,
and that rules are for our freedom and not to restrict life.
May all who teach and preach lead us
towards the glorious freedom of the children of God.

Silence

Lord, your kingdom come,
your will be done.

We look for the time when the kingdoms of this world
will be the kingdom of God.
We long for the time when God's rule
will be what guides us all.
We remember all who are suffering from injustice –
people robbed of their homes or their living.
We pray for native people being driven off their land
due to the greed of others.

Silence

Lord, your kingdom come,
your will be done.

Teach us, Lord, to live in love and harmony
with those around us.
Let there be peace in our dealings,
in our homes and in our hearts.
May we never oppress or hurt anyone
through word or deed.

Silence

Lord, your kingdom come,
your will be done.

We are sorry for all the harm done to the earth
by the greed and the insensitivity
of powerful groups or individuals.
We pray for all who seek to clean up our rivers
and the air we breathe,
all who work in conservation.
We remember before you all who are ill
or in trouble at this time.

Silence

Lord, your kingdom come,
your will be done.

We give thanks that you are ever with us
and offer us life eternal.
We remember friends and loved ones departed from us.
May they rejoice with your saints in glory.

Silence

Merciful Father,
accept these prayers
for the sake of your Son,
our Saviour Jesus Christ. Amen.

Memory verse

Let the words of my mouth and the meditations of my heart be acceptable in your sight, O Lord, my strength and my redeemer.
Psalm 19:14

Suggested music

Father, hear the prayer we offer
Father, Lord of all creation
We love the place, O God

CANDLES

Aim

To help the children understand we are called to love God and each other.

Teaching

Moses loved God and wanted to do what God wanted him to do. He was the leader of a lot of people and he was taking them through the desert. (Who knows what a desert is? Explain.) For a long time they lived in the desert and they wanted to do what God wanted them to do. Moses went up a mountain called Sinai. (Does anyone know what a mountain is?) Moses climbed high up the mountain until he was out of sight. The mountain was wrapped in fire and smoke because God was on the mountain waiting to meet Moses. There was a loud noise like the sound of a trumpet. Moses was not full of fear because he was meeting with God. God wanted to tell Moses what he wanted the people to do. God wanted the people to love him and to love each other. To help them, God gave Moses some rules about what they could do.

The rules were called 'The Ten Commandments'. (Let us count to ten.) There were four commandments which said we had to love God more than anything else and six which told us we had to love other people also. (Four and six: who knows how many that makes?) There were four which told us to love God, one that told us to love our parents, and five that told us to love other people. (4+1+5 = ?) Let us count again to ten. Some people find it hard to remember ten different things so Jesus told us how the Ten Commandments could be remembered as two. Listen, this is what Jesus said: 'You shall love the Lord your God with all your heart, and with all your soul, and with all your mind. This is the greatest and the first commandment. And the second is like it: You shall love your neighbour as yourself.' (Let someone read these verses out to the class.) What do you think Jesus was saying we should do? Yes, it sounds quite simple: we should love God and love each other. (Let the group talk about how we can do this). Let's look at our paper and read the words together:

LOVE GOD
LOVE OTHERS

God wants us to keep a special place for him in our hearts. He wants to know that we love him. We can show our love by talking to him each day in prayer and by doing what he wants us to do. God wants a place in our love and in our lives.

We can show our love to our parents by doing what they ask us to do and saying how we love them. We can show our love to others by being kind and generous. We are asked to LOVE GOD and LOVE OTHERS.

Activity
Play 'Musical chairs'. Have one chair on which there is a notice saying, 'Reserved', and tell the children that no one can sit in that chair as it is being kept for someone special. When the game is over sit in the reserved chair and say, 'I am lucky for this was kept for me.'

Prayer
God, you love us.
God, we love you.
We love our parents.
Help us to love each other.
Amen.

Song
Two little eyes

LAMPS

Aim
To encourage our love of God in our daily lives.

Teaching
Start by playing 'Musical chairs'. Has anyone ever had a reserved place, maybe on a train or a plane, at a theatre or at a football match? Talk about a reserved place and what it means. No one else should be able to take your place when it is reserved for you.

When Moses came down from the mountain with the Ten Commandments, he wanted to tell the people what God wanted them to do. On the two stones Moses brought down from the mountain were carved things that God would like us to do. The first of the Commandments was very important because God was telling us he wants a special place in our hearts and in our lives. He wants us to keep a place reserved for him. The first commandment says, 'I am the Lord your God. Do not let anything take my place.' In another commandment God asked us to keep a day reserved for him each week. (At this stage you may like the children to look at the Ten Commandments and discuss what they mean. Could they divide the Commandments into two clear groups: how we deal with God and how we deal with others?)

When Jesus was asked about the Commandments, he made it easier to remember them by saying there are two basic commandments: love God and love each other. Let us look at the words of Jesus in Matthew 22:37-39. 'You shall love the Lord your God with all your heart, and with all your soul, and with all your mind. This is the greatest and the first commandment. And the second is like it: You shall love your neighbour as yourself.'

(Let someone read these verses out to the class.) What do you think Jesus was saying we should do? Yes, it sounds quite simple: we should love God and love each other. (Let the group talk about how we can do this.)

Activity
Play 'Musical chairs'. Have one chair on which there is a notice saying, 'Reserved', and tell the children that no one can sit in that chair as it is being kept for someone special. When the game is over sit in the reserved chair and say, 'I am lucky for this was kept for me.'

We will make a reminder to take home and put where we can see it. We will make a scroll and write on it: LOVE GOD. LOVE OTHERS. Let us put it where we can touch it every morning and evening, and let us say the words every day this week.

Prayer
God, you made us out of your love
and you want us to love you.
We give our love to you this day.
Help us to show your love to others
by the way we deal with each of them.
Amen.

Song
Jesus wants all of me

TORCHES

Aim
To show that some rules are necessary and that it is also right to be angry about any evil acts.

Teaching
Jesus went up to Jerusalem for the Passover. This was a special holy time for all Jews. They celebrated gaining their freedom from slavery and leaving Egypt for the Promised Land. When he came to where the money-changers were, he became very angry because he saw these men were cheating people by charging very high prices. It was worse as these men were supposed to be helping in the work of God. They were giving God and his Church a bad name. They were not keeping the rules that God gave them for guidance in the Ten Commandments. Jesus made a whip and drove out the cattle, overturned the moneychangers' tables and spilled their money on the ground. He said they were using God's holy place like a robbers' den. I cannot believe they liked him for doing that to them. Perhaps Jesus wanted them to know that the days of offering animal sacrifices were coming to an end. But it was more likely he was angry because they were not showing any love for God or other people. They were selfishly looking after themselves and did not worry how it made a lot of poor people suffer to have to give them so much money.

There are things happening in the world that should make us angry. Rainforests are being destroyed and people put out of their homes, to provide cheap wood for the rich part of the world. Animals are being hunted until they become extinct due to the foolishness and greed of people. We should be angry when we hear that birds die due to pollution, or that people die when their country is invaded. We should be angry when we hear how someone was killed by the carelessness of another person. There are times when it is right to be angry. There are times when we should speak out against evil and not let weak or helpless people suffer. (See if you can get some examples from the group.)

To protect the poor and the weak, and to guide all in living a good life, God provided ten rules. What are these rules called? They are called the Ten Commandments. Let us read them and see if we can understand the meaning of each one. (Get ten different children to read them and seek comments after each one is read.)

Activity

Let us pretend we are cars. We will run around the room carefully. If you pass anyone, they must always be on your left. If someone is coming in the opposite direction they must pass on your right. Do you know why? I am going to be a set of traffic lights. If I shout, 'Red', what will you do? If I shout, 'Green', what will you do? Yes, you stop for red and move on green. If I shout, 'Amber', do you know what to do? If you are moving, keep moving but very carefully. If you have stopped on red, do not move until I say, 'Green'. Anyone who makes a mistake at the traffic lights must sit down. If we are to enjoy the game, the rules are important.

Prayer

God, you made us to love and obey you.
Help us to do what is right and to stand against evil;
to show our love for you
by the way we care for each other
and the world around us.
Amen.

Song

Do what you know is right

Fourth Sunday of Lent
Mothering Sunday

Aim

To help us to appreciate the love that is given to us through our mother.

Preparation

Give everyone or every family a candle to light as a 'Thank-you' and a prayer for their mother. Have a large box filled with sand that can hold the candles in an appropriate place when they are lit. Remember, all people who come in have had or have a mother; let no one be excluded. You may like to give them a printed copy of the opening prayer that will be sung.

Opening activity

Invite all to come forward in family groups, or, if they are on their own, as individuals, with their candle to light as a 'Thank-you' for their homes and especially their mothers. During or after this we will sing our opening prayer.

Opening prayer

Bless our mother, Lord, every day. *(3)*
O Lord, bless her now.

Keep her safe, O Lord, every day. *(3)*
O Lord, bless her now.

Give her joy, O Lord, every day. *(3)*
O Lord, bless her now.

(Tune: 'Kum ba yah')

(If there are lots of candles to light, different groups of children could sing this through during the candle lighting.)

Opening song

For the beauty of the earth

Readings

Exodus 2:1-10 or 1 Samuel 1:20-28
Psalm 34:11-20 or Psalm 127:1-4
2 Corinthians 1:3-7 or Colossians 3:12-17
Luke 2:33-35 or John 19:25b-27

Thought for the day

Whichever set of readings you use today, they have something in common. What do Moses, Samuel and Jesus have in common? The clue is in the readings. Like us, they all have a mother. Each has a mother who loves them and wants to care for them. The mother of Moses had to hide him from the cruelty of Pharaoh. If she had not done this, Moses would not have survived and all of history would be changed. For three months the mother of Moses fed him, cared for him and hid him from the soldiers, all at a risk to her own life, because she loved him. This brave woman changed the pattern of history and yet hardly anyone knows her name. Does anyone here know the name of the mother of Moses? She was called Jochebed (see Exodus 6:20, Numbers 26:59). She saved another son from Pharaoh and his name was Aaron. Jochebed and her daughter Miriam were brave women who risked their lives because of their love.

Who knows the name of Samuel's mother? She was called Hannah. For a long time Hannah thought she could not have children and it made her sad. One year when she was praying at the Temple church at Shiloh, she told the priest Eli of her troubles. He told her that she would have a child. When her baby was born Hannah called him Samuel, which means 'asked of the Lord'. Samuel was an answer to her prayers. As God gave her a child, she promised when he was old enough she would give him to the Lord. So she took him to the old priest Eli and let Samuel work for him and for God.

Without Mary saying 'Yes' to God, Jesus could not have been born. Because of Mary and her obedience to God, the Saviour was able to come into the world. Mary was amazed at the things that were said about Jesus when he was still a baby. She was warned that she would suffer because he would suffer. We learn in a family when one person suffers all share in the pain: mothers often suffer deeply for their children. It is not just sleepless nights and giving time and attention; it is the pain in a mother's heart at the suffering of her child. When Mary stood by the cross and saw the suffering of her son it must have caused her tremendous pain.

Today we rejoice in the love of our mother. We give thanks for her constant care and grace. Let us make sure that today our mother knows that we appreciate what she has done and is doing for us.

Question time

Do we truly recognise the love and sacrifice that our mother gives us? Are we in danger of taking love for granted?

How can we show our appreciation for all that we receive through grace? Remember grace is what is given freely.

Illustration

By tradition this middle Sunday in Lent was a time when young children who had left home to work in a big house or on a farm were allowed home for the first time in the year. Lots of children had to work for very low wages, sometimes only their keep, and it was very hard. They missed their homes and the care of their mother. At home much had been done for them. Now they had to look after themselves. It was lovely to come home and be looked after and loved. Usually the children had little they could bring as they had little. They may have been allowed to make a cake. More often they would bring a posy of flowers they picked on the way. Perhaps the first time they had thought of giving their mother flowers and saying 'Thank you' for all that their mother had done for them. It is very easy to take our mother for granted and not notice all the work she does for us. She does this work freely, gratis, out of her own grace and goodness. What most of us learn about love, grace and goodness has its foundation in our own homes.

Do you know how much a cup of tea or coffee costs in a café? How much is a meal? What would it cost you to hire a servant to clean for you? Our mother does all this out of love. We should show we appreciate all she does and that we are truly grateful. We should never take our mother for granted or make her work more difficult. As we grow we should know we have a share in that work, because as she loves us, we love her.

Intercessions

Blessed are you, Lord God of all creation.
You have loved us from the beginning
when you gave us life through our parents.
You have showered blessings upon us
through our homes and our loved ones.
Blessed are you now and for ever.

We give you thanks for our own mother
and all she has done for us.
We thank you for her grace and goodness.
We remember all who have cared for us
in our church and society,
all who have shared in our learning and loving.
We ask you to bless the church to which we belong.

Silence

Lord, as we are loved,
help us to love.

We give thanks for all who are newly born into this world.
We ask your blessing upon them,
especially any who will suffer
from neglect, violence or abuse.
We remember all unwanted children,
all who are vulnerable or in danger,
all who are born into poverty or famine.
We rejoice in the gift of life
and the loving care that is around us.

Silence

Lord, as we are loved,
help us to love.

Lord, thank you for our homes and loved ones.
We thank you today especially for our mother
and all loving relationships.
As we are given tender loving care,
let us show our appreciation by returning that love
in the way we live and in our dealings with each other.

Silence

Lord, as we are loved,
help us to love.

We remember, in your presence,
all who are separated from their loved ones
through illness or circumstance.
We bring before you the needs of the homeless and refugees.
We pray for children who have been taken into care.

Silence

Lord, as we are loved,
help us to love.

God, comfort and strengthen
all who have lost loved ones this year,
especially those who have lost their mother.
We remember all our loved ones departed.
We look forward in faith and in hope to the time
when we can be at home with you in your kingdom.

Silence

Merciful Father,
accept these prayers
for the sake of your Son,
our Saviour Jesus Christ.
Amen.

Memory verse

Children are a heritage from the Lord, and the fruit of the womb is a gift.
Psalm 127:3

Suggested music

The King of love my shepherd is
Welcome to the family
Now thank we all our God

CANDLES, LAMPS and TORCHES

Today is a day for the family to worship together, to rejoice in being a family and to give thanks for their mutual love. Involve as many of the children as possible in doing things. Let them bring up the bread and the wine, and take the collection. The children may carry banners expressing thanksgiving for the love of their homes and the love of God. Children could be encouraged to bring a photograph of their mother with them when they come to the altar rail. Let the young people lead some of the intercessions and some of the readings. A mother and a child could share in a reading. If flowers or cards are given out, remember that all of us have a mother. Encourage all to come forward. Some may then like to place their flowers or card near the candles if their mother has died and is now in God's kingdom and love.

Fifth Sunday of Lent

Aim

To look at the Passion of Christ and beyond to the resurrection.

Preparation

Have a crucifix towards the front of the church on a table, and a bowl in front of it to hold the gifts of grain. You may like to have a sheaf of wheat at each side of the crucifix – this can usually be obtained from a florist. Have two children at the door giving a single grain of wheat to everyone as they come in. (It will be necessary to have extra for those who lose the grain before the opening activity.)

Opening activity

We all have a grain of wheat. One little grain can produce a whole ear of grain (hold one up) with many seeds. But if our grain is not buried in the ground it will not have a chance to grow. It will shrivel and die. Let us offer our grains to God who sent his Son to die for us, that we may all have eternal life.

Opening prayer

Loving God, we thank you for the miracle of growth.
We give thanks for the mystery of new life
from seeds that are buried.
May we give ourselves fully to you
and in the service of others,
and so may we rejoice in the gift of life eternal.
Amen.

Opening song

I will offer up my life

Readings

Jeremiah 31:31-34
Psalm 51:1-12 or Psalm 119:9-16
Hebrews 5:5-10
John 12:20-33

Thought for the day

Philip told Andrew about some Greeks wanting to see Jesus. Andrew in his usual fashion brings them to Jesus. Here were seekers who were not Jews coming to meet the Saviour. It was an exciting moment. Jesus increases the excitement by saying, 'The hour has come for the Son of Man to be glorified.' The disciples would see this as the coming of the promised kingdom of God. This was exciting indeed. So the next words came as a shock as Jesus started to talk of death. He told them how troubled his soul was. Like any human being he did not want to die. He was only 33 years old; he did not seek out death. But he came to do whatever was the will of the Father.

On this Sunday we turn to look at the Passion of Christ in more detail and this will continue until his death on Good Friday.

For grains of wheat to grow, their burial is necessary. Only by death comes new life. If we hide the grain in a box to keep it safe and secure, it will be useless. Only when it is put in the cold earth can it rise to new life. Only by giving it away to the earth can we receive a good return.

Often we seek comfort and safety. We avoid conflict or having to put ourselves out. We look after ourselves. Jesus tells us that anyone who hoards their life or their talent will lose it. It is no use just surviving; we need to live life to the full. This will involve risk and danger. But of life it can be said: 'Use it or lose it.'

Bearing in mind what the world did to Jesus, whoever wants to serve him must realise they will not escape from similar troubles.

Today we end with a vision of the future. When Jesus has triumphed over the rulers of this world. 'When I am lifted up from the earth, I will draw all people to myself.' Looking back through two millennia, we can see how the cross has drawn all nations to come before him. We come to him who understands our suffering, who has borne our grief and our sins. We come to him who has triumphed over evil and through death opened to us the way to eternal life.

Question time

How often do we give the wrong impression by suggesting that life becomes less troubled if we follow Jesus?

Can we find ways of lifting Jesus up and drawing others towards him?

Illustration

Lazy Jack was given a sack of grain. His task was to sow the seed for the village so that they would have a harvest in the autumn. Jack looked at the seed. It was golden and beautiful. He thought it would be a shame to bury it in the ground. So he took it home and put it in a cupboard. No one knew that he had not sown the seed. Jack took it easy. It was only later in the year when there were no shoots, no signs of new wheat growing, that the village realised there was something wrong. Obviously the seed was not in the ground. After a search they found it in Lazy Jack's cupboard. The mice had eaten some, but most of it was still intact. Jack had almost allowed a community to starve by not sowing the seed. Like much in our lives, it was a case of use it or lose it. The villagers put the seed in the ground – it was late for sowing but they trusted in the power within the seed to grow and it did. In the end nothing was lost and the harvest was good.

Intercessions

Blessed are you, Creator of life and joy.
We give you thanks for the promise of eternal life
offered through the death and resurrection
of your Son, Jesus Christ.
As we rejoice in the gift of this new day
we seek to delight in you and in your great love.
Blessed are you for ever.

We give thanks for all who have helped us
to grow in the faith,
for teachers and preachers, for shining examples,
for friends and relatives.
Bless all who seek to bring others to you,
all who by their goodness
show the world of your goodness.
We remember all who work in mission and outreach.

Silence

Holy and strong God,
help us to reveal your glory.

We give thanks for explorers and inventors,
for all who extend our experience
of the world and its mysteries.
We remember especially all who are involved in research.
We ask you to bless all who work in farming
and agriculture,
all who seek to provide us with food.
Help us to care for the hungry and the homeless.

Silence

Holy and strong God,
help us to reveal your glory.

We give thanks for those
who regularly sacrifice their time and energies for us.
We remember especially our parents
and all who care for us.
Lord, as we are loved, help us to show love to others.
We ask your blessing on all who feel unwanted or lonely.

Silence

Holy and strong God,
help us to reveal your glory.

We give you thanks for all medical research,
for the caring of doctors and nurses.
We pray for all who work in the emergency services
and those who risk their lives for others.
Lord, bless all who are ill, in pain or in danger
with an awareness of your love and care.

Silence

Holy and strong God,
help us to reveal your glory.

Glory be to you, O God,
for through our Saviour Jesus Christ
you have opened to us the way to eternal life.
We rejoice in the fellowship of all your saints.
We remember before you
our loved ones who are departed from us.

Silence

Merciful Father,
accept these prayers
for the sake of your Son,
our Saviour Jesus Christ.
Amen.

Memory verse

Create in me a clean heart, O God, and renew a right spirit within me.
Psalm 51:10

Suggested music

Now the green blade riseth
Lift high the Cross
When I survey the wondrous cross

CANDLES

Aim

To look towards the crucifixion and resurrection.

Teaching

Has anyone ever planted seeds or bulbs? What did you do? You buried them in the soil. You covered them over and then waited until they grew. If you did not bury the seeds, but kept them in a packet in your house, what would happen to them? Nothing.

Go over the story of Lazy Jack. Have him look at the seed and admire it but not plant it. Have him keep the seed 'safe'. In doing this there was no growth and the harvest was lost. If seeds are to grow, they have to be planted in the ground.

Jesus told his disciples that what was going to happen to him was like planting seeds in the ground. He would die on the cross. He would be buried. But like seeds he would rise again. Let us think of the days when this happened. Jesus died on a Friday. Does anyone know what it is called? It is called Good Friday. On that day Jesus was on the cross. (Show a crucifix or a picture of the crucifixion and talk about it.) On Good Friday Jesus died and was buried – just like seeds are buried in the earth. On the Saturday nothing happened. Then on the Sunday Jesus rose again – he was alive and seen by his friends. Does anyone know what we call the day Jesus rose again? It is called Easter Day. It is the day we get Easter Eggs and are glad that Jesus is alive. It will soon be Easter and we will say, 'Thank you' to God that Jesus is alive. We will plant some seeds in a box and see if they can grow by Easter.

Activity

Have a seed tray full of seed compost and a packet of cress or some other quickly germinating seed. You may like to mark out a seed planting area in the shape of a cross. Give the children two or three tiny seeds each (with spares for those who lose them). It is better to give a child the seeds when it is their turn to plant them and to direct them in the planting. Do not forget to water the seeds and keep them in a warm place. After the seed is planted the children can sing and act out:

This is the way we plant our seeds,
plant our seeds, plant our seeds.
This is the way we plant our seeds
on a Sunday morning.

This is the way the seeds do sleep,
seeds do sleep, seeds do sleep.
This is the way the seeds do sleep
on a Sunday morning.

This is the way they rise again,
rise again, rise again.
This is the way they rise again
on a Sunday morning.

(Tune: 'Here we go round the mulberry bush')

First verse: bend down, sowing seeds in the ground.
Second verse: curl up on the ground.
Third verse: jump up and wave your hands.

Prayer

God, we thank you for all things that grow;
that buried seeds rise again.
We thank you for the love of Jesus.
Amen.

Song

Jesus' love is very wonderful

LAMPS

Aim

To look at the forthcoming events in the life of Jesus.

Teaching

When some people from Greece came to Philip and asked to see Jesus, Philip told Andrew. It was Andrew who brought them to Jesus. Can you remember whom else Andrew brought to Jesus? He brought his own brother Simon, whom we call Peter, and the boy with five barley loaves and two small fish. Have you ever thought of bringing someone to Jesus?

More and more people were coming to Jesus, and the disciples were pleased he was so popular. Not only Jews, but now even Greeks were coming, people from other nations. The disciples believed that this was what the Christ would do – bring all nations to God. They got more excited because Jesus talked to them of his 'glory'. It must have been lovely to be with Jesus. But now Jesus wanted to warn them of the troubles that lay ahead. He knew that some were plotting to kill him. Jesus did not want the disciples to worry but he did not want them to be unprepared. He talked to them about what was happening and said it was like planting a grain of wheat; they had to look ahead to its growth.

Let us look at planting. Who has ever planted a seed or a bulb? Tell us what you did. Were you not afraid to bury it in the ground? Sometimes you have to wait a long time for things to grow. Bulbs put in the soil last year are only growing now. If you keep your seeds in their packet, they will be safe, but they will not grow. You have to risk planting them if you want them to grow. You have to let them be buried if you want them to rise.

Jesus was warning the disciples that there was danger ahead. He would be taken from them and killed. Who can tell me how Jesus died? What do you call the day on which Jesus died? (Get the children to be aware of the crucifixion – show them a crucifix and let them talk about it. Also make sure they know why we keep Good Friday.) If it was a Friday, what was the day after called? Yes, Saturday, and on that day Jesus lay in the tomb – buried in the earth like a seed. The world had to wait, the disciples had to wait. No one knew what would happen. The next day, early in the morning, something wonderful happened. Who can tell me what happened? Yes, Jesus rose from the dead. Just like a seed, Jesus broke out of the earth and was seen to be alive. What do you call the day when Jesus rose again? Easter. But it is not Easter yet; it is two weeks until Easter – we will have to wait to celebrate.

Activity

Get the children to look at the crucifix on the worksheet. Why have we put seeds at the bottom and sheaves of wheat at the sides? We want to remind everyone that the cross was not the end. Dying was not the end. We know a secret that a lot of people do not know. Do you know what that secret is? Because it is a secret, I have written it in invisible ink.

Show your copy of the worksheet with the words 'Christ has died'. Below this you will have printed in lemon juice, 'Christ is risen. Christ will come again.'

With a hairdryer apply heat to the paper and the children will see the secret appear. Now offer the children the chance to show the secret to their parents. Let them write the secret in lemon juice to take home to receive the hairdryer treatment.

Perhaps they could decorate around the secret word with secret flowers.

Prayer

God, we thank you that seeds and bulbs grow in secret
without us seeing them.
We trust they will rise out of the earth.
We thank you for Jesus who,
though crucified, dead and buried,
rose again for us.
Amen.

Song

Push, little seed

TORCHES

Aim

To look towards the events of the crucifixion and resurrection.

Teaching

Has anyone ever planted seeds in a seed tray or in a garden? Do you know what happens to a seed that is buried? The seed will split open, sending roots into the ground and shoots that will grow up through the soil. It will produce leaves to capture air and sunlight to make plant food. When it is fully grown it will produce seeds, lots of seeds, sometimes hundreds, even thousands of seeds. In God's wonderful plan the seed knows what it is; if you plant flower seeds, you will not get the seeds growing vegetables. If you plant wheat, you will not get rice growing.

Why do you think Jesus compared himself to a grain of wheat? He would watch seeds being thrown on the ground. He would know that seeds are buried. But he also understood that is how new growth and new life comes. (Let the young people talk about this. Encourage them to talk about the death and resurrection of Jesus.)

If possible, at this stage have a 'resurrection plant': they can often be bought at novelty shops. This plant looks dead but when water is added to it new life appears almost immediately. Ask why it is called the resurrection plant.

Jesus was aware as he went towards Jerusalem that there would be trouble ahead. Though he was popular with lots of people, there were others who were jealous, some were angry and others just wanted to stop him. Jesus knew that his big battle against evil was about to begin. For this reason, he tried to warn his disciples. It must have been very hard for them to understand because he seemed so popular. He had to warn them of the danger and the possibility of his being put to death. If this did happen, they had to trust that goodness would still defeat evil, and life would triumph over death. Because it had never happened before, the disciples found it hard to understand when Jesus talked of his resurrection. As Christians we know something that many people do not. DEATH IS NOT FATAL because it is not the end but the beginning of a richer, fuller life.

Activity

Colour in the crucifix and the sheaves of corn at each side. Write in big letters 'Christ has died'. Show them how to write a secret message with lemon juice and then heat the writing with a hairdryer. Get each of them to write 'Christ is risen. Christ will come again' under the words 'Christ has died'.

Ask them to take the sheet home and demonstrate how the secret is revealed. Make sure they know the names of Good Friday and Easter Day.

Prayer

We give you praise and glory, Lord God,
for you give us the seasons:
a time for sowing and a time for reaping,
a time for burying seeds
and a time for watching them rise.
Help us to understand
the power of the death and resurrection of Jesus.
Amen.

Song

A man there lived in Galilee

Palm Sunday

Aim

To share in the joy of the triumphal entry into Jerusalem, and in the sorrow for the events that followed.

Preparation

Make sure there are enough palm crosses for everyone. It is a good exercise to get a few of the older children together to make your own. You may prefer to get palm crosses from Africa and so support a village that spends a good deal of the year making palm crosses. These can usually be obtained from SPCK shops or one of the missionary societies. You could also have palm branches to wave or branches from an evergreen tree. It is good to have a few tambourines, castanets and shakers for the younger children.

Opening activity

Use the Liturgy of the Palms, or at least a prayer for the blessing of the palm crosses, and then get everyone to come out and receive one. Have two children to hold the trays of palm crosses and two other children to distribute them. (During the distribution all could sing the words 'Praise God' over and over to the tune of 'Amazing Grace'.) Then have a procession and sing as you go. Have at least one hymn the children can easily sing, such as 'We have a king who rides a donkey' or 'Give me joy in my heart'. If you are fortunate enough to be able to borrow a donkey the procession could go outside and around the church.

Opening prayer

Lord Jesus, as you approached Jerusalem
the crowds welcomed you with loud 'Hosannas';
may we welcome you into our homes and our hearts
as our Saviour.
Amen.

Opening song

All glory, laud and honour

Readings

Liturgy of the Palms
Mark 11:1-11 or John 12:12-16
Psalm 118: 1, 2, 19-29

Liturgy of the Passion
Isaiah 50:4-9a
Psalm 31:9-16
Philippians 2:5-11
Mark 14:1–15:47 or Mark 15:1-39 (40-47)

Let the dramatic readings of the Passion narratives replace the sermon today. Allow the Scriptures to speak for themselves. Use as many people as possible to share in the readings. I have provided ideas for the Liturgy of the Palms rather than comment on the Passion: I hope Holy Week will be used to do that.

Thought for the day

It would seem that Jesus had planned ahead for this visit to Jerusalem. The donkey was where Jesus said and the password 'The Lord needs it' would allow the disciples to take it. The fact that the colt had never been ridden made it especially suitable for religious purposes. The cart on which the ark of the Lord was carried had never been used for any other purpose (1 Samuel 6:7).

Jesus was received like a king as he approached Jerusalem. People spread their cloaks in front of him. This is what the friends of Jehu had done when he was proclaimed king (2 Kings 9:13). People waved palm branches as they did when Simon Maccabaeus came to Jerusalem after a great victory (1 Maccabees 13:51). The words of welcome came from today's Psalm 118, which was used to welcome pilgrims to the feast. The word 'Hosanna' means 'Save us now': people used it when addressing their king or their God.

The prophet Zechariah talked of the king to come entering Jerusalem upon an ass. Jesus is fulfilling a Messianic prophecy. The ass was seen as a noble animal but not an animal to ride to war with. Jesus was coming to conquer but with love and not by force. The ass was seen as an animal of peace and Jesus enters in peace. He comes not to destroy or condemn but to set free and to encourage. He will not force himself upon the people: love will be his restraint. In the days ahead we will see how people edge him out of their lives, out of their city and out of their world. We need to welcome him into our lives and into the world in which we move.

Question time

Have we truly welcomed Jesus into our homes and our hearts?

Do we see him as our Lord, our King and our Saviour?

Intercessions

Blessed are you, Lord God of all creation.
You have created us out of your love and for your love.
Help us to welcome you with songs of 'Hosanna',
knowing that you are our strength and our shield.
Help us to welcome Christ our Lord into our lives
as our Lord and Saviour.

Silence

I will give thanks to you, for you answered me,
and have become my salvation.

Lord, by you we are wonderfully created.
Help us to use our talents and lives
to the benefit of others and to your glory.
May your Church be an instrument of peace in the world.
Lord, forgive the divisions of your Church
and help us to see we are one in you.
Help us to work together to bring in your kingdom.

Silence

I will give thanks to you, for you answered me,
and have become my salvation.

Lord, we long for the time
when the kingdoms of the world
may become the kingdom of God.
Help us to work for peace and justice.
Bless the work of all who strive
to maintain and increase peace.
We pray especially for the United Nations.

Silence

I will give thanks to you, for you answered me,
and have become my salvation.

Lord, come and rule in our lives,
that there may be peace in our hearts and in our homes.
We remember before you
homes where there is conflict and violence,
where there is division and distress.

Silence

I will give thanks to you, for you answered me,
and have become my salvation.

God, we bring before you
the troubles and distress of peoples and nations.
We remember the hungry and homeless.
We ask you to bless
all who are not at peace with themselves,
all who are disturbed in mind or spirit.
We ask that all who are ill at this time
may know your love and your presence.

Silence

I will give thanks to you, for you answered me,
and have become my salvation.

We rejoice in the fellowship of all your saints.
We commend ourselves, our loved ones
and the faithful departed
to your love and your saving power.

Silence

Merciful Father,
accept these prayers
for the sake of your Son,
our Saviour Jesus Christ.
Amen.

Memory verse

Give thanks to the Lord, for he is good; his mercy endures for ever.
Psalm 118:29

Suggested music

For the Liturgy of the Palms
All glory, laud and honour
Ride on, ride on in majesty
Hosanna, hosanna

(This last hymn is useful for repeating over and over and getting the children to join in.)

For the Liturgy of the Passion
When I survey the wondrous cross
Glory be to Jesus
There is a green hill far away
Were you there when they crucified my Lord?

CANDLES

Aim

To enjoy the triumphal entry into Jerusalem.

Teaching

If someone important comes to where you live, people usually crowd the streets to see them. (Ask the children for examples – athletes and sports people, the Queen, a pop star.) They often come in special cars or buses. This is a story of Jesus when he came to Jerusalem riding on a donkey. Has anyone ever had a ride on a donkey?

There was once a young donkey that lived with its mother. No one had ever been on its back. It would run and kick its heels and then go back to its mother and snuggle up close.

The donkey had a kind master. His master loved to hear Jesus talk and tell people about the love of God.

The little donkey dreamt that one day someone would ride upon him as they did on his mother. One day, two strangers came and started to unloose him from where he was tied with his mother. 'I wonder what they want?' thought the donkey. Someone was going to stop them but they were told, 'The Master needs him.' And they let the donkey go. The little donkey was going to carry the Lord Jesus. He felt so proud as he was led away. When he got to where Jesus was, people were so excited. Some people took off their coats and put them on the donkey to make a soft seat for Jesus. At first the donkey was surprised when Jesus got on his back – he had never carried anyone before – but soon he found it exciting. It was wonderful because people spread their cloaks on the ground for the donkey to walk on. This did not usually happen to donkeys but Jesus was a special person.

People started to wave and cheer. They cut down palm branches and laid them for the donkey to walk on. They shouted, 'Hosanna!' (Let us shout it again, but this time shout a little louder. Now let us shout it three times.) 'Hosanna' means 'Save us now'. (Sing the chorus from 'Give me joy in my heart'.) The people shouted and sang to Jesus because they thought he had come as their king. They did not understand Jesus wanted to be king of peace and to rule in their hearts.

People crowded around as Jesus entered Jerusalem. The little donkey knew it was doing something very important for it was carrying Jesus.

Activity

Show the children the donkey on the worksheet. Let them put Jesus on the donkey and then colour them in. Use glue to fix Jesus on the donkey.

Prayer

Dear Jesus, we want to sing songs of Hosanna to you.
We are so glad you rode into Jerusalem on a donkey.
We would like to help you do your work.
Amen.

Song

Give me joy in my heart

LAMPS

Aim

To share in the experience of Jesus riding into Jerusalem.

Teaching

Go over the main details of Jesus' entry into Jerusalem. Get one or two children to read aloud the reading from Mark or John. Let them make their own play of the story. Using a blanket or coat, two strong children can be the donkey. Choose a small child to be Jesus. Use the palm branches that were used earlier in church for waving, or some evergreen branches.

Let two disciples come and loosen the donkey. Someone could object to the donkey being loosened. A disciple could say, 'The Master needs it.' Disciples can put their own jackets on the donkey and then after Jesus gets on follow behind. (You may need to take the weight of Jesus as he travels on the donkey.)

At the other end of the room have people saying, 'Jerusalem, Jerusalem' over and over quietly; others saying, 'City of peace' in the same way. The donkey can add an occasional 'Hee-haw'. As Jesus approaches the crowd, let them change their words to 'Hosanna' and 'Save us'. At the same time they could wave their branches and welcome Jesus. Let Jesus dismount and all can sing 'We have a king who rides a donkey' or the chorus from 'Give me joy in my heart'.

Do not worry if this is slightly chaotic – the event was probably not very orderly.

Activity

Make a donkey out of newspaper. You will need lots of newspaper, sticky tape and glue.

The main activity today should be for them to take part in a Palm Sunday procession.

Prayer

Lord Jesus, we want to sing your praises.
We give thanks that you rode into Jerusalem
and that people accepted you with joy.
We invite you into our homes and our lives.
Hosanna.
Amen.

Song

We have a King who rides a donkey

TORCHES

Aim

To get the young people to understand the events leading up to Good Friday and Easter.

Teaching

If you were keeping a file on Jesus, the entry into Jerusalem would not necessarily come as a surprise. Jesus was popular with many of the people. Let us list the things that made him popular:

- Healing miracles
- Feeding miracles
- Storytelling (parables)
- Forgiveness (Zacchaeus, Mary Magdalene)
- Actions (cleansing the Temple, stilling the storm)

He cared for people and showed God's love. People saw him as the Messiah, their Saviour. They shouted, 'Hosanna', meaning 'Save us now'.

Some saw him as a revolutionary to drive out the Roman army.

Let the young people offer the reasons for popularity and only use the above as a prompt. Let each write a sentence to express a reason why Jesus was popular.

Then let the group explore the reasons for the events that led to the crucifixion. Much was due to what Jesus said:

- He spoke against evil.
- He spoke against injustice.
- He spoke against hypocrisy.
- He spoke against the Scribes and Pharisees: he upset the established Church.
- He overturned the tables of the moneychangers.
- He healed on the Sabbath.

Some wanted him to use force and lead an army, and they were angry that he chose an animal of peace to ride on into Jerusalem. Instead of pomp and power, he came in peace and poverty.

Some wanted him to lead them to freedom from the Romans; others feared he would cause a revolution.
Some were just jealous of his popularity.

The authorities easily manipulated the crowds.

Activity

There should be as much involvement as possible in making palm crosses, sharing in the procession and in the readings for the day. Instead of a sermon, one group of the young people could put forward ideas why Jesus was welcomed on his entry to Jerusalem. They should have no more than a sentence or two at the most. Others could express reasons for his capture and crucifixion. Keep the sentences crisp and simple. After each sentence there could be a waving of palm leaves and cries of 'Hosanna'.

Prayer

Blessed are you, Lord Jesus,
for you are our Saviour.
As you were welcomed into Jerusalem,
may we welcome you into our homes and our lives.
Let our lives sing Hosannas to you,
that we may be full of your praise.
As we carry palm crosses
may we know the great sacrifice of love
that you made for us,
Jesus our Lord and King.
Amen.

Song

Hosanna, hosanna

EASTER
Easter Day

Aim
To rejoice in the resurrection and in the presence of the risen Lord.

Preparation
There can be a lot of preparation for Easter and it is good to involve as many children as possible. The church will be decorated with flowers – let the children help in the decorating. Let the children help to prepare the Easter garden and an empty cross covered in spring flowers. Banners can be made with words such as 'Jesus is risen!'; 'Christ is alive!'; 'Jesus is here.' If possible, everyone should be able to light a candle from the Easter candle.

Opening activity
Let there be a procession where banners are carried and the flower-covered cross leads the way. Stop at the Easter garden for a rolling away of the stone from the tomb (let a child do this). Shout, 'Christ is risen! Alleluia,' with the response, 'He is risen indeed! Alleluia.' Light the Easter candle (again, let a child do this). Once more shout, 'Christ is risen! Alleluia,' and have the same response as before.

Opening prayer
Blessed are you,
God and Father of our Lord Jesus Christ.
To you be praise and glory for ever.
From the darkness of death
you have raised your Son to eternal life.
Through him death is destroyed,
light conquers darkness,
love defeats hatred
and your redeeming love is offered to us all.
Blessed are you, Lord God, for ever.
Alleluia.
Amen.

Opening songs
Alleluia, alleluia, give thanks to the risen Lord
Jesus Christ is risen today

Readings
Acts 10:34-43 or Isaiah 25:6-9
Psalm 118:1, 2, 14-24
1 Corinthians 15:1-11 or Acts 10:34-43
John 20:1-18 or Mark 16:1-8

Thought for the day
Regularly someone will say, 'I would believe in the resurrection if someone came back from the dead.' Well, today we rejoice because someone has. Christ is risen. Alleluia!

Let Mary Magdalene and Peter tell their story. (Have three voices – Mary, Peter and Jesus.)
Mary starts.
I had another sleepless night. My eyes are red with crying. One of those nights when the darkness seems to last for ever. When Jesus died something in me died also; it was all so cruel. He forgave me my many sins, he loved me dearly and now he is dead. There is a weight on my heart like a heavy stone; like the stone rolled on to the tomb. Such a weight, for I saw him die, I saw his agony, I saw him deserted by his friends. It turned my heart to stone. Who can lift the stone from my heart? Jesus could but he is dead and a stone is rolled against his tomb.

I will go and be beside him. It is still dark – it is about 5am – but I will go. If only someone would roll the stone away.

Please, God, lift the stone from my heart and from the tomb.

O Lord! Somebody has been here, somebody with great strength. The stone has been moved. I will go and see my Lord. Oh no! They have taken away my Lord. They have stolen his body. O Lord, what have they done? I will go and tell Peter.

Let Peter take up the story.
I haven't cried in years. I do not like to see grown men cry. I am so ashamed of myself. How can I forgive myself? I said that I did not know Jesus; I denied him . . . At about 5.30 there was a banging on the door . . .

I was afraid. Then I realised it was Mary Magdalene, shouting and weeping. I could hardly get any sense out of her. She kept saying, 'They have taken away my Lord.' Young John and I were quickly on the road, running to the tomb. I am not as young as I used to be and John got there first. But he did not go in. I went in and saw the grave clothes discarded but there was no body. It was the way the clothes were wrapped that was odd; it looked as if he had just vanished from them or come through them. John came in and later he said, 'The empty grave clothes convinced me he had risen.' But at that moment we went back home. We passed Mary on the way.

Mary continues the story.
I went back hoping to find someone who had moved him. But I could not see for tears. I cried and asked aloud, 'Where is he?' . . .

But I must get a grip of myself. My vision is blurred. My heart aches. (*Jesus joins Mary*) Who is this? Is it the gardener? He seems to be looking at the spring flowers that have burst into life. Sir, they have taken away my Lord. Do you know . . .

'Mary.'

No, it can't be! Is it really you? This is madness.

'Mary.'

It is you! Jesus, it really is you!

'Mary.'

Master, Master. Let me stay here close to you. Let me hug you and be with you for ever.

'Mary, do not cling to me. You cannot keep me to yourself. You will have to let me go. You will have to go, Mary. Go and tell the disciples that I am alive, I am risen. Tell them you have seen me.'

I did not want to go but he asked me. I ran again to the house and told the disciples, 'I have seen the Lord! Alleluia!'

Question time

Do we think too much in the past tense of Jesus and so fail to acknowledge that he is the living Lord and present in our lives?

Are we in danger of talking *about* Jesus when we could be talking *to* him?

Illustration

Napoleon escaped from his island prison. His armies regathered under the French flag and Europe was plunged into war. The British army under Wellington landed in Belgium and prepared to fight near a small village called Waterloo. There was no way of communicating to England the news except by semaphore. Day after day a man watched from the tower of Winchester Cathedral, peering towards the south coast. On a misty day the watcher received a message: 'Wellington defeated.' The mist came down and a sadness filled Winchester and spread over England. The watcher stayed at his post. After a long while the mist lifted and the message was repeated: 'Wellington defeated.' But now two more words were added and they made a great difference: 'Wellington defeated the French.' The assumed defeat was a victory. A new message sped to London. Bells rang out and flags flew. The message, which seemed one of defeat, was in fact the start of the news of victory. Likewise we must move from the crucifixion to the joy of the resurrection. We are able to proclaim, 'Death is conquered. We are free. Christ has won the victory.'

Intercessions

Blessed are you, God and Father of us all,
giver of life and life eternal.
By the love of your Son you have triumphed over hatred.
In his power, light has conquered darkness
and life has overcome death.
You have opened for us the gate of eternal life.
Blessed are you, O God, now and for ever.

Silence

Lord, we are Easter people:
let 'Alleluia' be our song.

We give you thanks and praise
for the resurrection of our Lord Jesus Christ
and for his appearances to his loved ones.
We rejoice with the whole Church
in the joy of the risen Lord.
May we who know the Good News
go and tell others that he is risen.
Grant that your Church may help to bring peace and hope
to a troubled world.
We ask you to give courage to all who have not seen
and yet believe.

Silence

Lord, we are Easter people:
let 'Alleluia' be our song.

Risen Lord, we seek your peace:
peace for our war-torn world;
peace between nations and people;
peace in our dealings with each other;
peace in our hearts and homes.

Silence

Lord, we are Easter people:
let 'Alleluia' be our song.

As you appeared to the disciples in the house,
come enter our homes;
come enter into our fear and darkness;
come enter into our enclosed lives and our fear to venture.
Come with the glorious freedom you offer
to the children of God.

Silence

Lord, we are Easter people:
let 'Alleluia' be our song.

We come with all who weep by gravesides,
all who mourn the loss of a loved one,
all who feel lonely or deserted.
May all who mourn find new hope and joy in you.
We remember all who are terminally ill
and those who are caring for them.
We think of those who have a heavy weight
on their hearts and minds
and tears in their eyes.
We ask that we may all know the hope of eternal life.

Silence

Lord, we are Easter people:
let 'Alleluia' be our song.

We rejoice with the disciples and all your saints
in the joy of the risen Lord.
We ask you to bless all our loved ones departed
with the fullness of your light and peace in eternal life.

Silence

Merciful Father,
accept these prayers
for the sake of your Son,
our Saviour Jesus Christ.
Amen.

Memory verse

I have seen the Lord.
John 20:18

Suggested music

Thine be the glory
Now the green blade riseth
The strife is o'er, the battle done

CANDLES

Aim

To experience the joy of the resurrection.

Teaching

Look at the Easter garden, beginning with the stone rolled against the tomb. Make sure they know who was buried there on Good Friday. (Get them to repeat, 'Good Friday.') Tell how no one would go there on the Sabbath day. Now it was Easter Day and Mary wanted to go to be near the body of Jesus. If the church has figures of Jesus and Mary, show Mary, or you may be able to show her from an Easter card. Mary wondered who could move the stone. It was big and heavy; it would take a few men to move it. We know that before she got there the stone was rolled away. (Let a child roll the stone gently aside.) Mary looked for Jesus but could not find his body. Mary was very sad. Mary was crying. (Let the children repeat, 'Mary was crying.') She went and told Peter and John, and they came and looked into the tomb but saw no one. They went away and Mary came back. Mary was crying. (Get all to repeat.)

She thought she heard someone coming along the path. Perhaps it was the gardener. She would ask him if he knew where the body of Jesus was. 'I am looking for Jesus and I cannot find him. Do you know where they have taken him?'

Then she heard a voice she knew saying her name, 'Mary, Mary.'

There was only one person who could say her name like that. Who is it? Yes, Jesus, and he is alive. Repeat after me: 'Jesus is alive.' At this point show the figure or a picture of Jesus. Let all look at it and make comments. Jesus is not a ghost: he is alive.

Then Jesus told Mary, 'You must go and tell the disciples you have seen me and that I am alive.' Mary did not want to leave Jesus but she did as he asked her. She went and said to the disciples, 'I have seen the Lord.' Let us say what Mary said: 'I have seen the Lord.'

Activity

If possible, all the children should take part in the activities in church. You may like to have an Easter-egg painting competition or a miniature Easter-garden competition. Eggs could be brought hard-boiled and decorated during their class if you have one. An Easter-egg hunt is always fun, especially if it can be outside. You could have an egg-rolling competition or even and egg 'jarping' contest (this is a little like conkers: the children clash eggs and see which break first). Easter cards to take home could be made.

If the story is told, get the children to mime it. Let half the children be Mary and the other half Jesus. You could keep a few to be the disciples.

Prayer

Let us all say, 'God, we thank you that Jesus is alive and loves us. Alleluia.'

(You may like to help them to sing 'Alleluia'.)

Song

This is the day

(Let a leader or a group sing it in parts and the children repeat the same words.)

LAMPS

Aim

To enjoy the fact that Jesus is risen.

Teaching

Let today's Gospel (John 20:1-18) be read by a narrator, with Mary and Jesus speaking their parts.

Tell the group they should listen carefully so that they can act the story out after it is read. It may be wise to choose who will take the different parts before the reading so that they can concentrate on what they are called to do.

Give prompts like:

It is early on Sunday morning and Mary prepares to leave the house . . . She goes to the tomb. She finds the stone rolled away. She does not find the body of Jesus. She starts to cry because she is so upset. She hurries to tell Peter and John . . . Peter and John run to the tomb. John gets there first. Peter goes in to the tomb. Then John goes in. After this they go home. They meet Mary on her way back to the tomb. Mary is weeping and she sees someone. She thinks it is the gardener and says to him, 'Sir, do you know where they have taken Jesus?'

He says, 'Mary.'

Mary is amazed. Can it be Jesus?

Again he says, 'Mary.'

It is Jesus! She runs to him and hugs him. He is not a ghost. He is alive.

Jesus says, 'Do not cling to me. Go and tell my disciples the Good News.'

Again Mary runs to tell Peter and the disciples, 'I have seen the Lord.'

Jesus is alive. Alleluia.

Get everyone to say aloud, 'Jesus is alive. Alleluia.'

Activity

If possible, all the children should take part in the activities in church.

You may like to have an Easter-egg painting competition or a miniature Easter-garden competition. Eggs could be brought hard-boiled and decorated during their class if you have one. An Easter-egg hunt is always fun, especially if it can be outside. You could have an egg-rolling competition or even and egg 'jarping' contest (this is a little like conkers: the children clash eggs and see which break first). Easter cards to take home could be made. Perhaps during Holy Week banners could have been made for the church procession.

Prayer

Lord Jesus, we rejoice today in your resurrection.
We are pleased that you appeared to Mary Magdalene
and you showed her that you were alive.
May we trust in you as our risen Lord,
for you are ever with us and always ready to help us.
Amen.

Song

He is Lord, he is Lord

TORCHES

Aim

To share the joy of Mary Magdalene.

Teaching

Look at today's song and learn it. Mary was worried about Jesus not having a proper burial. She wanted to bring spices to the tomb to see he was buried properly. But she knew there was a great big boulder in the way. It was too heavy for her to move. There was a heavy weight of sadness on her heart and mind. As she left the house, she wondered, 'Who will roll the stone away?' She quietly prayed, 'God, help me; get someone to roll away the stone.'

What she did not know was that the stone had already been rolled away.

Sing:

The angel rolled the stone away,
the angel rolled the stone away,
it was early Easter Sunday morning,
the angel rolled the stone away.

Let someone be Mary as the verse is said or sung. Let Mary show amazement at the empty tomb.

Sing the chorus.

In verse two let Mary sing or say the second line alone. The same with verse three. Have the chorus after each verse. Before verse four continue the story of today's Gospel.

Such wonderful news cannot be kept to ourselves. Jesus told Mary she needed to go and tell the disciples. She did not want to leave Jesus but she did as he asked her. Mary was the first to see the risen Lord Jesus. She hurried to tell the disciples, 'I have seen the Lord.'

Sing verse four with the chorus.

This would be a good hymn for the young people to sing during Communion with all joining in the chorus.

Activity

The young people should be in church for the whole service unless it proves impractical. They should help to carry banners, bring up the bread and wine, perhaps say a prayer and also take the collection. You may also like to have an Easter-egg painting competition or a miniature Easter-garden competition.

Prayer

Jesus stand among us
in your risen power;
let this time of worship
be a hallowed hour.

(This prayer could be said at the beginning of the service in church by one of the young people, or four of them each saying a line.)

Song

The angel rolled the stone away

Second Sunday of Easter

Aim

To share in the wonder of the resurrection.

Preparation

Have a large candle – the Easter candle – and ask a child to light it. As it is lit, let the child say, 'Alleluia. Christ is risen.' The response by all is: 'He is risen indeed. Alleluia.'

Four other children could gather around and say a line each of:

Jesus, stand among us
in your risen power;
let this time of worship
be a hallowed hour.

Opening activity

Have four children with the words LIFE, OF, BREATH, THE on sheets of paper, move up and down the aisles. Let them come together at the front of the church and in the right order. Let them say in chorus:

Breathe on me, Breath of God,
fill me with life anew,
that as you love so may I love,
and do what you would do.

Breathe on me, Breath of God,
so shall I never die,
but live with you the perfect life
of your eternity.

You can light 10 + 1 small candles near the Easter garden or the Easter candle. Why ten? There were only ten disciples in the locked room. Who was missing? Thomas and Judas. Judas is dead; Thomas comes as number 11 later. You can add another candle for Mary Magdalene who saw Jesus first.

Opening prayer

Jesus, risen Lord, you are here and with us now.
We welcome you to our church, our homes
and our lives.
We seek to know you better and to love you more.
Amen.

Opening song

Jesus, stand among us

Readings

Acts 4:32-35
Psalm 133
1 John 1:1–2:2
John 20:19-31

Thought for the day

The disciples were locked in through fear. The room they were in was like the tomb; they were sealed in and afraid to venture out. They had lost their Lord and leader. They felt powerless, lifeless. How often do we feel like this, locked in and unable to do what we ought to do? Then Jesus came. There was no fuss. Suddenly he was there, alive and well. He greeted them as normal: 'Shalom. Peace be with you.' But this was a new peace, for the risen Lord offered it to them. He showed them his hands and his side (interesting to note not his feet; feet were usually bound to the cross and not nailed). 'Then were the disciples glad when they saw the Lord' must be one of the great understatements of the Scriptures. What joy, what wonder must have been theirs. Then Jesus again said, 'Peace be with you.' Jesus said that as God sent him out, he would send them out.

Jesus needs disciples to continue his work. He will work in them and through them but he needs disciples. Think on these words concerning the risen Lord by St Teresa of Avila:

Christ has no hands, but your hands
to do his work today.
Christ has no feet but your feet
to speed men on his way.
Christ has no lips but your lips
to tell men why he died.
Christ has no love but your love
to win men to his side.

We are called to be Christ to others and to see Christ in others. This is only possible if we are filled with his Spirit. Jesus breathed on his disciples. There can be little doubt the Gospel writer saw this as a new creation. With the resurrection, a new world was dawning for us all. It is his Spirit that equips us for the work we need do. It is not in book learning but in the power of his Spirit that we are able to go out in mission.

This happened to ten disciples; Judas was already dead and Thomas was away from the company. When Thomas was told, he refused to believe. Faith can be handed down but it must become first-hand for us. We need a relationship with the risen Lord. Thomas wanted to experience this wonderful event for himself. But to do it he stayed with the fellowship of the faithful. Jesus came again. Again we hear the words, 'Peace be with you.' Thomas is invited to touch and feel; this is no ghost – Jesus bears the marks of the crucifixion. Then Jesus says, 'Blessed are those who have not seen and yet have come to believe.'

Question time

Have we allowed the risen Lord to offer us his peace?

Do we accept his commission to go out in his power and do his work?

Illustration

Suddenly a man fell to the ground. He had stopped breathing and it would not be long before he was totally dead. But help was at hand. Someone was willing to give him mouth-to-mouth resuscitation. They breathed their breath into him, filling his lungs, and then helped his lungs to expel the air and then receive some more breath. This process went on for a while at ten breaths a minute;

without it the man would have died. By the time the ambulance came the man was breathing freely on his own. The person had saved his life. Jesus breathes new life into us and gives us eternal life. Jesus defeats death and brings us to eternal life.

(You may be able to get a St John's Ambulance person or a paramedic to offer to demonstrate 'Breath of Life' – they also provide a useful card with this title.)

Intercessions

Blessed are you, Lord God of our salvation.
To you be praise and glory for ever.
You have delivered us from the darkness of death
through your beloved Son.
In him, light has conquered darkness;
life has triumphed over death.
He has breathed into us your life-giving Spirit.
Blessed are you, Father, Son and Holy Spirit,
our God for ever and ever.

Lord, we give you thanks for the light of the Gospel
and that it shines in our hearts.
We rejoice in the resurrection and in your saving power.
We remember all who are struggling with their faith,
those who doubt,
any who sit in darkness or who live in fear.
We bring to mind all who have fallen away from the faith,
especially any known to us.

Silence

Lord God, you are light:
in you is no darkness at all.

We remember peoples and nations who feel drained
and lack energy.
We ask your blessing upon all who suffer
from poverty or oppression.
We pray for any who are separated
from their loved ones and their homes;
we remember all who are in prison.

Silence

Lord God, you are light:
in you is no darkness at all.

We give thanks
that you appeared in an ordinary home, O Christ.
We ask that your presence and your peace
may be known in our homes and among our loved ones.
We bring before you homes
where faith is mocked or persecuted,
and pray for all who are struggling to remain faithful.

Silence

Lord God, you are light:
in you is no darkness at all.

We think of all who are struggling with life:
homes where there is tension or lack of peace;
people who are ill and afraid of the future;
all who are lonely and facing a time of crisis.
May all know your presence and your peace.

Silence

Lord God, you are light:
in you is no darkness at all.

Father, we give you thanks
for the new life that you offer to us in your Son,
for you offer us eternal life.
We come to you with confidence
and pray for friends and loved ones departed.
May they know the fullness of joy in your presence
and in eternal life.

Silence

Merciful Father,
accept these prayers
for the sake of your Son,
our Saviour Jesus Christ.
Amen.

Memory verse

He showed them his hands and his side. Then the disciples rejoiced when they saw the Lord.
John 20:20

Suggested music

Breathe on me, Breath of God
Jesus lives! thy terrors now
Jesus is Lord

CANDLES

Aim

To share in the resurrection joy of the disciples.

Teaching

Show some keys on a bunch and let the children guess what they might be for. Have a variety of keys: a large key, a yale or chubb lock key and a tiny key. Establish that keys are for locking and unlocking. Ask for suggestions why places should be locked or unlocked.

The disciples locked themselves in a room. Do you know why? They were afraid after Jesus was killed that the same people might come looking for them. So the disciples were hiding in a house with a locked door – no one could get in. They were talking very quietly. Suddenly Jesus was there with them. He was alive and said, 'Shalom'; that means 'Hello' or 'Peace be with you'. Jesus was saying, 'Hello, I am back.' Mary said he was alive and that she had seen him in the garden. Now there he was in the room. Strange, because no one had unlocked the door but Jesus was there inside. He suddenly appeared. He was not a ghost – he was really alive again. The disciples were really pleased to see him. They would have liked to ask all sorts of questions. Jesus had some work for them to do. He wanted them to tell others that he was alive. He wanted them to do the work he had been doing. To help them he came to each one of them and breathed his Spirit into them. The ten disciples were really glad to see Jesus. Why was there just ten? There should have been twelve. Do you know who was missing? Judas was missing because he had died. Thomas was also missing because he had gone away. When Thomas came back he was sorry that he had missed Jesus. The disciples said, 'We have seen the Lord.' (Let us repeat: 'We have seen the Lord.') Thomas said, 'I cannot believe that he is alive; I saw him die. I will only believe if I see him, if I can touch him. I would like to feel the nail holes in his hands and put my hand in his side where the spear made a hole. Then I will believe.'

It was a week after Easter and Jesus came again to where the disciples were. This time Thomas was with them. Jesus spoke to Thomas and said, 'Thomas, come here – put your finger in the nail holes, put your hand where the spear has been.' Thomas did not know what to do. He came before Jesus and touched his hands and his side and said quietly, 'My Lord and my God.' (Let us repeat: 'My Lord and my God.')

Now all of the disciples had seen Jesus. How many were there who saw him?

Let us say what they said: 'We have seen the Lord.'

Let us say what Mary Magdalene said: 'I have seen the Lord.'

They all knew that Jesus who had been dead was alive again and wanted to be their friend.

Activity

Tell the children that one is to be blindfolded and placed in the middle of a circle. The others sitting in a circle will pass the keys around. At a command they will stop and the person with the keys hides them behind their back. Everyone puts their hands behind their back. Now the blindfold is removed and the person in the middle has three chances to guess who has the keys. To help, the person with the keys should give them a gentle shake (especially when the person in the middle is looking away). If they guess correctly, the person with the keys should go into the middle and the game begins again.

Prayer

Jesus, we are glad that you are alive
and that you want to be our friend.
Let us remember you every day
and speak to you in our prayers.
Amen.

Song

Sing verse 3 of 'Away in a manger' and relate it to the resurrection.

LAMPS

Aim

To share in the wonder of the resurrection.

Teaching

(Tell the class to listen very carefully because at the end of the story we will act it out.)

On Easter Day, who was the first to see Jesus in the garden? Yes, Mary Magdalene found the tomb empty, and she went and told the disciples. Two disciples ran to the tomb (grave) but it was empty. Jesus was not there – they did not see Jesus. They went back to the house. Do you know who they were? It was Peter and John. Mary went back to the tomb and this time she saw Jesus alive and risen from the dead. Mary wanted to hug Jesus and stay with him. But he asked her to tell the disciples that he was alive. Mary ran and told them, 'I have seen the Lord.' (All repeat Mary's words.) The disciples found it hard to believe.

Now Peter and John were locked in a room with another eight disciples. Two and eight make ten. Who was missing? One disciple was dead and one had left Jerusalem. Judas was dead. Thomas was away somewhere else. Do you know why the ten locked themselves in? Because they were afraid; they were afraid to go outside or be seen in case they were taken prisoner and killed like Jesus was killed. They locked themselves in and spoke quietly. They hoped no one would find them. It was a bit like being locked in the tomb. There into the locked room, to the frightened disciples, came Jesus. He said, 'Shalom', which is like us saying 'Hello'. What a surprise – Jesus really was alive. He was not a ghost. Here he was, saying 'Hello, I am back.' They had not lost their friend. He had come back to them even from the dead. Every one of the disciples was full of happiness. Jesus touched each of them and breathed his new life into them. He wanted them to do the work he started to do. The disciples were really, really glad.

When Thomas came, they were all talking at once. He could see something wonderful had happened to them. Some were saying, 'He is alive.' And others were saying, 'We have seen him.' When Thomas asked who it was, they told him it was Jesus and said, 'We have seen the Lord.'

Thomas refused to believe them. He said, 'When you see someone die like Jesus, you know he is dead. He is dead and buried. When you are dead, you are dead. I will not believe unless I can put my fingers into the nail holes in his hands, unless I can put my hand in the hole in his side.' The disciples could not persuade him. A whole week later, when they were all together in the room, Jesus came again. Jesus again said 'Hello' to everyone. Then he turned to Thomas and said, 'Thomas, reach out and put your finger in the nail holes, put your hand in my side where the spear made a hole.' Thomas came and touched Jesus and knew that he was real and alive. He quietly said to Jesus, 'My Lord and my God.' Then with all the other disciples he could say, 'I have seen the Lord.' (Let us all repeat the two things that Thomas said.)

Activity

Choose Mary, Peter and John, Jesus, eight disciples and Thomas. Give them as few prompts as necessary for them to act out the story. You could mark the hands of Jesus for Thomas to see and feel.

Prayer

Lord Jesus,
you came to the room where the disciples were
and wanted still to be their friend –
come and be our friend.
Help us to know that you are alive and with us always,
Jesus Christ our risen Lord.
Amen.

Song

What a wonderful Saviour

TORCHES

Aim

To share in the joy of Thomas.

Teaching

After the crucifixion the disciples went into hiding for fear of being captured and maybe killed. If people could do such things to Jesus, the disciples were in great danger. They locked themselves in a room and did not go out. Two of the disciples were missing. Do you know who they were? Judas was missing. After betraying Jesus he went out and killed himself. Now he would never know what happened next. Thomas was missing; he had gone off somewhere else.

On Easter Day, Jesus appeared to Mary Magdalene in the garden and to the ten disciples in the locked room. This was a most wonderful moment, when they saw Jesus again and knew that he had risen from the dead. Jesus had spoken to them and given them the task of telling others about him. Thomas missed out on this. When the disciples told him, he could not believe it. He had seen Jesus die and knew that he was buried. They must be mistaken; how could it be Jesus? They kept telling him, 'Jesus is risen. We have seen the Lord.' Thomas was a practical sort of man and said, 'I will believe when I see him. If he is alive, I would like to meet him. In fact, to prove it is Jesus, I would like to touch him, put my finger in the nail holes in his hands and put my fist in his side where the spear went in.' It was obvious that the mind of Thomas was still full of the crucifixion. He would need to be moved on to the resurrection. Arguing and talking with the disciples was not enough. Thomas needed to experience the presence of the risen Lord for himself. How he wished he had been there with the ten; then he would have believed.

It was the next Sunday that Jesus came to them again. Thomas had stayed with the disciples and was waiting and hoping. Jesus came and said, 'Peace be with you.'

Thomas could hardly believe it when Jesus turned to him and said, 'Thomas, stretch out your hand and put your finger in the nail holes. Come, put your fist into my side.' Thomas actually touched Jesus. This was no ghost. There was no doubt that it was Jesus. Jesus had risen. Jesus is alive. Jesus even knew what the disciples had been saying. Thomas was overcome with wonder and awe and said to Jesus, 'My Lord and my God.'

Jesus then said to Thomas, 'Have you believed because you have seen me? Blessed are those who have not seen and yet have come to believe.'

Activity

Let us write down in a few sentences 'Why I believe Jesus is risen' and 'How I can make Jesus my friend'. It may help to talk for a while about how you make friends and keep friends.

Prayer

Jesus, as you came to the disciples, you come to us.
You want us to be your friend
and to help in the work that you do.
Jesus, we ask that we might be true friends
and know that you are with us always.
Amen.

Song

The Spirit lives to set us free (Walk in the light)

Third Sunday of Easter

Aim

To rejoice in the presence of the risen Lord.

Preparation

Ask three children to recite a verse each of 'Jesus, stand among us'. Another child should be prepared to read dramatically 'Jesus is my friend'. Have the Easter Candle in a central position.

Opening activity

The children will recite the three verses. A fourth child will light the Easter candle, saying, 'Alleluia, Christ is risen', with the response 'He is risen indeed, Alleluia.' The fifth child will read 'Jesus is my friend'.

Opening prayer

Father of us all, we give you thanks
for the wonderful resurrection of Jesus.
As he is our risen Lord and ever present,
may we enjoy his company
and know he is our friend always.
Amen.

Opening song

The King is among us

Readings

Acts 3:12-19
Psalm 4
1 John 3:1-7
Luke 24:36-48

Thought for the day

Two of our readings today come from the writings of St Luke. He wrote the Acts of the Apostles as well as the Gospel according to St Luke. In Acts we hear of Peter telling his fellow Jews that the power he has comes from Jesus, whom they killed and God raised from the dead. Peter tells how the disciples are witnesses to the risen Lord. He invites the people to repent and to turn to God, just as Jesus asked him to do. The change in the disciples, from locked in and fearful men to being men willing to die for the Gospel, is the great proof of the resurrection. Peter points out that it is not in their power but in the power of the Lord that they are able to heal the lame man.

Luke's account of Easter Day differs slightly from the account of Mark and Matthew. Interestingly, Luke has the eleven disciples together (did he not know the Thomas story?). He also tells us of 'companions' being present: here is a brief insight into the fact that there were others and not all male. Suddenly Jesus is there among them, saying, 'Peace be with you.' This was the group that knew all about the crucifixion and burial – they had seen him die. They had watched his burial. Now they were startled and terrified for they thought it must be a ghost. Jesus tells them not to be afraid or doubting. It is Luke who mentions the feet of Jesus when Jesus invites the people to touch him and to look at his hands and feet. He wants them to know he is solid. Yet they still found it hard to believe. Jesus had to deal with them quite gently. He asked for something to eat and they gave him some fish. Ghosts do not eat. Jesus ate the fish in their presence.

Only when they are more relaxed does Jesus talk to them of the prophecies in the Scriptures, of how the Messiah would suffer and rise from the dead. They are to proclaim repentance and forgiveness of sins. They are to be his witnesses. St John, in today's second reading, witnesses and calls for awareness that we are children of God and so we should turn away from evil and turn to God.

Question time

Are we truly people of the resurrection or do we get stuck at the cross?

How can we learn to walk with and witness to the risen Lord?

Illustration

Have you ever been caught in the fog? The whole world becomes cold and grey. Vision is greatly restricted. Everything around appears to be dull and damp. Then suddenly there is a shining, an extra amount of light; there is a radiance that begins to appear all around. The sun breaks through and the fog lifts and disappears. The day seems so glorious and bright. This was the experience of the disciples with the resurrection. They shut themselves in and shut the fullness of life out. They were locked in by sorrow and fear. They just wanted to hide. It was then he came. He came because he was needed. He came back from the dead. He came to be with them. He came to guide them. He came to help them. He came to be friends. He came to transform their world. He comes now and he comes to us. He comes to chase away our darkness and fear and to make our world bright.

Intercessions

Blessed are you, mighty God,
creator of light and darkness.
To you be praise and glory for ever.
By the resurrection of your Son to eternal life
you have destroyed the darkness and fear of death.
Radiant life is ours through him who loves us,
Jesus, our Lord and our friend.
Blessed are you, Father, Son and Holy Spirit,
our God for ever and ever.

We give thanks that you have called us
to witness to your resurrection and to your presence.
Help us, Lord Jesus, to turn away from sin
and to follow you.
May your Church reveal your glory to the world.
We remember today all who are persecuted for their faith,
all who are struggling to make your name known
in difficult areas.
We pray for all who are full of doubt or fear.

Silence

You set us free when we are hard-pressed.
Have mercy on us and hear our prayer.

We bring before you the fearful and the anxious;
all whose lives are in danger through violence or war.
We remember all who are locked away,
in prison or by painful memories,
all who are striving for new freedom and for hope.

Silence

You set us free when we are hard-pressed.
Have mercy on us and hear our prayer.

We give thanks for your presence in our homes:
that you are always with us.
May we know you as a friend and helper.
Bless our family and our loved ones
with your abiding presence.
Be known among our friends and our companions.
We remember all who live alone
and are worried about their lives or their future.

Silence

You set us free when we are hard-pressed.
Have mercy on us and hear our prayer.

We give thanks for the healing power of faith.
We ask you to bless and guide all who heal.
We remember our own doctor and surgery.
We ask that the ill and the weary may know you
as their companion and helper.
We pray to you for all who are hard-pressed
and struggling at this time,
especially for . . .

Silence

You set us free when we are hard-pressed.
Have mercy on us and hear our prayer.

Blessed are you, Lord Jesus Christ,
for you have triumphed over darkness and death,
opening for us the way to eternal life.
We remember in your presence
friends and loved ones who are departed from us.
May they rejoice in the fullness of life eternal.

Silence

Merciful Father,
accept these prayers
for the sake of your Son,
our Saviour Jesus Christ.
Amen.

Memory verse

Repent therefore and turn to God so that your sins may be wiped out.
Acts 3:19

Suggested music

What a friend we have in Jesus
Do not be afraid
Peace, perfect peace, is the gift of Christ our Lord

CANDLES

Aim

To encourage the children to know Jesus as their friend.

Teaching

Once there was a little boy who was going to walk home from school in the dark. It was a long way and the teacher was worried that he might be frightened. He said he was not. Just before he went home the teacher again asked him because she was worried about him walking in the dark. The boy again said he was not frightened because he had a big torch and it had a lovely light. After this he said he was not worried for he would not be alone as his father would be outside waiting for him.

What makes you frightened? Encourage the children to talk of fears – and to see it is sometimes good to have fears.

After Jesus died, the disciples were frightened that they might be captured, so they hid. They locked themselves in, so that no one would find them. They did not dare go out. Then Jesus came. At first they were frightened of Jesus. Do you know why? They thought Jesus was a ghost. But he was not. He came to them as their friend to help them not to be afraid. He had to show them he was not a ghost. He let them touch him, feel the nail holes in his feet and hands. Then he asked for something to eat; they knew that ghosts did not eat.

Jesus came to be their friend and to give them courage. He asked them to go out and to tell people that he was alive. He promised that he would go with them, so that they were not alone. They could talk to him and get strength from him.

Jesus wants us to be his friend. He wants us to know he is with us and that we can talk to him. He wants us to tell other people that he is alive and will be their friend.

Activity

This is a variation on 'What time is it, Mr Wolf?' Choose one person to be 'Spook'. As Spook walks away, the children follow behind asking the time. Spook can say any time he likes leading the children further away. When he says, 'Midnight', he turns, chasing the children and crying, 'Whoo, whoo, whoo'. The first person caught or the last back to base is the next Spook.

Prayer

Jesus, friend of the disciples,
be a friend of mine.
Let me know that you love me and you are with me.
Let me learn to talk to you every day.
Amen.

Song

Jesus, we thank you

LAMPS

Aim
To encourage the children to make a friend of Jesus.

Teaching
When Jesus was captured and crucified, the disciples ran away because they were afraid. They felt that they might be killed also. They watched from a distance but kept hidden. Once Jesus was buried, the disciples went into hiding. They stayed in a large room and locked the doors and closed the shutters. St Luke tells us there were eleven of them. Who was missing? Judas was missing because he had died.

They were almost as locked in as they thought Jesus was in the tomb. The windows had shutters and they were in the dark. At least no one could get to them. Suddenly Jesus was there. The doors were locked but Jesus was there. How could this be? They had seen him die – how could he be there? Some were whispering, 'It's a ghost', and many of them were frightened. 'It must be a ghost. How did he get here?' But Jesus was not a ghost: he had risen from the dead and was as solid as they were. He needed to prove he was not a ghost. He invited them to touch him and know he was solid; to give him a hug as they would a friend. To prove it was no one else, he asked them to look at the nail holes in his hands and his feet. Do you remember when those holes were made?

Some of them still could hardly believe it. Jesus needed to convince them so he asked them for something to eat. Well, ghosts do not eat. They had some fish already cooked so they gave some to Jesus. They watched him as he ate. It really was their friend: it was Jesus and he was really alive.

After this, Jesus told them how it was said in the Old Testament that the Messiah – the Christ – would suffer and rise from the dead. Once they understood this, they were to ask people to turn to God, to stop being wicked and to do what God wanted. Then he asked them to go out and be witnesses for him: to go out and tell people of the resurrection. They would have to be brave to do this but they were not alone; their friend Jesus was with them.

Jesus wants us to be his friend and to tell others about him. How can we do this? How can we be friends of Jesus?

Activity
One person is sent out of the room while someone else is chosen to be the risen Lord. All sit around in a circle. Jesus gives life to people by winking at them! When a person is winked at, they jump up, run around the circle and back to their own place. The person who has been out of the room has to discover who is the risen Lord. When 'Jesus' is discovered, he or she has to go out of the room and a new Jesus is chosen.

Prayer
Jesus, we are so happy
that you rose again from the dead.
You are alive and with us wherever we go.
Help us to keep in contact with you through our prayers
and so know that you are our friend and Saviour.
Amen.

Song
Jesus is my friend

TORCHES

Aim
To show how Jesus gives courage and hope to his friends.

Teaching
Once Jesus was captured, the disciples scattered because they were afraid. They had seen the cruelty that had been inflicted on Jesus. They watched at a distance, unable to help when Jesus was crucified. They felt useless and afraid. They saw his slow death and then his hasty burial. The tomb was sealed and their friend was dead. The disciples came together but locked themselves in because they were very frightened. The room they were in must have felt like the tomb. Would they ever be able to get out again?

Suddenly he was there, saying, 'Peace be unto you. Do not be afraid. Why are there doubts in your hearts?'

'Who can this be? Jesus is dead.'

'It looks like him – it must be a ghost.'

'It cannot be Jesus – we saw him die.'

'How did he get in here?'

The disciples were more afraid now. Who could this be?

Jesus had to show them that he was not a ghost, that it really was him and he was alive. He asked them to come and hug him, to know he had a body and it was real. He showed them the nail holes in his hands and feet. This was Jesus for sure. They were so surprised that they still found it hard to believe. Jesus asked them for something to eat. Ghosts do not eat. In front of them all Jesus ate the broiled fish. Now they were able to relax a little.

Jesus told them of how the Scriptures foretold that the Christ would suffer, die and rise again. Moses and the prophets talked of this. Now that he is alive he wanted them to go and tell others, starting in Jerusalem. They would have new courage and power because he would go with them. They might be weak but they would have his power also. After Jerusalem they were to go to all the nations so that the world would know that Jesus is risen.

How can we make friends with Jesus? We can gain strength from him to tell others of his resurrection.

Activity
Cut Easter cards into three parts and spread them around the room face down. Tell the young people how many pieces they are allowed to pick up. See if anyone has made a whole card. Now let them exchange pieces

of card among themselves. If it works out properly, everyone should have the same number of whole cards.

Prayer

Jesus, we thank you for the power of the resurrection
and the courage you give to your people.
Help us to know we are never alone
but that you are with us always
as our friend and Saviour.
Amen.

Song

Peace is flowing like a river

Fourth Sunday of Easter

Aim

To show how much the Good Shepherd cares for us and will do for us.

Preparation

Have pictures of the rescue services around the church and near the Easter candle. Your local emergency services will be glad to provide these.

Opening activity

One child lights the Easter candle and says, 'Alleluia. Christ is risen.' The response by all is 'He is risen indeed. Alleluia!'

Then have a dramatic reading of Psalm 23. Perhaps various people could say a verse that they have learnt.

Let one of the well-known members of the congregation say, with some feeling:

> Amazing Grace! How sweet the sound
> that saved a wretch like me.
> I once was lost, but now am found;
> was blind but now I see.

Opening prayer

Look down, O Lord, from heaven
upon your flock and lambs;
bless their bodies and souls
and grant that they who have received
your sign, O Christ, on their foreheads
may be your own on the day of judgement:
through Jesus Christ our Lord.
Amen.
Prayer of Egbert, Archbishop of York (734)

Opening song

Father, hear the prayer we offer

Readings

Acts 4:5-12
Psalm 23
1 John 3:16-24
John 10:11-18

Thought for the day

In most jobs there are those who work because they love what they are doing and those who only do it for the money. The people who only work for money rarely get as much pleasure out of their work. Those who are in it just for the money rarely choose dangerous work or work that demands some personal sacrifice.

In the time of Jesus, being a shepherd was recognised as a dangerous occupation. When he was a shepherd, David had to battle with a lion and a bear (1 Samuel 17:34-36). Isaiah tells of a group of shepherds coming together to chase a lion (Isaiah 31:4). Added to the risk from wild animals was the risk from thieves and robbers. A shepherd was called to risk his life for the sheep.

The false shepherd, when he saw trouble coming, would run away. He did not really care for the sheep; he certainly would not risk his life for them. It is not sensible to die for a few sheep. They were not worth it.

The good shepherd loved his sheep. He knew them by name and they knew him. Because of his love he would risk his life for the sheep; he would lay down his life for them. The false shepherd would say that was stupid. Is not a human worth more than the sheep? You will not be able to answer that question unless you understand about love.

Jesus died on the cross for us before we ever turned to him or loved him. You could argue it was not worth the Son of God suffering for us. He did it because of his love for us. Not even because we loved him but because he loved us. He could have avoided the crucifixion; he could have called down help from heaven. Then he would not have died for us and we would not have been saved from death. Out of love and obedience to the will of the Father, Jesus gave himself willingly for us and rose again for us.

Jesus reminds the Pharisees that his love was not exclusive: 'There are other sheep not of this fold.' Because of the outreach and love of Jesus, the Church can never be exclusive. We need to reach out and share in his rescuing and redeeming work.

Question time

Do we recognise the love that Jesus has for us and how he sacrificed himself for us?

Do you recognise those who work for their own gain only and those who are willing to sacrifice for others?

Illustration

There was a group of shepherds who often talked about caring for their sheep. Yet, when trouble came, some did not want to bother; others said the sheep were not worth the risk; one or two took the money and left. One could be heard saying, 'You cannot believe a lamb is worth the life of a shepherd.' The reply from a hired man was, 'Of course it is not.'

Listening to all this was the good shepherd. It made him sad to think that the sheep were not truly loved. He loved his sheep dearly and would do anything to save them. Suddenly an old man came to him and said, 'I have been looking at your flock and you have a ewe lamb missing. She has wandered off and is in danger of death.' The shepherd left the comfort of home and the safety of his surroundings and began the search. Some were sure he should not have bothered. There were plenty of other sheep; why bother with a wayward one? The shepherd's life was more precious than the lamb's. The shepherd was soon travelling dark valleys. More than once he was at risk himself. Briars tore at his hands and his feet. There was a gaping hole in his side. Thorns had pierced his head. He was calling the lamb by name. At last there was a weak response. It was down a steep slope and in danger of falling further. The shepherd did not fear but descended into the depths. The darkness was trying to hold on to the lamb. The shepherd reached into the thorn bushes and became entangled; he was caught alongside the lamb. Even now he reached out to comfort it. There he lay, life ebbing out of him. He was trapped for more than 48 hours. But on the third day he broke free and rising up brought the lamb with him. He carried it all the way home. When they saw him they rejoiced. 'Just see how much he loves his flock and what he was willing to suffer for one little ewe lamb.'

Intercessions

Blessed are you, Lord our God.
When we were lost in our sin
you sent our Lord as the Good Shepherd to bring us home.
He descended into the depths to raise us to the heights;
he tasted death for us to know eternal life.
Blessed are you, Father, Son and Holy Spirit.

We give thanks for all who are called
to be shepherds of your people,
all who are guides and protectors.
We remember bishops and especially our bishop;
we pray for all priests and especially our own pastor.
Bless all who teach us the faith
and help us to walk in the way of holiness.

Silence

The Lord is my shepherd;
I shall fear no evil.

We ask you to give courage and strength
to all who work in the emergency services.
We pray for all ambulance crews and paramedics,
for air and sea rescue services
and for coastguards.
We remember the police and the fire crews.
Bless, O Lord, all who work
for the relief of poverty and suffering
among the poor of our world.

Silence

The Lord is my shepherd;
I shall fear no evil.

We give you thanks
for the safety and comfort of our homes.
We ask you to protect our loved ones
and guide them in the ways of peace.
Give wisdom and love to all who work
in the social services.
Comfort all who are lonely or feel unwanted.

Silence

The Lord is my shepherd;
I shall fear no evil.

God of love, we remember all
who have been involved in accidents this week.
We pray for all who have been injured
and those who are bereaved.
We pray for those who have gone into hospital
and all who are ill at home.

Silence

The Lord is my shepherd;
I shall fear no evil.

Good and gracious God,
you have rescued us from the darkness of death
and opened for us the way to eternal life.
We bring before you all our friends and loved ones
who are now with you in your kingdom.
Lord, grant them your love and light.

Silence

Merciful Father,
accept these prayers
for the sake of your Son,
our Saviour Jesus Christ.
Amen.

Memory verse

The Lord is my shepherd: I shall not want.
Psalm 23:1

(It would be better to learn all of this Psalm.)

Suggested music

The King of love my shepherd is
How sweet the name of Jesus sounds
Faithful Shepherd, feed me

CANDLES

Aim

To show how Jesus, the Good Shepherd, loves us.

Teaching

Have you ever lost anything that you really cared for? Perhaps you lost a favourite toy? Do you remember how you looked and looked for it until you found it? Were you not really glad when you found it? (Let the children talk about lost things.)

Now, has anyone here ever been lost? It is horrible to be lost and it makes you sad and afraid. But Mummy and Daddy would look for you – other people might help. Sometimes people wander away from God and get lost but he will seek and seek until he finds them. He will not give up because he loves them.

Jesus said that he is a shepherd caring for his sheep. He is a good shepherd because he loves his sheep and will risk his life for any that are lost.

Let us think of a little sheep that has gone astray. It has wandered from its mother and gone to where it is dangerous. Soon it will get dark and the wolf will come looking for the lamb and if it catches the lamb, it will gobble it all up. The little lamb does not know which way to go. It cries (let the children make lamb sounds) The wolf pricks up his ears; he hears a cry and it sounds like his supper. The lamb cries again (let the children cry). The wolf licks its lips. But this time the shepherd heard the lamb and started to move quickly towards it. The wolf was also moving. Suddenly the shepherd called the little lamb by its name. This time it cried out with joy (let he children still make lamb sounds). The shepherd ran and rescued the lamb just in time. He picked it up, put it around the back his neck and carried it home safely.

Everyone was so happy when the little lamb was safe. The shepherd did this because he loves his sheep. Jesus loves us and seeks us if we are lost. He rescues us from danger and brings us to safety. This is why we sometimes call Jesus the Good Shepherd. Let us all say, 'Jesus is the Good Shepherd.'

Activity

Play 'What time is it, Mr Wolf?'

Mr Wolf is chosen and walks away with the rest following. Now you say loudly, 'What time is it, Mr Wolf?' Mr Wolf can say any time he likes as he leads the children further from the fold. When he answers, 'Twelve o'clock – dinner time', all must run back to the fold, making the sound of sheep. Mr Wolf runs after them. The person he catches is the next Mr Wolf.

Prayer

Jesus, you are the Good Shepherd;
you love us all
and seek all who are lost or in trouble.
May we learn to follow you
and to love you all our days.
Amen.

Song

Little lamb has lost its way,
lost its way,
lost its way.
Little lamb has lost its way.
Let the shepherd find it.

Little child has lost its way,
lost its way,
lost its way.
Little child has lost its way.
Good Shepherd, find it.

(Tune: 'London Bridge is falling down')

LAMPS

Aim

To show the courage and love of the Good Shepherd.

Teaching

Some people do very dangerous work because they care for other people. Sometimes they risk their lives for others. Can you think of any who risk their lives? We can make a list. Police, ambulance crews, lifeboat crews, air rescue, fire crews. Do you think they just work for money? Of course not, or they would have found a safer job. They care for people and do not want them to suffer.

In the time of Jesus, being a shepherd was a dangerous job. It often meant you had to work at night and in the dark. You had to keep a big fire burning to keep danger away. What made the shepherd's life dangerous? Wild animals like the lion, bear or wolf. Then there were robbers and thieves who came with knives and swords. The shepherd had to be brave and alert. Sometimes when the shepherd put his sheep in a pinfold he would lie across the entrance to stop them getting out or danger getting in. The shepherd was laying down his life for the sheep. Some who were just doing it for money and not really bothered about the sheep would run away when they thought the wolf or any other danger was coming. They were bad shepherds and left the sheep defenceless.

Jesus said that he was the Good Shepherd. He cared for all his people and he was willing to die for them. How do we know that Jesus was brave? He loved us so much that he died for us and he rose that we might have eternal life. He rescued us from darkness and death by his own offering on the cross. No one else was able to do what Jesus did and he did it out of love for each of us. He cares for each of us and knows us by our name.

Activity

One person is sent out of the room while someone else is chosen to be the killer wolf. All sit around in a circle. The wolf kills people by winking at them! When a person is winked at they fall forward into the circle and lie as still as possible. The person who has been out of the room has to discover who is the wolf. When the wolf is discovered, he or she has to go out of the room whilst a new wolf is chosen.

Look at the worksheet and list. Which do you think are the good and bad shepherds or carers?

Prayer

God, we thank you for all brave and courageous people,
for all who rescue and help others in need.
We thank you for Jesus, the Good Shepherd,
as he rescued us from darkness and death.
Amen.

Song

Loving Shepherd of thy sheep

TORCHES

Aim

To help the young people see that the Good Shepherd is our rescuer and redeemer.

Teaching

If you were asked to join one of the emergency or rescue services, which would you like to join? If you would not like to join any, you might like to say why.

Let us talk about a recent rescue that showed the emergency services at work. Often men and women were risking their lives to save others. Do we recognise heroism when it takes place? Who are some of our favourite real-life heroes?

In the times of Jesus, being a soldier was often a heroic job, but so was being a shepherd. When King David was still just a shepherd he had to fight a lion on one occasion and a bear on another (1 Samuel 17:34-36). A shepherd had to watch during the night in case wild animals or sheep rustlers came. The rustlers often came armed with swords and spears. The shepherd had to be brave to stand alone in the dark. When trouble came, the shepherd would stand firm because he loved his sheep and did not want them to be destroyed. Sometimes a shepherd died caring for his sheep.

Jesus called himself the Good Shepherd. He was well aware of the shepherd's work and bravery. He wanted us to know that he cared for us and was willing to die for us. Like a shepherd, Jesus looks for the straying and the lost, and seeks to bring them to safety.

Let us try to understand what it means for us if Jesus is our Good Shepherd. (Let the young people offer their suggestions and write them on a flip chart.)

Activity

Have illustrations of rescues by the emergency services. Have them all numbered. Ask if the young people can name which rescue services are present. There could be an ambulance crew, fire fighters, paramedics all working together; the coastguards could be working with air rescue and the lifeboat crew; the air rescue could be working with the mountain rescue; the police could be working with the AA or RAC. If you have time you may be able to collect information from some of the major rescue services.

The young people should learn all of Psalm 23 off by heart. Ask them to put some passion and drama into their reading of it.

Prayer

Lord, you are my shepherd,
my protector and my guardian.
You have given your life that I can have life eternal.
You will lead me into the way of peace
if only I will follow you.
I thank you for your love and sacrifice for me.
Amen.

Song

The Lord's my shepherd

Fifth Sunday of Easter

Aim

To show we are one with Christ and that we are called to bear fruit.

Preparation

Around the Easter candle have some grapes and a few growing plants.

Opening activity

Ask everyone to join hands for the lighting of the Easter candle and the following prayer. If possible, be in a circle around the Easter candle. Let a child light the candle saying, 'Alleluia. Christ is risen.' All respond, 'He is risen indeed. Alleluia.' (As we say this, let all joined hands be raised.)

Let another child proclaim, 'Christ is the whole vine.' Response: 'We are the branches.' (Let the raised hands be lowered and shake up and down a little.)

A third child says, 'We dwell in him.' Response: 'And he is in us.' (Look at the people on our right and our left as we say this and squeeze their hand gently.)

Keep holding hands as the opening prayer is said. Squeeze hands gently at the second line of the prayer.

Opening prayer

Christ, this day, within and about us.
Christ be near at either hand.
Christ before, behind me stand.
Christ above, around, below.
Christ be on the path I go.
Christ, this day, within and about us.

Opening song

Be still, for the presence of the Lord

Readings

Acts 8:26-40
Psalm 22:25-31
1 John 4:7-21
John 15:1-8

Thought for the day

The vine was one of the most common plants in Israel. It would grow almost anywhere: it grew on walls, up trellises, around the doors of houses; it grew up sticks. It also grew in the wild. For the vine to grow well, it needed the ground to be prepared carefully and it needed regular attention. If you wanted good fruit, you could not just leave it to chance.

Could it be that with Jesus who says, 'I am the vine', we need to give the same attention? There is no one in whom he will not grow if only the preparation of the 'soil' is properly done. Today we expect instant results, instant responses, instant changes in people, instant conversions, and they do not happen because we ignore what is going on at ground level. We tend to ignore the weeds, the poor environment, the lack of sustenance; we want growth without having to make an effort.

Let us learn from the preparation of the vine. First it is necessary to prepare the ground, to see that the atmosphere is as good as possible for growth. We need to be sure that it will not be choked by weeds or die from lack of attention. Many who are young in the faith are lost because we do not give them the sustenance they need.

It is lovely when growth begins. For a long time it seems little is happening and then suddenly growth speeds up. The vine is so luxuriant in its growth that young slips are usually set at two metres apart: to have room to grow is important. In the first three years the vine is not allowed to fruit so that it can conserve its life and energy. We often send people out before they have grown, and so they exhaust themselves and their fruiting is lost. Too often we rush young Christians into action, and they expect it, when we have spent little time building them up in the faith. We need those who are mature in the faith and who have the resources for bearing fruit.

The vine has two kinds of branches: one is fruit-bearing and the other is not. The non-fruit-bearing branches are drastically cut off so that they will not take away energy and strength from the plant. The vine will not produce a good crop without pruning. We are all meant to bear fruit in one way or another.

Lastly, though of utmost importance, we need to note that Jesus says he is the whole vine and we are the branches. We are not separate from Jesus. Without him we cannot bear fruit. But we are not without him. In fact, we dwell in him and he is in us. Without him, our lives will wither and die. If we abide in him and he in us, his life flows in us and through us. We are one with him and one in him. Then, in turn, we are the vine and we are called to be Christ to the world.

Question time

Do we enjoy the reality of abiding in Christ and knowing that he abides in us?

Do we see that we are called not only to worship but to bear fruit?

Illustration

We hear little of the disciples after the resurrection but we know they all bore the fruit of being with Jesus. After the death of Stephen, the disciples scattered because of persecution. We know Philip went to Samaria and told the story of Jesus. He preached of the love of God. Through the disciples the Church was growing rapidly and beyond the boundaries of Jerusalem (see Acts 8:5-13). Peter and John also went to the Samaritans.

A road from Jerusalem went by Bethlehem and, just south of Gaza, joined the main road to Egypt and beyond. St Luke points out that this is the Old or Desert Gaza, not the more modern one. Along this road travelled the Chancellor of the Exchequer of the queen of Ethiopia. He had been to Jerusalem to worship. He is at least a seeker of God. He was in his chariot reading Isaiah 53.

Philip simply asked if he understood what he was reading. The Ethiopian said how could he without a guide? Philip was invited into the chariot and they looked at the words: 'He was led like a lamb to the slaughter.' Philip talked of Jesus of the crucifixion and resurrection. The Ethiopian was moved and wanted to be baptised in the nearby water. After being baptised the Ethiopian went on his way rejoicing. Again we see Philip bearing fruit as he does the work of Jesus. Tradition has it that the Ethiopian went home and started to evangelise Ethiopia. And through the witness of many the Church grew in the faith and in number.

Intercessions

Blessed are you, Lord our God,
for you have created us out of your love
and for your love.
We know that we abide in you and that you are in us
by the Spirit that you have given us.
As you love us, help us to love one another,
Father, Son and Holy Spirit.

Lord, bless the Church with the knowledge
of your indwelling presence.
May we learn to abide in you and know that you are in us.
Give wisdom to all who go out in mission
and all who preach your word.
We pray for the young in the faith,
that they will be given the opportunity
to grow and bear fruit.
We remember all study groups, Bible classes
and Sunday schools.

Silence

Lord, you abide in us;
we ask that we may abide in you.

We remember the nations of the world
and especially those who are not at peace at this time.
We ask your guidance on all who care
for the world's poor, refugees and war-torn peoples.
We pray for the time when the kingdoms of this world
may become the kingdom of Christ our Lord.

Silence

Lord, you abide in us;
we ask that we may abide in you.

We give thanks for all who have shared their faith with us.
In our turn may we also bear fruit
and bring others to the love and presence of our God.
Lord, bless our homes with the glory of your presence.
Help us to live in and share your peace.

Silence

Lord, you abide in us;
we ask that we may abide in you.

We bring before you all who doubt or despair,
all who are surrounded by darkness or illness.
May they come into the light of your love
and know that you are with them.
We ask you to bless all who have been involved
in accidents or in violence this week.
Give courage and hope to all
who seek to bring your healing and peace.

Silence

Lord, you abide in us;
we ask that we may abide in you.

Lord, you abide with us through life
and we abide with you through death.
In your love you have given us eternal life
through Christ our risen Lord.
We give you thanks for this great gift.
We ask that you bless all our loved ones departed
with the joy of your love and your presence.

Silence

Merciful Father,
accept these prayers
for the sake of your Son,
our Saviour Jesus Christ.
Amen.

Memory verse

Abide in me as I abide in you.
John 15:4

Suggested music

We have a gospel to proclaim
For I'm building a people of power
You are the Light of the world

CANDLES

Aim

To help the children to share and pass on Good News.

Teaching

Show a bunch of grapes and ask if they know what sort of plant they come from. Vines grow lots of grapes and because of this we can buy them in our shops. How do you think grapes are grown? What do they need to grow?

The vine needs to be planted. It needs soil. It needs sun. It needs rain. (If it is in a greenhouse, it will need someone to water it.) It needs someone to care for it if it is to grow well.

These grapes have been well looked after: they have grown beautifully. Because they have had proper sun and rain they taste lovely. Who would like one? Let us share them. Let everyone have one. Who would like to give them out? (Let two children go around the class giving out a grape or two if there are plenty.)

The grapes were mine – but I like sharing. I like sharing the stories of Jesus and his disciples. It is a pity when people are greedy or keep good things to themselves. Jesus wants us to grow in what we believe and to share with others. We grow:

by coming to our class,
by saying our prayers,
by showing our love for God,
by doing what God wants,
by caring for the world,
by having someone to care for us.

Activity

Hide paper vine leaves around the room. Ask the class to find them. Let there be only one for each child. Anyone who finds two must give them both away and look for or receive another. Let this go on until everyone has a leaf. Have on the vine leaves simple words: 'Jesus', 'God', 'Love', 'Pray', 'Care', 'Share'. Help the children to read them and see if they can say what they mean. The leaves can be coloured green.

Prayer

Jesus, you shared your life with us,
you gave us your love.
We love you and want to share with you.
Amen.

Song

Lord of the loving heart

LAMPS

Aim

To show how we need to share with each other in the work of Christ.

Teaching

There was only one slate off the roof; it made only one tiny hole. Surely this did not matter. Let us forget there is one slate missing. The rain sneaked in through the one hole. It was not a flood. It was not obvious at first. It let water into the loft which then seeped through to the upstairs ceiling. Then, because it was soaked, the ceiling fell down. All this happened because one slate was missing.

Imagine being asked to play for your local team at the weekend. During the week you turn up for every practice. You are part of a team. Strategy is worked out and you are part of the plan. When the weekend comes it is lovely weather and you have the chance to go camping. You decide to go. The team is one member down. They will play one person short. Even if they get someone else that person will not know the tactics. The team loses by a single goal. Do you not see that if you were there, it could have been different? You were chosen and you let your team down. They might not ask you again.

Jesus has chosen you to be part of his team. He wants you to share in his work and to bring others to know him. There are some people only you can bring. If you do not tell them of Jesus, it could be that no one else will. Sometimes we show how important Jesus is not by our words but by our actions, by the way we live and react to what is around us. Can we be seen to be part of the Jesus Team? We have been selected: do we make sure we are active players?

Jesus compared his team to a growing vine. All branches, every single one, are expected to bear fruit. If a branch does not bear fruit, it is cut off so that it doesn't take energy and strength from the plant. (See how much the children understand about bearing fruit as part of their Christian life, and what it means for them.)

Sometimes we can only bear fruit by being part of a team. If you have a coal fire and you take one piece out, that piece is likely to go out. We need each other's encouragement and company. We need each other to learn and to grow in our faith. We are chosen to work as a team and to win others to Christ.

Activity

Divide the class up into equal groups and ask them to appoint a leader for each group. Get each group to stand in line. Now place in front of each group two saucers. One saucer will have two peas for every team member and the other will be empty. Every one is given a drinking straw and must take it in turns to transfer two peas from one plate to the other by sucking the peas one by one on to the end of the straw. Encourage them all to see that we depend on each other to achieve anything.

Prayer

Lord Jesus, we thank you that you have called us
to be part of your team.
You have called us to work with you
and to tell others of you.
Help us to do our best in showing how we love you
and to bring others to know you.
Amen.

Song

God is love: his the care

TORCHES

Aim

To show that we need to share in the work of Jesus.

Teaching

When Jesus said he was the vine, he knew that the people would understand his claim. The people of Israel had often been called 'God's planting, God's vine'. But, like many plants, they had grown wild and degenerated. They were no longer doing what God wanted them to do. Outside the Temple the door was covered in carvings of the vine, because God's people are the vineyard of God. Again God's people were not listening to and obeying God's word. Jesus was saying he was the true vine, the true beginning of the people of God, because of his obedience and love. In Jesus there is a chance for the people of God to start again. Again and again he called them to repent, to turn around and walk God's way.

Jesus calls himself the vine and says we are the branches – that means we are one with him and one with each other. We are expected to produce fruit together, to grow in the faith together. A Native American was taught the Lord's Prayer. He began by saying, 'Our Father', then he stopped in amazement. 'Is God my Father?' 'Yes' was the reply. 'And God is your Father?' Again the reply: 'Yes.' 'That is truly wonderful. God is your Father and mine – that means we are brothers.'

The Church needs to discover again its unity in Christ. We are one in the Lord. Jesus said he is the vine. He is the whole vine, trunk and branches. We are part of the vine: We are to be one with him. He asks us to abide in him and let him abide in us. We are asked to let his life flow through us: our union with him is to bear fruit. What fruit will show if we abide in him and let his life flow through us?

There is an old legend that tells of Jesus returning to heaven and the angels asking who will continue his work. Jesus points to the disciples. 'But they are so weak, so human,' protest the angels. Jesus replies, 'I trust them and know they will not let me down.'

Can this be said of us?

Remember the words of St Teresa of Avila:

Christ has no hands, but your hands
to do his work today.
Christ has no feet but your feet
to speed men on his way.
Christ has no lips but your lips
to tell men why he died.
Christ has no love but your love
to win men to his side.

Let us work with Christ and for Christ.

Activity

Pick out from today's Gospel the important points and write them out on a flip chart. Get the group to comment on what each bit means. We cannot go it alone; we need to be linked to Jesus. We have to bear fruit: unfruitful branches are cut off. If Jesus is the whole vine, we are part of him. He asks us to abide in him and promises he will abide in us. See if they can give examples of abiding.

Prayer

Abide with us, Lord,
abide with us today and for ever.
Abide with us in our joys and our sorrows.
Abide with us in darkness and light.
Abide with us, and your whole Church.
Abide with us in time and eternity.
Amen.

Song

If Jesus is de vine

Sixth Sunday of Easter

Aim

To know that we are chosen by God.

Preparation

Cut out from magazines well-known advertisements but hide the brand name. Number these and display them near the entrance to the church. Beside the Easter candle have, if possible, a copy of Dürer's 'Praying hands', some fruit, a big red heart and a sign saying, 'GO'.

Opening activity

At the beginning of the service see if they can identify the products in the advertisements. After this, remind everyone they have been chosen to be God's advertisements. They need to make sure the message they give is good and clear.

A child should light the Easter candle, saying, 'Alleluia. Christ is risen', with the response, 'He is risen indeed. Alleluia.'

Various people can then say sentences, with the response 'Alleluia' after each sentence:

Jesus has chosen us.
He wants us to enjoy his presence.
He asks us to love him and one another.
(Show the heart)
He wants us to be his friends.
(Pass the heart around)
He wants us to tell others of him.
(Continue to pass the heart around)
He wants us to bear fruit.
(Pass the fruit around)
He wants us to pray.
(Show the praying hands and ask for silence and stillness)

Opening prayer

Lord Jesus, in the stillness
let us know that you love us
and help us to give our love to you.
As you love all of us
help us to love each other.
You have called us to be your friends;
send us out in joy to witness to you,
to your power and your glory.
Amen.

Opening song

What a friend we have in Jesus

Readings

Acts 10:44-48
Psalm 98
1 John 5:1-6
John 15:9-17

Thought for the day

Have you ever been chosen to play for a team or to represent your school or firm? You are chosen because you can do certain things. You do not choose but you are chosen. You can try to earn a place but you cannot choose to be in the team. You are chosen.

A lot of people talk about choosing to be a Christian or not as if the choice was theirs. The choice is not ours; it is Jesus who chooses us. Jesus says, 'You did not choose me but I chose you.' We are asked to respond by saying whether or not we want to be part of his ministry and have a relationship with him. Any who excuse themselves exclude themselves.

Out of his love and grace God has called us. In today's Gospel we can see what that calling implies.

(1) We are chosen for joy. No matter which way the road goes, whether life is tough or easy, we are called to rejoice in the Lord (see Philippians 4:4). The Christian is a person of joy, knowing that God calls them and knowing that the Lord is with them. This is a joy no one or nothing should be able to take from us. Amidst all the gloom a Christian is to show joy, for we are loved and have an eternal destiny.

(2) We are chosen for love. Jesus gives to us an awareness of the love of the Father. He gives us his own love. What greater love can he give us than laying down his life for us? Jesus demonstrated his deep love for us on the cross. We are called to respond to this love by loving him. Then he has chosen us to love one another as he loves us. 'This is my commandment, that you love one another as I have loved you.' Warring factions among Christians betray the love of Christ.

(3) We are chosen to be friends of Jesus: 'I do not call you servants (slaves) any longer.' It was counted a great honour to be called slaves or servants of God. Moses was called the 'slave of God' (Deuteronomy 34:5); so was Joshua (Joshua 24:29); so was David (Psalm 89:20). St Paul also was proud to call himself a slave (Titus 1:1). One of the titles of the Pope is 'Servant of the servants of God'. But Jesus has called us to a far greater privilege: we are to be his friends and friends of God. We need not stand far off; we have immediate access to the presence of our friend. We are not like someone who gets a rare glimpse of the king; we are able to enter into his presence whenever we want. He has chosen us to be his friends. Because Jesus is alive he is not a theory or an idea; he is a person. We need to talk to him and make friends with him.

As always, with privileges come responsibilities. We have been chosen to 'go': Jesus sends us (in the way some are 'sent' by their favourite pop star). We need to learn to 'go for Jesus'. We are all called to share in the outreach and mission of our Lord.

We are called to bear lasting fruit, to be ambassadors for Christ. We are to show by our way of living that it is a joy to be a friend of God and to love as he loves us. We are his witnesses and witnesses to the riches of his glory. We are advertisements to our God and his love – or we ought to be.

To be able to do all this we are asked to pray to the Father in the power of Jesus. We cannot achieve this work in our own strength but only in the power and presence of God.

Question time

Do we take seriously the fact that God has chosen us, not that we have chosen him?

How can you be a good advertisement for God?

Illustration

Once upon a time there was an explosion that radiated out through the world. Countless people were touched, infected: many found it contagious as someone who was already touched passed it on to them. The explosion happened on a hill called Calvary just outside Jerusalem. Here love broke out in great power, defeating darkness. In a flash of blinding love, the Christ released a new way of life for the world. The love of God radiated through the whole earth and all times. The results of that explosion are still being felt today because he who died rose again. He lives and seeks to share his love with us. He comes to us and wants to be our friend. There are always those who will protect themselves against such an event; who will ignore his presence and avoid his radiant love. But he will transform all who come to be touched and give them the power to become the true children of God. They will shine with his presence and his love.

Intercessions

Blessed are you, Lord God, who through your Son
has revealed your great love for us
and in his resurrection gave us a Friend and a Saviour.
We rejoice in your presence this day
with the joy and the freedom of the children of God.
Blessed are you, our God for ever.

As you have called us to be friends,
to reveal your love and the joy of your presence,
we come with sorrow for the divisions
of the Church and the world.
We seek forgiveness for rivalry and disunity
within the Church.
Lord, strengthen us in love
and lead us to a unity that reflects that we are one in you.
May any divisions within our community be healed
and well-being restored.

Silence

Lord, as you love us,
help us to love one another.

We come before you as part of a world
caught up in violence, war, hatred, greed and hunger.
There are people who are oppressed and treated as slaves.
There are people who are counted as nothing,
rejected and unloved.
Lord, forgive us and change us.
Strengthen all who work
for the peace and well-being of all.
May we share in the care of all suffering people.

Silence

Lord, as you love us,
help us to love one another.

We give you thanks for all our loved ones,
for their generosity and sacrifice for us.
We remember all who feel unloved and unwanted.
We pray for homes where there is hatred or violence,
where there is little respect for each other,
where there is neglect.
We ask your blessing upon all
who have been taken into care.

Silence

Lord, as you love us,
help us to love one another.

Lord of love, we remember before you all who are lonely.
We ask your blessing upon those who are ill or injured.
We pray for all who are raging against life
and all who are not at peace with themselves
or the world.
We pray for all who have hardened their hearts
against love.

Silence

Lord, as you love us,
help us to love one another.

We rejoice in your saving love
and that you have called us to eternal life.
We remember loved ones departed from us.
As we give thanks for their friendship
we pray that they may know you as their friend
in your eternal kingdom.

Silence

Merciful Father,
accept these prayers
for the sake of your Son,
our Saviour Jesus Christ.
Amen.

Memory verse

As the Father has loved me, so have I loved you; abide in my love.
John 15:9

Suggested music

Beloved, let us love
God is love: let heaven adore him
My God, I love thee

CANDLES

Aim

To encourage the children to see Jesus as a friend.

Teaching

Do you know what a slave is? A slave is someone who always has to do what they are told. They do not share in the good things. Sometimes they are fastened by chains; they are not free to go out or in when they want. They cannot share in the riches of the master. Sometimes the master can be cruel to them. (Maybe the children know a story of a wicked king.)

Cinderella was a sort of slave to the ugly sisters. They made her do all the horrible jobs and were unkind to her. Cinderella was rather sad and not allowed to do nice things. (Tell the story briefly.)

Jesus wants us to be his friends. He does not want us to be servants or slaves. He wants us to work with him and to enjoy being with him. Let us all choose a friend in the room. (Get the children to join up in pairs.) How do we keep our friends? By talking to them and by sharing with them. I am now going to give one of each pair a picture to colour and I will give to the other one the felt tips or crayons. No one will be able to do the work unless we share with our friend. Let us share the pictures and the colours. Let us say which colours we would like to use and share with each other. Let us work as friends.

To be a friend of Jesus we need to learn to talk to him every day. What do you call talking to Jesus? Yes we call it 'praying' or 'saying our prayers'. Let us all say the prayer on our sheet. I will say it first and then you can say it after me, line by line.

Activity

'Do as I say.' Everyone faces the leader and must do what the leader tells them. They must not follow the actions of the leader if these are different. When the leader says, 'Touch your nose', they all touch their noses. If the leader says, 'Stand up', they all stand up. If the leader says, 'Sit down', they all sit down. If the leader says, 'Stand still', and then jumps, any who jump are out. If the leader says, 'Raise one arm', whilst lifting two, anyone who raises two arms is out.

Prayer

Jesus, friend of little children,
be a friend to me.
Let me learn to love you
and know you are with me.
Jesus, be with me always
as a friend and a helper.
Amen.

Song

Jesus is a friend of mine

LAMPS

Aim

To understand what Jesus means when he calls us 'friends'.

Teaching

At the foot of a cliff there are two lots of people. A chain around their feet ties the first group together and they are fastened to a wall. They are told they have to wait until the master returns from climbing a mountain. They are not free, they have no choice and they must obey. Anyone who tries to escape will be punished. These people are slaves. Their lives are often hard and their masters are often cruel to them.

The other group are fastened together by a rope. The rope is around their waist. They are chatting together and deciding on which way they will go up the mountain. They will all follow their leader and trust him because he is a friend. On the journey they will help each other and if anyone slips or needs help the others will be there: they will get encouragement and strength from each other. There is a lot of joy and gladness amongst this group, because they love being in each other's company. Not one of them could climb the mountain alone, but with the help of friends all will reach the top and have a great view.

Jesus says he does not want us to be like the first group. He does not want us to be servants or slaves. He wants us to be free people, to be able to choose. He would like us to choose to be his friend. Remember, Jesus is alive because he rose from the dead. Although we cannot see him, he is with us and wants to be our friend. He would like to help us and to encourage us. He would like to give us strength and adventures. But he can only do this if we become his friends.

How do we make friends with Jesus? We need to know he is with us. We need to speak to him in prayer. We need to trust him in troubles. He does not want us as slaves or to boss us about. He wants us to work with him as friends.

Activity

Play 'The Boss says.' You must do whatever the Boss commands. If she says, 'The Boss says jump', you must jump. If she says, 'The boss says crawl', then you must crawl. But if she gives and order without saying, 'The Boss says', you must stay perfectly still. Anyone who moves or even wobbles is out. The one who stays in the longest is the winner and becomes the next Boss.

Prayer

Lord Jesus, you have chosen us to be part of your team.
You ask us to come and work with you as your friends.
You give us the choice to respond to your love or not.
Help us to enjoy your presence
and to tell others of your love.
Amen.

Song

Father, we adore you

TORCHES

Aim

To see what it means to be friends of Jesus.

Teaching

There are many people who talk of Jesus as history. They tell you of what he did 2000 years ago. But we know more than that because *Jesus is alive.* We know that Jesus is risen and dies no more. We have a living Lord who has promised to be with us for ever. We know even more: *he wants us to be his friends*. Whilst some people talk *about* him, he wants us to talk *to* him and to enjoy his presence. I wonder when we make a list of our friends if we include Jesus. He wants us to be friends; have we sought to be a true friend of his? We do not ignore our friends or refuse to speak to them. We enjoy going about with them and sharing with them. Jesus seeks to be our friend and for us to share with him in his mission. In Acts 4:13 Peter and John are recognised as friends of Jesus. Would you be recognised as a Jesus Friend? How do we make friends? We come together. We talk together. (Relate this to prayer and speaking daily to our eternal friend.) We cannot be friends if we ignore or betray him. It should be seen that we enjoy his presence: it is by this we know we are friends. (Do we talk to him often? Can we chat to him as we do to our other friends?)

When we have a friend we try not to distress our friend or do what they would not like us to do. Not because they command us but because we are friends. We are not bound to Jesus by obedience but by love. He wants us to learn to love the world with the great love that he has for the world. His own love will inspire and strengthen us.

He has chosen us to continue the work he began and to share with him. We have the honour in sharing in his redeeming of the world. Jesus trusts us as friends. How can we prove worthy of him?

Read again today's Gospel, John 15:9-17. Let individuals read a verse each and let the group comment on each verse.

Activity

On the worksheet explore the impact of having a Living Lord and not just someone we know about. See how this should have an influence on our relationships. Encourage everyone to write a letter of thanks to Jesus for his friendship.

Prayer

(A good prayer to learn by heart and say each day.)

Thanks be to you,
O Lord Jesus Christ,
for all the benefits which you have won for us;
for all the pains and insults you have borne for us.
O merciful Redeemer, Friend and Brother,
may we know you more clearly,
love you more dearly,
and follow you more nearly,
day by day.
Richard of Chichester (1197–1253)

Song

Love is like a circle

Ascension Day

Aim

To rejoice in the presence of the ascended Lord.

Preparation

Light the Easter candle.

Opening song

Hail the day that sees him rise

Activity

This takes place after the Gospel at the Easter candle. It replaces the Opening activity and prayer and also the intercessions. There is a diagram of a traditional Easter candle at the end of today's resources. If you want to add the crown of thorns, the nails and the spear hole before the service you could use five drawing pins. Different people could do a section each.

Affirm the Alpha and Omega
God, you are the beginning and end of all things.
In you all things have their being.
You are the Alpha and the Omega;
Creator of time and space;
Saviour beyond time and space;
Spirit within time and space.
We worship and adore you.

Withdraw the incense grain for the crown of thorns (or touch the top of the candle)
The head that once was crowned with thorns
is crowned with glory now.
Lord, we remember before you
the troubled in mind,
all who have painful memories,
the depressed and the despairing,
the mentally disturbed
and all who cannot cope with life.
Ascended Lord, may we, in heart and mind,
ascend to where you are in glory.
Alleluia.
Alleluia.

Withdraw the grains of incense for the hands (or touch two places further down the candle)
We are in the hands of God.
We are in our Lord's nail-torn hands.
Underneath are the everlasting arms,
the arms of our Lord stretched out in love.
He descended to lift up all who are down.
We remember in your presence
all whose hands are idle.
We pray for the unemployed and redundant,
the handicapped and all with waning or failing powers.
We remember all who are in prison
or whose lives are restricted.
He descended that we might share
in the glorious liberty of the children of God.
Alleluia.
Alleluia.

Withdraw the incense grain for the pierced side of Christ (or move further down the candle)
Love was crucified – yet love is come again.
He comes the broken-hearted to restore.
God so loved the world that he gave of himself.
God, we remember before you
all who are betrayed in love,
the heart-broken and the deserted,
the rejected and the lonely.
We thank you for our loved ones and our friends.
The ascended Lord calls us friends.
Alleluia.
Alleluia.

Withdraw the incense representing the feet (or place your hands near the bottom of the candle)
He who was firmly fixed is set free.
He has triumphed over the captivities of the world.
Lord, we remember before you
all who are striving for freedom,
all who are held captive,
all who yearn for a better world.
Rejoice for death is conquered.
We are free.
Christ has won the victory.
Alleluia.
Alleluia.

Extinguish the candle
The Lord has gone up on high. Alleluia.
Alleluia.
The Lord is here. Alleluia.
Alleluia.
His Spirit is with us. Alleluia.
Alleluia.
Jesus said, 'I am with you always.'
Alleluia.
Alleluia.
'I go to prepare a place for you
that where I am you may be also.'
Alleluia.
Alleluia.

Lord, we remember in your presence
all who are in the dark.
May they come to your love and light
and know you as their ascended Lord and friend.
We remember all our loved ones departed
and rejoice that we are one in you.
The Lord is here.
His Spirit is with us.
Alleluia.
Alleluia.

The candle is removed to somewhere out of sight.

Readings

Acts 1:1-11 or Daniel 7:9-14
Psalm 147 or Psalm 93
Ephesians 1:15-23 or Acts 1:1-11
Luke 24:44-53
(*The reading from Acts must be one of the readings for the day*)

Thought for the day

The Ascension is of the utmost importance: it marks a new stage in the ministry of Jesus and a new stage in the history of humankind. Jesus did not come down just to walk the earth and be friendly; he came down to lift us up that we might share with him in his kingdom. At Christmas we celebrate 'God made flesh'; at Ascension we celebrate our humanity being raised to God. Jesus became human that we might share in the divine!

When on earth, Jesus, like all humans, was restricted by space and time. There was no way that Jesus could be in two places at once: if he was in Jerusalem he could not be in Nazareth; while he was in Galilee he could not be at Bethany. He was late in coming to his friend Lazarus because he was not nearby when his friend took ill. After the resurrection it seems to be a little different as he suddenly appears in the room with the disciples or in the garden to Mary. But he still seems to be in one place at a time. A new stage is marked by the Ascension: it is summarised in the words, 'Remember, I am with you always' (Matthew 28:20).

Mark, at the end of his Gospel, tells of Jesus being taken up into heaven and then say how Jesus continued to work with the disciples (Mark16:20). Jesus is freed from the restrictions of space and time; he is now available to us wherever we are. He is here and with us now. We begin many of our services by saying, 'The Lord is here. His Spirit is with us.' It is sad that we do not acknowledge the wonder and the full meaning of this great truth: The Lord is here.

Jesus returns to the Father. Luke in his Gospel says, 'He was carried up to heaven' (Luke 24:51). In Acts, Luke says, 'He was lifted up and a cloud took him out of their sight' (Acts 1:9). This is no ordinary cloud; it is to be seen like the cloud that hid the presence of God from Moses and the people of Israel. The cloud is about the hidden glory of God ever present in our midst. In returning to God, Jesus has taken our human flesh into the fullness of God's kingdom. Jesus remains our friend and in him heaven and earth are one.

Question time

Do we really celebrate that Jesus is here and that we have a common union with him?

How can we make Ascension Day more important and show that it is a special stage in our history and in the life of Christ?

Illustration

At first there was a silence, as if we had been left to our own devices. Through our foolishness we had been caught by a rising tide. We had sent up a plea, by means of a telephone in the refuge box that was placed on stilts above the waves. Some caring people had built this place of comparative safety on the sands to accommodate fools who disobeyed the guidelines of safe crossings.

Suddenly there was a whirring sound from on high. It was no vision. It was a Sea King helicopter. A man was coming down from the safety of the helicopter and being lowered to where we were. He was very friendly. He did not tell us off. He did not say he came to admire the scenery! He said to each of us in turn, 'Do not worry. You will be all right. Fasten yourself to me.' Once one of us was fastened to him he signalled to the helicopter above and we were raised to safety. He came down four times altogether. He told us sometimes he was actually dropped into a raging sea to pick someone up. His purpose was always the same: he came down that we might be lifted up; he descended that we might ascend with him. Then we were taken to dry land. I looked back on my poor old car with water flowing almost over its roof. It would be a write-off. But we were safe. A little like the resurrection of the body and our being lifted to heaven. Words of Psalm 18:16-19 came to mind: 'He reached down from on high, he took me; he drew me out of mighty waters . . . He brought me out into a broad place: he delivered me because he delighted in me.'

Jesus came down that we might be raised up on high.

Memory verse

Remember, I am with you always.
Matthew 28:20

Suggested music

Rejoice, the Lord is King
The head that once was crowned with thorns
Alleluia, sing to Jesus

CANDLES, LAMPS and TORCHES

As this is a working day and a school day, I have assumed there will be no separate teaching for the children and young people. However, I feel, if the opportunity is there, the children should be encouraged to go up into the church tower or a high place and release balloons with tags on them celebrating the Ascension. I have included suggestions for tags and banners that could be made during the sermon if the young people have the opportunity to withdraw. I have also included a hymn for each group. This is an important event and if missed on Ascension Day the material could be used on the Sunday following.

Song

Candles – I'm singing your praise, Lord
Lamps – Jesus isn't dead any more
Torches – Come and join in the song

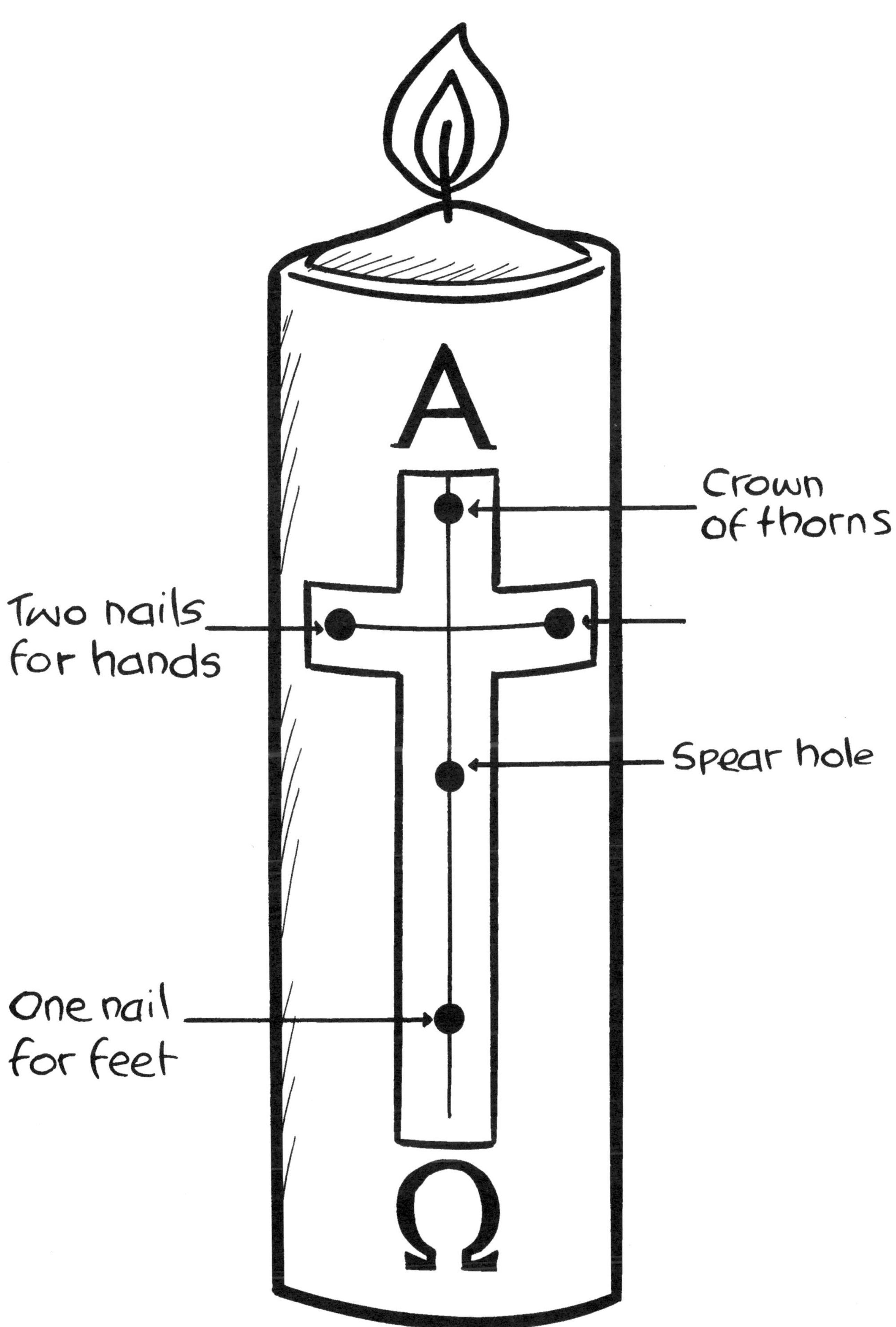
A
Crown of thorns
Two nails for hands
Spear hole
One nail for feet
Ω

Seventh Sunday of Easter

Aim

To show the importance of knowing Jesus personally.

Preparation

Give everyone a pencil and a piece of paper. This is only to write a single name on, so it can be quite small.

Opening activity

Ask everyone to write the name of someone they want to pray for on the paper. Emphasise they should choose carefully as this name is to be placed before God. Small children could draw the face of the person they want to pray for. Have two young people collect these prayers as you would take a collection. Now the prayers are to be placed on the communion table. Let the two young people invite everyone to kneel. One says, 'Pray silence.' The other says, 'We will keep two minutes' silence, knowing Jesus prays with us.'

Opening prayer

Lord Jesus, we thank you that you are always with us
and ready to hear our prayers.
As you have chosen us to be your friends,
may we be faithful to you and ready to do your will.
Amen.

Opening song

He is Lord

Readings

Acts 1:15-17, 21-26
Psalm 1
1 John 5:9-13
John 17:6-19

Thought for the day

If you had to help to choose your next priest or minister, what qualifications would you look for? In some parishes it is easy: they look for an Oxford or Cambridge graduate only. That would weed out an awful lot. We want a learned man, but is intellect of the prime importance? A degree in theology may impress but it does not guarantee that the owner is a committed Christian! There is a big distinction between knowing about Jesus and knowing Jesus.

The disciples had to face this problem with the death of Judas. They were used to working as a team. They went in twos: rarely did they work alone. So eleven was definitely an odd number. Twelve is a special number, like the twelve prophets or the twelve tribes of Israel. If the apostles were like the new Israel they would need to make up their team to twelve. If we play with a team member short, it will affect our overall performance. They needed to find a replacement, so they got together and asked what was required. It is worth noting that at this stage there were about 120 gathered together – that could be ten for every apostle.

They decided together it should be someone who had been with Jesus from the beginning, from the baptism of John until Jesus was taken up from them. (Here we discover there were more than just the twelve going around with Jesus, but nevertheless twelve is a special number.) Then they would require that person to witness with them to the resurrection. Definitely called as a team member and definitely called to witness to the resurrection.

If they were able to put an advert in Situations Vacant it might sound like this:

> Due to the untimely death of an apostle,
> one person needed to join a team of twelve.
> Will normally be required to work with others.
> Needs to know Jesus personally
> and to be ready to witness to the resurrection.

The important things became obvious. They wanted someone who knew Jesus, not someone who had just heard of him. The person had to have followed and loved Jesus. What mattered was their personal experience of the Lord.

What would such a man see as his work?

Take services, look after churches, do social work? Above all he would have to witness to the resurrection. He would have to show others that Jesus is alive. Jesus is not a figure of history or just a holy man of the past: he *is* the *Living Lord*. We need to know him in the present tense, to know him now.

There seemed two obvious candidates, Joseph and Matthias. Now the followers of Jesus wanted to show that it was God's choice, not theirs. They prayed, 'Lord, you know everyone's heart. Show us which one of these two you have chosen.' Then they cast lots. We may find this a little strange but they wanted the choice to be God's and in those days this was a natural way of seeking that choice. The names of the candidates were written on stones. They were then placed in a vessel and shaken until one stone fell out. He whose name fell out was the chosen one. In this case Matthias' name came out and he became apostle number 12.

Question time

Do we make sure we spend some time each day with our Lord so that we can say we know him?

As we sure we speak of a risen Lord? Do we speak of Jesus in the present tense?

Illustration

In the film *Oliver!*, Oliver Twist is in the poorhouse with many other young people. They want someone to complain that they are hungry and want more food. In this case no one wants to do it for they know they are likely to be punished. They decided to pick straws and whoever draws the shortest straw has to do it. If you draw the shortest straw, it means you are chosen. Oliver draws the shortest straw. The others have elected him. So though he is frightened, he goes to the front and asks for more. 'Please Sir, I would like some more.' In the poorhouse this is unthinkable and, as the young people expected, Oliver is punished for asking.

Intercessions

Blessed are you, Lord our God.
You are always with us and ready to hear our prayers.
You have called us by our name
and wait for us to turn to you.
You have chosen us to work with you
and you seek to fill us with your Spirit.
Blessed are you, Father, Son and Holy Spirit.

We give you thanks for men and women of prayer
who have revealed your love
and helped us to know of your presence.
We remember before you
all who are evangelists and ministers,
all who proclaim your love for us.
May we share in the ministry and the outreach
of your Church.

Silence

Lord, as we wait upon you,
hear our prayer.

We bring before you the troubles and the sadness
of our world.
We pray for all who have lost their vision,
who are blind to goodness
and unaware of your presence or your love.
We remember especially
all who feel that life is without purpose and meaningless.

Silence

Lord, as we wait upon you,
hear our prayer.

We thank you for all who love us,
for our families and our friends.
We know that you reveal your love through their love.
We ask your blessing on homes where there is little love
or where there is violence and neglect.
May we welcome you into our homes
and into our friendships.

Silence

Lord, as we wait upon you,
hear our prayer.

We give thanks to all who have been called
to share in your healing powers.
Bless all doctors and nurses,
all who work in hospitals or are part of ambulance crews.
We remember before you all who are struggling with life,
those who are ill or lonely, anxious or depressed.

Silence

Lord, as we wait upon you,
hear our prayer.

We rejoice that our Lord shares in our prayers
and makes intercession for us in heaven.
We pray for all our loved ones who have died
and are now in your keeping.

Silence

Merciful Father,
accept these prayers
for the sake of your Son,
our Saviour Jesus Christ. Amen.

Memory verse

. . . become a witness to his resurrection.
Acts 1:22

Suggested music

Jesus is Lord
Help us, O Lord, to learn
Will you come and follow me

CANDLES

Aim

To show that Jesus is always present and working with his disciples.

Teaching

Some days when there is a lot of cloud we cannot see the sun shining. Where has the sun gone? Yes, it is there behind the cloud. It has not gone away; it is just hidden. Sometimes you can tell the sun is behind the clouds because the cloud has a silver lining or rays of light escape from behind the cloud. Even when it is very cloudy we know the sun has not gone away. Tell the Ascension story. Help the children to understand that Jesus had not gone away; rather, he is hidden from our sight but always there. Let the children visualise the cloud that hid Jesus. Tell them how the same cloud was hiding the Father from the eyes of the disciples. Jesus and the Father are hidden from us but they are here. Remind them of the last words of Jesus as he was hidden: 'Remember, I am with you always' (Matthew 28:20).

Let the children colour the cloud on the worksheet. Encourage them to make the cloud dark and to add a silver lining.

The disciples watched Jesus enter into the cloud. Then they went back to Jerusalem. They kept thinking about the last words Jesus said to them. When we leave someone what do we usually say? 'Ta-ta', 'Goodbye', 'See you soon', 'Cheerio'. Jesus did not say goodbye because he was not leaving his disciples. They would not be able to see him but he was with them. They learnt they could still talk to him and he would still help them. Jesus is with us and he wants us to talk to him.

Activity

If the space allows, play hide-and-seek. If this is not possible, hide a few small articles before the children arrive and ask them to find them. You could tape things to the underside of seats or to curtains. Encourage them to know there are lots of things hidden and they will only be found if we look for them.

Help them to trace around the words 'I am with you always'. Tell them this is what Jesus says to us.

Prayer

Jesus, you are with us always.
We come to give our love to you
and we want to be your friends.
We cannot see you but we still love you.
Amen.

Song

Come on and shine

LAMPS

Aim

To show that Jesus wants a full team and we are part of that team.

Teaching

Look at the list of apostles in Acts 1:13. Let us find their names. Peter and John, James and Andrew, Philip and Thomas, Bartholomew and Matthew, James the son of Alphaeus, and Simon the Zealot, and Judas the son of James. How many are there? It would seem they are in twos until you come to the last three; it looks as if Judas the son of James (let them know this is not Judas Iscariot) did not have a partner. Even if the disciples kept changing partners there would be an odd one out because eleven is an odd number. There was meant to be twelve disciples, like the twelve tribes of Israel; Jesus chose twelve on purpose. If they were to have a full team of workers, they would need someone else to join them. They wanted to have twelve so that they could continue working for Jesus with a full team. When they met together to talk about it they decided whoever was chosen had to know Jesus. He had to have been with Jesus and been a follower of Jesus. It was no use choosing someone just because they were a good speaker. It had to be someone who knew Jesus and loved Jesus. Then they had to be sure that he knew what the work would be. He would have to go and tell people that Jesus who was dead is alive: he had to be someone who could tell about the resurrection. The new apostle would have to be a person who knew the risen Lord.

Well, the group chose two men who knew and loved Jesus. But 2 + 11 = ? That was no good; they could only have one of them. They could have Joseph or Matthias in place of Judas Iscariot, but not both. Anyway, they wanted to show that God had the choice. So they wrote the names of the men on two small stones. Then they put the stones in a container and shook them up. They said that whichever stone fell out of the container first would be the one chosen to be an apostle. When a stone fell out they picked it up and on it was the name of Matthias. So Matthias joined the team and worked for Jesus. He went around telling people that Jesus is alive. I am sure that Joseph probably did as well, but he would be part of another team.

Jesus would like us to work for him. But before we can work for him we have to get to know him. How do we get to know Jesus? By our prayers, for then we speak to him and learn to listen to him. By meeting in church, because then we are with other members of the team and they can tell us more about him. We can also read about him in the Gospels that were written by those who got to know him. He would like us to tell others that he is alive and wants to be friends with them. He wants us to join his team but we need to be ready to do what Jesus our captain asks.

Activity

Play a game of forfeits. Give everyone a card to write their name on. Collect the cards and mix them up. Now ask someone to pick out one card. The person whose name comes out must do a forfeit. After the forfeit let the person who did it pick out another card and so on.

Prayer

God, we thank you that you have chosen us
to be members of your team.
Help us to tell others that Jesus is alive
and that we can be friends of his
because he has risen from the dead.
Amen.

Song

Alleluia, alleluia, give thanks to the risen Lord

TORCHES

Aim

To understand better the meaning of the Ascension.

Teaching

Look again at the Ascension story. Jesus is on the mountain with his disciples. Do they remember the story of the Transfiguration? On that occasion there were only three disciples. This time they are all there, except Judas Iscariot. (Why is he missing?) On the mountain of the Transfiguration, God the Father was heard speaking from the cloud. God the Father is present but hidden by the cloud. The Jewish people believed that no one could look at God and survive. So when God appeared it was often in a cloud to protect the people from destruction. God is present but does not fully reveal his presence. God is with us even though we cannot see him.

Jesus made God known to us. But, as a human on earth, he was restricted by time and space just as we are. There was no way Jesus could be in two places at once. If he was to be with each of us, he had to be freed from the restrictions of time and space. The Ascension would make this possible. The Ascension is the time when Jesus returns to the full presence of the Father. The disciples could not possibly see this – it was too much for their human minds – so the cloud hid the Father and when Jesus went to the Father it hid him also. Jesus was gone from sight but he did not say, 'Goodbye' or 'Cheerio'. He said, 'Remember, I am with you always.' It would be a strange thing to say if he were leaving, but he was not leaving them. He would be with them always. They would not see him but they would learn he was working with them. In a wonderful way the Ascension freed Jesus from being limited by space or time. Wherever his disciples met, he was there. When we come to worship him, he is with us. In fact, he is with us always and he wants us to be one of his friends.

Activity

Let the young people discuss the meaning of the Ascension. What does it mean to be freed from space and time? See if they can find any images that help. For example, a man who lived in a village wanted to talk to all the people at once but some could not leave their homes. The man went to a television studio and broadcast to each house. The people were able to reply to him over the telephone or the Internet. By leaving one place he was seen and heard in many places at once.

Prayer

God, we know the sun is there on the cloudiest of days.
Help us to know that Jesus is always with us.
He is ready to hear our prayers and to help us.
Lord Jesus, we thank you for being with us
and for praying for us.
Amen.

Song

Oh! Oh! Oh! How good is the Lord

Pentecost

Aim

To rejoice in the presence and power of the Spirit.

Preparation

Have 12 candles or night lights waiting to be lit. Around the church have banners or posters of the tongues of fire. Have a large banner or poster with the words 'His Spirit is with us'. You will need 12 balloons for young children to carry. Also have something that needs a power pack.

Opening activity

Every Sunday we make a very exciting statement when I say, 'The Lord is here,' and you reply, 'His Spirit is with us.' Today we will hear it said by young people as they light 12 candles for the disciples and 12 young children bring down balloons (to be tied around the lectern). When each young person shouts, 'The Lord is here,' let us reply with a strong voice, 'His Spirit is with us.' We will have it said 12 times.

Opening prayer

O God, as you sent your Spirit to your disciples,
giving them courage and power
to go out and preach the Gospel,
so fill us with your Spirit.
May we also have power and courage
to proclaim the Good News,
through Jesus Christ our Lord who,
with you and the same Spirit,
is to be worshipped and adored.
Amen.

Opening song

Come down, O Love divine

Readings

Acts 2:1-21 or Ezekiel 37:1-14
Psalm 104:24-34, 35b
Romans 8:22-27 or Acts 2:1-21
John 15:26-27; 16:4b-15

Thought for the day

Today we lit the 12 candles and carried the 12 balloons to remind us what happened to the disciples at Pentecost. We heard in the Acts of the Apostles how there was a great wind that rushed through the house where they were, and that on each of the disciples there appeared to be tongues of fire.

Now here is something else to look at: it is a drill but it is useless (you could use anything that needs a power pack). It should be able to work but it does not. Who can tell me why it does not work? It could be that its batteries are flat or, like this one, it needs a power pack. Now if I snap this power into place, away it goes (demonstrate).

Pentecost was a time when all the Jews who lived near Jerusalem came to give thanks for the giving of the Law to Moses on Mount Sinai. It was also time to give thanks for the barley harvest. Pentecost was 50 days after the Passover, so for us it is 50 days after Easter. If you do not count Easter Day itself, it is only 49 days, 7 x 7, a week of weeks. Sometimes this was called the Festival of weeks.

The disciples were all together in a room. Perhaps they were still afraid to venture out. They did not show any signs of going out and talking about Jesus. In fact, they were waiting to be given the power. They had known Jesus; they had seen the risen Lord and they knew his presence in their lives. They had been commissioned by him to go out and preach the Gospel. But they were waiting for the power to go out. Jesus had foreseen this and had asked them to wait: 'Stay here in the city until you have been clothed with power from on high'(Luke 24:49). It was there, in the room where the disciples were, that the Spirit came with the sound of wind and tongues of fire. Wind and fire were symbols of great power in the ancient world and both were associated with the presence of God. Wind, breath and spirit were all linked together in the ancient world and all were signs of the Spirit of God.

Whatever happened, we know that on this day the disciples were empowered. They were given courage and the ability to go out and proclaim the Gospel. These 12 ordinary men were given the power that would transform the world. If we look at what they were like before the coming of the Spirit and what they were like after, we have proof that something great happened. They would all tell you the Spirit came. He comes to us too.

The Lord is here.
His Spirit is with us.

Question time

Do we really rejoice in the reality that 'His Spirit is with us'?

Too often we go it alone and seek to do all in our own power. How can we learn to wait upon the Spirit, to be strong in the Lord and the power of his might?

Illustration

One of Europe's leading ecologists has said the energy crisis we face is not so much in energy supplies but in our own thinking. There is enough energy in the ebb and flow of the tides, in the running of rivers, in the winds and in the rays of the sun to supply our needs if we would give time and attention to these. Three things are obvious:

(1) Many energy supplies are limited and will run out.

(2) Wrong thinking or lack of proper attention makes us do nothing.

(3) All around there is power that we do not realise.

Too often the Church tries to go along in its own resources and strength, and it can be seen to be running out of supplies. We spend too much of our attention looking in the wrong direction.

The power of God is here, for the Lord is here: His Spirit is with us.

We need to learn to wait upon the Lord and the power of his might.

Intercessions

Blessed are you, Lord our God.
Your Spirit comes to our weakness with his power.
In the strength of your Spirit
you enable us to live and work to your praise and glory.
May we who have received the gifts of the Spirit
use them for the benefit of your creation
and to reveal your love in the world.
Blessed are you, Lord God, Father, Son and Holy Spirit.

Lord, as we rejoice in the coming of the Spirit
we give thanks for all who proclaim your presence
and power.
We remember all preachers and evangelists,
all who celebrate the sacraments and minister to us.
May all your people share fully
in forwarding the Gospel and revealing your love.

Silence

We rejoice that you fill our world.
Your Spirit is with us.

Lord, you give great gifts and talents to your people.
We ask you to bless and guide all leaders
of nations and peoples,
all who make decisions that will affect our lives
and the future of the world.
We pray for scientists and research workers,
for all who work in providing us with news
or influence us through the press and television.

Silence

We rejoice that you fill our world.
Your Spirit is with us.

We give thanks that your Holy Spirit
came upon the disciples in an ordinary home.
Bless our homes with your presence
and grant that there we may grow in the fruits of the Spirit.
Let us know you are with our loved ones and us.
Protect us from all evil
and guide us by your Spirit
in the ways of peace and love.

Silence

We rejoice that you fill our world.
Your Spirit is with us.

Lord of life, we remember all who are dis-spirited,
the distressed, the depressed and despairing,
all who have lost hope or joy in their lives.
We pray for all who fear the future,
all who have lost sight of you and your love.
We remember also all who are struggling
with poverty or hunger,
the homeless and the refugee.
We pray for all who are ill.

Silence

We rejoice that you fill our world.
Your Spirit is with us.

We give you praise, Lord, giver of life and life eternal.
We rejoice that you renew, refresh and restore us.
We remember in your presence
your blessed saints and our loved ones departed;
may light perpetual shine upon them
as they share in the glory of your kingdom.

Silence

Merciful Father,
accept these prayers
for the sake of your Son,
our Saviour Jesus Christ.
Amen.

Memory verse

All of them were filled with the Holy Spirit.
Acts 2:4

Suggested music

Breathe on me, Breath of God
For I'm building a people
O Breath of Life

CANDLES

Aim

To celebrate the power of the Spirit.

Teaching

Have some toys that need batteries or power packs. A car that can be controlled would be ideal. Show the children the toys without their batteries and ask if they know what is wrong with them. Why do they lack power? Get the children to push them and see how they still do not go properly. Now produce the source of power. If they can, let the children snap on power packs or add batteries. Will this make a difference? Let the children see the difference it makes. If necessary, remove the batteries and replace them again to emphasise the difference they make.

The twelve disciples had been asked to tell the world about Jesus. They were to be strong and brave and not be afraid, but they did not have the power to do this by themselves. Jesus told them to wait in Jerusalem until the power of the Spirit was given to them, to wait until they were given power from God. At Pentecost they were waiting in a room in Jerusalem when there was a powerful sound like a big wind. (Let us make a sound like the wind.) It was a really big sound. (Let us make a bigger sound.) The sound was heard because the Spirit of God had come to give the disciples power. The wind, which was the Spirit of God, filled the whole house where they were. The power of God had come and was filling the disciples.

Then on each of the twelve disciples there was what looked like flames of fire. It did not burn them because it was really the Spirit of God. Over the head of each disciple were these wonderful flames.

Now the disciples were given power from the Spirit of God. They were made brave and strong. They were not afraid any more. They knew God was with them. Now they would go out in power and tell the people about Jesus.

Activity

Let the children play with the toys that have batteries and power packs. Show the children how they work and how they need to be switched on. Tell them how power goes from the batteries to the toys and how the toys will not work properly without this power.

Make paper hats of flames of fire that can be worn for the end of the service if the children return to church.

Prayer

Holy Spirit, come to us.
Fill us with your power.
Help us to be strong.
Help us to be brave,
and to know you are with us.
Amen.

Song

I'm a pow, pow, powerpack

LAMPS

Aim

To celebrate the coming of the Spirit.

Teaching

Today we are going to make kites. Does anyone here have a kite? Who has ever flown a kite? What do you need for a kite to fly? You need the wind. A kite cannot fly without the wind.

There was a young girl who was given a beautiful kite. It had a painting of a bird on it. She was so excited and she wanted to go out and make the kite fly. She ran along the beach and the kite went a little way into the air but it soon crashed to the ground. Her brother held it and then when she had a good length of string he threw the kite into the air. But it came down very quickly. She wondered if there was something wrong with the kite and asked her mother. Her mother told her it was not a good day for flying kites because there was no wind. The girl would have to wait for a windy day. Well, she had to wait for nearly a week. Then one morning there was the sound of the wind blowing. She went out with her brother as soon as she could. When they tried to fly the kite it went straight up into the air: it flew beautifully. The girl and her brother flew the kite all that morning.

Jesus asked the disciples to go and tell the world the Good News about his life and resurrection. But the disciples were afraid. They did not seem to have the power. Jesus knew this would be so and asked them to wait in Jerusalem until power was given to them.

Pentecost is 50 days after Easter, seven whole weeks, and the disciples waited all that time. They did not feel any braver or stronger. The city was crowded with people early that morning. Suddenly in the house was a sound like a mighty wind (Let us make the sound . . . I am sure it was louder than that . . . let us make a louder sound.) The sound filled the whole house where they were. It did not seem to be anywhere else. They knew this was what they were waiting for. God was sending his Spirit to them. God was giving them the power to go out and tell others about him.

Suddenly it was as if all of them were alight like candles. There seemed to be flames of fire above them. This was a wonderful sign that they were being filled with the power of the Spirit. Their waiting time was over. Now the frightened disciples were made strong. They were given courage and the power to go out and tell the people about Jesus and his love.

It was only 9 o'clock in the morning but the streets were crowded because it was Pentecost and people were on their way to the Temple to praise God. The disciples went out into the streets. They were full of new power: they were full of the Spirit of God. Now they would tell all peoples about Jesus and his love.

Sometimes we think of Pentecost as the birthday of the Church because it was on this day the Spirit came. Let us say, 'Happy Birthday, Church.'

Activity

If possible, some time should be spent flying a kite or even the kites that have been made following the instructions on the worksheet. Banners could be made with gold and yellow flames and the words, 'His Spirit is with us'. See if the children can make a banner depicting the wind with the words, 'Spirit of God'.

Prayer

Come, Holy Spirit,
we wait for you;
fill us with your power.
Come, Holy Spirit,
we wait for you;
fill us with your presence.
Come, Holy Spirit,
we wait for you;
fill us with your peace.
Amen.

Song

Spirit of God, as strong as the wind

TORCHES

Aim

To understand the waiting upon and the coming of the Spirit.

Teaching

Have you ever been in a power cut when you needed electricity? It is amazing how many things depend on electric power. (Ask for examples of things that the young people use.) If you are lucky you may have a back-up or a generator which will supply you with at least basic power. But usually all you can do in a power cut is wait, wait until the power has returned.

Sometimes athletes and sportspeople suddenly run out of energy. They use up all their powers in trying to win and suddenly they have no strength left. No matter how hard they try, they cannot go on; in fact, the harder they try, the worse they usually become. They need to rest and renew their strength. Isaiah said, 'Those who wait for the Lord shall renew their strength' (Isaiah 40:31). Jesus told the disciples to wait in Jerusalem: 'Stay here in the city until you have been clothed with power from on high' (Luke 24:49). The disciples had to wait until God sent his Spirit to fill them and to give them strength. They waited and waited.

Waiting is quite hard. It is awful waiting in the dentist's. It is difficult when we have to wait on exam results or a doctor's diagnosis. Sometimes it is hard to wait until our birthday to get what we had hoped for. Waiting demands patience and trust. The disciples waited 50 days after Jesus' resurrection. They waited for the power that Jesus promised them; they waited for the gift of the Holy Spirit. They could not make this happen. They had to trust Jesus; that he would send his Spirit upon them as he had promised. As they were waiting, they did not feel very strong or confident. They lacked power in themselves. Perhaps they thought that as Jesus died in Jerusalem at the last great festival, the Passover, something might happen at this, the next great festival: Pentecost. If they thought and hoped this, they were right.

Suddenly before 9 o'clock in the morning it happened. The disciples were all in one place. There was a sound like a rushing mighty wind. It filled the house where they were but it seemed to be nowhere else. Then it was as if all the disciples had flames of fire above them. It did not last long but the effects were to last, for they had received the promise. They had received the Holy Spirit and all the power the Spirit brings. They were no longer afraid: they had courage and new abilities to speak boldly. If anyone doubts what happened at Pentecost, they just need look at the difference it made to the disciples. They were changed from fearful and powerless men to men who would go out boldly to speak for Jesus and to change the world.

Listen to what St Peter said to the people. Get someone to read Acts 2:14-21.

Activity

Get the young people to try and re-enact this event. Get them to talk about the importance of waiting and trusting. Help them to understand the two great symbols of power. Finally, get them to act out the difference the Spirit makes when he comes.

Prayer

Lord, we wait for you.
Come, Holy Spirit.
Lord, take away our fear.
Come, Holy Spirit.
Lord, give us courage to proclaim your Gospel.
Come, Holy Spirit.
Lord, fill our lives with your power.
Come, Holy Spirit.
Lord, teach us patience as we wait.
Come, Holy Spirit.

Song

Holy Spirit, Holy Spirit

ORDINARY TIME
Trinity Sunday

Aim
To encourage a greater awareness of the Trinity.

Preparation
Have blank badges for people to draw on and felt pens for them to use. Tell then to draw on their badge a symbol of the Trinity. As an aid have a few symbols around the church: a triangle, a Celtic knot of three parts, words such as 'One in Three: Three in One.' If possible have some clover or shamrock.

Opening activity
Get everyone to gather around the font. Have some water in the font. Let the people profess their faith:

Do you believe in God the Creator,
who made heaven and earth,
who made us out of love?
I believe and trust in him.

Do you believe in God the Son,
who shared in our humanity,
who died and rose again for us?
I believe and trust in him.

Do you believe in God the Holy Spirit,
who is the Lord and giver of life,
who sustains us in our need?
I believe and trust in him.

This is the faith of the whole Church.
I believe and love one God,
Father, Son and Holy Spirit.

Using a spray branch dipped in the water, sprinkle the people and say aloud, 'You are baptised – totally immersed – in the presence, power and love of Father, Son and Holy Spirit.'

Opening prayer
Lord, all the world belongs to you.
Father, you created us out of your love and for your love.
Christ, you redeemed us by your love and for your love.
Spirit, you sustain us with your love and for your love.
We come to give our love to you, Holy Three,
Father, Son and Holy Spirit.
Amen.

Opening song
Father of heaven, whose love profound

Today is a good day to sing the 'Peruvian Gloria' and let children wave streamers or their hands during the Alleluias. You can also sing the Creed in the words of 'Firmly I believe and truly'.

Readings
Isaiah 6:1-8
Psalm 29
Romans 8:12-17
John 3:1-17

Thought for the day
Do you have a proper diet? We do not all need to eat the same things but we do need a balanced diet. The body cannot live for long without the proper sustenance – fasting can be useful but starving yourself is useless. Many starving people get weak and disorientated. While most of us are not likely to starve, even a slight deficiency can reduce our well-being. A lack of calcium or iron or even zinc in their minute quantities can affect our health.

There was a farm that was not prospering. The cows were losing weight and dying. The family was being reduced to poverty. It seemed disaster was inevitable. Then the vet discovered a chemical deficiency in the cows' feed. The necessary chemical was added and, almost immediately, cows, farm and family improved.

Why are we talking about deficiency? It is because so many people are deficient in their Christian life; there is an element lacking and that leaves them poor when they should be rejoicing in the great riches that are offered to them. They have not experienced the Trinity: they have latched on to one of the persons of the Trinity and missed out on the other two. Quite often if you look at your prayers, you will discover you neglect to have a relationship with one of the three, either Father, Son or Holy Spirit. In the words of Saint Paul: 'The grace of the Lord Jesus Christ, the love of God, and the communion of the Holy Spirit be with you all' (2 Corinthians 13:13).

Check your own experience. Are you aware of a loving Creator who cares for his creation? Do you know he made you out of his love and for his love? He surrounds you with love and wants you to respond to him with love. Do you rejoice to know that nothing in this world can separate you from the love of God? He is with you, the Almighty, the Creator and seeks your love.

Have you discovered the grace – that is, the free gift and the beauty – of our Lord Jesus Christ? Know that he came to earth for you. He lived and died and rose again for you. You do not have to earn his love; it is a free gift (gratis). When you cannot help yourself, he comes to your aid. He is your Saviour and Redeemer. He loves you and he seeks your love.

Are you in common union – communion – with the Holy Spirit? He is with you at every encounter; he shares in every bond of fellowship. The Spirit brings gifts and talents for you to use. As last week, all need learn to wait upon the Spirit.

Father in heaven, you are our Creator.
Jesus, you are our Saviour.
Spirit, you are our Guide and Strengthener.

Make sure you know this and rejoice in Father, Son and Holy Spirit, in the Holy Trinity.

Question time

Do you feel there is a Person of the Trinity that you or the Church neglects? If so, how can we correct this?

We cannot imagine the Trinity but we can love the Trinity. Do we spend too much time theorising and not enough time giving our love and attention to Father, Son and Holy Spirit?

Illustration

A child went down to the beach and dug a hole in the sand. She then went down to the sea and brought some water to fill the hole. In a moment the water disappeared. She went back for more water, and then more. But the same thing happened each time. The little girl became exhausted and began to cry. Meanwhile the tide had been coming in. Her father showed her how to make a channel for the sea, so that it would flow naturally into the hole and fill it. We are like the little girl: we try to fill our minds with ideas about God and often exhaust ourselves. We talk too much. We need learn to wait upon God, knowing he will come to us. Trying to understand the Trinity is like trying to pour the whole sea into a small hole. Yet we can rest in the Trinity and enjoy the love of Father, Son and Holy Spirit.

Intercessions

Blessed are you, Lord God, Father of all creation.
To you be praise and glory for ever.
Your Son Jesus Christ brings light
to dispel our darkness and hope to banish our fears.
He sends upon us your promised Spirit
to strengthen and guide us.
Through your great grace and goodness
help us to reveal your love in all the world.
Blessed are you, Father, Son and Holy Spirit.

Father, we give thanks
for the wonders and mystery of creation.
We thank you for life and for your love.
We ask you to bless the nations of the world
as they strive for unity and peace.
We remember all who work in caring for our planet,
all who work in conservation
and in growing our food.

Silence

Holy, holy, holy God,
hear us and help us.

Jesus, you are our Redeemer.
You gave yourself in love for us.
We come to give our love to you.
We remember in your presence
all who lack any knowledge of love.
We pray for all who are scorned and rejected,
especially those who suffer
from the cruelty and wickedness of others.
We ask you to bless all who are struggling at this time.

Silence

Holy, holy, holy God,
hear us and help us.

Holy Spirit, inspirer and giver of talents,
we thank you for artists and crafts people,
for all who beautify and enrich our earth.
We remember in your presence
all who are unable to use their talents
because of the situation in which they live.
We remember those who are restricted
by poverty or tyranny.

Silence

Holy, holy, holy God,
hear us and help us.

Holy and blessed Trinity, Three Persons and One God,
we thank you for your love which is eternal.
We thank you for the gift of personality.
We remember in your presence
friends and loved ones who are departed from us.
May they rejoice in the fullness of life eternal
in your presence and in your kingdom.

Silence

Merciful Father,
accept these prayers
for the sake of your Son,
our Saviour Jesus Christ.
Amen.

Memory verse

The grace of the Lord Jesus Christ, the love of God, and the communion of the Holy Spirit be with you all.
2 Corinthians 13:13

Suggested music

Father God, we worship you
Thou, whose almighty word
Father, Lord of all creation

Use the 'grace' today as part of the blessing.

CANDLES

Aim

To remind the children of their baptism.

Teaching

Who knows what happens at the font? Yes, babies and sometimes grown-ups are christened, baptised. Do you know what happens? Let us act it out. We have a bowl of water and a doll. We will have to decide on a name for the doll. (Let the children make suggestions.) What do we do? We put water on the baby's head three times (put three drops on the doll and explain): one for the Father, one for the Son and one for the Holy Spirit. We do this because God made us and loves us. (Repeat with another three drops.) One drop because the Father loves us and wants us to love him, one drop because Jesus loves us and wants us to love him, and one drop because the Holy Spirit loves us and wants us to love him.

Who would like three tiny drops of water on their head to remind us that God, the Father, Son and Holy Spirit, loves us? Go round all volunteers saying their name and saying, 'God the Father loves you' and place a tiny drop of water on their heads. Repeat the action saying, 'Jesus loves you.' A third time go round saying, 'The Holy Spirit loves you.' (If someone does not want to take part, see if they would like to help putting drops on the doll or a friend with some help. Try gently to discover why someone may not want to take part.)

Now we know God loves all of us. Let us sing our song to Father, Son and Holy Spirit.

Activity

To show the children the meaning of baptism, and to help them to know God loves them, make a big poster that says, 'God loves me.' Let the children draw their faces or themselves on the poster. If possible, add their names underneath their drawing. Let the poster be displayed in church.

Prayer

Father God, you love me.
I love you.
Jesus, you love me.
I love you.
Holy Spirit, you love me.
I love you.
Let us love each other always.
Amen.

Song

Father, we adore you

LAMPS

Aim

To introduce the children to the experience of the Trinity.

Teaching

Who likes sunny days? We like them because they are bright and warm. Let us think about the sun and sunshine. The sun burns so brightly in the sky that we cannot look at it without hurting our eyes. We cannot look at it but it gives light and heat to our earth. Even when the clouds cover the sun, it is still there.

From the sun comes light, and that light gives life to the things on the earth. Without that light all creatures would die. The light destroys darkness and helps us to walk in the light.

From the sun comes warmth. The sun heats the earth and encourages growth. If there were no heat, all creatures would die. We need light and heat. We cannot see the heat but we can feel it.

The sun in the sky, the light of day and the heat of the day are all joined together. If you took the sun away there would be no heat or light and we would not be able to live on the earth. Sun, light and heat are joined in one and you cannot have one without the other.

The sun can remind us of God the Father who is the maker of all things. God the Father made us out of his love and made all things from that love. God is so wonderful and mysterious that no one can see him, but he is there, giving us life. God is always present, always with us, giving us life and love.

Jesus is like the light of the sun. In fact, Jesus called himself the 'Light of the World'. He came to drive away darkness and to help us walk in the brightness of the day. He rose from the darkness of death and the grave so that we might have the light of eternal life. Jesus is always with us, giving us light and love.

The Holy Spirit cannot be seen, just as heat cannot be seen. Like heat, he gives us life and helps us to grow. The Holy Spirit encourages us to grow strong and to be able to do all sorts of things. The Holy Spirit is always with us, giving us power and love.

The sun gives us heat and light. The three belong together; you cannot separate them.

The Father, the Son and the Holy Spirit are one. They belong together; you cannot really separate them, yet you can know each of them by themselves. Who knows what you call the three persons of God when we think of them together? The Trinity. The Trinity means TRI (three) UNITY (together as one). Father, Son and Holy Spirit are one God: God who made us out of his love and for his love.

God is always with us – like the sun in the sky. When was this first said for us? When were the names of Father, Son and Holy Spirit said over us? (Give clues if the children are stuck.) At our baptism, when we were shown to be in the presence of God – Father, Son and Holy Spirit.

Activity

If possible, go out into the sunshine and talk about the sun, light and heat. If it is cloudy, all the better, for you can tell them how the sun is still there even though we cannot see it.

Have a lot of wool of three different colours. Give each child a good length of a single colour, and ask them to join up with two other people who have different colours. Show them how to knot together the three at one end and then plait the wool into one. Get them to understand the three are making one, yet not one colour is lost. If the original lengths were long enough, it should be possible to make three small bracelets from the length for each child to wear. If they do this tell them they have to remember in their prayers the other two friends who helped to make this possible.

Prayer

Father, thank you for the world and for loving us.
We give our love to you.
Jesus, thank you for loving us,
for dying and rising again.
We give our love to you.
Spirit, thank you for loving us,
for helping us and guiding us.
We give our love to you.
Amen.

Song

Father, we love you

TORCHES

Aim

To encourage the group to give attention to all the persons of the Trinity.

Teaching

Today we are going to try some simple prayer writing. First, it is necessary that you divide into three groups. One will be the Father group, another the Son group and another the Spirit group. Group one will make a simple statement such as 'The Father is God.' Group two will reply, 'Jesus is God,' and group three will follow up by saying, 'The Spirit is God.' Keep the statements simple, for example: 'The Father is here,'; 'The Father loves us.'

If the starting group hesitates too long, let the Jesus group begin; the Spirit group will follow and the Father group will finish off. Here are a few words that might help you to get going: holy, wonderful, mysterious, caring, ready to hear us, almighty, powerful. Let us be thoughtful about what we say as this is to be like our creed, this is what we believe. (Let this last as long as it is going well. Perhaps to establish a rhythm you could suggest after a group makes a statement there should be three claps before the next group follows on.)

Now we will seek to do the same on paper. We will write some simple prayers to the Trinity. Let them all begin in the same way:

> Father, I (love you, need you, adore you, etc.)
> Jesus, I (then the same words as addressed to the Father)
> Spirit, I (then the same words as addressed to the Father and Son)

For example:

> Father, I worship you.
> Jesus, I worship you.
> Spirit, I worship you.

See if you can write three prayers to the Trinity, without using any of the examples used in the spoken prayers or the examples given in the lesson. At the end of our time together we will use one prayer from each person as a short act of worship.

Activity

Today's session has been one of activity where we have shown the unity of the Trinity. If there is still time, we could now try to express the uniqueness of each of the persons of the Trinity. To help, look at a hymn expressing the Trinity, such as 'Father in heaven'. Write a prayer that rejoices in the Father as Creator, the Son as Redeemer and the Holy Spirit as our Guide and Sanctifier.

Prayer

Glory to you, Father,
for you have created us out of your love.
May we live to your glory.
Glory to you, Jesus, Son of God, our Saviour,
for you have redeemed us by your love.
May we share in your saving work.
Glory to you, Holy Spirit,
for you refresh and restore us through your love.
May we walk before you in newness of life.
Glory for ever to you, Father, Son and Holy Spirit.
Amen.

Song

Be still, for the presence of the Lord

Proper 4

Sunday between 29 May and 4 June inclusive (if after Trinity Sunday)

Aim

To show that lives are richer than the keeping of rules – but that rules are necessary.

Preparation

Have an earthenware pot that is of no value; if it is cracked, all the better. Fill the pot with coins and old jewellery. Place it in a prominent place in front of the congregation.

Opening activity

Arrange for a youngster to come out and take hold of the pot. (Pre-arrange for the youngster to drop it; to pretend to let it slip from their fingers. You need a hard surface for this.) Let the child say, 'Sorry'. Now explain how it was all arranged. The pot was not important but its contents are. The pot can easily be replaced. St Paul compared us to pots – maybe crackpots! – that contain a great treasure.

(During the hymn let two or three children pick up the spilled treasure. Let an adult sweep up and collect the shards.)

Opening prayer

Lord God, you give us great treasures.
You fill our life with your love and your presence.
You give us talents and abilities.
You give us your Spirit.
Help us to be aware of the great gifts that are ours,
that we may use them to your glory,
through Jesus Christ our Lord.
Amen.

Opening song

A man there lived in Galilee

Readings

1 Samuel 3:1-10 (11-20) or Deuteronomy 5:12-15
Psalm 139:1-6, 13-18 or Psalm 81:1-10
2 Corinthians 4:5-12
Mark 2:23–3:6

Thought for the day

Self-righteous church people can be very frightening. They are usually full of negative goodness. 'I don't smoke, I don't drink, I don't chase after women (or men), I don't swear.' I want to ask, 'What do you do? What is your positive contribution to life?' It is sad when religion is portrayed as something that is life-restricting and negative. Jesus said, 'I came that they may have life and have it abundantly' (John 10:10).

In today's Gospel we meet religious people who are opposed to Jesus and his ways; in fact, they are out to kill him. We should not be surprised when we are faced with opposition as Christians: Jesus faced it throughout his ministry.

It begins in a cornfield. As the disciples were going through the field they plucked the ears of corn and ate them. It was all right to do this as long as they did not use a cutting instrument such as a sickle. Travellers were allowed to take and eat corn, but not on the Sabbath. Then it was not lawful because it was counted as work; in fact, it broke at least four rules of working on the Sabbath. The disciples could be accused of reaping, winnowing, threshing and preparing a meal! You wonder who was spying on them.

The Pharisees expected Jesus to tell his disciples not to do such things. In reality, the Pharisees were out to stop Jesus. If he gave in to this pettiness, he would hardly lead people to freedom. Jesus replied by telling them how David, when hungry, ate the sacred bread that only priests could eat (see 1 Samuel 21:1-6), citing this as a precedent for what the disciples were doing. Religion was not about rules and regulations but about a relationship with God. It is no use keeping the rules without a loving relationship. God wants our obedience but not as slaves. He wants us to do his will out of love. It would appear there was little love among these Pharisees.

The opposition continued in the synagogue. It is sad when a church reflects all too human feelings of violence and hatred. The Pharisees almost wanted Jesus to heal the ill man so that they could condemn him. Jesus does not play for safety. He could have healed the man after the Sabbath. He asks the man to come forward to let it be seen what he is doing. He faces the Pharisees and asks them, 'Is it lawful to do good or to do harm on the Sabbath, to save life or to kill?' Jesus had come to heal and to save; the Pharisees were plotting the death of Jesus. Such an attitude angered Jesus; he was saddened at their hardness of heart. Like Pharaoh dealing with Moses and the people of Israel, hardness of heart comes through regularly hardening ourselves.

Jesus heals, giving new life to the man with the withered hand. The Pharisees go out and make an unholy alliance with the Herodians. Normally, the Pharisees would have no dealings with the Herodians who were considered untouchable. Opposition mounts as members of government and church join forces to destroy Jesus. So often there are groups in our society that still seek to do this and we need be aware of it.

Question time

Are we sure we have a faith that is about relationships with God and others, rather than rules and regulations?

Are we aware of areas of opposition to the Christian faith in the media or our local region?

Illustration

Rules and regulations are there to help us and the society we live in. Occasionally you hear of some absurd application of the law, usually by someone who says something like, 'It's more than my job's worth.' A young motorcyclist was knocked off his bike in an area of parking meters. His bike was put carefully at the side of the road. Even though the traffic warden knew of the event, he placed a parking ticket on the bike. Fortunately, the city council was more understanding when a plea was made. Some people find it very hard to understand that rules are there to help us rather than hinder us.

Intercessions

Blessed are you, Lord our God,
for you have created light to dispel the darkness
and have shone in our hearts
to give the light of the knowledge of the glory of God
in the face of Jesus Christ.
We rejoice that all power and might come from you.
Blessed be God for ever.

Loving God, we pray for all who do not know or love you.
We remember especially
those who have hardened their hearts against you.
We pray for all whose life is joyless
or governed by rules rather than love.
May your Church be willing to accept and welcome
all who come seeking you and your love.
Teach us to be generous in our dealings with each other.

Silence

Lord, bringing light out of darkness,
let us share in your love.

We give thanks for the many talents and abilities
of your people.
We rejoice in each other's gifts and uniqueness.
We pray for all who are restricted
by tyranny or the dominance of others.
We remember all who are in refugee camps
or are homeless.
We pray for all who feel unloved and neglected.

Silence

Lord, bringing light out of darkness,
let us share in your love.

We thank you for our homes
and the love and acceptance that is there.
We pray for homes where life is oppressive
or adventure smothered.
We remember all who are leaving home for the first time
and all their loved ones.
We give you thanks for homes
where there are new members of the family
and where all are growing in love.

Silence

Lord, bringing light out of darkness,
let us share in your love.

Loving God, we pray for all who walk in darkness
and live in fear.
We think especially of those who are persecuted,
abused or neglected.
We remember before you
all who are depressed and lonely,
all who are struggling to survive.
We remember also all who are ill
and all who have been injured in accidents
or acts of violence.
We think especially of those who are now disabled
or restricted by illness.

Silence

Lord, bringing light out of darkness,
let us share in your love.

Lord of life, we rejoice
that you have destroyed the darkness of death
and opened for us the way to eternal life.
In love we bring before you our dear ones departed,
praying they may rejoice in your light.
In fellowship with all the saints,
we offer you our love and ourselves.

Silence

Merciful Father,
accept these prayers
for the sake of your Son,
our Saviour Jesus Christ.
Amen.

Memory verse

Speak, Lord, for your servant is listening.
1 Samuel 3:9

Suggested music

Take my hands, Lord
Take my life, and let is be
Lord of all hopefulness

CANDLES

Aim

To let the children see the love of Jesus.

Teaching

Once a long time ago there was a man who worked with his hands. He enjoyed making things. He often used a large hammer and chisel. Some days he hit the chisel many times, more than a hundred times. One day a piece of stone broke off the large piece and the man's hand holding the chisel slipped. As it did, he accidentally hit it with the hammer. It caused him a lot of pain. He had to go home and he went to a doctor. His hand could not be made better and it meant he could not use it. His fingers would not work properly. He could not grip the chisel, so he could not do his work. There are lots of things we cannot do if we cannot use two hands.

Who can tie their laces? You cannot do that if you have only one hand. It can be hard to put on your clothes and fasten buttons if you can only use one hand. (Explore the idea of only being able to use one hand.)

The man went to church and often prayed that his hand might get better but it did not. One day Jesus came to the church with his disciples. Jesus wanted to help the man with the injured hand but some of the people said, 'Not today. We do not think God would like you to do it today. Come back another day.' What do you think the man thought? What do you think Jesus thought?

Jesus wanted to make the man better. He wanted to heal him. Jesus said to the man, 'Stretch out your hand.' Everyone could see the hand was hurt and the man could not use it. Jesus hoped they would be sorry for the man and help him, but they would not. Yet while they were all watching, the man's hand got better – it was healed. What do you think this meant for the man? Who do you think made it better? Jesus loved people and wanted them all to be well.

Activity

Let the children draw around their hands and add underneath them, 'Thank you, God, for our hands.'

Play a game of pass the parcel where they must only use their left hand. (This will have to be explained carefully.) The other hand should be kept behind their back. If the parcel is dropped, the person who drops it is out. If two hands are used or the wrong hand, that person is also out. The last person in is the winner and should be given a clap. (Point out that we need two hands to clap.)

Prayer

God, we thank you that you have given us hands.
We clap our hands to thank you:
CLAP, CLAP, CLAP, CLAP.
We clap our hands because we love you:
CLAP, CLAP, CLAP, CLAP.
We clap our hands for Jesus healing the man
with the injured hand:
CLAP, CLAP, CLAP, CLAP.
God, we clap our hands because you are here:
CLAP, CLAP, CLAP, CLAP.

Song

Hands, hands, fingers, thumbs

LAMPS

Aim

To show Jesus cares for individuals.

Teaching

Start with the activity and then talk about how many things would be difficult if only one hand was working properly. What jobs would be difficult to do? Could someone drive a car? Could they use a hammer and nails?

This is a story about a man who used to work with his hands. He was a clever man and worked with stone. He used a heavy hammer and sometimes a chisel. He held the chisel in one hand and hit it with the hammer. He was paid for his work, and that meant his wife and children could have food and clothing. They were a happy family.

One day the man came home from work early. He had wrapped a bandage around his hand, and his family wanted to know what had happened. He told them how he was working on a large stone trying to break a piece off with his hammer and chisel. Suddenly the stone split and the hammer hit his hand instead of the chisel. His hand was badly bruised and he could not move his fingers. He went to a doctor but the doctor could not help and told him to wait until the swelling went down. After a week the hand looked better but it would not work. He could not use his fingers; he could not grip anything. This was bad news for the family because they would not get any money from his work, and they would not be able to buy food or new clothes. Sadly, his hand did not get better and it withered like and old leaf.

The man went every Sabbath to the synagogue to say his prayers. (Talk about what the Sabbath is and what a synagogue is.) He hoped one day he would be better but it did not happen. Then, one Sabbath, Jesus came to the synagogue. He came to pray but he noticed the man with the withered hand. Because it was the Sabbath some people in the church – the Pharisees – were watching Jesus to see if he would heal the man. If he did, they would be very angry because healing is work and you should not heal on the Sabbath. They were not worried about the man; they did not think of his family. They were more concerned about rules and themselves. Jesus was more concerned about the man. The man was more important than a rule. It is more important to love and care than to say, 'I have kept the rules.' Jesus cared for the man and asked him to come out: 'Now stretch out your hand.' The man lifted his withered hand to show them all and as he did his hand became healed. Who do you think healed the man? Jesus did it on the Sabbath and for this reason the Pharisees were very angry. Jesus came to give people life and healing, and these people plotted to kill him. This did not stop Jesus healing because he cared for people.

Activity

Give the children various tasks that are difficult to do with one hand. Have a jar that needs opening and a bottle that needs unscrewing. Ask them to loosen and fasten their laces. Have some peas on plate and a fork and ask them to transfer the peas to another plate. You can make this a team game and have as many peas on a plate as there are members in a team.

Prayer

Take my hands, Lord Jesus,
let them work for you.
Let me share in helping
and in caring for others.
Let my hands show your love,
Jesus our Friend and our Healer.
Amen.

Song

I will wave my hands

TORCHES

Aim

To show God seeks a relationship, not a set of rules.

Teaching

Look at the Ten Commandments: use Deuteronomy 5:6-21 and let ten people read a commandment each. Who had the longest reading? The person who read the fourth commandment about the Sabbath had the longest reading. The Sabbath was very important to the Jews. Which day was it? What was the rule about the Sabbath? That no one should do any work. It was a special day of the week when everything should be allowed a rest. This day was for the benefit of all who were overworked and too busy.

Do you think the disciples were working when they plucked the ears of corn? (Have a show of hands.) Under strict Jewish law concerning the Sabbath, the disciples were seen as working. By picking the wheat the disciples were harvesting and by separating the grain from the husks they were winnowing: by chewing they had ground it as if it were milled and in eating it they were seen to have prepared a meal! Here were four rules about not working that they broke. Can you see each of the actions? God wanted the Sabbath to be a time of rest, but for many it had become a day of rules and regulations that hindered life. It is important that we rest and have time for God, but a relationship with God is even more important than rules. Jesus said, 'The Sabbath was made for humankind, not humankind for the Sabbath.' What do you think this means?

Jesus, as was his custom, went to the synagogue on the Sabbath. There were some Pharisees who were waiting to trap him if they could. This was surely not the right thing for godly people to be doing. In the synagogue was a man who had a withered hand. There is a tradition that says he used to be a stonemason and his hand was injured at work. The word that describes his injury suggests that he did not always have a withered hand. Think how difficult it would be for this man. He would not be able to work and so could not look after his family. All of the family would suffer because of his injury. As healing was work, the Pharisees were looking to see if Jesus would break the rules. Jesus could have waited until the evening and healed the man, but it was important that he did not let a rule spoil a relationship. It was also important he did not let the Pharisees call the tune. Jesus knew if he healed the man he would not be popular with the Pharisees. It made him angry to see how hard-hearted they were. They cared for rules rather than the needs of the man. Let us see the contrast: Jesus came to give life and to heal; the Pharisees were planning to destroy life and to kill Jesus. Which do you think was right?

Jesus did not seek his own safety or popularity with the Pharisees. He came to show the love of God, to heal and to save. He called the man out, saying, 'Come forward.' Then he asked the man to stretch out his hand. As the man stretched it out, his hand was restored. This was something to give thanks to God for – healing and restoration. Sadly, the Pharisees wanted no relationship with Jesus and could only think of how to plot his death.

Activity

Look again at the Ten Commandments (there is a shortened form of them on the worksheet). All are written for the benefit of community and people. Could we make any suggestions for a new commandment? Look at the summary of the law and decide how our church could show this love more towards God and towards individuals.

Prayer

Lord God, we thank you for a day of rest and reflection.
May we make room for you and your love daily
and on this day each week come together
to rejoice in your presence.
May we keep a day each week as a special holy day
to remind us that we all belong to you.
We ask this in the name of Jesus Christ our Lord.
Amen.

Song

I'm putting my hand in your hand

Proper 5

Sunday between 5 and 11 June inclusive (if after Trinity Sunday)

Aim

To show how Jesus risked safety and security for us.

Preparation

If possible get the game Diabolo (available at many toy shops) and get a few people to come out and try it. The art of the game is to throw the bobbin in the air by means of the string and to catch it again. Diabolo means to throw apart.

Opening activity

Let various age groups come and try Diabolo. Afterwards explain that diabolo is a word that is sometimes used for the devil. This is because the devil seeks to divide us. The devil understands well the meaning of 'divide and conquer'. He seeks to divide families and communities. He delights when things fall apart.

Opening prayer

Lord God our Father,
we rejoice that we cannot be separated from you
and that in you we are joined together as a family.
May we seek to keep the love and unity
that you offer us,
through Jesus Christ our Lord.
Amen.

Opening song

Lord Jesus Christ (Living Lord)

Readings

1 Samuel 8:4-11 (12-15) 16-20 (11:14-15)
or Genesis 3:8-15
Psalm 138 or Psalm 130
2 Corinthians 4:13–5:1
Mark 3:20-35

Thought for the day

Jesus was very popular with the ordinary people: wherever he went crowds followed him. He went into a house and the crowd that followed was so large that Jesus and his disciples did not even have time to eat. It was not the first time this had happened and his family was worried for him. They loved him and wanted to protect him. They came to where he was because people were saying, 'He has gone out of his mind.'

Jesus had left the security of Nazareth for a life on the road. His work as a carpenter in Nazareth must have provided Jesus with a good way of life. He would have his family around him; there would be love and care. His family thought it was foolish to leave this to become a wandering preacher who did not have time to eat.

Not only did Jesus leave his security behind; he left the safety of a peaceful life. He was running into trouble with the religious leaders. There are some people whom it is better not to upset and Jesus was upsetting them. Very soon, if not already, Jesus' life would be in danger. He would be safer at home in Nazareth.

He wanted to lead people and show them a better way of life. But look at the people he gathered around him – they were neither learned nor great strong characters. He chose fishermen, a traitorous tax collector and a freedom fighter to be part of his team. He risked society laughing at him. Out of love, his family wanted to take him home.

Jesus could not go with them. He would risk his life for us. He would leave safety and security behind and go on the road towards the cross.

As his family loved him, another group was out to condemn him. The Scribes had followed from Jerusalem, not because they believed or loved him but because they wanted to find fault. They could not deny that Jesus healed people: they actually saw it happen. They tried to frighten people off Jesus by saying he was in league with Beelzebul. This was a pagan god and the name means 'lord of the flies'. They suggested that Jesus worked for Satan, the ruler of demons.

Jesus pointed out how wicked it was to say this. Evil would not fight evil (evil fights goodness). To call good evil is wicked and perverts life.

Jesus accepted that life is a struggle between good and evil, and there is no doubt on which side he stood. Jesus regarded healing as a defeat of evil. He wanted people to be whole and healthy. Jesus cared for the whole person – body, mind and spirit – and not just part of them.

He confronted the Scribes. This was a great risk but he was determined to stand against evil. By their attitude, the Scribes separated themselves from Jesus.

Question time

Are we sure we recognise goodness when it is at work and seek to help it?

How can we express in a better way that we are all part of the family of God our Father?

Illustration

Jesus risked his own safety and security for us. As Christians, we are often called to share in this risky adventure. The call is often like the call to the man with the withered hand: 'Come forward . . . stretch out' (Mark 3:3, 5).

Very often the Church hides behind set services and conventions. The words and the patterns are fixed so that no one is disturbed. Jesus calls, 'Come forward.' Stand where everyone can see you. Where every fault-finding eye can fall upon you. Where those who reject Jesus can vent themselves upon you. 'Safety first' is not our policy: the Church is not meant to be hidden – 'Come forward' for Jesus. Then 'stretch out', even if you feel your talent has withered. Attempt the impossible for God, trusting in his power. Take risks for God and let him work through you. The call of Jesus to the man with the withered hand is a call to the Church to let him work through us. Come forward . . . stretch out.

Intercessions

Blessed are you, Father, Son and Holy Spirit,
for you reveal your love to us
through our families and friends.
We learn of your care and protection
through the goodness and grace of our loved ones.
Teach us to learn to love as you love us.
Blessed are you, Father, Son and Holy Spirit.

We rejoice in the family of the Church.
May all who come find love and fellowship.
May they find acceptance and friendship.
Lord, help your Church be an instrument
of peace and healing in the world.
As we come together,
let us show the unity that is ours in Christ Jesus;
let us show one faith, one Church, one God.
We pray especially for unity among Christians,
that they may show a unity to the world.

Silence

Father, in your mercy,
hear your children's prayer.

We praise you, O God,
for the wonderful variety of people and talents
in the world.
We ask your blessing
on all areas of growth in goodness and grace.
We pray for schools, colleges and universities.
Lord, guide all who influence the minds of young people;
we pray for those who work with television
and in the pop-culture of today.

Silence

Father, in your mercy,
hear your children's prayer.

We give thanks
for all that enriches and encourages family life.
We pray for the social services
and all who support any families that are in difficulty.
We remember before you families
where there is great debt
or where love is absent.
Lord, bless our homes with your love and care.

Silence

Father, in your mercy,
hear your children's prayer.

We give thanks that you are a God who heals and restores,
that you care for our whole being –
body, mind and spirit.
We remember in your presence
all who have been injured in accidents
or through acts of violence,
all who have taken ill suddenly
and those whose illness has no cure.
We pray for their well-being
and the knowledge of your love.
Lord, bless all who share in healing.
We pray for our doctors and nurses
and all who work in hospitals.

Silence

Father, in your mercy,
hear your children's prayer.

Lord, in your power
all are restored and renewed in your heavenly kingdom.
We give thanks for all the saints
and we pray to you for our loved ones and friends
who are departed from us.

Silence

Merciful Father,
accept these prayers
for the sake of your Son,
our Saviour Jesus Christ.
Amen.

Memory verse

It is God who said, 'Let light shine out of darkness,' who has shone in our hearts.
2 Corinthians 4:6

Suggested music

The King is among us
There's a wideness in God's mercy
Stand up, stand up for Jesus

CANDLES

Aim

To show how not everyone loved Jesus.

Teaching

Jesus was very busy helping people. Wherever he went, large crowds followed him. They wanted to hear him speak, to learn from him. Some wanted to be healed and to be made well by him. (Tell the story of one of the healing miracles to the children, as they need the pictorial images.) Sometimes the crowd was so large Jesus could hardly breathe. When he was by the seaside he sometimes spoke to people from a fishing boat and that stopped the crowds pushing around him. A friend of Jesus told his family at Nazareth that Jesus would wear himself out. He was working too hard and not getting enough rest. Sometimes there was not even time for him to eat.

Mary was worried about her son. She loved him and wanted to protect him. Jesus' brothers came with Mary to the house where he was. They wanted to take him home and look after him, to feed him properly and to care for him. Jesus knew they loved him and cared but he could not go with them. He had to do some special work for God his Father. He wanted everyone to know that God loves them. He wants you to know that God loves you. Even though they loved him, Jesus could not stay at home; he had work to do. (The children can understand this, as parents need to work.)

There were some other people who did not love Jesus. They followed him from Jerusalem to spy on him. They were saying nasty things about him. They knew Jesus was healing people and making them better. But they said Jesus was doing this because he was working with the devil. They tried to say that Jesus was not doing good work. They were against him and his work. This made Jesus very sad because they were telling lies and could not see the goodness.

But Jesus did not stay sad, because he knew that his family loved him and he knew that lots of people were wanting to do what God would like them to do.

Activity

We will draw a picture of our family and say thank you to God for them.

Prayer

We thank you, God, for our homes.
We thank you for food to eat.
We thank you that we can rest.
We thank you for all who love us.
We thank you, that you are with us always.

Song

Jesus' love is very wonderful

LAMPS

Aim

To understand that division can be harmful when it comes to community.

Teaching

There is no doubt that Jesus healed people. Last week we heard about the man with the withered hand and how Jesus made him well again. Do you remember that there was a group of people who were not pleased with Jesus? (Who were they and what had upset them?)

Wherever Jesus went, he cared about sick people and healed them. Crowds came for his help and for his teaching. Often the crowds were so large and Jesus was so busy that he did not get time to eat.

There was a group who followed him around, not because they liked him but to spy on him. They followed him from Jerusalem and were saying strange things about him. They said Jesus had 'Beelzebul'. Sounds horrible, like a disease! Can you say it? Beelzebul. It means 'lord of the flies' and it was a name that some used for the devil or Satan. They tried to tell people that it was through evil powers that Jesus was able to heal. They said Jesus was using evil to do good. They wanted people to stop following Jesus.

Jesus knew what they were doing and spoke to them about division, about when things are not on the same side, but on opposite sides.

Jesus said, 'How can Satan cast out Satan?'

If a kingdom is divided against itself, that kingdom cannot stand. The kingdom will fall apart. If people on the same side were fighting themselves, then the enemy would win. If someone kept scoring goals for the other side, then his team would lose. (Imagine a team where the main scorer got all the goals he could for the other side.) Satan could not be divided against himself. Jesus had come not to score goals for evil, or to be on the same side as the devil, but to conquer all evil and to win people back to God. Sin separated people from each other. Evil causes divisions. Jesus came to unite people and bring them together in the love of God. These people following him had to stop telling lies to the people. The majority could see the good work he was doing.

Activity

Encourage the children to run around until the music stops. Then they must form a group of whatever number you say. Call out, 'Divide into . . .' and then say a number. Start with a large number that will keep everyone in if possible. Have groups of 7, 5, 4, 3, 2. If someone cannot find a group, they are out; if a group has the wrong number, they are out. Get them to see that by dividing you are separating them until they are all out except one, and you cannot have a group of one!

If there is time let the children have another go at Diabolo (see Preparation, page 134).

Prayer

Lord Jesus, we would like to be on your team
to fight against evil and to do good.
Help us to be your friend
and to work for you and your kingdom.
Let us not give in to evil but seek to help you.
Amen.

Song

One, two, three, Jesus loves me

TORCHES

Aim

To make decisions about whose side we are on.

Teaching

I want you to imagine a football team where the striker was a most wonderful player. He could defeat his rivals and score great goals. Now imagine during the game he suddenly started scoring for the other side, not once or twice but often. Your own team would not have a chance. Your striker had gone over to the enemy. If he did this game after game, you would soon be at the bottom of the league and your team would fall apart. If someone does not know which side he is on, he is not a good member to have on the team.

There were two groups that followed Jesus around. One group, which included the disciples, wanted to be with him in the good work he was doing. The disciples wanted to work with him as part of his team. They wanted to share in the good work he was doing. We actually come to church to share in that work, to continue the work of Jesus. We are here to be on the same side as Jesus.

The other group followed Jesus from Jerusalem. They wanted to find fault with Jesus; they wanted to stop the work he was doing. They could not deny that Jesus was healing people because this was done in public and everyone knew he was a healer. So, they said that Jesus was not working for good but for evil: Jesus was a friend of Beelzebul, the lord of the flies. They were trying to frighten people away from supporting Jesus.

Jesus asked them how he could be supporting Satan, the evil one, when he was doing good. If he was supporting Satan, then Satan's powers were being divided because Jesus was doing good, not evil. (Get the young people to discuss this. Talk about teams and scoring for the opposite side.) Jesus pointed out that his goodness was defeating evil. If he was supposed to be on Satan's side, then Satan was about to lose. He was about to lose anyway. Any kingdom with divisions in it would crumble. Jesus was on the side of good and not evil, and all need understand this.

As we seek to be Christians, do we make sure we do not score against our own side by doing things that Jesus would not like us to do? (Spend time talking of how we can be on the side of Jesus and what would be like scoring for the other side.)

Activity

Have two teams to play any soft ball game. From the start choose a player from each team who will try to score for the other team if he or she gets a chance. See how the teams deal with such a player.

If there is time, let the group discuss, 'How can we avoid evil and do good?'

Prayer

Lord Jesus, you have called us to work for you
and with you.
Help us to be faithful to you,
to work against evil
and to seek to do what is right and good.
May we be ready to stand up
for all who strive for goodness and peace.
We ask this in your power and in your name,
Jesus Christ our Lord.
Amen.

Song

Oh! Oh! Oh! How good is the Lord

Proper 6

Sunday between 12 and 18 June inclusive
(if after Trinity Sunday)

Aim

To show that the kingdom of God is waiting to grow in us.

Preparation

Have various seeds for recognition. Have obvious ones like a pea, a bean and an avocado. You may like to have some still in their protective cases, such as an apple and an orange. Have a large amount of mustard seed or cress to give out. If possible, have a Bible Society poster with their logo of a sower as large as possible (Bible Society, Stonehill Green, Westlea, Swindon SN5 7DG).

Opening activity

Have a time for seed recognition. Let the children be chosen by a show of hands to say which they recognise. Show the sower on the poster and ask what he is sowing. He is sowing the seed, which is the 'word of God'. Promise to give to everyone a small mustard or cress seed as they leave. Tell them it must be looked after carefully, planted and watered. Promise to put any results on show in three weeks' time.

Opening prayer

O God, you have made many things
from small beginnings.
In the seed you have hidden life and growth.
In us your kingdom is waiting to grow.
Lord God, may your kingdom come in us
as we do your will and seek to serve you.
We ask this through the power of our Lord Jesus Christ.
Amen.

Opening song

The King is among us

Readings

1 Samuel 15:34–16:13 or Ezekiel 17:22-24
Psalm 20 or Psalm 92:1-4, 12-15
2 Corinthians 5:6-10 (11-13) 14-17
Mark 4:26-34

Thought for the day

The Church is in the growth business. We are called to sow seeds and to encourage growth. Today's Gospel has two of the parables of Jesus about the kingdom of God and growth.

'The kingdom of God is as if someone would scatter seed.' There has to be a sowing: the Church must proclaim the message. We may often feel we have failed but we need to have patience and to trust in God. The seed must be given time to germinate. Once the sowing is done, the farmer gets on with other things, including other sowings. While he sleeps and does other things the seed starts to grow – remember it can only do this if it was sown in the first place.

'The earth produces of itself'; it does this automatically for that is what the Greek word means. We do not create the kingdom. We can prepare for its growth in us and in others, but God gives the increase. Growth is often imperceptible, sometimes slow; sometimes it takes much patience. But if we sow, we should trust that God is at work. There will be a harvest – that is, if you have sown the seeds.

(Show a mustard seed.) Most of you will not be able to see this because it is so tiny. In fact, I must be careful I do not lose it. It is a mustard seed. When talking of something small, the people who lived in the Holy Land would say, 'as small as a mustard seed' because it was the smallest of things. Yet in our amazing world, packed into this tiny seed is a large shrub. In the Holy Land it grows to something that looks like a tree, nearly two and a half metres high. Often you see birds sitting in its branches picking off the little black seeds. This is a wonderful thing if you think about it. God's kingdom is also amazing in the way it grows. Again, we have to do the sowing but God will give the increase.

To the early Church which was often facing opposition and setbacks, like the Church now, these were parables of encouragement. Sow the seed and trust God. The faith spread, the Church grew, the kingdom increased against opposition and persecution. This happened because the early Christians continued to sow the word of God in the hearts of people and the society in which they lived.

Question time

How is our church sowing the word of God in the community in which we live? (Remember: no sowing, no harvest.)

We need to sow but we also need to learn patience. How can we tend what is sown without forcing results?

Illustration

Jonathan Chapman used to travel around farms in America with his Bible. In the evenings he would read to the family; not many of them could read themselves. They looked forward to his visits and they called him 'Johnny Appleseed'.

This is how he got his nickname. On some farms he noticed the men busy making cider. The apples were pressed and when the juice was extracted the pips were thrown away. 'What a waste,' thought Johnny: those little pips could grow into fine trees. So Johnny asked if he could have some seed. The man replied he could have as much seed as he wanted. Johnny filled his saddlebag with seeds. When he visited a farm, in the evening he read from the Bible, then before he left he would make some holes in the soil and plant some apple seeds. He then made a little fence around them to protect them and to give them the chance to grow. For over 40 years Johnny did this work, sowing the word of God in the hearts of people and sowing apple seeds in the ground. Everywhere he went he left something behind to give pleasure and nourishment to the farming people. He understood well that seeds could not grow unless they were planted.

Intercessions

Blessed are you, Lord God.
You give the increase to our sowing,
to our work and to our plantings.
You are the giver of life and life in abundance.
May we put our faith in your goodness
and, when we have sown, trust the increase to you.
Though our faith is often small, it is in a Mighty God.
Blessed are you, Father, Son and Holy Spirit.

We give thanks for those who taught us the faith,
who sowed the seed of the Gospel in our hearts.
We ask your blessing upon preachers and teachers,
upon ministers of the word and the sacraments.
We remember homes where the word of God is sown
and children are given the chance
to grow in the kingdom.
We pray for the Bible Society,
for all who produce and translate the Bible.

Silence

Lord our God,
your kingdom come in us as it is in heaven.

Lord, we long for the time
when the kingdoms of the world
will become the kingdom of Christ our Lord.
May the rulers on earth reflect the gentle and loving rule of your kingdom in heaven.
We pray for all who are striving to do your will
in their places of work and in their homes,
for all who witness to you by their way of life.

Silence

Lord our God,
your kingdom come in us as it is in heaven.

We give thanks for those who love us
and show us through their lives
a glimpse of your kingdom.
We ask your blessing upon our homes
and our loved ones.
We remember all who suffer from violence or neglect
in their homes,
all who feel uncared for or unwanted.
We pray for the lonely
and those who have been taken into care.

Silence

Lord our God,
your kingdom come in us as it is in heaven.

We give thanks for the work of healing in our hospitals
and through the healing professions.
We pray for our own doctor.
We remember areas of the world where there is little care
or where the problems seem to overwhelm
those who seek to help.
We remember peoples caught up in disasters,
in floods, in drought or in war.
We pray for relief agencies and all who contribute to them.

Silence

Lord our God,
your kingdom come in us as it is in heaven.

We give thanks for all the saints,
for those who spread the word of God,
for those who witnessed to your love,
for those who brought the Gospel to this land.
We remember all our loved ones who are departed from us
and pray that they may rejoice
in the fullness of your kingdom.

Silence

Merciful Father,
accept these prayers
for the sake of your Son,
our Saviour Jesus Christ.
Amen.

Memory verse

It is a good thing to give thanks to the Lord, and to sing praises to your name, O Most High.
Psalm 92:1

Suggested music

God is working his purpose out
Thy kingdom come, O God
Will you come and follow me

CANDLES

Aim

To discover how the kingdom of God can grow.

Teaching

Tell the story of Johnny Appleseed (see page 138). Make a point of showing how all the apple seeds are just thrown away after the cider is made. The seeds are counted as useless. Yet in each seed there is life. In each seed there is an apple tree waiting to be born. If no apple seeds were planted, there would be no apple trees. If you want apple trees, you have to plant seeds. If you want flowers or vegetables in your garden, you have to plant seeds. You will be given a seed or seeds to take home. As long as you look after them, plant them and water them they will grow.

Johnny Appleseed planted seeds in the farms he went to. He also told Bible stories and planted the word of God in the people's hearts. He wanted the people to grow in their love for God. Lots of people grew to know God better and to enjoy the beauty of apple trees because of the work of Johnny Appleseed.

We cannot make things grow. We can plant seeds and water it. But God makes it grow. God has given each seed its own special life. If we do not plant seeds, there will be no new flowers or vegetables. In the same way, if we do not do things for God, his kingdom will not be able to grow in us. God wants us to sow seeds of kindness, of love. He wants to know that we love him as he loves us.

Activity

Let us plant some seeds (give each child a yoghurt carton with a drainage hole in the bottom, seed compost and a runner-bean seed. Get them to fill the cartons with compost. Then make a hole in the compost for their seed. Tell them if they do not put the seed in the hole, it will not grow. Once the seeds are planted, they need to be watered (this could be done at home). We cannot make them grow but we can help them to grow by making sure they are looked after.

Read again Mark 4:26-29 or tell it in your own words. God's kingdom will grow in us if we try to be kind and loving, if we seek to be good and generous.

Make a date in about three weeks' time for them to bring any growing seeds.

Prayer

God, we thank you for seeds,
for the seeds of flowers, fruit and vegetables.
We thank you for seeds of trees and bushes and grasses,
for seeds that make bread and for rice seeds.
May we grow in our love for you
and be part of your kingdom.
Amen.

Song

There are hundreds of sparrows

LAMPS

Aim

To show the need to sow the seeds of the kingdom.

Teaching

Lazy Jack was given a job in a market garden. He had to prepare the soil for planting and then sow the seeds. The owner of the garden told him how important this work was, for the future depended on it. Lazy Jack seemed to understand. He was soon digging the soil and getting rid of weeds. But then he felt tired and wondered if it would matter if he did not plant some of the seeds – no one would know. Some seeds he left in their packets; other seed he spread over the land regardless of what they were and where he should have planted them. He was able to sit back and listen to music on his personal CD-player. For a long time no one knew anything was wrong. Then slowly the chief gardener noticed problems in the garden: one area was growing nothing at all and another area had a lot growing but it was flowers and vegetables all mixed together. The garden was a mess and it would take a long time for the owner to get it sorted out. Jack could have lost his job, but the kindly gardener kept him on and hoped that he would learn that seeds must be planted properly if they are to grow.

Jesus said the kingdom of heaven is like that: if you want the kingdom to grow, you have to plant the seeds of the kingdom in your heart, your home and in the area in which you live. If we plant the seeds of God's presence, God's love and God's peace in the places where we live, we will help his kingdom to grow. God will work through us and make the kingdom increase. (Get a member of the group to read Mark 4:26-29.) Remember, seed cannot grow if it is not planted.

Sometimes we are discouraged from planting awareness of God's presence or his love because we feel our efforts are so small. Remember how small most seeds are. (Show a tiny seed. Talk about how little acorns make mighty oaks, how sunflower seeds grow, etc.) If we sow the seeds, God will have the opportunity to make them grow. We show our trust in God by sowing the seed. If we do not sow, we cannot hope for growth. (Get a member of the group to read Mark 4:30-32.)

At the end of the session remind the children they will be given an ordinary seed to plant and watch it grow. Talk about how we share in the growth of God's kingdom. If we do our part, God will bring in the kingdom. Remember, wherever the king is obeyed, there is his kingdom. Wherever we co-operate with God and seek to work with him, even in a small way, the kingdom has come.

Activity

On the sheet there is a further opportunity for seed recognition. Give each child a sunflower seed and see if they recognise it. Now provide them with a pot and some compost so they can plant it. Tell them when it grows they will have to transfer it to the garden; before that it needs sunlight, water and a warm place. You may be able to have a 'tallest sunflower' competition later. Though we plant and water, we must remember God gives the growth. On the checklist let us see if we are planting seeds of God's kingdom.

Prayer

God, you have given us certain powers:
we can make the world around us a good place
or a bad place.
We can live at war
or seek peace.
Help us to sow the seeds of love and peace –
the seeds of your kingdom –
in our hearts, in our homes
and in the world around us.
Amen.

Song

For ever I will live my life by faith

TORCHES

Aim

To show God's kingdom comes through our actions.

Teaching

A young man went away to sea. He was off to unknown lands and did not know when he would see his mother again. He sailed far, far away. In a distant land he saw a beautiful bush with bell-shaped flowers. He had never seen such a beautiful bush and it made him think of home and his mother. He remembered that his mother loved flowers. He decided to take one of these bushes home for her. He dug it up carefully and planted it in a pot. On the long journey home he looked after it and kept it alive. His mother loved the bush and put in on show in her front window.

One day a botanist, passing the window, noticed the bush and realised he had never seen one like it. He knocked on the door and asked if he could buy the bush. The woman was very poor but did not want to part with the bush. The man promised she would get a bush from a cutting and that he would also give her a lot of money. When her son returned from his next voyage there was still a bush in the window.

That is how the first fuchsia came to England (if possible, show a plant or a picture). Perhaps you have one at home that descended from it. It all happened because of one young man's love and care. If we do not sow seeds of love and care, how will they grow? God's kingdom comes whenever we do his will and obey his word. When we seek to live by God's rule we sow the seeds of the kingdom of God. When we do deeds of kindness or act with forgiveness we share in God's acts and sow the seeds of the kingdom. God will bless our works and it is he who gives the increase.

A young girl told her mum she was going to work for the kingdom of God. Her mum's reply was, 'Well, you can start by tidying up your room.' God's kingdom is never far away but it will not come without our sowing. He waits for us to say, 'Your kingdom come: your will be done.' Wherever we do acts of kindness, wherever we seek to improve our world, wherever we seek to do his will, we are sowing the seeds of God's kingdom. Obviously, by hatred, evil thoughts or violence we can hinder God's kingdom. Let us pray each day, 'Your kingdom come in us as it is in heaven.'

Activity

Let the group discuss how we sow the seeds of the kingdom. What, in our area, prevents the growth of the kingdom, and what helps? God sows the kingdom in our hearts: what do we need to encourage the growth that God gives?

Prayer

God, you are the maker of all things.
In the seed you have placed great potential for growth.
In our lives you give us the power
to share in the growth of your kingdom.
May your kingdom come in us,
and your will be done in us
today and always.
Teach us to sow the seed of your word
and to do deeds of kindness and love.
Amen.

Song

Let your kingdom come

Proper 7

Sunday between 19 and 25 June inclusive (if after Trinity Sunday)

Aim

To learn to turn to Jesus in the storms of life.

Preparation

Have posters from the Mission to Seafarers showing the work they do (Mission to Seafarers, St Michael Paternoster Royal, College Hill, London EC4R 2RL). You could also have a display of the work of the Royal National Lifeboat Institution.

Opening activity

Have people look at the posters. Play or sing 'When you walk through a storm (You'll never walk alone)' – *BBC Songs of Praise*, 320.

Opening prayer

Lord, you know that our lives are lived
in the midst of so many dangers:
there are storms and events
that can so easily overwhelm us.
Help us at all times to know your presence,
to be aware of your power
and to rest in your peace.
Amen.

Opening song

Lead us, heavenly Father, lead us

Readings

1 Samuel 17:(1a, 4-11, 19-23) 32-49
or 1 Samuel 17:57–18:5, 10-16 or Job 38:1-11
Psalm 9:9-20 or Psalm 133 or Psalm 107:1-3, 23-32
2 Corinthians 6:1-13
Mark 4:35-41

Thought for the day

Jesus was exhausted. People had been coming day and night. He had hardly had time even to eat. He had been pouring himself out until there was little left and he needed space and refreshment. He got into the boat and was asleep almost straightaway. There he is in the stern sleeping.

Peter scans the sky and does not like the look of it. The wind is rising; the sea is becoming restless. From the heights of Mount Hermon and the hills and valleys around, funnelled through the ravines, winds descend without warning and with great force. Voyagers on the Sea of Galilee often met such storms. The disciples understood that only God could still the storm and bring calm; humans would do best to stay out of it if they could.

Suddenly the storm hits the little boat. There is little the fishermen can do. They cannot escape and their boat is filling with water. Jesus continues to sleep. The boat is in the midst of chaos: the canvas is out of control, the helm won't respond, timber and tackle groan. Like many before them it seems they could be lost at sea. They are fighting for survival and they call upon Jesus, 'Teacher, do you not care that we are perishing?'

Jesus wakes up and rebukes the wind and says to the waves, 'Peace! Be still.' Then the wind ceases and there is a dead calm.

(Read from Psalm 107:28-29.) The words of the Psalm were applied to God only. No wonder the disciples were filled with awe and asked, 'Who is this that even the wind and the sea obey him?' To this there is one answer only: Jesus is God.

Question time

What storms is our church facing at this time?

Have we allowed Jesus to sleep and trusted too much in our own strength and devices?

Illustration

Do you know the story of Aladdin and his lamp? The lamp had wonderful powers but most people did not recognise it. The lamp standing unused was no better than any other. It could give out a little light but its great power remained untapped. It is no use having a wonderful power if you do not use it. In the same way, it is no use saying you believe in a Saviour if you do not call upon him.

Too often we allow Jesus to sleep in our lives. We struggle on alone and are often overwhelmed because we do not call upon him in the storm. While we allow fear to mount and energies to be overpowered, we fail to call upon the greatest power, which is our Lord.

In the storms of fear and sorrow, when we are feeling overwhelmed, we need to know the presence and the power of our God. We need to know again that God can bring order out of chaos and that Christ can give us his peace. Do not let Jesus sleep in your life; call upon him each day. Take heed these words from Julian of Norwich:

> He said not: 'Thou shalt not be tempest-tossed; thou shalt not be work-weary; thou shalt not be distressed.' But he did say: 'Thou shalt not be overcome.'

Intercessions

Blessed are you, Lord our God,
for you are ever with us
and your presence brings us close to your power
and your peace.
You are ready to hear our cry
and to help us in our troubles.
We rejoice in your love and in your care.
Blessed are you, God, for ever,
Father, Son and Holy Spirit.

Almighty and loving God,
we seek to rest in your presence and in your peace.
The Church is often buffeted
by storms of antagonism and opposition.
We remember before you all Christians
who are struggling to survive in areas
where they face violence or ridicule for their faith.
We pray especially for those
whose lives are at risk at this time.

We remember also young Christians
who have to face opposition
from their friends and relatives.

Silence

Lord, in the storms of life we call upon you:
grant us your peace.

God our Creator, we rejoice in the well-being that is ours.
We remember in your presence
all who are suffering at this time
from storms, from floods, from drought.
We pray for all who are caught up in war,
in violence and acts of wickedness.
We remember all who are suffering from poverty
or who are in great debt.

Silence

Lord, in the storms of life we call upon you:
grant us your peace.

We give you thanks
for the love and protection of our homes.
Lord, grant that our loved ones may know your peace
and your presence.
We remember homes where people are not coping well,
where there are struggles in relationships.
We remember especially homes
where there are great tensions
between parents and their children.
Bless, O Lord, all whose homes have fallen apart
and all children who have been taken into care.

Silence

Lord, in the storms of life we call upon you:
grant us your peace.

God, you are ever-present.
We ask you to strengthen and support
all who are overwhelmed by the storms of life.
We remember those whose sickness finds no cure.
We pray for loved ones and carers who feel exhausted
and unable to cope any more.
Bless, O Lord, all who have been injured this week
or who have gone into hospital,
and all their loved ones who are anxious for them.

Silence

Lord, in the storms of life we call upon you:
grant us your peace.

Mighty God, when the last great storm overwhelms us
help us to know you are there
as the Lord and Giver of life;
to know we are not alone
and you will not let us perish.
Bless our loved ones who are departed
from the storms and troubles of this world
with your presence and your peace.

Silence

Merciful Father,
accept these prayers
for the sake of your Son,
our Saviour Jesus Christ.
Amen.

Memory verse

They cried to the Lord in their trouble, and he delivered them from their distress.
Psalm 107:28

Suggested music

Will your anchor hold
Eternal Father, strong to save
Do not be afraid

CANDLES

Aim

To show how Jesus keeps us safe.

Teaching

Begin by talking how the children feel safe when they have a parent or someone to look after them. Discover how they are not afraid of the dark if someone who loves them is near.

One evening Jesus was very tired. He had been working very hard and needed to rest. The disciples who were fishermen took him into their boat away from the crowds. Soon Jesus was asleep on a seat in the back of the boat. The disciples raised the sail and pulled on the oars and soon they were right out at sea. (Get the children to pretend to raise the sails and to row.) They were now out in the middle of the sea and the water was very deep. Jesus was fast asleep.

Suddenly the wind started to blow. Let us make the sound of the wind. It was much louder than that – let us make the sound bigger! The wind rushed down the hills and blew on to the sea. The waves rose up and they slapped into the boat (clap your hands as you say this). The wind got louder and the waves grew higher. Let us make the sounds of the wind and the waves. The disciples were frightened their boat was going to sink.

If they did not get some of the water out of the boat, the boat would sink and they would all be in the sea. They took the sail down and rowed hard (actions). They tried to get some of the water out of the boat (actions). The wind kept blowing and the waves got bigger (actions).

All this time Jesus was asleep in the back of the boat. He trusted in God his Father and was able to sleep even in the storm. The disciples needed his help. The boat was rocking from side to side (action). The disciples were frightened and they woke Jesus up, shouting, 'Teacher, save us.' Let us shout those words again.

Jesus awoke to the sound of the wind and the waves and the boat rocking (actions). He stood up and said in a loud voice, 'Peace! Be still!' The wind and the waves obeyed him. The wind stopped blowing and the sea became calm. All was quiet. The disciples were amazed: only one person could make the wind stop and the waves to be still and that was God. So who must Jesus be? Jesus is God. The disciples were very happy because they were not afraid any more. They felt safe to be with Jesus.

Activity

If possible, have a little boat and a large bowl for it to sail in. Let the children make the water stormy and put little bits of water in the boat. Rescue the boat before it sinks. On the worksheet there is a boat and a stormy sea to be coloured.

Prayer

Jesus, we thank you that you stilled the storm
and saved the disciples.
You are with us always.
Help us when we are afraid.
Amen.

Song

Wide, wide as the ocean

LAMPS

Aim

To show that Jesus is our Saviour.

Teaching

If you look at the list of ships a lifeboat crew has saved, you will see what wonderful work they do. They rescue people from the danger of the sea. But also written in the list is 'Standing by'. What do you think that means?

The lifeboat crew go out and come close to a ship that is in trouble. They wait to see if there is a call for help or if they will have to suddenly go to their aid. They make sure that the other ship's crew can travel in safety until they come to a harbour.

Jesus often stands by, waiting for us to call upon him. He watches over us and wants to make sure we have his peace and know of his presence. He will not force himself into our lives; we have to invite him.

Picture the tired fishermen trying to get a little rest in their fishing boat. It is lovely on a calm sea when the sky is blue. Suddenly a great storm comes up. They are not prepared for this. The wind whips up and the waves climb higher. Soon water is washing into the boat, and the more water that comes in, the lower the boat is in the water. Soon the little boat will sink. The fishermen understand the danger and begin to panic. They cannot keep the water out of the boat. All the time Jesus is there, asleep in the stern of the boat. Maybe another pair of hands could help. They awaken Jesus, calling, 'Teacher, do you not care that we are perishing?' Of course Jesus cares and he cares about anyone who is perishing (get a child to read John 3:16). What Jesus did surprised the disciples. He stood up in the rocky boat, and, shouting above the storm, he rebuked the wind and said to the sea, 'Peace! Be still.' The storm stopped, the wind dropped and the sea became calm. The disciples wondered at the strange power at work and asked, 'Who is this that even the wind and the sea obey him?' Well, only God can control the wind and the waves. There was only one answer: Jesus is God and he is also their Saviour.

Jesus is our Saviour. He is always with us. When we are in trouble we can call upon him. He comes to rescue us because he does not want us to perish.

Activity

Let the children mime rescue services: ambulance, coast-guards, fire brigade, mountain rescue. After each mime talk about how people have been saved and how others risk their lives.

Talk about how Jesus risked his life for us. Make sure the children know about the cross and the resurrection. Jesus is our Saviour.

Prayer

Lord Jesus, when we are in trouble you are close by.
You, Lord, are our Saviour and are ready to help us.
We give thanks for your presence
and rest in your power and peace,
Jesus Christ our Lord and Saviour.
Amen.

Song

O the dark waves were raging
or Calm me, Lord

TORCHES

Aim

To show that Jesus is our Lord and Saviour.

Teaching

Have a dramatic reading of Psalm 107:1-3, 23-32 with the refrain.

Let verses 1 to 3 be read by different people and the refrain – 'Give thanks to the Lord for he is good, and his mercy endures for ever' – is to be said loudly after each verse. If your group is large, let the refrain be divided into two parts.

For verses 23-25, use three new readers. Let the refrain start loudly but get quieter for each verse.

Verses 26-27 are said in a loud voice with actions of waves and people reeling about. The refrain is whispered.

Give verse 28 great emphasis; the refrain is said with equal emphasis.

Verses 29-30 are said quietly, and the refrain is said quietly also.

Verses 31-32 are declared with confidence. Let these last two verses be said by four people as half a verse each with the refrain after each half verse.

Practise this reading a couple of times and then perform it as a dramatic piece. It would be good if the readers could learn their lines.

How can we affirm the goodness of God when a storm is raging around us? Can we see that by acknowledging his presence it makes a difference to how we feel in the storm?

Tell how the Jews feared the sea and saw it as an image of chaos. Yet they were sure God was always present and in control. Even when the storms raged and the sea was in danger of overwhelming them, they would put their trust in God. They remembered how Moses brought them through the Red Sea by the power and presence of God. Listen to the song 'When you walk through the storm (You'll never walk alone)' and let everyone join in the chorus.

Activity

Let someone read the stilling of the storm (Mark 4:35-41). Discuss how the boat was being overwhelmed and how the disciples called on Jesus. Talk about what overwhelms us in this world and how we often go it alone. How can we assure ourselves of the presence of our Saviour? We discover in the storm that we are perishable goods. We learn from the Bible that Jesus came to save us from perishing. Colour in the text of John 3:16.

Prayer

Lord our God, we come in our weakness to your strength.
We know that in Jesus we have a Saviour.
May we know his presence, his power and his peace
in our daily lives.
Amen.

Song

With Jesus in the boat

Proper 8

Sunday between 26 June and 2 July inclusive

Aim

To show Jesus is the giver of hope and life.

Preparation

Have the five words DO NOT FEAR ONLY BELIEVE on separate cards big enough for the congregation to see. Give them to children to fasten around their neck. Prepare the children for the following.

Opening activity

'Only' comes down and says, 'Hello, I am lonely only.' 'Do' comes down and says, 'I am all of a do.' The two children raise hands from their sides and touch with one hand.

'Not' comes down and says, 'I'm a negative', joining raised hand with the others. The sentence now reads ONLY DO NOT.

'Believe' comes down and says, 'You need faith but I find it hard.' 'Believe' raises hand and joins the others. The sentence is now ONLY DO NOT BELIEVE.

'Fear' comes down and the rest scatter for a moment, leaving 'Fear' to say, 'I am good at scaring people.'

All return and join raised hands. The order of the sentence is now DO NOT FEAR ONLY BELIEVE. The five children say in a loud voice their individual word and then say the whole five words together: 'Do not fear; only believe.'

Opening prayer

Lord our God,
we thank you for your love and care towards us.
When the way is dark and life is hard
help us to believe in you and not be afraid.
Let us trust in your power and your love
and know that you are our Saviour.
Amen.

Opening song

Christ's is the world in which we move

Readings

2 Samuel 1:1, 17-27 or
Wisdom of Solomon 1:13-15; 2:23-24
Psalm 130 or Psalm 30 or Lamentations 3:23-33.
2 Corinthians 8:7-15
Mark 5:21-43

Thought for the day

Here are two sad stories, one of a young girl and the other of an older woman. It would seem the young girl was an only child. She would be the light of her parents' life, their joy and a living expression of their love. Now it would seem that light was about to go out. What darkness and pain it must have caused the loving parents that their child was so ill.

This young girl was 12. That is to say she had grown into a woman. In the land where Jesus lived when you were 12 years and a day you were counted as grown up and could even get married. (Maybe all the girls over 12 would like to stand for a moment.) Sadly, just as she should have been starting her adult life, she was going to die. Her father called doctors and healers but the girl could not be made well. He was desperate and that made him go to Jesus.

The man was called Jairus and he was the ruler of the synagogue. He was the administrator: he saw to the good running of the synagogue and to the list of who would take services and preach. He was an important man, respected and of good standing. Now he threw himself at the feet of a wandering preacher. No doubt he was not sure of Jesus and maybe even thought Jesus was a heretic, but he threw himself down before Jesus. He put aside any prejudice. He put aside any pride and begged repeatedly, 'My little daughter is at the point of death. Come lay your hands on her, so that she may be made well and live.' Jesus went with him immediately.

The crowds held up their progress. People were all around and seeking to see Jesus or hear him. It was a slow journey and suddenly Jesus stopped. Everyone stood still. Jesus turned and looked at the crowds and asked, 'Who touched me?' The disciples said, 'Look at the crowds. How can you ask such a question? Lots of people must have touched you.' But Jesus knew power had gone out from him to someone. He asked again, 'Who touched me?' and looked at the faces in the crowd. A woman came forward and confessed. She suffered from haemorrhages and should not even have been there. Any contact with people would render them unclean by the law. She should not have touched Jesus. Maybe she thought she could steal some power. It sounds as if she was rather superstitious but, whatever she was, she was desperate for healing. Jesus said to her, 'Daughter, your faith has made you well. Go in peace, and be healed of your disease.'

This was wonderful but it was a delay, and while Jesus was there a message came that the daughter of Jairus had died. Jesus looked at Jairus and said, 'Do not fear; only believe.' At the house the professional mourners were weeping and wailing, the flute players were playing sad songs. The girl was dead. Jesus said to them, 'The child is not dead but sleeping.' They didn't believe him and continued their wailing and crying. Jesus put everyone out of the house except the girl's parents. Then with Peter, James and John he went up to where the girl was and taking her by the hand he said to her, 'Talitha cum.' This was the local Aramaic language that the child would know; it meant, 'Little girl, get up.' Immediately, with Jesus holding her hands, she arose. Jesus told them not to tell anyone – they would know soon enough. The girl needed rest and food.

Question time

Are we sure we make an effort to make contact with Jesus? Can it be said we have touched him and he has touched us?

Do we bring our faith to bear on our fears?

Illustration

How often do we lose contact with friends because we do not make the effort? To maintain a relationship with anyone we need to meet them and talk to them. If they are far away we can at least write, telephone or send an e-mail. A once-a-year Christmas card could hardly be called contact.

In a car the contacts give a vital spark that fires the engine. If the contacts are broken, the engine will not fire properly. Even if we have plenty of fuel and the battery is charged, the car will not go if there are no contacts at work.

When Jesus asks, 'Who touched me?' could you say, 'It was I, Lord'? Do you keep in proper contact with Jesus? When the woman touched him, power travelled from Jesus to her. We so often fail to achieve because we go it alone and do not touch base with Jesus.

(You might like to use the hymn 'What a friend we have in Jesus'; let the people read it during a silence.)

Intercessions

Blessed are you, O God,
our Lord, King of the Universe, God of our fathers,
our Creator, Redeemer, Sustainer.
From you come life, renewal and refreshment.
In you we find hope, restoration and well-being.
We believe in you, we trust you.
Blessed are you, Father, Son and Holy Spirit.

We give thanks for the Church throughout the world;
for people who are growing in the faith
and being made strong by their beliefs.
We remember all who are struggling
with opposition and evil
and all whose lives are in danger.
We remember all who feel oppressed and let down.
We pray for all whose faith is being challenged
and those who have lost contact with you.

Silence

Lord, through contact with you
help us to rise.

Lord, we rejoice in the lives and talents
of the people of our world.
We pray to you for all whose gifts are being wasted
through poor education or through tyranny.
We remember all whose ambitions and livelihood
have been destroyed through war or natural disasters.
We ask your blessing upon all who
are counted as untouchable or are rejected by society.

Silence

Lord, through contact with you
help us to rise.

We give you praise and thanks for all who care for us.
We ask your blessing upon our families and friends,
all whom we love and all who love us.
We remember homes were there is serious illness
and where loved ones are carers.
We pray especially for all who are struggling
to keep their homes together,
all whose physical or financial resources are running out.

Silence

Lord, through contact with you
help us to rise.

We give thanks for all healers,
for doctors and nurses, for social workers and carers.
We remember all who are strengthened
by their faith and trust in you.
We ask you to bless all whose sickness finds no cure.
We pray for the terminally ill
and all who are in a hospice
or need permanent care in a home.
We pray for all who feel their life is wasting away.

Silence

Lord, through contact with you
help us to rise.

Lord, you are the giver of life and life eternal.
We rejoice in your presence and in your love.
We give you thanks for the resurrection
and the hope of eternal life.
We remember in your presence
our friends and loved ones who are departed from us.
We rejoice in the fellowship of all your saints.
We commend the whole world and ourselves
to your unfailing love.

Silence

Merciful Father,
accept these prayers
for the sake of your Son,
our Saviour Jesus Christ.
Amen.

Memory verse

Do not fear; only believe.
Mark 5:36

Suggested music

New every morning is the love
Have faith in God, my heart
Bless the Lord, O my soul

CANDLES

Aim

To show that by touching the girl Jesus gave her life back to her.

Teaching

Begin by welcoming back to the class anyone who has been ill. When (Sam) was poorly his mother and father were really sad. They wanted him to be well and happy. Now that he is well again they are very happy. Today's story is about a little girl who was very ill and it made her mother and father very sad. This is also a story about Jesus and the girl's father Jairus. (Let us say his name together.)

Jairus lived in a lovely white house with his wife and daughter. He was an important man and looked after the church. One day when he came home he noticed the house was very quiet – there was no little girl running about. Mummy came and said their girl was in bed because she was not very well. Jairus got the doctor to call but he said she could not be made well. Mummy and Daddy sat by her bedside. They held her hands but the little girl did not open her eyes. She was very poorly and they did not know what to do.

Suddenly Jairus turned to his wife and said, 'I know what to do. Remember there is someone who has been healing people and making them well again. Do you remember he cured the man with the withered hand? (Explain.) Well, I am going to find him and bring him to our home and to our daughter. 'Good,' said Mummy, 'go as quickly as you can because she is very poorly.'

Jairus ran as fast as he could. He pushed through the crowds to where Jesus was and knelt down at his feet. Everyone was amazed to see the man who looked after their church kneeling before Jesus. 'Oh Jesus, come to my house and heal my little girl or she will die.' Everyone heard and they were so sad for the man. They wondered what Jesus would do. Jesus said he would go now and they set off for the house. Then a very sad man came running and said, 'Don't bother to bring Jesus: your little girl has died.' Jairus began to cry because his little girl was dead. Jesus said to him, 'I will still come with you. Do not be afraid; only believe.' When they got to the house people were playing sad music, others were crying loudly – it was all very sad. They told Jesus he was too late to do anything. Jesus asked them all to go outside the house. He went in with the girl's mummy and daddy and three of his disciples. They all went into the bedroom and saw the little girl lying very still upon the bed with her eyes closed. Jesus went over, took hold of her cold hands and said to her, 'Get up, my little girl.' He could feel her hands get warm. She opened her eyes and smiled at Jesus. Then she got up out of bed and stood up on her own two feet. Jesus told them to give her some food to make her strong again. How happy her mummy and daddy were, because Jesus had come to their house and by touching the girl had made her well again.

Activity

Play a game of tag. Once a person is touched they join the person who started and go around touching others. The last person to be touched becomes the new leader. All who were touched have to sit or lie on the ground until the new leader goes around and touches them and gives them 'new life'. If time allows, play this three or four times.

Prayer

Lord Jesus, we thank you for our lives
and that you love us.
We thank you that you healed the little girl
and we ask that you will look after us.
Amen.

Song

Jesus, friend of little children

LAMPS

Aim

To show Jesus is the Lord and giver of life.

Teaching

Today's story is about two different people: a young girl and an older woman. Both were poorly and could not be made better by doctors. In fact, both were just getting worse.

The girl was just 12 years old, but in the country where she lived that was counted as the age when she became grown up. Sadly, at this point, she was in bed and facing death. This made her parents very sad. They had tried all sorts of things but their daughter's life was just fading away. It seemed there was nothing they could do. Then her father Jairus remembered the healer Jesus and wondered if he could help. Jesus was a poor teacher wandering around the country and Jairus was a rich man who looked after the synagogue. Jairus knew his money could not save his daughter but maybe Jesus could.

Jairus knew that Jesus was in his town and ran to where he was. The crowds made way for him as he pushed through to see Jesus. Then everyone was amazed as he threw himself at the feet of Jesus. Jairus knelt before Jesus and asked him to come and heal his little girl. Jesus said he would and they set off immediately. The crowd followed and this made their travelling slower.

In the crowd was a woman who was also ill. Her life was wasting away because she could not stop bleeding. The Jews believed our whole life is in the blood and that if blood was ebbing away, so was life. They also said that anyone with such an illness should not touch other people. She must have touched lots of people in the crowd but she especially wanted to touch Jesus. When she touched him, it was as if the whole world stopped. Jesus stood still. The crowd stood still. Jesus turned around and said, 'Who touched me?' Jesus knew power had gone from him. The woman was afraid and confessed it was her. Jesus looked kindly on her. She had made contact with him and by that contact with the living Lord she was healed. Jesus said to her, 'Daughter, your faith has made you well; go in peace, and be healed of your disease.'

Sadly, due to this delay Jesus did not get to the house of Jairus before a messenger came and said the little girl was dead. Jairus was heartbroken. Jesus said, 'Do not fear; only believe.' They continued to the house. As they approached they could hear the mourners crying with loud piercing cries. They could hear the flute players playing very sad music. Jesus told them to stop because the girl was just asleep but they laughed at him and said, 'She is dead.' It was a pity Jesus could not have come earlier.

Jesus asked all the people to leave the house. Then, with the girl's parents and three of his disciples, Peter, James and John, he went into the room where the girl was. They could all see she was dead. Jesus went over and took hold of her hands – they were so cold. Then in a gentle voice he said, 'Little girl, get up.' He helped her to sit up. She opened her eyes and smiled. Everyone was amazed. Jesus told them not to tell anyone yet as the girl would need rest. She would also need some food as she had not eaten for a while and was weak. Jairus was so thankful that he had made contact with Jesus.

Activity

Everyone sits down in a circle. Choose someone to walk around the circle and touch another person who jumps up. The one who touched her runs around the circle in a clockwise direction and she runs in an anticlockwise direction. The race is to get back to the empty place and sit down. The one who is last has to go around and touch someone and it begins again.

Prayer

Lord Jesus, you help all who come to you
and never turn anyone away.
We thank you for your healing of the daughter of Jairus
and the curing of the older lady.
Help us to trust in you
and to keep in contact through our prayers.
Amen.

Song

I'm putting my hand in your hand

TORCHES

Aim

To show Jesus is the Lord of life.

Teaching

Let us look at two people who have a lot in common: one was 12 years old and the other had been ill for 12 years. The younger one was about to die and the older one was excluded from life by her illness. One was the daughter of Jairus; Jesus calls the other one 'Daughter'. Both needed healing and their only hope was in Jesus.

The child had suddenly taken ill in the year she was to be counted as grown up. At 12, the same age as some of you, she was counted as a woman and old enough to get married. She should be beginning to find life exciting but it was not to be because she was ill. Her parents had tried to find help but no doctor could cure her. Jairus decided to ask Jesus for help. Jairus was a rich man but money cannot buy health. He was a man in authority but he could not have command over life and death. He hoped Jesus, who had been healing people, might be able to do something for his daughter.

When he found Jesus there were already crowds around him seeking help and listening to what he said. Jairus managed to get through the crowd and threw himself down at the feet of Jesus and begged for help. The rich man begged from the man who did not own anything. Jesus saw the sadness in the man's eyes and offered to go home with him.

The crowd followed and were all jostling each other. Suddenly Jesus stopped and asked, 'Who touched me?' The disciples tried to say it could have been anyone because there were so many people in the crowd. Jesus knew power had gone out from him and said again, 'Who touched me?' Obviously, every time Jesus healed, power was used and it cost him something. The woman who suffered from constant bleeding admitted she had touched him. She should not have been there because her illness made her unclean in Jewish law. Touching Jesus would make him unclean. But Jesus saw her need. In faith she had made contact. Jesus said, 'Daughter, your faith has made you well; go in peace and be healed of your disease.'

How wonderful for her, but for Jairus it was a sad moment. Someone came to tell him his daughter was dead and it was no use bringing Jesus. Jesus saw the pain in the man's eyes and the tears, and promised to still go with him. He said, 'Do not fear; only believe.' Jairus wanted to but what could Jesus do now? Already the professional mourners and flute players were making sad sounds. Jesus told them the girl was not dead, only sleeping, but they just laughed at him. He sent them all out of the house and went in with the girl's mother and father, and with Peter, James and John. They went to where the little girl lay dead on the bed. Jesus went over and took her by the hands. Her hands were cold and Jesus held them until they felt warmer. Then he said, 'Little girl, get up.' He helped her and she arose from the dead as if out of sleep. Jesus then told the parents that the girl would need something to eat, as she had not been able to eat for a while.

Activity

Talk about people making contact with Jesus. You may like to show that Jesus often touched people. Let the group act out this story. You need main characters such as Jairus, the woman in the crowd, the little girl and Jesus. After talking about it for a while choose those who seem to have a good idea of what the story is about.

Prayer

Lord Jesus, we are sorry
when we have lost contact with you,
when we have forgotten our prayers
or thought we were too busy.
We seek your presence and your healing power
in our lives.
Amen.

Song

Jesus, touch me now

Proper 9

Sunday between 3 and 9 July inclusive

Aim

To show Jesus has work for us but will not force himself or his work upon us.

Preparation

Have a large print of Holman Hunt's picture 'The Light of the World'.

Opening activity

Three people are needed for this.

Person 1 Knock, knock.
Person 2 Go away, I am too busy.
Person 1 Knock, knock.
Person 2 I cannot be bothered, I'm watching television.
Person 1 Knock, knock.
Person 2 I have had enough of this. (Puts on a personal CD player)
Person 1 Pity there is no one at home. They were chosen to receive £1000. I will give it to the person next door.
Person 3 Jesus says, 'Behold, I stand at the door and knock.' He will not force his way in to your life. Will you let him in?

Opening prayer

Lord, awaken us to your call.
Open our ears to hear your words,
open our eyes to your presence,
open our hands with your generosity,
open our hearts to your love,
that we may live and work for you,
Jesus Christ our Lord.
Amen.

Opening song

Will you come and follow me

Readings

2 Samuel 5:1-5, 9-10 or Ezekiel 2:1-5
Psalm 48 or Psalm 123
2 Corinthians 12:2-10
Mark 6:1-13

Thought for the day

Not everyone welcomed Jesus: that should be obvious from the crucifixion. Jesus was often scorned and rejected and not always popular. It is to be expected that if Jesus was not popular, then his disciples and followers would not be popular either.

Often what stops people accepting Jesus is their pride and prejudice. Jesus is not given a chance because people have made up their minds before they meet him.

It was quite natural for Jesus to turn up at Nazareth where he lived most of his life. He went to the synagogue and taught but the people could not hear him because of their prejudice. 'How can he preach? Is he not a carpenter? Let him get back to making furniture.' They saw Jesus as a craftsman, but could not see him as a preacher. They could see him as he was, but could not accept him for what he had become. He had changed but they were unwilling to. Sadly, some would think he could not have a great message because he was just a working man. Where did he get his wisdom from, for he was no scholar!

They knew his family, his mother Mary, his four brothers James and Joses, Judas and Simon, and his sisters. Here we get a glimpse of home at Nazareth. Jesus was not an only child. He grew up in what we would consider a large family. Joseph is not mentioned so it is likely he was dead. As Jesus was the first-born, he probably had to work hard to help to bring up this family, and that is why he is still at Nazareth until he is about 30 (Luke 3:3). The people who knew his family would not accept that Jesus could achieve anything special because he was so ordinary in their eyes, and so they rejected him. How can a carpenter preach? Such prejudice has hindered many a good man or woman. Even though Jesus cured some sick people, the people of Nazareth could not see his power. There is none so blind as those who do not want to see.

Jesus was amazed at their unbelief. He knew them and did not expect it from them. Before he left he said, 'Prophets are not without honour, except in their home town, and among their own kin, and in their own house.' This is a very sad statement from Jesus.

When people refuse to hear, Jesus moves on; he goes to other villages. Jesus never forces himself on anyone. We all have the choice to accept him as our Lord and our Friend or to ignore him. Many are not antagonistic to Jesus; they just cannot be bothered to put themselves out. When Jesus is ignored or rejected he will move on unless we call him back.

He also sent his disciples out in twos giving them some of his power over unclean spirits. They were to go out in his strength, not their own. They were to go out in faith without taking provisions, financial protection or the security of extra clothing. They were to travel light. Likewise, we do not need degrees or theological training; we do not need special qualifications. We need to know Jesus. We need to be sent by him. This is what makes an Apostolic Church: people who are called and sent by Jesus. They were not to take a collecting bag because they were to give rather than seek to receive. The Church needs money to survive but if raising money is its priority, it is giving out a wrong message. Like our God, we are to give more than we demand.

The disciples were not sent out to create a message. They went out as Christ's messengers; evangelists are 'good news tellers'. In a sense all are called to be 'angels' – that is, God's messengers. The mission of the disciples is to share in the mission of Jesus. 'As the Father has sent me, so I send you' (John 20:21).

The message of the disciples begins as Jesus began: 'Repent' (Mark 1:15). It is a call to turn around: turn around because you are going in the wrong direction. This is a call that disturbs, a call to be aware of where we are going and to accept that we can change.

The disciples revealed the mercy – the loving kindness – of God in bringing liberty and healing. Like Jesus, they were not to force themselves on anyone. God respects our freedom. 'If any place will not welcome you and they refuse to hear you, shake off the dust that is on your feet as a testimony against them' (Mark 6:11).

Question time

How does our church express the mission of Jesus? When do we proclaim the message to those outside and show them acts of mercy, revealing the loving kindness of God?

Do we see that all who are called by Jesus are involved in his mission, including every one of you?

Illustration

In the totalitarian state you are not allowed free choice. You must do as you are told. If you do not open your door to the officials, it will be broken down. You cannot hide because they will seek you out and make you do what they want.

Jesus is different. He has the power but he will not force himself upon you. The choice is yours: he respects your free will. You can edge him out of your life and home if you so choose. You can be too busy to bother to keep in contact with him if you so desire. He will not force you.

If you look at Holman Hunt's picture you will see the door has not been opened for a long time. Jesus stands there knocking and waiting to bring his light upon those who live within. There is no means of opening the door from the outside. If he is to enter, you have to let him in. It is good to think of these words of Jesus every day: 'Behold, I stand at the door and knock' (Revelation 3:20).

Intercessions

Blessed are you, Lord God, giver of life and light.
You give us of your love:
you give us of yourself.
Open our ears to your call and our hearts to your love.
Send us out in the power of your Spirit
to proclaim the Good News of your saving love
as revealed in our Saviour Jesus Christ.
Blessed are you, Father, Son and Holy Spirit.

We give thanks that you sent Jesus to live among us.
We pray that we may share in his mission,
that we may pass on the message of the Gospel
and show acts of mercy that reveal God's love.
May your whole Church be moved to share
in the ministry that is theirs.
We remember today all involved in the healing ministry.
We ask you to bless all counsellors, spiritual directors
and all who lead us in our ministry.

Silence

Lord, hear us:
show us your loving kindness.

We remember all who are suffering
under totalitarian states,
all who are oppressed
and forced to do what they do not want to do.
We ask your blessing on all who are seeking
to bring liberty and freedom to captive peoples.
Give courage and strength
to all who are working for relief agencies
and generosity to all who are called upon
to support them in their work.

Silence

Lord, hear us:
show us your loving kindness.

We give thanks for our homes and loved ones.
Through our families teach us to be sensitive
to the needs of others;
help us to listen carefully and to respond quickly.
We ask your blessing upon all
who have stopped communicating properly
with each other,
that they may again be awakened
to those with whom they live and work.

Silence

Lord, hear us:
show us your loving kindness.

We give thanks that you, O God, care for us,
body, mind and spirit.
We remember in your presence all suffering people.
We pray especially for those who feel no one listens
or cares.
We ask you to bless all who are homeless,
all who are deeply in debt.
We pray for all who are drug addicts
and all who cannot cope with life.
We remember all who are ill in our own community.

Silence

Lord, hear us:
show us your loving kindness.

We rejoice in the Good News of eternal life.
We remember in your presence
friends and loved ones who are departed from us.
We share with them in the fellowship of all your saints
and commend them and ourselves to your unfailing love.

Silence

Merciful Father,
accept these prayers
for the sake of your Son,
our Saviour Jesus Christ.
Amen.

Memory verse

Behold, I stand at the door and knock.
Revelation 3:20

Suggested music

Lord, you call us to a journey
Thy hand, O God, has guided
We have a gospel to proclaim

CANDLES

Aim

To show that Jesus wants us to listen and to talk about him to others.

Teaching

Who knows how many disciples Jesus had? It was twelve. (Let us count to twelve.) They were his special friends who went with him and listened to all that he told them. They listened carefully to him. (Let us be very quiet and listen. Do you hear any sounds?) We will play a listening game. (Choose someone to make the sound of an animal and the rest have to guess what it is. The one who gets it right can make the next sound.)

Naughty Nigel never listened. When someone was talking to him he often talked as well. He did not want to hear when he was told to go and do something so he kept his ears shut. At school he did not learn because he would not listen. When his mummy spoke to him he did not hear because he was listening to the television. When his daddy asked him to do something he did not hear because he was thinking about his toys. Naughty Nigel would not listen. He was told not to go into an old building because it was dangerous. Nigel would not listen and went in with another naughty boy. They climbed some old stairs but when they got near the top, the stairs all fell down and so did Nigel and his friend. Nigel had to go to hospital with a broken leg. He knew this had happened because he would not listen. From now on he promised to listen carefully.

Jesus wanted his twelve disciples to go and tell other people about him. He chose the twelve because they listened to him and went around with him. They knew him best of all. He sent them out to villages and towns to tell people the Good News of God's love and to heal people and make them well again. He sent them out in twos so that they could help each other and be friends with each other. If there were twelve and they were sent out in twos, how many twos were there? (Get twelve children to come out and divide them into twos to show it was six twos. Let the children count the twelve and the six.)

Wherever the disciples went people welcomed them because they had Good News to tell them. The disciples showed the people the power of Jesus by healing and helping them. But there were some people who would not listen. Some people said they were too busy. Some could not be bothered. Others talked too much to hear anyone else but themselves. So some people missed the Good News and some people missed being made well again. It was rather sad that they would not listen. When the disciples came back and told Jesus, he was sorry that some would not listen. But some did not listen even to him.

Now I will see who has been listening. I will ask you some questions. (Review today's lesson, which is quite hard for little ones.) Jesus likes people who are able to listen carefully and then tell others about him. Tell me what you know about Jesus.

Activity

We will play 'Sleepy tigers'. One person must sit out in front and count to ten. She watches whilst the others lie down and go to sleep. The tigers must not move at all. Anyone who is seen moving must sit out with the person at the front and watch for twitching tigers. The last person is the King of the Jungle and becomes the next one to count.

Prayer

Jesus, we love you and like being quiet with you.
We like the stories about you
and that you want us to be your disciples.
Amen.

Song

I'm singing your praise, Lord

LAMPS

Aim

To show how Jesus sends us out to be his heralds.

Teaching

Jesus went to his hometown. Who knows its name? He had brothers and sisters who lived there and his mother lived there. He had lots of friends who lived there. They remembered when he worked as a carpenter. Now he came back as a teacher with twelve of his followers. But people could not believe he was anybody special or that he had a message. 'How can he be special? We know his mum and all his family. He only trained as a carpenter – how can he teach us?' They closed their ears and would not listen. Not everybody listened to or followed Jesus, not even in Nazareth. In fact, Jesus found it harder to speak to people in Nazareth than in lots of other places.

Because the disciples listened to Jesus and loved him they were ready to be sent out to tell others about him. Can you remember the names of the disciples? There were four at least who were fishermen: Andrew, Peter, James and John. Andrew and Peter were brothers. James and John were also brothers.

Matthew was a tax collector and before he became a disciple people did not like him. Because he listened to Jesus when Jesus said, 'Follow me', he became a much nicer man. We know that Thomas was a twin and that Simon was someone that longed for freedom. We know that Judas would later betray Jesus. The names of the other disciples were another James, possibly called Junior, Philip and Bartholomew and Thaddaeus. We know very little about some of them except that they listened to Jesus when he called them and they went with him listening to his stories and teaching.

Jesus sent the twelve out in twos, so that they could support each other and put across the message of Jesus with more power. They went out to share in the work of Jesus, teaching and healing in his name. When they came back, all had the same sort of report. People were healed; people listened and decided to turn to God. But some would not listen. Some closed their ears and their doors to the message. The disciples could not reach them. Jesus told them they should not be surprised, for even at Nazareth some would not listen to him. Wherever people listened the church grew and a new way of life was discovered.

If our community, our village, our town or your friends are to know about Jesus, it needs someone to tell them about him. We learn about Jesus and his love not to keep it to ourselves but so that we can go out and tell others about him.

Activity

Play 'Chinese whispers'. Get the group to gather in a circle. Pass a message around and see how much it changes as it comes back to the beginning. You might like to pass around, 'God gave us two ears and one mouth so that we should listen twice as much as we speak.' People must pass on as much as they think they remember. At the end of each round congratulate them on a well-passed-on message, or have a laugh at such distorted messages and comment on listening.

Prayer

Lord Jesus, you call us to be your disciples.
Give us ears to hear your call and the will to obey you.
By listening to you
may we be able to tell others of your love and your power.
Amen.

Song

Jesus is a friend of mine

TORCHES

Aim

To discover that Jesus sends us to be his heralds.

Teaching

Who is your favourite pop star or footballer? Do you bother to listen to them or to go where they are? Would you put yourself out to go to a match or a concert? Maybe you collect photographs, cuttings, booklets about them. Then you tell your friends how good the star or the player performs: you will often talk about them. It is you and people like you that help to make them popular. You make their name and their actions known. You can call yourself a fan. Sometimes, when talking about stars, we say, 'He/she sends me.' This is short-hand for saying they send us into raptures of joy; they send us to copy them as best we can; they send us to tell others about them. We will give as much time as we can to be with them, to listen to them, to talk about them.

So it was with Jesus and his disciples. They gave up their jobs as fishermen, tax collector and whatever else to be with Jesus, to listen to him and to do what he asked. They were with Jesus when he went to his hometown of Nazareth. They thought he would get a good hearing there but they were wrong. Many people would not listen to his teaching because they remembered him as just a carpenter or as a lad from the town. Prejudice stopped them hearing. It is amazing how many cannot hear Jesus because they keep their ears, their minds and their hearts closed. Some keep their doors firmly closed. Yet the Church grows because there are always people who need to hear and who need the help of Jesus.

When they had been with him long enough to know of him and his teaching, Jesus sent the disciples out. They became 'Apostles'; that means 'those who are sent'. They were sent by the love and the power of Jesus. They were sent out in his name and his strength. Jesus sent them in twos for their own safety but also so that they could help and encourage each other. He sent them with no extra resources except to have faith in him. They did not go out to collect money; only to tell of Jesus and give of their time. Jesus sent them as heralds to proclaim the Good News. They had a mission – they were sent by Jesus. They had a message – they spoke about Jesus and the love of God. They did acts of mercy; they healed and brought peace in the name of Jesus.

Jesus has called us to know him so that we might experience his love and power. And we are to pass it on. We are called to be Apostles, those sent by Jesus. We have a mission and a message, and we are to show acts of mercy. This is the joy and duty of every church member – to proclaim the Good News, to be heralds of Jesus.

Activity

Get the group to split up into threes with one listener and two speakers. The speakers have to tell the listener what they know about Jesus. Get the speakers to understand they have to talk of Jesus in the present tense and not relegate him to history. The speakers should encourage one another and fill gaps in what the other says. One of the speakers should end with a short prayer to Jesus.

Prayer

Loving Father, help us to listen carefully
to the call of Jesus.
Give us a love for him that sends us out
to tell others of his power and his greatness.
May we share in his mission and in his message
by the way we live and speak.
Amen.

Song

I believe in Jesus

Proper 10

Sunday between 10 and 16 July inclusive

Aim

To compare the rule of Herod with the rule of Jesus.

Preparation

Have posters from Amnesty International. Show people who are in camps and in prison because they disagree with the regime of their country.

Opening activity

Have a group who are tied with ropes or chains walk down the church and sit down. Choose people who can sing 'We shall overcome', and have a verse, 'Our God shall make us free'.

Opening prayer

O God our King, we thank you
for the glorious liberty you give to us.
We rejoice in our freedom
and pray that we may use it
to your praise and glory;
through Jesus Christ our Lord.
Amen.

Opening song

The King is among us

Readings

2 Samuel 6:1-5, 12b-19 or Amos 7:7-15
Psalm 24 or Psalm 85:8-13
Ephesians 1:3-14
Mark 6:14-29

Thought for the day

You could present today's Gospel as a history lesson and show the dangerous times John the Baptist and Jesus lived in. But on its own none of that is very uplifting. As Mark and Matthew put the feeding of the 5000 next to the murder of John the Baptist, it is good to compare the events. We can look at the rule of Caesar compared to the rule of God: a way of death compared to the way of life.

Herod Antipas was the puppet ruler of Galilee. He served Rome and used military force to make his rule work. If anyone opposed him, he had them imprisoned or even put to death. John the Baptist had two faults in the eyes of Herod. First, John was popular with the people. Herod was afraid he might lead a rebellion. Like all tyrants he lived nervously and was suspicious of any popular person. Second, he saw John as dangerous because he spoke out against him and told the truth. Herod did not want to know the truth. To keep himself secure in power he had John imprisoned in the Castle of Machaerus on the east side of the Dead Sea. It is perched up on bare rocks and is one of the grimmest castles in the world. You can still see the dungeons where John the Baptist was imprisoned.

On his birthday Herod threw a feast for the rich and the famous. It was for members of the royal court, political leaders and officials – for people of influence. Herod was out to get what he could. His wife Herodias, who had been his brother's wife, was there. She had a seething anger against John the Baptist because he had objected to her marriage, and she wanted him killed. Their daughter Salome was also there and danced before them. This shows how decadent the court was as it was usually only loose women and prostitutes who danced before them. The ordinary women and slaves were counted as nobodies, not people but things to use, and they waited on the company. For their entertainment Salome danced, and to add to the entertainment she is offered whatever she would like. At the direction of her mother, she asks for John the Baptist's head. John was beheaded in prison and his head presented on a platter to Salome and she in turn presented it to her mother. Obviously this is not a safe place to be. This is the rule of force where people count for little and life is cheap.

The feast Jesus has is for any who come. He does not want to force them to do anything. He looks on them with compassion, caring for their needs. The poor, the needy, the hungry, those whom the world counts as nobodies, come to him. He gives them his attention. Such people would not have got anywhere near Herod. Jesus treats the poor and needy like royalty. He asks them to sit down (the word he uses actually means lie down) and his disciples wait upon them. (You may like to read out Mark 10:42-44). Jesus practised what he preached. He came to give and to care; not to take life but to save life. Jesus came not to proclaim his own rule but to bring in the rule of God through his love and sacrifice. This is the rule of love where everyone is counted as important.

To proclaim God is King is to challenge that the earthly ruler is almighty. It acknowledges a greater power. For this, Jesus will meet death as John the Baptist did.

Question time

Do we show God's kingdom in the way we deal with people?

Has our church a programme for helping the needy and the rejected?

Illustration

So many rulers rule by force. They often think of their subjects as objects for their own selfish ends. If people do not obey, there are ways of dealing with them, which include torture, imprisonment and even death. Dictators throughout history have got rid of those who opposed them by exterminating them; there are many tyrannical governments in our world that still operate like this.

The kingdom of heaven is the free gift of God's presence and love to us. It is not forced upon us but is offered freely. God loves us before we even turn to him. We are not rejected from his kingdom. We leave it of our own free will when we do not obey the King in love.

Intercessions

Blessed are you,
the God and Father of our Lord Jesus Christ,
who has blessed us with every spiritual blessing.
You have destined us for the glorious freedom
of the children of God.
You have given us of your love and of yourself.
May we rejoice in your rule
and in the coming of your kingdom.
Blessed are you, Father, Son and Holy Spirit,
one God for ever and ever.

Father, we give you thanks for John the Baptist
and the way he stood against an evil regime.
We thank you for the gift of your kingdom to us.
We rejoice in our freedom
and the freedom of our Church and country.
We ask that your Church may reflect your love
in the way it cares for the outcast and the needy.
We remember all who are persecuted for their faith
or for making a stand against evil.
We pray especially for Christians who are seeking
to improve corrupt societies and governments.

Silence

Show us your loving kindness, O Lord,
and grant us your salvation.

We give you thanks for the work of the United Nations
and its efforts to bring peace and unity to our world.
We pray for all who are caught up in war and violence.
We remember those who have lost loved ones
and those who do not know where their loved ones are.
We ask your blessing
on the work of Amnesty International
and all who risk their lives for the freedom of others.

Silence

Show us your loving kindness, O Lord,
and grant us your salvation.

Father, may our homes reflect the love and unity
of your kingdom.
Bless our families and friends
with the joy of your presence.
We ask your love to strengthen
all who are in homes where there is oppression
and where lives are not valued.

Silence

Show us your loving kindness, O Lord,
and grant us your salvation.

God, we thank you for the freedom you have won for us
in our Saviour Jesus Christ.
We remember before you all who are slaves to sin and vice.
We pray for drug addicts, alcoholics,
those who gamble away their lives.
We remember also those who are imprisoned
by their illness or incapacity
and who long for a fuller and richer life.

Silence

Show us your loving kindness, O Lord,
and grant us your salvation.

Lord, we pray for the time
when your kingdom will come
on earth as it is in heaven.
We long for justice and freedom for all peoples.
We join our prayers with our loved ones departed
and all your saints,
praying that we may all know your rule
and enjoy your presence.

Silence

Merciful Father,
accept these prayers
for the sake of your Son,
our Saviour Jesus Christ.
Amen.

Memory verse

The Lord of hosts, he is the King of glory.
Psalm 24:10

Suggested music

Thy kingdom come, O God
On Jordan's bank the Baptist's cry
Compassion walks the city streets

CANDLES

Aim

To show the wickedness of Herod and the goodness of God's kingdom.

Teaching

Once there was a wicked king who lived in a big castle beside the Dead Sea. If he did not like what you said, he sent his soldiers to capture and put you in his prison. His prison was underneath the castle and it was dark and cold and damp. This king was called Herod. John the Baptist, who was a cousin of Jesus, said King Herod should not be so wicked. He should turn away from wickedness and do good. This just made the king angry. He sent his soldiers and took John a prisoner. He had him put in the dungeons of his castle.

The wicked King Herod had a birthday and he asked all sorts of people to his party. He asked people from his palace, and he asked important people, rich people. He asked those who would help him and give him things. At the party his daughter Salome came and danced for them. The king was very pleased with her dancing and offered her a present – anything she wanted. What do you think you would choose? She could have silver or jewels or gold, even part of the king's kingdom. She thought for a moment or two and then asked her mother what she should ask for. Her mother, Herodias, did not like John the Baptist and she asked for a terrible thing. She asked for the head of John the Baptist on a plate. Even though the king was wicked he did not want to do this. I think he was a little frightened of John the Baptist. But he promised. So he sent his soldiers down into the prison to where John was and had John's head cut off and put on a plate. It was a terrible thing to do but it pleased the wicked queen. John's friends came and took his body away and buried it.

Not far away was another King, though most people did not know he was a king. He did not have a castle and he did not wear rich clothes. He did not have soldiers to protect him. He only had twelve friends who went with him and helped him. He also had a party. It was not his birthday but he saw that the people were hungry and tired and he wanted to help them. He did not check to see if they were rich or poor. He loved them and got his friends, the disciples, to feed them. Who knows the name of this kind king?

Jesus wants us all to be happy and to be free to do what is good and kind in this world. He wants to help us as much as he can.

Which king would you like to look after you: the wicked King Herod or Jesus the King of love? (Let the children explore this for a while.)

Activity

Have five cards with a large club on one side and a large heart on the other side. The corners of the room will each have a person with a card and there will be someone in the centre of the room with a card. The children run around the room to music. When the music stops they must run to a corner. The people with cards in the corners will produce them and show a black club or a red heart. Black clubs are for the wicked king and all these children are out. If all cards are black, the person in the centre shows a red heart and all are set free to run again. The corners with the red hearts are corners for the King of love: when the music starts the children in red corners can join the game again.

Prayer

Jesus, you are the King of love.
We thank you for being so kind and gentle.
Help us to be kind and gentle too.
Amen.

Song

We're the kids of the King

LAMPS

Aim

To know the danger of speaking out and the call to be brave.

Teaching

High on rocky cliffs stood a grim castle. People who were taken there often disappeared. It was called the Castle of Machaerus and it had dungeons for putting prisoners in. This was Herod's castle and here he would have his birthday party. He invited all sorts of important people – politicians, members of the royal court and people with lots of money. He promised them a feast and good entertainment. There was one person already in the castle who would not be invited and that was John the Baptist.

Do you remember how John baptised Jesus in the river Jordan? John went around telling people to turn away from their wicked ways and to turn to God. Some people listened but some did not. Some wicked people were annoyed because John said their way of life was evil. Amongst those annoyed with John were King Herod and his wife Herodias. John had told them they should not have been married because Herodias was really the wife of Herod's brother. Herod was worried that John the Baptist was becoming more popular than he was and thought he might lead the people against him. So Herod put John in the dungeons, in the castle prison. He knew that John would still speak out against him if he were free, so he put him in prison.

Whilst John was in prison in the castle dungeon the party continued upstairs. There were slaves and ordinary people all waiting upon those who were counted as important. During the evening Herod's daughter Salome danced before the crowds. Herod thought it was a wonderful dance and offered her anything she would like, even half of his kingdom. Salome went to her mother, who was still very angry with John the Baptist, and asked what she should have from her father Herod. Her mother said, 'Ask for the head of John the Baptist on a platter.'

Salome went to her father and said, 'Do you promise I can have whatever I ask?'

'I promise,' said Herod.

'Then I would like the head of John the Baptist on a silver platter.'

Herod never expected this, but he had promised and said he would keep his promise. He sent soldiers down into the prison where John was. They made him kneel down and bow his head: then, with a large sword, they cut off his head. It was taken and given to Herod, who gave it to Salome, who gave it to her mother.

John died because he had spoken the truth. He spoke against evil and wanted people to serve God. It is often dangerous to speak the truth but as God's people we are called to do this without fear. We should know if we try to do good, evil will try to stop us. But evil would always win if good people did nothing.

John's friends came to the prison after the party and took away his body and buried it.

Activity

Choose a Herod. As Herod walks around the room everyone follows him. You all ask loudly, 'How are you today, Herod?' If he turns and replies, 'I am OK,' in a moment you start following him again. If he says, 'I am angry,' everyone must run as fast as they can back to the start. The one Herod catches or the last one home is the next Herod.

Prayer

God, we thank you for the bravery and courage
of John the Baptist.
Make us strong to stand for all that is good
and to show our love for you.
Amen.

Song

Jesus, you are my King

TORCHES

Aim

To show how speaking out for God can be dangerous.

Teaching

Because there is evil in the world and there are evil people, those who love God must speak out against evil. It has been said that evil triumphs when good people do nothing. As Christians we are called to stand against evil but we must realise how dangerous that can be. Many holy people have been persecuted and put to death because they spoke the truth.

John the Baptist was put into the prison of Herod's castle beside the Dead Sea because he spoke against King Herod and his evil ways. John also objected to Herod marrying Herodias, his brother's wife, because it was wrong.

During celebrations at the castle for Herod's birthday his daughter Salome danced before all the guests. Herod thought this was wonderful and he offered her anything she wanted. He was probably drunk at the time. Salome then asked her mother what she should have. Her mother said, 'Ask for the head of John the Baptist.' Salome went back to her father and said, 'You promised I can have anything I want. I want the head of John the Baptist on a silver platter.' Herod was not too pleased with this request but he kept his promise. John was beheaded in the prison and his head was presented to Salome and Herodias on a silver dish. For speaking the truth John had been put to death by wicked people. His disciples came after the party was over and buried his body.

In 1884 Mwanga became the king of Buganda (now Uganda). When three of his people, obeying a Christain missionary, disobeyed his instructions he had them executed. Mwanga was angered that Christians obeyed a higher authority than himself and ordered their execution. More than 46 Roman Catholics and Anglicans were martyred (explain this word): most of them died by being burnt to death on Ascension Day 1886.

In the 1970s, when Idi Amin and Obote were presidents of Uganda, Christians were always in danger for speaking the truth. Janani Luwum, who had been a goatherd but trained to be a teacher, was converted to Christianity. In 1969 he became the Archbishop of Uganda. Soon after Janani and his fellow bishops complained about the wickedness of Idi Amin in a letter, Janani was killed in a road accident. It was discovered that he had died at the instructions of Idi Amin: it was not an accident but a planned killing. Janani had been willing to risk his life because he believed in Jesus. He died for his faith on 17 February 1977.

Activity

Let the group explore the idea of martyrdom. Look at the quotations on the worksheet and let them discuss openly their reactions to what is said. Look at areas where we ought to speak out today. Are we making a stand against the evils of today? How do we personally make a difference?

Prayer

Holy and strong God, we trust in you.
Help us to stand against all evil
and to seek to tell others of your goodness.
Give us courage in troubles
but, above all, help us to know you are always with us.
We ask this in the name of Jesus
who died for us and who rose again.
Amen.

Song

Majesty

Proper 11

Sunday between 17 and 23 July inclusive

Aim

To show that we need times of quietness and rest.

Preparation

Have a large notice at the entrance to the church saying, 'Please switch off your engine.' Have the cards described below written out, and images of what each child is meant to be.

Opening activity

At the beginning of the service have five children running around the church: one using a mobile phone, one playing with a power-driven toy, one driving an imaginary car (making the noises), one with a drill (making the noises), one with a light. At a given signal they have to all run to the front and switch off. Standing in the order arranged beforehand, they will pick up large cards which read: 'We / have / run / out / of power.' They must stand as still as possible for 30 seconds and then turn over their cards to reveal 'They that / wait upon / the Lord / shall renew their / strength.' Give everyone time to see this and then the children run back to their places. Keep another silence.

Opening prayer

Holy and Strong One, ever-loving God,
we come into the stillness to rejoice in your presence,
to give ourselves to you
and to wait upon your renewing power.
Lord, help us to know you are always with us
and that you are our strength and hope.
Amen.

Opening song

Be still, for the presence of the Lord

Readings

2 Samuel 7:1-14a or Jeremiah 23:1-6
Psalm 89:20-37 or Psalm 23
Ephesians 2:11-22
Mark 6:30-34, 53-56

Thought for the day

When the disciples returned from their mission they gathered around Jesus and told him what they had done and taught. The crowds of people had kept them so busy they did not even have time to eat. Jesus said to them they should now go to a deserted place and rest. Here we see the balance of the Christian life. The Christian life is built up of going to the presence of God for refreshment, renewal and guidance and then going to people. The Christian learns to go to God with people in their heart and to people with God in their heart. No human can forever pour themselves out; there needs to be time for rest and renewal. If we have not spent time before God, we will not be able to introduce others to him.

There are two main dangers for everyone. The first is one of constant activity – and some church groups are like that. No one can work without rest: we cannot proclaim God unless we spend time quietly before him. Many Christians run out of resources or even faith because they have not learnt to be still and quiet before God. Our God is unable to be our strength because we are not still enough and quiet enough before him.

The second danger is that of too much withdrawal – though most churches cannot be charged with this. Devotion should lead to action. Awareness of God and his love should make us proclaim his goodness: prayer should lead to work. To turn to God is not to turn away from our fellow beings but to prepare us for caring and sharing with them in a better way.

Yet the rest the disciples sought was not to be. The crowds noted the direction Jesus took and they followed. The boat had a four-mile journey to cross the lake: it was a ten-mile walk for the crowd. No doubt some of this crowd set off and actually got there as quickly as Jesus. The boat journey was their only time of rest.

It would be easy to get frustrated with the demands of the people but Jesus was sorry for them. They were like sheep without a shepherd. They needed a guide and someone to care for them. They needed someone to love them and look after them. Let us see what Jesus meant by thinking of people as sheep without a shepherd.

Sheep without a shepherd lose their way. How right we are when we say, 'We have erred and strayed from your ways like lost sheep.' We need a guide and a travelling companion to prevent us from getting lost. Sadly, for so many today there is no knowledge of guidance or a companion.

Sheep without a caring shepherd can soon starve. So often people are undernourished in spirit. They might look well-fed but there is an emptiness within that nothing can fill except a relationship with God.

Sheep without a shepherd are in constant danger. The sheep cannot defend itself against wild beasts or from robbers. There are many things that can take away our life unless we discover eternal life in Jesus our Lord.

Question time

Is there enough quiet time in our church life and in our own private devotions?

Have we learnt to come to God with people in our heart and to come to people with God in our heart?

Illustration

There was a famous General who met a poor shepherd. The shepherd was distressed because he had lost a lamb and could not find it. The General offered to help and sent his soldiers in search of the lamb. One by one the soldiers returned to camp hungry, muddied and feeling too tired to carry on. It was dark by then and they felt they could do nothing more. The next morning, just as it was getting light, the General was seen coming into the camp carrying the lamb under his greatcoat to keep it warm. This is what made him such a great leader: he was not put off and he did not think of himself too much. He only stopped looking for the lamb when he found it. (You can compare this to the Good Shepherd.)

Intercessions

Blessed are you, Lord of our salvation:
to you be praise and glory for ever.
When we have erred and strayed,
you seek us out:
your love searches for us and desires to bring us home
to the light of your presence.
As we rejoice in your Son as the Good Shepherd,
stir in us the same compassion for others
as you have for us,
that we may help to reveal your glory in the world.
Blessed are you, Father, Son and Holy Spirit.

Loving God, we give you thanks that you have called us
to share in showing your compassion to the world.
Bless all who are called to be pastors, priests and ministers;
all who preach the word and administer the sacraments.
Give to your whole Church
a sense of mission and outreach,
that it may share in your redemption.
We remember before you all who lead retreats
and quiet days
and all who help us to see the value of silent prayer
and waiting upon you.

Silence

Lord, we come before you;
in you is our peace.

We give thanks for all those who care for sheep and cattle;
all who provide us with food and the necessities of life.
We ask your blessing
upon all who have been made homeless or stateless:
we pray for asylum seekers and refugees.
We remember in your presence
all who are suffering from hunger or poverty
and we pray for all who are seeking to care for them.

Silence

Lord, we come before you;
in you is our peace.

Loving Father, we give you thanks for our lives
and all that we have.
We seek your blessing upon our homes
and our loved ones.
We pray for members of our community
who are suffering from loneliness, debt
or the inability to cope with what is happening to them.

Silence

Lord, we come before you;
in you is our peace.

You are our hope and strength, O Lord.
We come to you for refreshment and renewal.
When we are weak, may we trust in your strength.
When we are fearful, may we turn to you and your light.
We pray for all who are struggling at this time.
We remember before you the troubled in mind
and the distressed in spirit.
We ask your blessing upon friends and loved ones
who are ill.
We pray especially
for any who have been recently taken into care.

Silence

Lord we come before you,
in you is our peace.

We give you thanks and praise
that through your Son we shall not perish
but have everlasting life.
We rejoice in the fellowship of all your saints.
We remember before you all our loved ones departed,
praying that they may know the fullness of your kingdom.

Silence

Merciful Father,
accept these prayers
for the sake of your Son,
our Saviour Jesus Christ.
Amen.

Memory verse

The Lord is my shepherd; I shall not be in want.
Psalm 23:1

Suggested music

Father, hear the prayer we offer
The King of love my shepherd is
Faithful Shepherd, feed me

CANDLES

Aim

To show that Jesus loves each one of us and wants us to love him.

Teaching

Do you know the story of the lost lamb? It was an adventurous little lamb which wanted to see what was around the next corner or over the top of the next hill. It walked and walked and walked, until it was tired. Then it lay down to sleep. When it woke it was still dark and it did not know where it was. It started to cry, 'Maa, maa, maa.' (Let us make that sound.) It was calling for its mother but its mother could not hear it. Again it cried, 'Maa, maa, maa.' (Let us make the sound again.) As it was getting light, the little lamb was very hungry and it was not very happy. It would never find its way home. Then it heard a lion growling and it was very frightened. It knew that lions eat little lambs. It stayed very quiet until the lion went away. Poor little lamb was lost and hungry. But the shepherd was a good man and he had been out all night looking for it. He shouted its name, 'Aggy.' For a long time he heard nothing; then, when he shouted 'Aggy', he heard a little cry. 'Maa, maa, maa.' He hurried to where the lamb was and picked it up, put it on his shoulders and carried it home to its mother.

Like the shepherd, Jesus cares for anyone who is hungry or lost. He looks for anyone who needs his help.

Jesus wants to help us if we are frightened or not very well. Jesus comes to be with and to help us. When people were hungry, Jesus fed them; when they were poorly, he made them well again; when they were in trouble, Jesus helped them. Jesus loves us and cares for us like a good shepherd cares for his sheep and lambs.

Activity

Play 'Lion and sheep'. This is another version of 'What time is it, Mr Wolf?'

The children follow behind the one chosen to be the Lion, saying, 'Baa, baa, baa, what are you doing?' The Lion replies, 'I am walking in the desert' and keeps on walking. When the Lion says, 'I am hungry', he chases the sheep and the one he catches or the last one back to the safety of base becomes the next lion.

Prayer

Jesus, thank you for loving us.
We know that you are the Good Shepherd
and that you care for us and come to us.
We give our love to you.
Amen.

Song

Jesus is our shepherd

LAMPS

Aim

To show that Jesus is never too busy to care for us.

Teaching

The disciples had been busy, busy, busy. Jesus had sent them out in twos to go and tell people about him. They walked a long way from village to village and town to town. They spoke about Jesus. They healed people who were sick. Crowds of people came to them and they hardly had time to have anything to eat. Sometimes they were very hungry and often they were tired. When they came back to Jesus, he saw that they were tired. It was time for them to rest. He suggested that they went on to the Sea of Galilee in a boat, probably belonging to one of the fishermen disciples, and cross to the other side of the lake. They would be on the sea for about four miles. During the journey they would get a little rest. It is possible the journey took about five hours.

Meanwhile, the people noticed the boat with Jesus in it going across the lake so they decided to follow him by walking around the lake. They walked about ten miles. That is as far as . . . (give an example) is from here. It was a long way for some of them to walk. Some hurried and got there as quickly as the disciples in the boat. When Jesus and the disciples were back on land, there were already people waiting for them. There were hundreds, soon thousands of people gathering around Jesus and the disciples. No one had any time for rest. They could have sent the people away but Jesus noticed how tired and hungry the people were: they also needed rest and looking after. He felt that the people were like sheep without a shepherd. They needed someone to look after them and help them. Jesus did not hesitate. He made sure all the people were fed and told them how God loved them. After this the disciples and Jesus would need a time of quiet and refreshment if they could get it. Whenever Jesus was very busy or had something important to do he always spent some time in quiet with God the Father.

Activity

Play 'Musical statues' with the emphasis on being absolutely still and quiet when the music stops. When the music plays, the group should rush about, mime activities, such as using a mobile, driving a car, doing schoolwork, playing sports. They can talk and shout when the music is on. But once the music stops the slightest sound or movement puts them out.

Prayer

God, teach us to be still and quiet before you,
so that we may know your love for us
and give our love to you.
In the stillness help us to know you are always with us
and that you care for every one of us.
Amen.

Song

Loving Shepherd of thy sheep

TORCHES

Aim

To encourage the group to create moments of stillness in their lives.

Teaching

Whenever Jesus was busy or had important decisions to make, he always spent some time in quietness and prayer. Jesus understood well that no human could for ever pour themselves out without some new in-pouring. Like a battery or a power pack, unless we are recharged every now and again, we will run out of power and energy. All humans need a time of rest and refreshment. How do you make sure you get yours? (Have a time when this is discussed. Follow it by a minute of silence.)

When St Patrick was 16 he was taken away from his home by invaders and made a slave in Ireland. He was kept busy working for his master and looking after sheep. This is what Patrick says of this time: 'In a day I prayed up to a hundred times and almost as many at night . . . Come hail, rain or snow, I was up before the dawn to pray . . . the Spirit was fervent in me.'

How often do you pray? Do you make sure there is time set aside each day for quiet prayer? (Spend some time discussing this.)

After the disciples had been busy sharing in the outreach of Jesus, Jesus said to them, 'Come away to a deserted place and rest a while.' The rest they got was possibly only a few hours on the Sea of Galilee because, as soon as they landed, crowds began to gather. At least they had that time with Jesus to themselves.

We need to make sure we get time with Jesus to ourselves. If the morning does not seem practical we have to make sure of another time in the day. Of course, if we are taking the power of the presence of God seriously, surely we need to start the day by affirming that we are in his presence.

Activity

Write prayers that can be used to start the day: prayers that affirm God is with us. As examples look at the beginning of a service. 'In the name (which means in the presence, in the love, in the power, in the peace) of God, the Father, Son and Holy Spirit.' Or learn to say every morning on rising, 'The Lord is here: his Spirit is with us (me).'

Prayer

Lord, unseen yet ever near,
your presence may we know
and rejoice that you are here,
your love and peace to show.

Song

The Lord's my shepherd

Proper 12

Sunday between 24 and 30 July inclusive

Aim

To show the care and concern of Jesus.

Preparation

Have a basket with five white bread rolls and two small fish. (The fish could be made of plastic or real.) The rolls could be used at communion if they have been kept away from the fish. Display a motorway sign for refreshments and have in large letters below it, 'Stop here to rest and be refreshed.'

You may also like to have a display of 'Feed the hungry' posters from one of the relief agencies.

Opening activity

Have three children come down. Two have lunch boxes with food in them but the one in the middle does not. (The food can be pretend or they can have a few small biscuits.) The two start to eat and then notice the one in the middle is not eating. They share their food. After this the one in the middle gets up and says, 'I was given some money to buy food; now I can give that money to help to feed the hungry. (Let him/her go and put a coin on the collection plate.)

Opening prayer

Lord God, in your love you have called us to seek you.
When we turn to you
we find you are waiting for us and come to us.
You meet our hunger and emptiness
with the richness of your presence.
This day, dear Lord, renew and refresh us
for all that we are called to do.
Amen.

Opening song

Alleluia, sing to Jesus

Readings

2 Samuel 11:1-15 or 2 Kings 4:42-44
Psalm 14 or Psalm 145:10-18
Ephesians 3:14-21
John 6:1-21

Thought for the day

The feeding of the five thousand reveals a good deal about Jesus and his mission.

First, there is the compassion of Jesus. He saw the hunger of the people who had been with him for a good while. He felt for these people who were physically and spiritually hungry. It would have been easy to say, 'There are too many of them; we cannot hope to feed them.' But Jesus has compassion: his heart goes out to them.

Second, there is the challenge of Jesus. He asks Philip, 'Where can we buy bread?' It must have been quite a daunting question when Philip looked at the crowd. Philip estimated that it would take about six months' wages to raise the money to buy enough bread. Jesus was challenging Philip and the disciples to look at their potential and resources. Though our resources are small, they can be greatly transformed if put in God's hands. Andrew seems to rise to the occasion by saying, 'There is a lad here who has five barley loaves and two fish. But what are they among so many?' We often wonder if our small efforts make a difference; well, here we learn they do.

Third is the command of Jesus: 'Make the people sit down.' The disciples were asked to get the people ready for a meal, and then, after the prayer, to distribute it. Jesus does not work alone; he works through us and with us. Without Jesus, we cannot do any great works. Without us, Jesus will not work; he wants us willingly to share with him.

Next is the concern of Jesus. Jesus says, 'Gather up the fragments left over, so that nothing may be lost.' Who would have thought that Jesus, who could feed five thousand with five loaves, would be bothered about crumbs and scraps? Jesus does not want waste: he is concerned how we use the things around us and how we deal with the world. It is good to know Jesus is concerned for the leftovers and that which is lost: they are precious in his sight.

Lastly, notice the caution of Jesus. The people were excited. Some saw the feeding as a 'sign', saying, 'This is indeed the prophet who is to come into the world.' They wanted to take him by force to make him king. Jesus did not come for this kind of kingship or to be a puppet of the people. The people were after Jesus for what they could get out of him. Jesus once again withdrew to the mountain by himself. Yet even in doing this there are hints that Jesus is like Moses who went up on Mount Sinai.

Question time

How does our church show compassion for those in need?

We may not have much to offer. Do we see that in God's power it can be transformed?

Illustration

There is a story about a boy walking along a beach. All along the shore there were thousands of starfish washed up. You could hardly walk on the sand for them. The boy was putting a few in his bucket and taking them back to the sea. A man came along and said, 'There are thousands of starfish stranded. Why do you bother? You will hardly make an impression. You will only be able to put a few back into the sea.' The boy replied. 'It will matter for these few and it will matter to me.'

Though our effort may be small, it is counted as worthwhile, and who knows what God will do with it?

Intercessions

Blessed are you, Lord our God,
in your love and care for your creation.
You do not turn away any who come to you.
You come to meet the seekers
and provide refreshment for all who hunger and thirst.
You care for the broken and the fragmented
and want nothing to be lost.
Blessed are you, Father, Son and Holy Spirit.

We come to you, dear Lord, as seekers;
we are hungry for your love and your care.
We ask you to bless all who are pilgrims and seekers,
all who long for an awareness
of your presence and your power.
We remember before you
all who bring healing and refreshment to your people.
We pray for preachers and pastors,
for leaders of prayer groups and retreat conductors
and for all places of pilgrimage.

Silence

Lord, have mercy:
let us know your compassion and care.

We give thanks for our daily bread
and for all who provide us with our food and shelter.
We pray for farmers and fishermen,
for those who work in our shops
and all who prepare food for us to eat.
We remember before you all who are hungry and weary.
We ask you to bless all who suffer
from poverty, from famine or from natural disasters.
We pray especially for the world poor
and those who are deeply in debt.

Silence

Lord, have mercy:
let us know your compassion and care.

We give you thanks for the comfort and security
of our homes.
Lord, give your blessing to all our loved ones
and friends.
We pray for any who may feel lonely or uncared for
within our community.
We remember all carers, social workers and helpers.

Silence

Lord, have mercy:
let us know your compassion and care.

Lord, we bring before you all whose lives are fragmented;
people who are broken in body, mind or spirit.
We remember all who feel shattered and exhausted,
all who long for your healing touch.
We pray for all who seek hope and peace,
that they may come to you and rest in your presence.

Silence

Lord, have mercy:
let us know your compassion and care.

You are the God who takes our weakness
and makes us strong.
We come to you as mortals
and you offer us immortality.
In your loving presence,
we remember friends and loved ones departed
and ask that not one is lost
but gathered into the fullness of joy in your kingdom.

Silence

Merciful Father,
accept these prayers
for the sake of your Son,
our Saviour Jesus Christ.
Amen.

Memory verse

The eyes of all wait upon you, O Lord, and you give them their food in due season.
Psalm 145:15

Suggested music

Break thou the bread of life
I heard the voice of Jesus say
Let all mortal flesh keep silence

CANDLES

Aim

To show how Jesus cares for people and seeks help even from children.

Teaching

Have you ever gone for a long walk in the country? What did you do for food? It is nice to take a picnic. (Talk a little about picnics.)

Once there were a lot of people walking around the edge of the sea. They wanted to go to where Jesus was and they were walking for about half a day. Most of them had set off suddenly and did not take any food with them, though there was one little lad who had a picnic. He had five little loaves – they were really rolls – and two tiny fish. (Bring out a basket at this point with five little loaves in it and two small fish, all made from playdough or plasticine). Look, this is what his mummy gave him. (Let them count the loaves and fishes and then put them away again until Andrew brings the basket to Jesus.)

More and more people gathered on a grassy hillside to listen to Jesus or to be healed by him. They were there until late in the afternoon and by now they were hungry. The disciples thought that Jesus should tell them to go home because it was getting late and they all looked hungry. Jesus knew what he was going to do but he asked Philip, 'Where can we get bread for these people to eat?' Philip said, 'There is nowhere to buy food and even if there was I would have to work for half a year just to be able to pay for them to have a little.'

Andrew noticed the little boy with the basket and told Jesus, 'There is a little lad with five loaves and two small fish.' Jesus asked if he could have the food and the boy said he could. 'But,' said Andrew, 'it is such a small amount, and there must be about 5000 people. You would have to share a loaf amongst 1000 people.'

Jesus smiled and told the disciples to ask the people to sit down. Then he took the loaves and fishes into his hands. He looked up to heaven and thanked God for this food the boy had given. He then began to break it and share it. He gave it to the disciples and the disciples gave it to the people. A wonderful thing happened. As Jesus gave the disciples the bread, it did not run out – there was enough for everyone there. He did the same with the fish. There was even a lot left at the end.

The little boy was so pleased that he had given Jesus his picnic. When he got home he would tell his mother how his picnic of five loaves and two fish had fed 5000 people.

In the large crowd Jesus and his friends had noticed one little boy and asked him to help them. Because one child was willing to help Jesus, Jesus was able to feed 5000 people.

Activity

Let each child make the loaves and fishes with playdough or plasticine. They can also colour the five loaves and the two fish on their worksheet.

Help the children to understand the song. Read it to them. Sing a verse and then get them to sing a verse.

Prayer

Jesus, thank you for letting the little boy help you.
We would like to help you
and do what you want us to do.
Amen.

Song

5 0 0 0 + hungry folk

LAMPS

Aim

To show how Jesus cares for our whole being and not just our spirits.

Teaching

When the disciples returned from their mission of preaching and healing they were tired. Jesus saw that they needed a time of rest and refreshment. Because there were still so many people coming to them, Jesus suggested that they crossed the sea in one of the fishing boats. This way they would get time of rest on the sea and find a quiet place on the other side of the sea. They were probably on the sea for about four or five hours. When they got to the other side, already people were rushing to see them. Soon there were thousands of people crowding around. There were so many it was hard to make your voice heard. There were about 5000 people.

Jesus saw that the people were also tired and hungry. If he sent them away, they would be exhausted and some would probably faint on their journey home. Jesus was concerned that they should not suffer in this way. He asked Philip, 'Where are we to buy bread for these people to eat?' Jesus actually knew there were no shops open to get this amount of bread. Philip worked out it would cost about half a year's wage just to provide them with a very small amount. It did not seem possible to feed them all. Then Andrew came forward with a young boy: 'There is a lad here who has five barley loaves and two fish. But what are they among so many people?'

Jesus asked the disciples if they would get the people to sit down. There was a lot of grass and soon the people were seated. Jesus asked the boy for the bread and fish. When the boy gave it to him, Jesus gave thanks to God for providing this food. Then the disciples went around sharing the food and it never ran out. There was enough food for everyone. The little lad could hardly believe it. Wait until he went home and told his mother he shared his picnic with 5000 people! Of course, he would have to tell her that Jesus made it possible. Everybody had plenty to eat; there was even a lot left over.

Jesus felt that the people would travel far more safely now that they had been fed. Just as Moses had led people to food in the desert, Jesus had provided food for those who followed him in this desert place.

Activity

Have two teams to 'Flip the fish'. The fish are made from a sheet of newspaper. Then two people, the leaders of each team, are given a magazine to waft the fish with and so make them move. The idea is to move the fish in this way from the start to a finishing line – it is not as easy as you think. Once it is over the line it can be picked up and the next person in the team has a turn. The first team to finish is the winner.

Prayer

Lord Jesus, you care for us and our needs.
May we learn to come to you for renewal and refreshment.
Help us to be aware of the hungry and the homeless
in our world
and to help them when we can.

Song

Two little fishes, five loaves of bread

TORCHES

Aim

To show that Jesus seeks to meet our hunger.

Teaching

People from all over the area were seeking Jesus. They hungered for something that the world could not provide. Some knew that no matter how much they filled themselves, they would still be empty. Inside them there was a hole that nothing could fill. That is because God made us for himself and nothing can really take his place. Sometimes you see people trying to fill themselves with food, with drink, with music, or with being busy, so that they can hide from the emptiness within. The people who sought Jesus hungered for more than food. They had not come into the desert to have a picnic, but now they were tired and weary and some were in danger of fainting through hunger.

Aware of their immediate need, Jesus sought to provide them with some refreshment. When he asked Philip about resources, Philip replied that it would take more than half a year's wage to provide this group with a small amount each. Andrew then came forward with a lad and his picnic of five loaves and two small fish. If the boy had refused to share, there would have been no miracle. Jesus asks us to share in his caring and redeeming work.

There is no explanation of the miracle but we can say Jesus acted out of care for the frailty and hunger of the people who were present. The food would meet an immediate need and Jesus would meet a deeper need within them.

Like the people who were seeking Jesus, we are all called to seek our God until we find him: we are to hunger after God. During the seeking some get weary; others are in danger of fainting or giving up. Let us remember that Jesus cares for everyone and does not want any to be lost; he cares for the smallest and least as much as he does for the greatest.

Activity

Have today's Epistle, Ephesians 3:14-21, read verse by verse by different people. Ask them to take to heart what they are to read and to direct verses 16-19 towards each other. Verses 14, 15, 20 and 21 are directed to God. This is a very powerful reading. See if the group can capture the beauty and majesty of the words. Practise it once or twice and see if the group can suggest actions to go with the words. If time remains, discuss how we are able to know that Christ dwells in our hearts.

Prayer

Glory to you, O God,
for you provide for our daily needs.
You have made us for yourself
and we hunger for your love
until we come to your presence.
In you alone are we truly refreshed
and restored to the fullness of life.
Glory to you, O God.

Song

I am the bread of life (And I will raise you up)

Proper 13

Sunday between 31 July and 6 August inclusive

Aim

To see Jesus as the Bread of Life.

Preparation

Have a freshly baked loaf at the back of the church ready to be brought to the offertory by a young member of the congregation. Near the entrance to the church display photographs of hungry people and also of people drinking and eating.

Opening activity

Let an adult come down with a bottle, pretending to be drinking a lot. Let them say, 'You have to be filled with something.' Let a thin young person with a cushion stuffed under their clothes enter pretending to be cramming food into their mouth. They also say, 'You have to be filled with something.' Then let someone come down with a personal CD and headphones on; dancing and skipping, they shout, 'You all need filling with something.' Let someone come down with a Bible and read the words, 'I am the bread of life. Whoever comes to me will never be hungry, and whoever believes in me will never be thirsty' (John 6:35).

Opening prayer

Lord our God, we hunger and thirst for your love
and for your presence.
Without you our lives have a great emptiness.
Come, Lord, fill us with love,
nourish us with your goodness
for you alone fully satisfy our needs.
Amen.

Opening song

Guide me, O thou great Redeemer

Readings

2 Samuel 11:26–12:13a or Exodus 16:2-4, 9-15
Psalm 51:1-12 or Psalm 78:23-29
Ephesians 4:1-6
John 6:24-35

Thought for the day

The early Church met regularly for the breaking of the bread. It is not surprising that there is a deep interest in Jesus as the Bread of Life. Today's Gospel ends with Jesus saying, 'I am the bread of life' (John 6:35).

It is worth looking at the questions raised in today's Gospel and the response Jesus gives to each of them as he seeks to clarify what true faith entails.

'Rabbi, when did you come here?' allows Jesus to discuss the motives of those who seek him: 'You are looking for me, not because you saw signs, but because you ate your fill of the loaves.' We often fail to read the signs that point us to God. We journey on, ever seeking, and ignore the God who can satisfy our emptiness and who is in our midst. We fill our lives with perishable goods and forget the One who alone gives eternal life. 'Do not work for the food that perishes, but for the food that endures to eternal life, which the Son of Man will give you.'

'What must we do to perform the works of God?' The work of God is to believe in him and in whom he has sent. The Greek word for 'believe' is far more than an assent to certain ideas about God; it is to have 'faith' in him: that is, to have a living relationship with God. Faith is about our personal relationship with the living God and with Jesus whom he has sent. If we do not have a relationship with God, we cannot truly perform his works. We are asked to give our heart to God. The German word 'belieben' is the root of the English word 'believe' and it means 'to belove'.

'What sign are you going to give us, then, so that we may believe in you? What work are you performing?' They hungered for more signs and more excitement and failed to seek the relationship that Jesus was offering. 'Our ancestors ate the manna in the wilderness; as it is written, "He gave them bread from heaven to eat."' Jesus responds by saying it was God not Moses that fed them in the wilderness and God gives you 'the true bread from heaven': that is, Jesus who came down from heaven and gives life to the world (John 6:33).

'Sir, give us this bread always.' The 'always' on this occasion is the Greek work 'pantote', which means again and again and again. Once more they have missed the point. Jesus clearly says, 'I am the bread of life. Whoever comes to me will never be hungry, and whoever believes in me will never be thirsty' (John 6:35). By saying, 'I am the bread of life', Jesus is saying he is linked to the 'I Am' who is God: he is God. The love of God is revealed in Jesus Christ and he meets the needs of those with inner hunger and thirst. In whatever situation we find ourselves we can trust in the unfailing power and love of God. There is no doubt that in writing his Gospel John was aware of the sacramental implications of the bread.

Question time

Are we aware that God made us for himself and nothing that takes his place can fully satisfy us?

Do we seek God for himself or for what we feel we can get out of him?

Illustration

Throughout our world there are people who seem to have to fill their lives with food, with things or with activity. No matter how much they get, they are still not satisfied. When young people say they are bored, it is usually when they have plenty happening around them but they recognise emptiness within. Bored means having a hole drilled in you. There is something in you that things cannot fill, no matter how you stuff yourself or your days. God made us for himself and nothing else will really fill the space he created within us for himself. In each of us there is a space for the eternal and nothing less than the eternal God can fill it.

Intercessions

Blessed are you, Father, Son and Holy Spirit.
You have created us out of your love and for your love.
You have made our hearts to long for you
and nothing else will fully satisfy them.
Help us to turn to you in our hunger and thirst,
that in you and your love
we may find refreshment and life.
You, Lord, are the giver of life in all its fullness.
Blessed are you, God, for ever.

We give thanks for all who sustain us in life
with their love and care.
Bless those who seek to bring us to the Bread of Life
and all who seek to help to provide us
with our spiritual needs.
We pray for all who celebrate the sacraments
and for those being prepared
to make their first Communion.
We remember in your presence all who are pilgrims
and seekers,
those who long for your love and wish to serve you.
We ask you to guide any who feel they have lost their way
and put too much trust in material things alone.

Silence

Lord, you alone
are our strength and hope.

We give you thanks for all who work to provide us
with food and refreshment.
We remember those who provide us with bread:
the farmers, the millers, the bakers and the shops.
We ask you to guide all who are caught up
in materialism and consumerism.
We remember especially all who have lost sight
of the deeper meaning of life.
We pray for all who are unemployed
and those who suffer from hunger or homelessness,
all who lack the necessary resources for their well-being.

Silence

Lord, you alone
are our strength and hope.

Lord, we give thanks for our homes
and for all who care for us.
We pray for our friends and our loved ones.
We remember our community:
its schools and its places of work.
May all reflect your glory and your love.
Let us be aware of any who are lonely or feel rejected.

Silence

Lord, you alone
are our strength and hope.

We give thanks for the renewing powers of our bodies
and for all who share in the healing and care of others.
We pray for all who feel their lives are empty
or meaningless,
all who feel they have wasted their lives
or never fully lived.
We remember also friends and loved ones who are ill.

Silence

Lord, you alone
are our strength and hope.

Lord, we put our trust in you.
We believe that in you is the gift of eternal life.
We pray that through you and your love
we may be brought at the last
to the fullness of your kingdom.
We remember in your presence the Blessed Virgin Mary
and all the saints departed.
We ask you to bless all our loved ones
whom we see no longer.

Silence

Merciful Father,
accept these prayers
for the sake of your Son,
our Saviour Jesus Christ.
Amen.

Memory verse

I am the bread of life. Whoever comes to me will never be hungry, and whoever believes in me will never be thirsty.
John 6:35

Suggested music

Bread of heaven, on thee we feed
I am the bread of life (And I will raise you up)
Jesus the Lord said: 'I am the Bread'

CANDLES

Aim

To show how God fed his people when they were hungry.

Teaching

Have you ever walked a long way in the countryside? Did you take a picnic or did you go and get some food somewhere? Once the people who escaped from the wicked king in Egypt walked a long way through the desert. They walked for days and for years. They had to walk and walk and walk. After a while all the food that they had brought with them had gone; they had eaten it. Some children began to cry because they were very hungry. But their mothers and fathers had no food to give them and they were hungry too. 'I wish we had stayed with the wicked king; at least we had food.' They went and grumbled to their leader Moses and blamed him for their being hungry.

Moses was very sad because he could not help them. But he was even sadder because they forgot that God was looking after them. 'Do you not remember that God helped you to escape from the wicked king? God has kept you safe and helped you to cross the sea. God has always cared for you – don't you think he will help you now?'

Moses went away to a quiet place by himself and said his prayers to God. God then told Moses, 'Do not worry. I will look after the people.' Then he told Moses what he was going to do.

Moses got all the people together and said, 'God is going to give you bread from heaven each day. You must go out every day and collect it. Do not be greedy; just collect enough for everyone in your family.'

The next morning there was something white scattered all over the ground. Everybody asked, 'Manna?' (which means 'What is it?'). They picked it up and said, 'Manna.' (Let us say it: 'Manna.') They turned it over and looked at it, and smelt it and asked, 'Manna? What is it?' Then someone tasted it and it tasted sweet and lovely. 'It tastes lovely, we can eat it.' Soon everyone was excited and they were collecting manna until there was a bowlful for each person. Some of the children would have gone on collecting but they were told only to collect enough for the day. God would give them some more the next day.

Everyone ate the manna. How nice it tasted! No one was hungry any more. God had sent the people food when they needed it. The next day there was more and they still called it manna. They scooped it up into bowls and collected it for their food. They all said thank you to God for giving them food and for loving them.

Activity

Have teams of about six children. Scatter a cupful of rice or confetti on large sheets of brown paper. Tell the children they are to pick it all up piece by piece and each time they have a few pieces to put them in the cup and, as they put it in, say, 'Manna'. It is not a race but we would like to see all the cups full again and nothing left lying about.

Prayer

God, thank you for loving us,
for giving us food to eat.
We know that you care for us
and for everything that you have made. Amen.

Song

There are hundreds of sparrows

LAMPS

Aim

To discover what it means for Jesus to be the Bread of Life.

Teaching

What would you do if you were in a car and it ran out of petrol? You could get out and push it, or you could get someone to give it a tow. But the car will not run properly unless it has fuel in its tank. We are a bit like a car: we will not run properly unless we have something in our stomach. We can only go so long without food before we become weak; we need food or we will die. For many people the worst thing comes when they no longer know they are hungry; they no longer want food. They have become too weak to bother.

Last week we heard how Jesus provided food for the people before some became weak and fainted. (Review the feeding of the five thousand.)

Some only followed Jesus for the chance of getting a meal. Jesus was worried that this was all they were after, because being full with food is not enough. We are not just bodies – we have minds and spirits – and all of us need to be fed. We spend a good deal of time feeding. How many meals do you have each day? There is the shopping, the preparation time, the eating and the washing up. You may only do the eating but a lot of time is spent on making sure you are fed. Then we spend a good deal of time feeding our minds: we go to school, we read, we listen to teachers, we learn by doing. A lot of time each day is spent feeding our minds. Sometimes our bodies and our minds are crammed full. But what about our spirits? Are we sure they are being fed? Jesus warned the people who came for food not to spend their whole lives just filling their bodies. Your spirit needs food as well. You need the food that will keep your spirit alive, that will keep you alive even when your body gives up. Spiritual food keeps you going. The people wanted Jesus to tell them where to get such food. They had not found any in the shops. They asked Jesus, 'Teacher, give us this bread. We would like the bread that feeds us for ever.'

Then Jesus said something strange: 'My Father has given you this bread. He has sent me. I am the bread of life; whoever comes to me will never hunger.' It is hard to understand but if you lived in the presence of lots of bread, you would never be hungry. If you live with Jesus and let him into your life, your spirit will not be hungry. If we come to Jesus each day, our spirits will not hunger and he will give us eternal life.

Activity

Let us mime filling our bodies with food. See if the others can guess what you are eating. Now we will mime filling our minds. Let the others guess if you are reading, listening, learning. Now the part of us that we sometimes forget: let us mime how we keep our spirits from emptiness. Explore the idea that boredom – saying, 'I am bored' – might mean we have let out spirits get empty.

Prayer

Lord Jesus, come to us.
Fill our days with your presence.
Fill our homes with your peace.
Fill our lives with your power.
Fill our hearts with your love.

Song

Praise and thanksgiving, Father, we offer

TORCHES

Aim

To show that Jesus is like Moses, but even more special.

Teaching

When Jesus fed the people in the wilderness it was the Passover time. This was the time when the people of Israel celebrated their freedom from slavery and their moving out of Egypt towards the Promised Land. It was the time when they remembered Moses and the mighty works of God. Here was a group of people in the wilderness, just like it was in the time of Moses. They hungered and Jesus provided them with food, just as God provided Moses and the people with food when they were hungry. Could Jesus be another Moses and bring his people to the Promised Land?

Some who followed Jesus did so only to see what they could get out of him. They wanted miracles; they wanted feeding; they also wanted someone to lead them and drive out the Romans. The crowds were there for bread. But bread is not enough. Jesus wanted to lead them to the Promised Land. He wanted to bring them to the kingdom of God. The people were too materially minded: they sought for and laboured for the food that perishes. It is no use just being fed, or simply existing. Jesus wanted people to have life in all its fullness (John 10:10). It's no use having a well-fed body and a mind full of learning if your spirit is dying of hunger. For the spirit to prosper, the people had to turn to God. God alone can fulfil the needs of the spirit. Jesus wanted the people to recognise that there is a greater hunger than hunger for food. There is an emptiness within each of us that nothing but God can fill. Our spirits were made for the eternal and only the Eternal will satisfy us – anything else is just a put-off. Jesus said to the people, 'The Son of Man will give you this bread. For it is on him the Father has set his seal.' Here Jesus is claiming to be the Messiah, the One sent by God. He says that God has authenticated him by setting his seal upon him. Now the people are asked to believe in Jesus, to trust in him, to have a relationship with him. The people want more proof and want to debate about credentials. Jesus cuts through all this and says, 'It was not Moses who gave you the bread from heaven but my Father' (see Exodus 16:15). When the people ask for this bread, Jesus replies, 'I am the bread of life.' Jesus is greater than Moses. Jesus claims to be 'I Am', which is a title of God. Jesus is God and Jesus is the Bread of Life. Only if we come to Jesus and through him to the Father can our spirits truly have life. Our spirits will die in the wilderness of this world unless we come to him who is the source of life (see John 3:16).

Activity

On the worksheet there are examples of different ways of feeding on Jesus as the Bread of Life. Talk about Holy Communion and how we seek to receive our Lord and be in common union with him.

Prayer

Lord of life,
come and fill us with your love.
We need your presence and your power:
come to us and fill us with your peace.
Lord, abide in us and let us abide in you
for in you alone is eternal life,
Jesus Christ our Lord.
Amen.

Song

Are you wired up

Proper 14

Sunday between 7 and 13 August inclusive

Aim

To show the calling of God and the stalling of our hearts.

Preparation

Have two loaves and a sandwich. At the entrance to the church have in large letters, 'Jesus said: I am the bread of life. Whoever comes to me will never be hungry.'

Opening activity

Let two people come down with the bread. The first person will place a loaf on the altar and say, 'Thank you, God, for our daily bread.' They will turn to face the people. The second person comes down and says, 'I am not eating this', and then reads from the wrapping the ingredients of a cut loaf. Meanwhile, the first person leisurely eats a sandwich. The second person ends by saying, 'I am not satisfied.' With a smile, the first person says, 'Well, I am.' Both then sit down.

Opening prayer

Lord God, open our ears to your call
and our hearts to your love.
You have given us Jesus as the Bread of Life.
May we know his presence in this Eucharist
and receive him into our lives.
Amen.

Opening song

I am the bread of life

Readings

2 Samuel 18:5-9, 31-33 or 1 Kings 19:4-8
Psalm 130 or Psalm 34:1-8
Ephesians 4:25–5:2
John 6:35, 41-51

Thought for the day

John's Gospel continues with the reactions of the people to the feeding of the five thousand. For John this is in the context of the Passover festival and of the Christian breaking of the bread meetings. The readings from John 6 obviously have a Eucharistic setting.

We begin today where last week's Gospel ended with Jesus saying, 'I am the bread of life.' Sadly the reaction of the people was to start 'murmuring', complaining about him (6:41). Jesus is offering himself to them and all they can do is grumble and complain. How often the great mystery of God's gift of himself to us is lost because of our attitude and prejudices. God has always worked through his creation and has come to us time and again through the ordinary, but we fail to see it because we are so prejudiced against it. We are forever looking for another miracle whilst God is actually offering himself to us. The people did not see that Jesus could be anyone special, and certainly thought he could not be God's Son, or the 'Bread of Life', because they knew where he lived. They refused to see beyond the obvious: that they thought they knew his mum and dad! Jesus tells them to stop murmuring, stop complaining and grumbling. The people with Moses had grumbled against him and therefore against God (Exodus 15:24; 16:2). It was believed that such grumbling prevented them coming into the Promised Land. 'Do not complain as some of them did, and were destroyed by the destroyer' (1 Corinthians 10:10). How often we miss out on the mystery and wonder of God's gift to us through our attitude of complaining and dissatisfaction. When Jesus offers himself to us we spend our time debating what we think of him! Let us learn to talk to God more than we talk about him; to come before the mystery with a sense of awe.

Jesus says, 'No one can come to me unless drawn by the Father.' The word which Jesus uses for 'drawn' is the translation of the Hebrew in Jeremiah 31:3 (the Authorised Version has 'With loving kindness I have drawn thee'). The word implies the tugging of God but it also suggests some resistance. The same word is used for tugging a heavy net ashore (John 21:6, 11). God tugs at us in love but we always have the power to resist him. In verse 45 of today's Gospel, Jesus says how all are taught by God, not only the Jews. All are called but all do not listen; all do not react to the tugging of God.

Jesus then repeats how he is the bread of life. Here is an invitation to come to him. Analysis and debate can easily keep you away. With words we can avoid the Word of God. How great is your resistance to his call and his love? There are none so deaf as those who do not want to hear.

Question time

Is there a danger of words preventing us from coming to the Word of God?

Do we see that we talk more about God than we talk to him?

Illustration

There was a brilliant scientist who was keen on analysis. He wanted to get to the basic elements of everything. A meal was set before him and he was hungry. But he wanted to check where this food came from and what was in it. He went into his laboratory and started on a loaf of bread. He did not eat any. He checked what its constituents were. He discovered wholemeal flour, water, yeast, vegetable fat, preservatives, emulsifiers and vinegar. He checked out the preservatives and found calcium propionate and potassium sorbate. By now he was starving but research must go on. The emulsifiers kept him busy for ages. He found mono- and diacetyl tartaric acid, esters of mono- and diglycerides, fatty acids. He was kept very busy but he grew weaker and weaker. He still had to analyse the wholemeal and check out the grains. Sadly he died of starvation whilst looking at the loaf. There was food all around him but he died of analysis.

Intercessions

Blessed are you, Lord our God,
for you provided for your children.
In the wilderness of this world
you give us the bread of life.
Lord, grant, as we journey towards the Promised Land,
that we may put our hope and our trust in you.
Blessed are you, Father, Son and Holy Spirit.

Father, we give you thanks that you have called us
to know you and to love you.
You have drawn us to you with bands of love.
Help us to listen and to obey your word.
We pray for all preachers and pastors,
for ministers of the word and of the sacraments.
We remember before you all who do not know or love you
and we ask your blessing upon all
who reach out in mission and love to them.
We pray for any who have lost faith in themselves
or in you.

Silence

Lord our God,
our hope is in you.

Lord God, creator of heaven and earth,
we pray for the nations of the world.
May they find a unity and a peace in you.
We ask your blessing upon the work of the United Nations
and upon all peacekeeping forces.
We pray for areas of the world
where there is strife and division,
where people are unable to trust each other,
where people do not listen to each other.
We remember displaced peoples and refugees.

Silence

Lord our God,
our hope is in you.

We thank your for the love and protection of our homes.
We ask your blessing upon our families and friends.
We remember before you
homes where there is division or distrust,
where families are divided.
We pray for all who have been betrayed or deserted.
We remember also all who are leaving home
for the first time.

Silence

Lord our God,
our hope is in you.

We give you thanks for our own well-being
and for all that feeds our bodies, minds and spirits.
We remember all who are struggling
with doubt, depression and despair,
all who are having difficulty in their daily lives.
We pray for all who are ill at home or in hospital,
especially those who have no one
to care for them or visit them.

Silence

Lord our God,
our hope is in you.

We rejoice that you sustain us with the Bread of Life.
Through our union with Jesus you offer us life eternal.
As we celebrate our communion with the saints,
we remember our friends and loved ones departed
and ask that they may rejoice
in the fullness of eternal life.

Silence

Merciful Father,
accept these prayers
for the sake of your Son,
our Saviour Jesus Christ.
Amen.

Memory verse

I am the living bread that came down from heaven. Whoever eats of this bread will live for ever.
John 6:51

Suggested music

Break thou the bread of life
I, the Lord of sea and sky (Here I am, Lord)
Jesu, thou joy of loving hearts

CANDLES

Aim

To show how God cares for Elijah, and to suggest he cares for us in the same way.

Teaching

Today we are going to learn about someone who worked very hard for God. He was called Elijah. (Would you like to say his name after me? Elijah. Would anyone like to say it by himself or herself?) Elijah was a strong man and not afraid to tell people about God. He showed the people how God loved them and cared for them. Elijah did wonderful works for God. He was a good and brave man.

But there was a wicked queen who did not like Elijah. She was called Jezebel (Would you like to say her name?) The wicked queen had an army and she wanted to capture Elijah and kill him. Poor Elijah felt so tired and now he was afraid. He would have to hide from Queen Jezebel. He went away into a wild place where no one lived. It was a desert place (see if the children know what a desert is); nothing much grew there and there was no food. There was a single tree – just one all by itself. Elijah tried to get some shelter from the sun under the shade of the tree. He was so tired and hungry. There was no food and he was sure he would die. He lay under the tree and went to sleep.

Suddenly there was someone shaking him and making him wake up. He opened his eyes and saw a messenger from God, one of God's angels. The angel touched him and said, 'Get up and eat, or the journey will be too hard for you.' Elijah rubbed his eyes in case he was dreaming. But there was the angel and there was a loaf baked on hot stones and there was a jar of water. Elijah got up and ate and drank. He knew that God cared for him and loved him. He then lay down again and had a good sleep. The angel of God came a second time and woke him again. There was a nice smell of wood smoke and baking. Again there was food for Elijah to eat. This would make him strong and able to go across the desert. Elijah felt so much better. God had sent him food and new strength. He would now be able to go to God's mountain and escape from the wicked queen.

Activity

Play the game 'Elijah and Jezebel'. Let two children be blindfolded; one is Elijah and the other is Jezebel. The aim is for Jezebel to catch Elijah. Jezebel calls out, 'Elijah!' and he has to reply 'Jezebel!' Jezebel keeps shouting to get a reply and guess where he is. Elijah keeps on the move. If Jezebel manages to capture Elijah, an 'angel' removes his blindfold and helps him escape before Jezebel's blindfold is removed.

Prayer

God our Father, we thank you for caring for us
and providing us with food.
We know that you love us
and this makes us happy.
Amen.

Song

Praise him, praise him

LAMPS

Aim

To learn to listen carefully and make room in our lives for Jesus.

Teaching

Sometimes at school it is not easy to learn something new because some of the children are talking or doing things that show they are not listening. If we do not listen, we do not learn. Can you think of a time when you or your friends did not listen?

Sometimes we do not listen because we do not want to hear what is being said, especially if we are being told to do something we do not want to do. (Can the children give examples?) Some people never listen to others because they have their minds full of other things.

The people would not listen to Moses in the wilderness. He told them God would care for them but they would not listen. They did not hear Moses or God. Instead they grumbled and complained about being hungry and thirsty. The complainers never got to the Promised Land.

Elijah listened to God and did wonderful things for God. The wicked Queen Jezebel did not want to listen to God and wanted to kill Elijah. Elijah had to escape to the wilderness where he could hide from Jezebel. Out in the desert he found a single solitary tree and lay down in the shade that it made. Elijah was very tired and soon fell asleep. He was so tired he just wanted to die. But God was listening to Elijah and sent a messenger to him. The messenger shook Elijah gently until he was awake and said, 'Get up and eat.' Elijah sat up and saw a fire smoking and bread baking on hot stones. There was also a jar of water. Elijah did what he was told and ate the food and drank the water. Then he lay down again and slept. The messenger of God – God's messengers are called angels – came again and touched him and said, 'Get up and eat; otherwise the journey will be too much for you.' Elijah listened to what he was told. He got up. He ate. Then he went on a journey for 40 days to Horeb, the mountain of God. Because he had listened he knew he had to make this journey.

Jesus found that a lot of people did not listen to him. Instead they talked and argued among themselves. They could not hear Jesus for the sound of their own voices. Jesus thought his words were like seed falling on rocky ground; they could not get into the hearts and minds of these people. They blocked out the Word of God with their own words. They could have enjoyed being with Jesus but instead they grumbled and complained. So they missed out on knowing Jesus and did not receive him into their lives and homes.

Activity

Play 'Chinese whispers'. Get the children to sit in a circle and to pass a message around by whispering in each other's ears. Pass sentences around about Jesus – 'Jesus loves all of us'; 'Jesus is here and speaks to us'; 'Jesus wants us to listen'. Praise the children if a sentence manages to go around without being altered. Point out that it is when we do not listen that words get lost or altered.

Prayer

God, we thank you that you have called us
to know you and love you.
Teach us to listen carefully to your call
and to come to you through Jesus Christ our Lord.
Amen.

Song

In the morning early

TORCHES

Aim

To discover how to respond to the drawing of God.

Teaching

Jesus had been trying to draw the people following him to a deeper knowledge of God and to know who he is. The people came for feeding but not for commitment. They avoided hearing the words of Jesus by murmuring and grumbling among themselves. Some could not see who he was because of their prejudice. They said they knew the parents of Jesus; they knew where he was born, so how could he say he had come down from heaven? They were talking about him rather than talking to him.

Jesus said to them, 'No one can come to me unless drawn by the Father who sent me.' If they did not allow God the Father to draw them, there would be little chance for Jesus. The word for drawing implies being tugged along and contains within it a suggestion of resistance. It is the same word that is used for pulling a heavy net to the shore (John 21:6, 11). The same word is used when Paul and Silas are dragged before the magistrates (Acts 16:19). In the Old Testament it is the word used for Jeremiah being pulled out of the well (Jeremiah 38:13). The same word is used in Jeremiah 31:3: 'With loving kindness I have drawn thee' (Authorised Version). In Hosea 11:4, God says, 'I drew him with cords of a man, with bands of love' (AV).

God tugs at our hearts and minds but we set up resistance by our attitude towards him. We do not want to know because God calls for a response to his tugging. We listen with divided attention; our minds are elsewhere. We listen but we remain untouched and unmoved, protecting ourselves by analysis, or by criticism or prejudice. We listen but we do not learn from the words. If we are truly to have communion with God and with our Saviour Jesus Christ, we have to respond to the call of God we hear in our hearts and minds. Sadly, too often God calls and the person stalls. Yet whoever believes has eternal life. The choice is ours – why do we put off?

Activity

Let us look at different ways that God calls and how we put off. Let us all pencil into a busy day a time when we will come before God in stillness.

Prayer

Good and glorious God,
you have made us out of your love and for your love.
Touch our hearts with the joy of your presence,
that we may give ourselves in love to you.
Amen.

Song

Break the bread and pour the wine

Proper 15

Sunday between 14 and 20 August inclusive

Aim

To seek to abide in Jesus and let him abide in us.

Preparation

Have a crucifix or a painting of the crucifixion at the main entrance. Underneath have the words, 'Remember me.' You may like to add a photograph of a chalice and paten.

Opening activity

Let someone walk down the church with either a loaf of bread or the paten with bread upon it. Before they place it on the altar let them say, 'God, we thank you for our daily bread and for Jesus who is the Bread of Life.'

A second person comes with a chalice containing a little wine. Before they place it on the altar they say, 'God, we thank you for wine that makes glad our hearts and for Jesus who poured out his life for us.'

Opening prayer

Holy and most wonderful God,
we thank you for the gifts of bread and wine
and for all that sustains us in life.
We remember this day
how the body of Jesus was broken for us
and his blood poured out.
May we know his presence with and within us.
Amen.

Opening song

Awake, my soul, and with the sun

Readings

1 Kings 2:10-12; 3:3-14 or Proverbs 9:1-6
Psalm 111 or Psalm 34:9-14
Ephesians 5:15-20
John 6:51-58

Thought for the day

The Passover and the Eucharist are the setting for this discourse on the 'bread of heaven', and it takes place in the synagogue at Capernaum. At the Passover the Jews are required to eat the unleavened bread and the paschal lamb amongst other things. The Passover remembers the exodus from Egypt, the wandering in the wilderness, including the provision of manna. The reading begins with the last verse from last week's Gospel: 'I am the living bread that came down from heaven. Whoever eats this bread will live for ever; and the bread that I will give for the life of the world is my flesh.'

Many claims are here. Jesus is still purposely using the words 'I am', which are used as a naming of God. God comes to us in Jesus Christ. It is Jesus who is the living bread. This is a greater offer than Moses', for the children of Israel ate the manna and still died: those who eat this bread from heaven will live for ever. 'The bread that I give for the life of the world is my flesh.' Jesus is not giving us things; he is giving us himself. He offers himself *to* us and offers himself *for* us. He wants us to take of him. We who receive Communion can understand this, and that we abide in him and he in us. The Jews murmured – as ever, analysis prevents the mystery from entering into our lives. The Jews said, 'How can this man give us his flesh to eat?' Surely it is a good question. Do we understand that Jesus was replacing the Passover lamb with his own sacrifice?

Jesus insists, 'Unless you eat the flesh of the Son of Man and drink his blood, you have no life in you.' Unless we take Jesus' life into our life, we will lack the fullness of life. Jesus continues with the theme of mutual indwelling: 'Those who eat my flesh and drink my blood abide in me, and I in them.' This mutual indwelling is the purpose and the joy of every Communion and with it the knowledge that through him we live for ever.

Jesus is not a figure in a book, not even the Bible. He is the living Lord and wants to be one with us. When we abide in him and he in us we have eternal life.

Question time

Do we come to Communion to be at one with Jesus, to have common union with the Holy One?

How can we learn to abide in him and know that he abides in us?

Illustration

There was once a man who bought a beautiful box for his wife. The box had flowers on the top and they would glow in the dark. As it was for her birthday he hid it away in a drawer and left it there for a few weeks. On her birthday it was given to her all wrapped in a lovely parcel. She was delighted and could hardly wait until the evening. When it got dark she looked at the box but it did not shine; it had not changed at all. They both waited until it got really dark but the box never did shine. They felt a little cheated because the box was bought to shine. Then a little note fell from the packaging. It said, 'If you want me to shine all night, you need put me in the sun all day.' The box would only glow if it was left out in the daylight. They left it out all the next day and, true to the words, all night it glowed with a splendid light.

If we are to glow with eternal life, we need to be placed in the presence of the Son of God to let him abide in us and for us to know we abide in him.

Intercessions

Blessed are you, Lord our God,
you give us life and love.
We rejoice in your presence that is ever with us.
We give thanks for the offering of Jesus on the cross
and for the memorial we have this Eucharist.
May we remember that he comes to us
and asks us to offer ourselves to him.
Blessed are you, Father, Son and Holy Spirit.

Father, we thank you for the revealing of your Son
in the breaking of the bread and in the taking of the wine.
We pray for all who celebrate the memorial
of the death and passion of Jesus.
We ask you to bless all who strive
for unity and fellowship within the whole Church.
May we show that we are Christians
by our love and our sharing.

Silence

Lord, may we abide in you
and know you are with us.

We give thanks for the fruits of the earth
and for all that you have given us.
As we give thanks for our daily bread
we remember all who are celebrating
growth and increase in their lives.
We pray for those in new work
or preparing to go to new schools.
We ask you to bless all artists and craftspeople,
all who enrich our world with their talents and goodness.
We remember all who provide us with food
and our daily needs.

Silence

Lord, may we abide in you
and know you are with us.

We give you thanks and praise for our homes,
for their peace and protection.
We ask your blessing on all homes
where there is disunity or discord.
We pray for all who are suffering
from a breakdown in relationships.
We pray for homes where there is a new birth
or someone newly admitted into their family.

Silence

Lord, may we abide in you
and know you are with us.

We give thanks that Jesus has shared our grief and sorrows.
As we give thanks for the wine of communion,
we remember all whose lives are being out-poured.
We pray for all who are facing pain or weakness,
all who feel diminished by the trials of life.
We remember those whose energies are failing
and any who are finding it hard to cope with life.

Silence

Lord, may we abide in you
and know you are with us.

We celebrate our Communion with you, O God,
and with the whole Church on earth and in heaven.
We rejoice in the resurrection of our Lord.
We pray for all our loved ones departed from us:
may they, with all the saints,
enjoy the fullness of your presence and your kingdom.

Silence

Merciful Father,
accept these prayers
for the sake of your Son,
our Saviour Jesus Christ.
Amen.

Memory verse

Abide in me as I abide in you.
John 15:4

Suggested music

Bread of heaven, on thee we feed
Here is bread
Eat this bread

CANDLES

Aim

To introduce the idea of the bread and wine as a remembrance of Jesus.

Teaching

How do we remember our relatives and friends? We have photographs and presents that they gave us. Have you got photographs at home of your grandmother or grandfather? You may have a photograph of a brother or sister who has left home. Sometimes we have photographs or pictures of places we have been to remind us how nice they are. Here are some of my photographs of my family and some of the places I like. (Show photographs – if you prefer you can show photographs of famous people from magazines and see if the children recognise them.)

In the time of Jesus there were no photographs or magazines. If you wanted someone to remember you, you had to give him or her something that would make them think of you. Jesus decided to give his disciples two things to remind them always of him. (If possible, show a chalice and a paten and see if the children recognise what they are for – a photograph could suffice.) Jesus did not give silver or gold; he gave the disciples bread and wine. He wanted them to remember him through bread and wine. To remember he fed 5000 people. Do you remember? To remember he took bread, broke it and gave it to them. He said he would be with them when they broke bread. (Explain how they did not cut bread but broke it. Take a piece of bread, break it and give it to the children and say, 'Remember Jesus'.)

Jesus also gave the disciples wine. 'Remember how I turned water into wine at the wedding.'

The disciples met often to break bread together and to drink the wine and to remember Jesus. The wine was red and it reminded them how Jesus died on the cross and gave his life for them. They remembered that Jesus was with them even though they could not see him. Every time they took bread and wine they gave thanks for Jesus: that he gave his life for them and that he rose again.

Activity

Have a pack of cards – you can buy packs with nice pictures on them – and turn them all face downwards. The children have to pick two that are the same. If they fail, they show the two cards and put them back carefully.

If there are less than 26 children in the class, make sure there are only enough cards for two each.

Prayer

Jesus, help us to remember you each day
and to give our love to you.
Amen.

Song

Jesus' love is very wonderful

LAMPS

Aim

To seek to introduce the children to the meaning of the Eucharist.

Teaching

Show the group a chalice and paten or a photograph of them. What are these for? What do we put on the plate and what do we put in the cup? (You may like to teach them the words 'chalice' and 'paten'.) They are for the bread and wine of Communion. We use bread and wine because Jesus said that we should use them to remind us of him. Can you think of a story that reminds you of Jesus using bread?

Jesus took the five loaves that the little boy gave to him and fed 5000 people. We remember the miracle of the feeding of the 5000. He fed them at the Passover festival. At the next Passover festival he again took bread. This time it was at a special meal with his disciples, and he gave thanks and broke the bread and gave it to the disciples, saying, 'Do this in remembrance of me.' He wanted them to remember how he fed people in the wilderness. He wanted them to remember how his body was broken on the cross. He wanted them to remember he was with them always.

At the same Passover supper Jesus took the wine and after he had given thanks he gave it to them, saying, 'Drink this in remembrance of me.' Remember the first miracle at Cana of Galilee. When the wine ran out at the wedding feast what did Jesus do? Remember that Jesus turned the ordinary water into wine. He wanted the people to enjoy themselves and not feel sad.

Jesus wants us to remember him every time the wine is poured out. Wine looks like the colour of blood – and Jesus poured out his life for us on the cross. The wine reminds us of the death of Jesus, how he died to save us. But we are to remember also that he rose again and that he wants us to invite him into our lives.

Holy Communion has its name because we can have common union with the Holy One. Through the bread and wine Jesus reminds us of his presence and comes to us.

Activity

Have about a dozen objects on a tray. Show them to the group for a minute. Then give them pencils and paper to write down what they saw. If they write down something that was not on the tray, they lose a point. All with full points are counted as the winners, the ones with good memories.

Prayer

Father, we thank you for Jesus
and that he offered his life for us.
We remember that he died on the cross for us
and rose again
that we might share in life eternal.
We thank you for Jesus.
Amen.

Song

Praise God from whom all blessings flow

TORCHES

Aim

To look at today's Gospel with the Last Supper in mind.

Teaching

The setting for today's Gospel is the Passover time. What does the Passover celebrate? It was the escaping of the Israelites from death in Egypt, their escape to freedom and their journeying to the Promised Land. Every year the Passover is celebrated. For Jesus this year it is with the feeding of the five thousand, with the breaking of the bread and the giving of thanks. The next Passover he will celebrate the Last Supper and the breaking of the bread with his disciples in the upper room. At the Passover the Passover lamb is sacrificed and eaten. Jesus is the Lamb of God and talks of 'eating his flesh and drinking his blood'.

St John does not record the Last Supper but it is there behind most of his writing. Just as the Jews kept the memorial of their escape from Egypt, Jesus was offering his people a chance to keep remembrance of him. When he took the bread and broke it he said, 'This is my body.' In the bread we remember that Jesus was truly human and that he suffered, was broken for us. We are reminded that he was scorned and rejected, that he was betrayed and deserted, that he was crucified, dead and buried. In the breaking of the bread we remember his suffering and death. In the taking of the bread we remember how he fed the weary people and provided new life for them. We remember his resurrection and that he comes to us to give us of his life that is life eternal. He asks us to break the bread in remembrance of what he offers to us now and that he comes to us.

In wine, we may remember the wedding feast at Cana, the first miracle of Jesus. Jesus says at the last Supper, 'This is my blood given for you.' In Jewish thought, 'blood' stands for 'life'. This is easy to understand because if your blood is lost, so is your life. The Jews believed that life was in the blood. With the wine we are reminded of Jesus dying for us; we are reminded how his life was poured out in love. He says, 'Drink this in remembrance of me.'

Because Jesus is alive, all these remembrances are to remind us of his presence with us now. We are reminded that he is risen and comes to us again and again. The words that Jesus said to the Jews in today's Gospel have to be accepted by us: 'Those who eat my flesh and drink my blood have eternal life, and I will raise them up on the last day; for my flesh is true food and my blood is true drink. Those who eat my flesh and drink my blood abide in me, and I in them' (John 6:54-56). (Let the group seek to understand and talk about these verses and about Communion.)

Activity

Make a collage of how bread and wine are produced. Try to show the cost of labour, and how the bread and wine symbolise life. Use the worksheet to see how Jesus gave us a remembrance to keep in the bread and wine.

Prayer

Lord Jesus, who in a wonderful sacrament
has left us a memorial of your life offered
and of your death and passion,
help us to understand and respect this wonderful mystery
and to know the joy of your resurrection
and your presence with us.
Amen.

Song

Jesus took a piece of bread

Proper 16

Sunday between 21 and 27 August inclusive

Aim

To affirm our commitment to Christ.

Preparation

Have a 'Polling Station' notice outside the church door. Give people the choice of placing a cross on a voting form with the following:

VOTE FOR	
Jesus Christ and eternal life	☐
The World without God and an uncertain future	☐
The Put-it-off Party	☐

Let the votes be counted before the service begins and announce the outcome.

Opening activity

Get the congregation to gather around the font and re-affirm their baptismal promises. You may like to ask simply:

> Do you seek the ways of God?
> Do you choose to follow Christ?
> Do you want to be led by the Holy Spirit?

After they answer 'I do' to each question, say, 'Be strong in the Lord your God, Father, Son and Holy Spirit, and seek to serve him.'

Opening prayer

Lord God, you have called us to know you
and to love you.
Help us to be faithful to our calling
and to serve you all our days.
Amen.

Opening song

Be thou my vision

Readings

1 Kings 8:(1, 6, 10-11) 22-30, 41-43 or Joshua 24:1-2a, 14-18
Psalm 84 or Psalm 34:15-22
Ephesians 6:10-20
John 6:56-69

Thought for the day

God does not force himself upon us. He has given us the freedom to choose whether we serve him or not. He gives himself to us in love and we can choose whether to return that love or to ignore him. Some definitely choose to ignore or go against God; others ignore him by default – that is, they let other things and people squeeze God out. If we are to love and serve God, we have to be sure we have made this a definite choice.

Joshua called the tribes of Israel together and asked them to dedicate their lives to the true God. If they were unwilling to serve the Lord, they should at least choose whom they were going to serve, whether it was the gods of Egypt or the gods of the Amorites. There is always the danger of not making a clear choice. Joshua gave a lead by saying, 'As for me and my household, we will serve the LORD.'

Once they were given a lead, the Israelites declared they would not desert the LORD and follow other gods. They then recited how the LORD delivered them from Egypt and from slavery: the LORD did great wonders in their sight and the LORD protected them. 'Therefore we will also serve the LORD for he is our God.' The Israelites made a definite decision to serve the LORD.

In today's Gospel we find two definite groups of people. Those who find the teaching too hard, who take offence and do not believe, belong to the first group. They turn away from Jesus and no longer go with him. There are many who do this. The second group are those who seek to stay with him and be loyal to him. Amongst those are the disciples. Jesus asks them, 'Do you also wish to go away?' They are not forced to stay: if they want, they can leave. Judas will later prove the possibility of this. Simon Peter replies for the disciples and says, 'Lord, to whom can we go? You have the words of eternal life. We have come to believe and know that you are the Holy One of God.'

We are given the opportunity of turning away from him or committing ourselves to follow him. This is not just a one-off choice; we have to make it every day and sometimes many times in a day.

Question time

Do we recognise that in Jesus is eternal life and that he is the Holy One of God?

Do we truly give our allegiance to our Lord? If we feel that we do, how do we come to believe and know that he is the Christ?

Illustration

Here is a story of loyalty. A man and his dog walked in the hill country. The man saw an old mine in a hillside and went in. Whilst inside, the roof collapsed and trapped the man by his leg. For a while the dog stayed with him but it then went outside the mine and stood at the entrance. There it began to howl to attract attention. No one took any notice at first. The dog became hungry and thirsty but it did not leave its post. The weather became bad; the dog got wet and cold but it stayed put and continued to howl. Finally a nearby farmer decided there was something wrong with the dog and he climbed the hillside to find it. When he arrived, the dog stopped howling but would not let him touch it or even feed it. It tried to lead him into the mine. The farmer made to go away but as soon as he did this the dog started to howl and to walk towards the mine again. At last he decided to go to the entrance and call to see if there was anyone there. He heard a voice and so went cautiously inside. He saw the man was trapped and went for help. The dog seemed to understand because it now stayed with its master and remained with him until help came and he was rescued.

Intercessions

Blessed are you, Lord our God;
in you is life and life eternal.
You love us with an everlasting love.
You give us the freedom to turn to you
or turn away from you.
You do not compel us to love you
but invite us to know you and your love.
Help us in our desire to know you
and to be more faithful to you.
Blessed are you, God, for ever.

We give you thanks for all your faithful people.
We rejoice in the fellowship of your saints
and all who have been loyal to you.
We remember before you those who are new to the faith
and all who are seeking to deepen their faith.
We pray for all who are tempted to turn their back on you,
those who are troubled by doubt
and all those who are finding their faith a challenge.

Silence

Holy Lord,
our trust is in you.

We give thanks for the gift of power you have given
to peoples and nations.
May we use all our powers to your glory
and the benefit of others.
We remember all who suffer from the misuse of power,
all who are oppressed, the wrongly imprisoned
and those who suffer from violence.
Lord, grant us peace in our hearts and in the world.

Silence

Holy Lord,
our trust is in you.

We give you thanks for those who brought us
to know you and love you.
We remember our teachers and preachers.
We pray for our friends and our families.
May our relationships all reflect
a good relationship with you.
We remember all who have been betrayed in love.

Silence

Holy Lord,
our trust is in you.

We give thanks for all who have committed themselves
to work for your glory and the benefits of others.
We remember all who feel let down, deserted or lonely.
We pray for the persecuted and the marginalised in society.
We ask your blessing on all who are ill at home
or in hospital,
on all who seek healing or deliverance.

Silence

Holy Lord,
our trust is in you.

You, Lord, are the giver of life eternal.
We remember before you the faithful departed.
We ask your blessing upon loved ones and friends
who are at rest with you.
May they rejoice in the fellowship of the saints
and the fullness of life eternal.

Silence

Merciful Father,
accept these prayers
for the sake of your Son,
our Saviour Jesus Christ.
Amen.

Memory verse

Be strong in the Lord and in the strength of his power.
Ephesians 6:10

Suggested music

Stand up, stand up for Jesus
Break thou the bread of life
O Jesus, I have promised

CANDLES

Aim

To know that God loves us and protects us.

Teaching

If you are going out and it starts to rain, what do you put on? Waterproofs, a raincoat, wellingtons, and you might have an umbrella.

If it is very hot and sunny, what do you use to protect yourself? You might wear sunglasses, sun cream; you might have a parasol. What is the difference between an umbrella and a parasol? (If possible, show these to the children.)

Now, if it is very cold, what do you wear? Gloves, scarf, coat, snow boots: you wrap up to keep warm.

If you are riding a bike or on a skateboard, what sort of things do you wear? You need a helmet, some knee pads and some elbow pads to protect you in case you fall off.

Let us pretend we are getting ready to go out. It is raining: let us put on our rainwear and put up an umbrella.

Now it's hot and sunny: let us take off our rainwear and put on our sunglasses and put up a sunshade.

Now it is suddenly becoming cold: we put away the sunshade and get out our gloves and scarves and put on a big coat.

Show some toy armour or a picture of a Roman soldier in armour. Now, what do you think this is for? It is to protect the soldier from the enemy, to save him from getting hurt. His helmet is to stop his head getting hurt. His shield and breastplate are to stop arrows or someone with a sword from hitting him. The Roman soldier feels stronger and safer in his armour. (Let one of the children put on the toy armour if you have some.)

God knows that sometimes the world is a dangerous place and he wants to protect us. He comes to us to give us his strength. If we know he is there, it makes us strong. If it is dark and we have a light, it makes us braver and happier. When we know that God loves us and protects us, it also makes us braver and happier. God is always with us, and when we are in trouble, he especially wants to care for us and keep us from harm.

Activity

Play 'Musical hats'. Have two or three funny hats. The children stand in a circle all facing in one direction so that they look at the back of each other's heads. During the music a hat is placed on their heads from behind. They then take the hat off and place it on the head in front. Those caught with a hat on their head when the music stops are out. So it continues until the circle is small and only one is left.

Prayer

O God, thank you for your love.
We are happy that you care for us
and protect us from all evil.
Amen.

Song

We are marching in the light of God

(Have the second verse – 'We are marching in the strength of God'. Let the children march around as they sing this. The music could be used for 'Musical hats' so that the children become familiar with it.)

LAMPS

Aim

To discover that God is our strength.

Teaching

Look at various sports equipment that is used for protection. It would be good to have someone dressed for skateboarding and someone dressed for cricket; someone else could be wearing a cycling helmet. Look at whatever gear there is available and discuss why it is used.

Every time we get into a car what is the first thing we should do? Belt up. We do this for protection. We may not need that protection but if something suddenly happened, then we would be glad of it.

In the days before the use of guns and gunpowder the best protection for a soldier was his armour and a shield. Let us see if we can name different pieces of armour. (Use the worksheet or a representation of a Roman soldier to get the various pieces named. Can they find the helmet, the breastplate, the belt and sword, the sandals, the shield?)

When St Paul was a prisoner, he was chained by the wrist to a Roman soldier. There was always a soldier chained to him to make sure he could not escape. He must have often talked to the soldiers and asked them about what battles they had fought.

Paul thought of the troubles he had been in and how God was always with him and cared for him. Maybe the soldier was strong in his armour, but Paul was strong because of the power of God. Paul wants us to put on God's armour every day so that we might be protected against evil. He asks us to put the armour of God on by being in contact with him – that is, by prayer. In every battle it is important that the soldier keeps in contact with his leader and we need to keep contact with our God.

Activity

Using two or three soft balls, have someone in the middle of a circle with a bat and let the rest try to hit him/her. You can stipulate that the person in the middle is protected and therefore they cannot be hit on the head or chest. Once they are hit, someone else (perhaps the person that hit them) goes into the centre. (You can make soft balls with a sock stuffed with another sock.)

Prayer

Holy and strong God,
protect us from all that is evil.
Keep us in your presence,
surround us with your power,
and keep us in your peace.
Amen.

Song

I'm putting God's armour on

TORCHES

Aim

To seek strength from God through prayer.

Teaching

We are fortunate if we are strong. We can go to a gym or do exercises to increase or keep up our strength. We can do the same with our minds and exercise them by reading, by learning and by using them. In the time of St Paul many a man of strong body and sharp mind was in the Roman army. These men were trained to be strong, to use their might and their minds. To help them they were given armour so that they would be protected in battle.

Paul was a prisoner and chained to such a soldier. A chain around their wrists linked them to each other. Paul must have often asked the soldier about past campaigns and battles. The soldier fastened to Paul was one who had fought his battles; his strength was lessening and his powers were getting weaker. Paul saw that the man's armour could not protect him from everything in life.

We might be strong in body and mind but we need to be strong in our spirit also. Even more important, we need to be strong in the Lord.

As Paul looked at the man's armour he realised that we need to have on the armour of God and he gave us a list. The beginning and end of the list is of utmost importance. 'Be strong in the Lord and in the strength of his power . . . Pray in the Spirit at all times.'

Let us look first at the armour (use the worksheet.).

The belt of truth: the belt was used to help to hold things together and from it hung the sword. We need to wrap around us the truth that God made the world, God made us. God loves us and is with us. That is the truth. If feelings tell us otherwise, then feelings are liars.

The breastplate: apart from the shield this is the biggest piece of armour. Paul sees it as the protection of righteousness. This is not just being good; it is about living in a right relationship with God. Our protection comes from our relationship with God. We are strong not in our own efforts but in the Lord.

The shoes are signs of being ready for action. Paul says we need to be ready at all times to proclaim the Gospel of peace. We need to be alert to every opportunity of telling of Christ, including to ourselves.

The shield Paul talks about is not the little round shield but a big oblong one that can cover the whole body. One of the dangers of ancient warfare was fiery darts. But the large shield was a great protection. We have the shield of faith. Again, faith is about our relationship with God through prayer. It is in God that we are strong and protected.

The helmet has saved many a soldier. Our salvation is in and through Jesus Christ. Salvation is not just from our past; it also guarantees our future. Jesus has won for us eternal life.

The sword is the sword of the Spirit, which is the word of God. It is the word of God that is our defence against evil, especially the Word made flesh in Christ our Lord.

We are more confident and safer because of our armour. We are strong in the Lord and in the strength of his power. We maintain our armour and keep it by us through our relationship with God, through perseverance in prayer.

Activity

Against each piece of armour on the worksheet write what St Paul calls it. Let the group read out the name of a piece and say how St Paul wants us to use it. Discuss how we keep our relationship with God alive.

Prayer

Lord, you know that we have no power of our own
to help ourselves.
Keep us under your protection,
defend us against all the fiery darts of wickedness
and bring us into your peace.
Amen.

Song

Be strong, and put on the armour of God

Proper 17

Sunday between 28 August and 3 September inclusive

Aim

To make sure our traditions do not hinder our relationship with God.

Preparation

Have notices about washing hands near the main entrance to the church.

Opening activity

Mini-drama

Speaker 1 Mr X is always so lovely and clean. He smells of soap and after-shave. His clothes are always tidy.
Speaker 2 True, but I went to his house and it is a tip. There are unwashed dishes and clothes everywhere. It is all a front. He gives a show of cleanliness.
Speaker 1 But he always speaks so nicely and has kind words for everyone.
Speaker 2 Not everyone. You should have heard the way he spoke to his brother and sister – he was absolutely horrible. His language was foul.
Speaker 1 Some people are not all they seem to be.

Opening prayer

God, we rejoice in your love and in your forgiveness.
Though we are not worthy to come into your presence
you welcome us and forgive us our sins.
Make our hearts clean, O God,
and renew a right spirit within us.
Amen.

Opening song

Father of heaven

Readings

Song of Solomon 2:8-13 or Deuteronomy 4:1-2, 6-9
Psalm 45:1-2, 6-9 or Psalm 15
James 1:17-27
Mark 7:1-8, 14-15, 21-23

Thought for the day

It is hard to believe that the Pharisees would travel all the way from Jerusalem to Galilee to tell Jesus that he and his disciples had dirty hands. This meeting is about confrontation and it shows how Jesus was challenging the attitudes of the established church.

The Pharisees say that Jesus and his disciples are unclean. They have not washed properly before eating bread. Very often Jesus did things that made him unclean in the eyes of the Pharisees. He touched a leper; he touched a bier on which there was a dead man. A woman who was suffering from a haemorrhage touched him. Jesus was declared unclean by each of these acts, and anyone who was in contact with him became unclean also.

The Jewish rituals of washing were mainly good common sense. They were safeguards against infection and harmful contacts. In the same way, we know we ought to wash after doing a dirty job or going to the toilet. But with the tradition becoming fixed there was a danger that someone felt they could do something they ought not to and then just wash their hands and be clean. Within the Christian Church some people have misused the sacrament of confession. We cannot truly seek forgiveness of a sin if we intend to go on committing it. We cannot come to church on a Sunday for absolution if we intend to do the same things again.

Jesus replied that it was no use going through outward rituals if the inside is not cleansed. A show of being clean is just pretence. Jesus calls the Pharisees hypocrites. Originally a hypocrite was a play actor; it meant one who pretends or gives a set reply. It came to mean a person whose life was an act without depth or sincerity. Anyone who goes through the religious acts or rituals without a relationship to God is a hypocrite. Cleanliness does not depend on whether you have washed or eaten; it depends on your inner attitude, on your thoughts and your heart. It is no use being present at worship if we do not give ourselves to our God. This is why the Psalmist prayed, 'Make me a clean heart, O God, and renew a right Spirit within me.' We must be sure our human traditions do not come between God and us. Maybe this would make Christians take a careful look at how we keep Christmas.

Jesus lists among the things that defile a person evil intentions or designs. Every outward act of sin comes from an inward choice. We need to keep watch on our thoughts and our decisions. Very often our departure from goodness and from God begins with the attitudes and choices that we make. If we fail to give God the central place in our thinking, we will soon push him to the edges of our life.

Another word Jesus uses about defilement is translated as 'fornications'. It is from the Greek word 'porneiai' and means every kind of sexual vice. We must include all pornography and wrong attitudes towards sex. Anything that degrades others or ourselves makes us unclean. We need keep a close watch on our attitudes and what we expose our minds to.

Question time

Do we seek to come before God with a pure heart and good intentions? Assuming we do, we need to know God accepts us even when we fail, as long as we are seeking to do his will.

Are there things within our own church tradition that need changing so that we may have more living relationship with God?

Illustration

A devout Muslim carries his prayer mat around with him and prays a fixed number of times each day. At the fixed times he will unroll his mat and turn to God. This is a wonderful way of keeping in contact with his creator.

There was a certain Muslim who had great anger in his heart. He was in hot pursuit of a man whom he wanted to kill. He had a dagger and was intent on murder. Suddenly the call to prayer rang out from the mosque. The man stopped for a moment, rushed his prayers, then continued on his murderous chase. The prayer was part of his daily ritual but he did not let it touch his heart. This man could be seen to be a hypocrite.

Intercessions

Blessed are you, Lord our God.
You give us life, you give us love, you give us yourself.
We come to give our lives and our love to you.
Cleanse us from all our sin
and make a clean heart within us,
that we may do what you want us to do
and be the people you want us to be.

We give thanks for the examples of the saints
in their battle against evil and in their striving to do good.
We remember before you
all who are struggling with temptation,
all who are pulled by divided loyalties.
We pray for those who go through the rituals
but miss the reality.
We ask your blessing
on all who are scorned and rejected
because of their relationship with Christ.

Silence

Make our hearts clean, O God;
renew a right spirit within us.

We give thanks for the work of the Social Services
and all who work for the care of others.
We remember before you
all who are caught up in vice or degradation.
We pray for all addicts,
that they may find help and hope.
Bless all who struggle to keep standards
and make a stand against the evils that are around them.

Silence

Make our hearts clean, O God;
renew a right spirit within us.

We rejoice in our homes and in family life.
We thank you for all who have given their lives
in caring for us and in loving us.
We ask your blessing upon our families and friends.
We remember before you all who are lonely,
all who feel uncared for or unwanted.
We pray for all who suffer from neglect
or a breakdown in relationships.

Silence

Make our hearts clean, O God;
renew a right spirit within us.

As we rejoice in life, we remember all who feel
that life is meaningless and empty.
We ask your blessing on the despairing and despondent.
We pray for all who are treated as unclean
through illness or disability.
We remember all who work to combat disease
and infections.

Silence

Make our hearts clean, O God;
renew a right spirit within us.

We rejoice in the fellowship of all your saints.
We remember before you all our loved ones departed,
giving thanks for their life and their care.
We offer our hearts and minds and whole being to you,
good and gracious God.

Silence

Merciful Father,
accept these prayers
for the sake of your Son,
our Saviour Jesus Christ.
Amen.

Memory verse

Create in me a clean heart, O God, and put a new and right spirit within me.
Psalm 51:10

Suggested music

Father, who in Jesus found us
In an age of twisted values
O for a heart to praise my God

CANDLES

Aim

To show God wants all of us, not just our prayers.

Teaching

Who gets your breakfast ready? Who washes your clothes? Who sees that you are happy and loved? You are lucky that someone loves you and gives themselves to you. Your mother and father show their love by what they give you, but more important they give you of themselves. They give you their time, their attention and their love. It is good to know that you are not left alone. When you go home you can depend on someone being there.

Jesus likes us to speak to him in prayer. Jesus likes us to come to church. Jesus likes us to try and be good, but most of all he likes us to give ourselves to him – not just our prayers or our songs but our whole self in love. We will learn a new song that tells us this:

Jesus wants all of me,
Jesus wants all of me,
Jesus wants all of me,
that's what he wants.
(*Repeat*)

My heart, my mind, my hands, my feet, my ears, my nose, my eyes, my teeth, my arms, my legs, my toes, my knees.

Get the children to repeat the first verse a few times before they sing it.

Go through the second verse getting them to point at each part of the body. Let them wave their hands, jump with their feet, swing their arms, shake their legs, wiggle their toes and knock their knees together. Go through the actions a few times before they attempt it to music.

End with shouting, 'What does Jesus want?' and let them reply loudly, 'Jesus wants all of me'.

Activity

Play 'Simon says'. Choose someone to stand out in front. They are to tell the others what to do. You must obey when he/she starts with 'Simon says' But if he/she omits starting with 'Simon says', you must stand absolutely still. If you move the least bit you are out. The last person in is the next Simon/Simone.

Prayer

God, we love you.
You have made us and you love us.
We want to give ourselves to you.
Amen.

Song

Jesus wants all of me

LAMPS

Aim

To show how our inner thoughts and ideas are important.

Teaching

Once upon a time there was a sleepy village on the slopes of a mountain. The soil was rich and good, producing lots of food. People had built nice houses and farms, and they had a school and a church. Inside the mountain trouble was brewing. Steam, smoke and lava were building up power. The mountain often trembled but the people did not take much notice – not even when smoke came out of the top. It had done this before. It did not seem to bother them that they were sitting on a volcano. (Get the children to talk about what a volcano is.)

Suddenly one day the volcano blew its top. Lava and hot ash came tumbling down the mountainside. It destroyed houses and farms, school and church. Everything disappeared. It was all rather sad and it happened because the people ignored what was going on inside the mountain. They thought as long as the surface was all right it did not matter what was happening within.

Pharisees travelled all the way from Jerusalem to Galilee to tell Jesus that his disciples were unclean because they did not wash their hands. If the disciples were unclean, then anyone that touched them was unclean. This meant that Jesus was also unclean. No unclean people would be allowed to come into their church. They were beginning to stop Jesus and the disciples from attending the synagogue. Inside, in their hearts and minds, the Pharisees were very angry with Jesus because he was saying that it was no use having clean hands if your mind or your heart was dirty. He said it was like just washing the outside of the cup and not cleaning the inside. Jesus was saying that it was no use just going to church and saying prayers, you also had to lead a good life and to give yourself fully to God. It is no use looking nice and pretty if you are full of anger and bully people.

Sadly this would just make the Pharisees angrier with Jesus, they would plot to kill him and they would not be happy until Jesus was crucified.

When we come to church we need to know that God wants more than our prayers and our singing, he wants us to give our whole lives to him. It is no use coming looking clean if we have wicked thoughts or anger against someone in our hearts. God is willing to accept us as we are. He knows our thoughts and he still loves us. He wants us to seek to lead a good life and to offer the whole of our life to him. Let us see how we can give ourselves to him today.

Activity

Play a game of tag. Once the person, who is chasing, touches someone they have to hold his/her hand and continue the chase. As they touch someone else the chain of hands increase and they then continue until the last person is caught. The last person becomes the new starter of the game.

Prayer

God, I want to give my whole life to you.
I am sorry for when I have done wrong
and ask you to forgive me.
I will try to live a good life
and to do what you would have me do,
that your kingdom may come on earth
as it is in heaven.
Amen.

Song

In everything that I do

TORCHES

Aim

To show the danger of what we harbour within.

Teaching

Do you know what a UXB is? No, it is not a sort of bicycle. It is something quite dangerous. In means 'unexploded bomb.' Sometimes UXBs have been discovered in pretty parcels or in nice-looking travelling cases. They look fine on the outside but all the time a great danger is ticking inside. If people do not notice the danger, then their lives become at risk. Often it takes very brave people to defuse the unexploded bomb. It is terrible if someone with an unexploded bomb goes amongst a group of people.

The Pharisees had travelled all the way from Jerusalem to Galilee to argue with Jesus about his disciples eating with unwashed hands. Imagine your mum coming for over 70 miles to tell you to wash your hands – I am sure you would feel she had really come for another reason. Perhaps she was worried about you, or you had made her angry or sad.

The Pharisees were angry with Jesus and his disciples because they seemed to be challenging their traditions. If they looked at what the prophets had said in the past, Jesus was challenging not so much the traditions as the way people were using those traditions. Here they were talking about washing hands when they were full of hatred and anger towards Jesus and his disciples. By declaring the disciples unclean, it meant that all who made contact with them were unclean. Jesus was unclean and any with whom he made contact.

It would appear the Pharisees were more concerned with hygiene and rules about washing than Jesus was. Jesus said they were like people who would wash the outside of the cup and not the inside. They were dealing with outward appearances and ignoring the inward. Inside was ticking away a UXB, because inside was anger, hatred and resentment; these would suddenly explode and cause trouble. There are certain things we harbour in our hearts and minds that, unless we deal with them, will cause no end of trouble for us and for others. Jesus was far more concerned about what was going on inside than with the outward show.

Sadly, this only annoyed the Pharisees even more. They would let their feelings explode and seek to destroy Jesus.

Let us look at Mark 7:21-23 and see how these warnings apply to us today.

Activity

Play a game of UXB. It is like 'Pass the parcel', except when the music stops the person holding the UXB shouts, 'Bang', and then the people each side of them are out, not them. Once the music starts the UXB continues to be passed around. Let whatever is passed around look quite innocuous.

Prayer

Holy and ever-loving God,
we thank you for the forgiveness of sins
and the opportunity to start anew.
We pray that you will fill our hearts with your goodness
and our minds with your love.
Amen.

Song

Teach me to trust you

Proper 18

Sunday between 4 and 10 September inclusive

Aim

To encourage our church to be open and welcoming.

Preparation

Have notice saying:

> This is part of the Catholic Church –
> meaning we are open for all people
> at all times
> and all places.
> Welcome.

Opening activity

Mini-drama

Speaker 1 I would like to be exclusive; only classy and well-spoken people for my friends.
Speaker 2 I would like all sorts of friends; I would like to be inclusive.
Speaker 1 I would like to mix only with the well-dressed and the well-known.
Speaker 2 I seek friends from all kinds of people.
Speaker 1 I only want people like me for my friends.
Speaker 2 I would like a few friends who are different to me.
Speaker 1 How is it you have so many friends and I am so lonely?
Speaker 2 You have managed to be really exclusive. You have no friends but yourself. But I will be your friend.

Opening prayer

Lord, open our ears to your call;
open our lips to sing your praises;
open our hearts to your love;
open our eyes to your abiding presence.
May we ever rejoice in your word
and proclaim your glory in all the world.
Amen.

Opening song

O for a thousand tongues to sing

Readings

Proverbs 22:1-2, 8-9, 22-23 or Isaiah 35:4-7a
Psalm 125 or Psalm 146
James 2:1-10 (11-13) 14-17
Mark 7:24-37

Thought for the day

The Pharisees had declared Jesus and the disciples to be unclean. This was a way of banning them and any who had contact with them from their synagogues. Therefore it is not surprising that the stories following this event come from a non-Jewish area.

Tyre and Sidon are famed for their Phoenician sailors who were the first to navigate the seas by the stars. Tyre is 40 miles north of Capernaum and Sidon is 60 miles away. Both cities looked to the sea and overseas for their trade.

Jesus is in Gentile territory. Just as the Jews would not soil their lips with unwashed pots, so they avoided contact with the Gentiles for that would also make them unclean. As Jesus challenged the distinction between clean and unclean foods, he is now challenging the distinction between clean and unclean people. The Jewish people survived through their exclusiveness. Jesus wanted to show that the love of God is inclusive. The rest of the world, the Gentiles, also have a place in God's kingdom.

Whilst there, Jesus is approached by two Gentiles. A woman comes asking help for her daughter and a man who is deaf with an impediment in his speech is brought to Jesus. The woman was a Greek, and adding to this that she was a Syrophoenician evokes the idea of the fractiousness there was between the Jews and the people of Tyre. There was a definite animosity between these groups. Jesus takes no notice of this division.

When Jesus replies to her plea for help, 'Let the children be fed first, for it is not fair to take the children's food and throw it to the dogs', he would have found many a Jew rejoicing, for they use the term 'Gentile dogs' as a term of contempt. Jesus used a diminutive word for 'dog' to soften this and there is no doubt his voice did not imply his rejection of the woman. Israel may be 'first' but only first; many others from the rest of the world would also be fed with the 'Bread of Life'.

The woman had sought Jesus out, and now from the Greek-speaking area of the Decapolis they brought to Jesus a man who was deaf and had an impediment in his speech. Again Jesus is to offer the healing and love of God to this Gentile. Isaiah said that a sign of God's kingdom would be when 'the ears of the deaf (are) unstopped . . . and the tongue of the speechless sing for joy' (Isaiah 35:5-6). On a deeper level we need to consider the Jewish idea of hearing and speaking. Hearing was the most important sense because it was through hearing and speaking that the covenant was given. It was Israel who heard; the Gentiles were deaf. The Gentiles cannot hear the word of God or sing his praises. Once more Jesus challenges this view by accepting the man who is brought to him. Jesus acts out the miracle as the man would not hear the words. When Jesus says, 'Ephphatha' – that is, 'Be opened' – it can be a call not only to the man but also to the opening of the Gentiles to the Christ. The ears of the Gentiles are opened to the Word of God. The man, representing the Gentiles, zealously proclaims what Jesus has done. The response is 'He has done all things well; he even makes the deaf to hear and the mute to speak.' The whole world is being opened to the Christ. Let not the Church act in exclusive ways.

Question time

Is our church really open to all who come, or do we send signals that say some are not welcome?

How can we reach out so that others are given the opportunity to hear God's word?

Illustration

There was once a very famous church. Every Sunday it was fashionable to go there and be seen. People came in their finery. Some of the most important people of the land attended it. The music and the choir were superb, the ordering of the service was of a very high standard; everything done was to the highest degree of excellence and in the best possible taste. For a good few Sundays a poorly dressed and shabby-looking person turned up at the door but was turned away for one reason or another. After a few weeks of trying to get in, the woman sat on the lowest step and prayed to God, 'Lord, why can I not get entrance into this church?' The Lord replied, 'My daughter, how do I know? I have been trying to get into this church for years.'

Intercessions

Blessed are you, Lord our God,
for you have called your people
from every tribe, nation and language.
We rejoice that you care for all peoples
and every single individual
and seek to offer each of them your love.
You have called us all to hear your word
and to proclaim your praises.
Blessed are you, Father, Son and Holy Spirit.

We rejoice that your Church is for all people
in all times and in all places.
No one who comes to you is cast out.
May we seek to make your Church
open and welcoming to all.
We ask your blessing upon all who are involved
in the outreach and mission of the church.
We remember especially those who seek
to proclaim your love by word and example.
We pray for all who have not heard of you
and your saving grace.

Silence

God, ever with us,
be our strength and our Saviour.

We give thanks for the peace
that you offer to us and to the nations.
We remember before you areas where there is conflict
and violence,
where people are caught up in war.
We pray for all who suffer from racial hatred
or prejudice,
all who are outcasts or refugees.
We ask your blessing upon the work of the United Nations
and all peacekeeping forces.

Silence

God, ever with us,
be our strength and our Saviour.

We give thanks for those who brought us
to know you and your love.
We pray for all who have taught us and cared for us.
We ask your blessing upon our families and our friends.
We remember before you all who are lonely
or feel uncared for and unwanted.

Silence

God, ever with us,
be our strength and our Saviour.

We give thanks for the gifts of hearing and speech.
We remember all who suffer from deafness
and those who are unable to speak.
We pray for all who suffer from autism,
all who are withdrawn from normal life
and all who find communication difficult.
We ask your blessing upon all ill and suffering people.
We remember especially
friends and members of our community who are ill.

Silence

God, ever with us,
be our strength and our Saviour.

We rejoice that you have opened for us
the fullness of eternal life and the way to your kingdom.
We remember friends and loved ones
who are departed from us.
May they enjoy knowing you in glory
and rest in the peace of your presence.

Silence

Merciful Father,
accept these prayers
for the sake of your Son,
our Saviour Jesus Christ.
Amen.

Memory verse

Faith by itself, if it has no works, is dead.
James 2:17

Suggested music

Listen, let your heart keep seeking
All things bright and beautiful
Jesus shall reign

CANDLES

Aim

To help the children understand the wonderful healing of the man suffering from deafness.

Teaching

There are many people in the world who cannot hear. Do you know what you call it when you cannot hear? Anyone who cannot hear is said to be 'deaf'. Say it after me: 'deaf'. If you suffer from deafness you cannot hear anything. You cannot hear the birds singing. You cannot hear someone speaking. What else would you not hear? Let us pretend we are not able to hear. Cover your ears with the flat of your hands. (Once this is done, mouth words to the children but do not say them.) Mime that they should take their hands off their ears.

If you do not hear words, you cannot learn them. So many people who suffer from deafness cannot speak properly either. They have never heard words so they do not know how to say them. They have to learn to talk through actions. If they want something, they can point or show it by actions. Try a few simple mimes and see if the children can understand. Mime 'I am hungry', 'I am tired', 'I will go upstairs', 'I love you'. Do not worry if the children do not get all the answers. Shake your head when they are wrong and nod when they are right. Help them to see how difficult it is.

Now we will use our ears and listen to a story. There was once a man who could not hear: he was deaf. So he could not hear about Jesus and how wonderful Jesus is. The man could not speak properly because he had not heard words. So he could not ask to be taken to Jesus. The man had some friends who cared for him and wished that he could get better. When the friends heard that Jesus was near where they lived they got very excited. Maybe Jesus could make their friend better. By signs they invited their friend to go out for a walk. (Indicate this by walking fingers.) They brought him to Jesus.

Jesus could see that the man was unable to hear so he took him away from the crowd. He led him by the hand. Then Jesus acted out what he wanted to do. He put his fingers gently into the man's ears. Then he touched the man's tongue. Looking closely at the man, Jesus said, 'Be opened.' Jesus was speaking to the man's ears and to his mouth. And the man heard him. This was the first time the man had heard anything. Jesus made the man able to hear and to speak.

Everyone was very excited and they said about Jesus, 'He has done everything well; he makes the deaf to hear and the dumb to speak.'

Activity

Show drawings of various things and ask what noise they make – for example, a cat, dog, alarm clock, bell, aeroplane, bird. Let the children make the noise of something for others to guess what it is. They may also like to react to sign language. Use your hands to welcome them – open arms and smiley face. Turn them away with pushing-out action of arms. Beckon them back with a wave of the hand. You could make this into a little game.

Prayer

God, we thank you for ears to hear
and a mouth to speak.
May we listen carefully to what we are told
and enjoy singing songs about you.
Amen.

Song

Lord, you put a tongue in my mouth

LAMPS

Aim

To show how Jesus is concerned for the individual.

Teaching

There was once a man who had never heard of Jesus. He lived in one of the ten cities that were known as the 'Decapolis'. This word is Greek for 'ten cities' and they were mainly filled with non-Jewish peoples. Maybe Jesus went there because the Pharisees were excluding him from the Jewish community. The man could not hear anything about Jesus because he suffered from deafness. He could not hear anything at all, not even the voices of his friends. (Discuss how difficult this must be and how they would have to use sign language.)

It was the friends of the man who heard that Jesus the healer had come to their area. They thought it would be a good idea to see if Jesus could make their friend hear and speak. The man could not speak properly because he had never heard words. Very often people suffering from deafness are unable to speak. The man found it very hard to communicate with others; some decided it was not worth trying to talk to him. The friends brought him to Jesus. This is a wonderful thing to do. We should learn to bring some of our friends to Jesus.

When Jesus met the man he soon realised that the man had problems with hearing and speaking. Jesus realised that he needed special attention on his own so he took him away from the crowds. The man needed special attention and Jesus gave it to him. Jesus acted out what he wanted to do. He put his fingers in the man's ears and then unstopped them. Next he spat on his fingers (spit was thought to have healing powers) and he put his fingers on the man's tongue. Only after this did he speak to the man, saying, 'Be opened.' Immediately the man's ears were unstopped and his tongue unloosened and he was able to hear and speak. The healing touch of Jesus had made him well.

Not only the man but also everyone in the area started to speak about Jesus. They were saying, 'He does everything well; he has made the deaf to hear and the dumb to speak.' These were people outside the Holy Land of the Jews hearing Jesus speak and opening their mouths to praise Jesus. This was part of the Gentile, non-Jewish world hearing of Jesus. In many ways this was Jesus reaching out to the rest of the world – and that includes us.

Activity

Let this story be acted out without words. Friends should come to the man and beckon him to go with them. They should take him by the hand and present him to Jesus. Show the actions of Jesus in taking him aside (no spitting!). Only after the actions let Jesus say, 'Be opened', and then let the man say, 'Thank you' to Jesus and 'Thank you' to God.

Let the children try and communicate, through miming, joy and sorrow, welcome and turning away. Let them try to be absolutely silent and yet communicate with each other.

Prayer

God, we thank you for our ears
and the sounds we hear.
We thank you for our voices
and the power of speech.
Teach us to listen carefully to each other and to you.
May we tell others of your love and healing power.
Amen.

Song

Open our eyes, Lord

TORCHES

Aim

To hear the call to have a new openness to God and to others.

Teaching

Jesus was away from the Holy Land and among people who were not Jews. But these people too had needs and troubles. Once they discovered that Jesus was a healer and that he cared for all people they came to him for help and healing. Jesus cared for all, whether they had heard of God or not.

Some people came with a friend. They brought him to Jesus. What a wonderful act this is to bring someone to Jesus. We know that Andrew brought his brother Peter to Jesus. Andrew also brought the boy with five loaves and two small fish to Jesus. Then when some Greeks wanted to speak to Jesus it was Andrew who brought them. The Church often grows this way when we seek to bring others to Jesus.

One man who was brought to Jesus suffered from being totally deaf, and because of this he could not formulate proper words. He could not have heard of Jesus. He was dependent on his friends to bring him to Jesus. When Jesus looked at the man and saw his trouble he took him aside. To try and communicate with him in a crowd was almost impossible. Jesus noticed the man's individual needs and sought to help him. As words would fall on deaf ears, Jesus acted out the healing and put his fingers in the man's ears. Then Jesus spat on his own hand and then touched the man's tongue. The ancient world believed in the healing properties of spit. The man was to understand that Jesus was seeking to heal him. Then Jesus looked up to heaven and said, 'Ephphatha' – that is, 'Be opened'. The man heard the words and was healed from that moment.

One of the weaknesses of the Church is that it appears to be deaf and unable to speak clearly. It does not speak out for God or joyously proclaim the Gospel. It rarely seems to be seeking to bring others to Jesus. We have lost a sense of mission and outreach and become the person who is tongue-tied and cannot speak clearly. Perhaps our inability to speak out is tied to our difficulty in hearing. How good are you at hearing the word of God? Did the readings of the Scriptures enter into your life today, or did they go in one ear and out the other? Too often people assume that they have heard when in fact they have never heeded a single word. We are conditioned to turning a deaf ear to so many sounds around us and so we fail to hear the Word of God. The Hebrew word for 'hear' meant to 'hear and react', 'to hear and obey'. If we close our ears to the call of God, or to the cries of the world, we become restricted – handicapped. Jesus calls us to openness with God and with the world. Let us hear again his words, 'Be opened.'

Open your ears to the call.
Open your mouth to proclaim his love.
Open your hearts to react to him.
Open your hands to reach out in generosity.
Be open.

Activity

Spend some time playing charades where they must communicate by actions and not use words. See if they can depict scenes from the life of Jesus without using words.

Prayer

Lord God,
you are always more ready to hear than we are to pray.
Forgive us when we have been deaf to your call
and when we have failed to proclaim you to others.
Open our ears to hear your word to us,
and our lips to sing your praises.
Amen.

Song

God be in my head

Proper 19

Sunday between 11 and 17 September inclusive

Aim
To encourage a personal relationship with Christ the living Lord.

Preparation
Have a crucifix or a painting of the crucifixion at the entrance of the church, with the words 'Come to me' underneath it.

Opening activity
Give everyone a cross made from red material or crêpe paper. Tell them it is red because Jesus gave his life that we may have life eternal. Ask everyone to hold their cross and think of something that is really bothering them. Ask them to bring their trouble to Jesus Christ. As an outward sign we will come to the front of the church one by one and place the red crosses in a bowl. (During this you may like to have some quiet music. I would suggest 'O my Saviour lifted'. You may decide to sing the hymn or at least the last verse.)

Opening prayer
Father, in your great love
you sent your Son to be our Saviour.
Help us to know Jesus as Christ,
as the living Lord who comes to us
and offers himself to us as our friend and redeemer.
Amen.

Opening song
Hail to the Lord's anointed

Readings
Proverbs 1:20-33 or Isaiah 50:4-9a
Psalm 19 or Wisdom of Solomon 7:26–8:1 or Psalm 116:1-9
James 3:1-12
Mark 8:27-38

Thought for the day
Jesus and the disciples are 25 miles north of the Sea of Galilee in an area that was well known for pagan worship. They are travelling around the villages of Caesarea Philippi. This area was famous for the worship of the god Baal in ancient times. The Greeks said it was the birthplace of Pan, the god of nature: the pipes of Pan could be heard in the woods and wood nymphs were to be seen dancing. It was here that Herod the Great built a gleaming white temple for the worship of Caesar. Herod's son Philip beautified the temple and added his name to the town, so that it became known as Caesarea Philippi. It was here, most likely under a starry sky by a campfire, that Jesus asked the disciples about their thoughts towards him.

Jesus asks first, 'Who do people say that I am?' Some were saying he was John the Baptist returned from the dead. No doubt this caused some amusement in the camp. Others were saying he was Elijah returned to herald in the coming of the Messiah. Yet others were saying he was a prophet, a good man and a wonder-worker. People still suggest all sorts of ideas about who Jesus is.

Jesus then asks, 'But who do *you* say that I am?' This is what Jesus wants to know from each of us. Not a summary of other people's ideas. He wants the reply from those who have spent time with him, the personal conviction of a disciple. It is not enough to be able to recite creeds or what others have said about Jesus. A person can be an atheist and still pass exams in theology. You can be able to recite stories about the historical Jesus and not be a Christian. Jesus seeks a personal response from each of us. He wants us to know him, to talk to him, and only then talk *about* him. Notice how personal Jesus is in his invitations:

> Come to me.
> I will refresh you.
> Abide in me and I will abide in you.

We can only be true disciples if we spend time with him, if we get to know him. Then we can respond as Peter does by saying, 'You are the Christ, the Messiah.' When we personally come to know Jesus as the 'Anointed One of God' we will acknowledge him as our Lord and Saviour. One of the reasons Jesus told the disciples to tell no one is that people had wrong ideas about what the Messiah should do. They would learn through Jesus that being the Messiah would involve his suffering, and they would discover that they will be called to suffer like him.

Peter tried to sway Jesus away from any conflict but Jesus knew he could not escape the battle if he had come to win people to God. He knew the powers of evil would rally against him and he could not run away. He did not want to suffer; that's what made Peter's words all the more dangerous. The Tempter often seeks to weaken our resolve through our friends. We need to learn to stand firm.

Question time
Have we built up a good enough relationship with Jesus to be able to say who he is?

Illustration
In his poem 'Gareth and Lynette', Tennyson tells of the struggle Gareth has to leave home. He wants to become one of the knights of Arthur but his mother does not want him to leave home. She has already lost two of her sons to Arthur's court. 'Hast thou no pity on my loneliness?' she asks. 'Stay, my best son, ye are yet more a boy than a man,' she pleads. The mother produces excellent reasons for Gareth to stay at home and ignore his vision. Here, the tempter is using someone who loves him dearly to stop Gareth serving his vision. Gareth replies:

> O Mother,
> How can you keep me tethered to you – Shame.
> Man I am a grown, a man's work I must do.
> Follow the deer? Follow Christ the King,

Live pure, speak true, right wrong, follow the King –
Else, wherefore born.

Gareth was not tempted through his mother but followed the vision as he saw it.

Jesus could not allow Peter to sway him from his purpose.

Intercessions

Blessed are you, Lord our God,
for you have sent your Son to be our Saviour.
In the darkness of this world he comes to be our light.
He has triumphed over pain and death
and opened to us the way to everlasting life.
He has revealed your love
and made us sons and daughters of God.
Blessed are you, Father, Son and Holy Spirit.

We give thanks for your saints
and for all who have stood against evil and temptation in the world.
We remember before you all who at this time
are struggling with their faith,
all who are tempted away by false promises
and bright lights.
We pray for those who have learnt the words
but not met the Saviour.
We remember any who go through rituals
that seem empty of your presence.
Bless all who are being prepared for confirmation
and all who are seeking to grow
in their relationship with you.

Silence

O Lord, our Strength and our Redeemer,
hear our prayer.

We give thanks for the beauty of this day
and for the wonders of creation.
We remember before you all who are suffering
from war or division within communities.
We pray for those who have lost their way in life
and feel life has no meaning or purpose.
We ask your blessing upon all who strive
to improve our world and to create works of beauty.

Silence

O Lord, our Strength and our Redeemer,
hear our prayer.

We give thanks for the support of our families and friends,
for all the encouragement and help they give us.
We pray for homes where there is little encouragement
or where adventure and the fullness of life
are smothered by false securities.
We remember all who are homeless
and uncertain of their future.

Silence

O Lord, our Strength and our Redeemer,
hear our prayer.

We thank you for your love towards us.
We ask you to bless all who are struggling
with temptation and vice at this time.
We pray especially for any who live
in areas of degradation or evil.
We pray for all who struggle with weakness or illness,
especially those who cannot cope on their own.

Silence

O Lord, our Strength and our Redeemer,
hear our prayer.

We give thanks that through Christ
we are offered eternal life.
We remember the saints in glory
and our loved ones departed.
May they rejoice in your presence
and the fullness of life in your kingdom.

Silence

Merciful Father,
accept these prayers
for the sake of your Son,
our Saviour Jesus Christ.
Amen.

Memory verse

You are the Christ, the Son of the living God.
Matthew 16:16

Suggested music

Christ, whose glory fills the skies
Follow me, follow me
Jesus calls us here to meet him

CANDLES

Aim

To review what the children know about Jesus.

Teaching

Lots of names have meanings. Perhaps even yours.

Peter = Rock or Rocky
John = Jonah = Dove
Abigail = Servant
Christopher = one who carries Christ

(Encourage the children to talk about names and meanings.)

Jesus = Saviour; the one who rescues people.

Who can tell me where Jesus was born? Yes, it was in Bethlehem, in a stable. Can you remember who his mother was? She was called Mary.

When Jesus was born there were shepherds on the hillsides and they heard angels singing, 'Glory to God in the highest.' The angels also said, 'To you is born in the city of David a Saviour, who is Christ, the Lord.'

What do you call the day when Jesus was born? Christmas Day. It has one of the names of Jesus in it. Who knows what it is?

Christ means that Jesus was God's special chosen one. It reminds us that God sent his Son Jesus to help us when we are in trouble.

Once when the friends of Jesus were sitting by a campfire Jesus asked if they knew who he really was. Peter said, 'You are the Christ.' He knew that Jesus was God's chosen one. God had especially sent Jesus to show us all about his love. (You could encourage the children to talk about some of the wonderful things Jesus did.)

Who knows how Jesus died? It was on Good Friday. He died on a cross. (Show a picture or crucifix and let the children talk about it.) After he died he was buried in a cave in a hillside. But that was not the end for Jesus Christ. What happened next? He was alive again and was seen by his disciples. Who knows what you call the day when Jesus awoke from the dead? It is Easter Day and we are all happy on Easter Day because Jesus Christ is alive.

We cannot see Jesus but we know he loves us and is with us always. How do we speak to Jesus? Through our prayers we speak to Jesus.

Activity

Play 'Stuck in the mud'. Whenever a person is tagged they have to stand with legs apart and arms outstretched. A player who has not been tagged can crawl through their legs and set them free again. You may need more than one 'It' to tag people or people will be freed too easily.

Prayer

Jesus, we are happy that you love us
and want us to be your friends.
We come in the quiet to be with you.
Amen.

Song

Wide, wide as the ocean

LAMPS

Aim

To begin to look at what the disciples meant when they said, 'Jesus is the Christ.'

Teaching

Jesus had escaped from the Pharisees, who were trying to harm him, by going north. He went to a place called Caesarea Philippi. It was called this because Philip, the son of Herod the Great, added beauty to the temple built by his father and dedicated to Caesar Augustus. The place had been called Caesarea after the temple was built. Philip changed the name to Caesarea Philippi. But, of course, it was wrong to worship a man or the power of the state; we can only worship God.

While they were away from trouble, Jesus wanted the disciples to know him better and why he was doing the things he did. They knew that he was a good teacher and that he was a healer. They were beginning to understand that God especially sent him. So, when they were sitting around the campfire, Jesus asked them, 'Who do people say that I am?' 'Well, we know that you are our friend and that you are Jesus. Some people say that you are John the Baptist back from the dead. But we know that is not true. Some think that you are the most famous of prophets come back to prepare the world for the chosen one, or that you are one of the prophets. We have been with you and we think you are more important than all of these.'

Jesus then asked them, 'Who do you say that I am?' For a minute they were all very quiet. Then Peter spoke out and said, 'You are the Christ, the Son of God.'

By staying with him and working for him the disciples had discovered that Jesus was the one God had chosen to show his love to the world. The disciples were discovering that Jesus is God's Son. By calling Jesus 'the Christ' they meant God's 'anointed one' – that is, the one who would bring salvation and healing to God's people. The disciples were beginning to understand that Jesus was very special and the person that had been promised to save them by the prophets of old. (You can expand this by conversation with the children about how people need a Saviour.) Jesus told them to keep it a secret because unless they knew him, people would not understand.

Then he told the disciples of the trouble that was ahead of them. Because Jesus is the Christ he had a special task to do and he could not let anything stop him. As the Christ he would be attacked, captured and crucified. But they were not to worry because he would rise again from the dead.

The disciples could not understand this. They would only know it was true after the crucifixion and resurrection. (Talk about these events.) Then they would know that Jesus is the Christ, the Son of God.

Activity

Play a pointing game. A person says, 'I believe that Jesus is', and then points at someone. They have to finish the sentence by saying a word or two (for example, 'alive', 'here', 'wonderful', 'lovely', 'the Christ', 'our friend'). You may have to prompt a little to get them going.

Prayer

Jesus Christ our Lord,
we thank you for all that you have done for us
and that you love us always.
Amen.

Song

I love to be with you, Jesus

TORCHES

Aim

To deepen awareness of who Jesus is.

Teaching

Begin by using the worksheet. Use this session as a revision of the use of symbols and at the same time extend the group's awareness of who Jesus is.

IHS = first three letters of the name Jesus. The name Jesus means Saviour.

INRI = Jesus of Nazareth, King (Rex) of the Jews. (Remind them this was the title placed on the cross.)

☧ This is called the Chi-Rho sign because of the two letters from which the sign is made up. These are the first three letters of Christ, or Christos, the Greek for the Hebrew word Messiah, which means 'God's anointed one'. It came specially to mean the one who would come as the Saviour of God's people.

ICHTHUS = Jesus Christ, God's Son, Saviour.
In one sense you can see the repetition of the idea of 'Saviour' here three times: Jesus = Saviour; Christ = the 'one anointed to be the Saviour'; and the word 'Saviour'.

The crucifix is a sign of the suffering of the Son of God. It reminds us of what he bore for us as a result of sin. It is a sign of his rejection and all the pain he endured. It is also a sign of his death and burial. (Discuss what Jesus has endured for us.)

The cross without a figure is a sign of the resurrection. The cross and the grave are empty because Christ has risen. Through death and the grave Jesus has triumphed and opened for us the gate to eternal life. (Encourage the group to talk about the resurrection.)

There was a time when Jesus seemed to be popular but soon the leaders of the Church – the Scribes and Pharisees – set out to trap him and condemn him. Jesus needed time for his disciples to learn who he really was. So he took the disciples away to the Phoenician area of Tyre and Sidon beside the Mediterranean Sea. After this, Jesus is still keeping a distance between himself and the Pharisees. He is in Decapolis, the 'ten towns' area 25 miles south of the Sea of Galilee. It is nearly time for Jesus to return to Jerusalem and face his enemies. He knows that trouble lies ahead.

During the evening around the campfire he asks his disciples, 'Who do people say I am?'

Most people thought he was special like John the Baptist come back to life (the disciples must have found this a little funny), or Elijah returned to prepare for the Christ, or a prophet. The answers were interesting but did the disciples begin to know who Jesus was? So he asked them a personal question. He did not want the answer that others were giving. He turned to them and said, 'Who do you say that I am?' No doubt the disciples encouraged Peter to speak. He said, 'You are the Christ, the Son of the living God.' If he had said, 'Jesus, (you are) the Christ, the Son of God', he could have been the first to use the words hidden by the sign ICHTHUS. It must have been a very special moment for them all. Jesus had been recognised as God's anointed one and as the Son of God. The disciples must have been at a loss what to say next. Jesus warned them not to tell anyone because people would misunderstand what he had come for, unless they got to know him like the disciples did.

Now that the disciples began to understand, Jesus would turn towards Jerusalem. He knew what would happen when he went there. He tried to warn the disciples but they would not understand until after the crucifixion and resurrection.

Activity

On the worksheet (Second Sunday of Christmas) are various symbols for Jesus Christ. See how many can be recognised and explore their meaning. See if the group can express what knowing Jesus means to them. Get them to use words like 'Christ' and 'Saviour' and relate them to the world they live in.

Prayer

Jesus, you are the Christ, the Son of God.
You came to our world and became human
so that you could lift us into your kingdom
and let us share in the Divine.
We thank you for your love
and your abiding presence with us.
Amen.

Song

Christ be with me

Proper 20

Sunday between 18 and 24 September inclusive

Aim

To show that Jesus calls us to serve each other rather than to lord it over people.

Preparation

On the main entrance have a notice, 'Servants' Quarters'. Have four people learn the mini-drama. You may like to have some posters displaying the work of Shelter or a local hostel.

Opening activity

Mini-drama

Voice 1 They asked me to help with the washing up. Who do they think I am?

Voice 2 I know they wanted me to help with the cleaning. They must be joking.

Voice 3 They asked me to spend two hours a week looking after some old woman. They could put her in a home.

1, 2 and 3 Who is that scrubbing the floor after that child was sick?

Voice 4 That is the Honourable Lady Rose. She often gives two or three hours a day to care for others and keep the place tidy. She says it is her Christian duty and she loves it.

Opening prayer

Father, we thank you that Jesus came to serve
and to give his life as a ransom for many.
Teach us to be generous
in the giving of our time and of ourselves
in the service of others,
through Jesus Christ our Lord.
Amen.

Opening song

Love divine, all loves excelling

Readings

Proverbs 31:10-31 or Wisdom of Solomon 1:16–2:1, 12-22 or Jeremiah 11:18-20
Psalm 1 or Psalm 54
James 3:13–4:3, 7-8a
Mark 9:30-37

Thought for the day

Today's Gospel splits into three parts. In the first part (9:30), Mark shows Jesus seeking to keep his whereabouts a secret. The reasons are twofold. It was a time for teaching his disciples and getting them to understand his purpose and message. It was also necessary to avoid conflict before the disciples had time to understand. This was a precious and important time for Jesus.

In the second part Jesus is predicting his death and resurrection. He is seeking to warn his disciples of what lies ahead, the dangers and the suffering, his death and resurrection. This is important for the disciples to grasp and it is repeated three times (9:31, 8:31 and 10:32-34). We are told that the disciples did not understand what Jesus was saying and were afraid to ask him. No doubt this is part of the reason for the repetition. The disciples found it hard to grasp that God's Anointed One, the Messiah, could be rejected and killed by his own people. To understand the idea of a suffering Messiah was beyond their comprehension. There are still some Christians today who suggest that if only we had more faith we would escape suffering. That is not the way of this world.

The third part is the turning towards Carpernaum and back towards Jerusalem and danger. The disciples still think in worldly terms of power – hence their rejection of any idea of the cross or a suffering Christ. They still expect a display of might and when they will share in ruling. When they were on the way back to Capernaum they argued with one another who was the greatest (9:34). In the ancient world, social position was highly ordered; people were expected to stay in 'their place'. The disciples wanted to know their place in the kingdom so that they could get the greatest gain from it. The phrase 'on the way' (33) is the same word as used in Mark 4:14 to describe the seed that got no entry because of Satan taking away any chance of growth. This must have been a very sad time for Jesus. He is willingly going to Jerusalem to offer his life for others and his disciples are arguing among themselves about position and power. Perhaps Judas believed that by betraying Jesus he would make Jesus use force against his enemies.

In 9:35 Jesus assumes the teaching position of a rabbi by sitting down and calling his disciples to him. What Jesus says turns their striving for position upside down – we do well to heed it. Standing, security, satisfaction are not gained by power struggles or beating the Joneses, but by serving. Not from getting and gaining but from giving and grace. The followers of Jesus are called to serve and to give their lives for others as he did.

Jesus illustrates what he means by picking up a little child and taking it in his arms and saying, 'Whoever welcomes one such child in my name welcomes me, and whoever welcomes me, welcomes not me but the one who sent me.' Children had no rights and could make no demands; they had the lowest place in the social order – of course, love made nonsense of such a statement. Being a follower of Jesus means to be willing to give of yourself and to serve. It is not being servile but choosing to give your life to others and for others. By this welcoming of children, or the least, we welcome into our lives not only Jesus the risen Lord but also God. Jesus will emphasise his own desire to serve when James and John are still seeking positions of power. Then he said, 'The Son of Man came not to be served but to serve, and to give his life as a ransom for many' (Mark 10:45).

Question time

Does our church show that it is a servant church and works for the needy in our community?

Do we still make status and self-seeking more important than service?

Illustration

There is a story about a fourth wise man who wanted to come and see the Christ. He started off well. He dressed in his best clothes, rode a fine horse and brought a present of precious stones. On his journey he met a group of poor people who were hungry, so he gave away half of his jewels for them to trade for food. Then he met a family who were taken into slavery because of a debt. He used the rest of his precious jewels to buy their freedom. Further on he found a merchant in deep distress. His horse had died on him and he would not get his goods to be sold on time. The generous wise man gave him his horse and all its trappings. Now he had to walk on foot and the going was slow.

He was old and very weary. He wondered if he would ever see the Christ. The way was very muddy and he met a young family trying to get their cart out of the mud. The wise man helped them but ended up very dirty. He now wondered if he should give up and go home. In a dream he was told, 'The Christ you seek is now only a little distance away. He will welcome you because he knows you. You have met him many times on your journey in the poor and the needy. You soiled your clothes in caring for him. Tomorrow you will meet him and he will welcome you.' And so it was.

Intercessions

Blessed are you, Lord our God.
You give us the opportunity to meet you
in the call of the poor and in the cries of the needy.
Give us the courage to serve
and to share in the love that you have for all people.
Teach us to be attentive and open to others
for in meeting them we meet you.
Blessed are you, Father, Son and Holy Spirit.

Father, we give you thanks for all who have cared for us
and brought us to know you and your love.
We ask your blessing on all who serve
as ministers and priests within your church.
May our churches be ready
to serve the needs of our community and the world.
We remember all who give their lives
to relieve the sorrows and suffering of their fellow beings.

Silence

Lord, as we draw near to you,
help us to know you are ever with us.

As we rejoice in your goodness and grace,
we remember all who hunger, all who are homeless,
all refugees and stateless peoples.
We remember ethnic minorities
who are suffering from persecution.
We pray for those who suffer through war and violence.
We ask your blessing on all who are underpaid
and treated as slaves
to provide richer people with cheap goods.
We pray for all Fair Trade organisations.

Silence

Lord, as we draw near to you,
help us to know you are ever with us.

We give thanks to you for the love and care
we have in our homes.
We remember how much we are served
and looked after by our parents.
May we never take them or any who care for us
for granted.
May we learn to help as much as we can
within our own homes.
We ask you to bless all homes
where there is poverty or great debt.
We remember also homes where some individuals
are ignored or taken for granted.

Silence

Lord, as we draw near to you,
help us to know you are ever with us.

Lord, we pray for areas of poverty and bad housing
throughout our world.
We remember all who do not have the basic needs
of care and attention.
We ask your blessing upon all who are ill
and those who feel lonely or neglected.
We remember especially children separated
from their loved ones
and children taken into care.

Silence

Lord, as we draw near to you,
help us to know you are ever with us.

Teach us, good Lord, to serve you as you deserve:
to give and not to count the cost.
Grant that we may learn to be generous and gracious
as are your saints who now rejoice in your kingdom.
We rejoice in the fellowship of all your saints
and ask your blessing
upon our loved ones who are departed from us.

Silence

Merciful Father,
accept these prayers
for the sake of your Son,
our Saviour Jesus Christ.
Amen.

Memory verse

Draw near to God, and he will draw near to you.
James 4:8

Suggested music

Christ's is the world in which we move
Brother, sister, let me serve you
Make me a channel of your peace

CANDLES

Aim

To show that by caring for others we find that Jesus comes to us.

Teaching

There was once a strong young man called Offero. He lived in a mountain area where there were great waterfalls and deep streams. Because he was strong he decided he would like to work for the strongest person of all. When he enquired, he was told about many strong people but then he was told the devil was even stronger than them all. He wondered if he should serve the devil. Then he saw someone making the sign of the cross and was told that they did it because Jesus Christ was stronger than the devil; that Jesus' love was stronger than wickedness. Offero decided he would like to work for Jesus Christ but did not know how to do it. A Christian told him that if he cared for people and was kind to them, Christ would be there and come to him.

Offero decided to stay by a very deep stream in the mountains and help people across the stream. He did this because the stream was dangerous and people had been swept away and some had died. He was strong and with the help of a large stick and a light he got many people across the stream safely.

He hoped Jesus Christ would come and ask for his help. One day as it was getting dark a child came and wanted to cross the stream. The winter snows had been melting and the stream was very deep. Offero took the child's hand and they stepped into the cold water. But the water got too deep and Offero had to lift the child up and carry him in his arms. After a short while the stream was so deep Offero had to lift the child on to his shoulders. Even then the strong man had to struggle to get to the other bank. Once on the other side of the stream, Offero put the child down and began to dry himself. When he was a little drier and warmer he looked around but the child had gone. Offero then knew he had met the Christ. The child he had helped across the stream was Jesus Christ and he had come to Offero. He thought of the words that he had heard from the Bible. They were words that Jesus had said: 'Whoever welcomes one such child in my name, welcomes me.'

Offero got his name from carrying people across the stream. Now he was called Christoffero or Christopher, which means 'Christ carrier', because he had met and carried Jesus Christ.

Activity

Play 'In the river'. Everyone stands in a circle. One person stands in the middle. When she calls out, 'In the river', all have to jump forward. When she shouts, 'On the bank', all jump backwards. This sounds easy but there is a catch. If the caller shouts, 'On the river' or 'In the bank', no one must move. Anyone who even wobbles must sit out. The last person left is the winner.

Prayer

Jesus, we thank you that you loved children
and took them in your arms.
Help us to be kind and loving to each other.
Amen.

Song

Jesus' hands were kind hands

LAMPS

Aim

To show we meet Christ in our caring for others.

Teaching

Francis was born in Assisi in central Italy. His father was a rich cloth merchant who traded with France. Francis' mother was a French woman. They lived in a fine house and wore fine clothes, and they were never short of money. It was expected that one day Francis would be a cloth merchant and take over from his father. Francis loved partying, he liked singing and going out with his friends. He was able to spend a lot of money. His father wanted him to take work more seriously but Francis just wanted to enjoy himself.

As part of his adventures he joined the army of his city and went to war against another local city called Perugia. During the battle he was captured and put in prison. His father would have to pay for his release. Being in prison and having seen how awful war is made Francis think differently about life: he became more thoughtful, though he continued to party for a while.

One day, while still dressed in fine clothes, Francis met a leper. This was a horrible sight. The man looked awful and smelt terrible. The very thought of a leper made Francis feel sick; he would have liked to chase the man away. Suddenly Francis was filled with deep sorrow for the man. He was aware how lonely and sad the leper was. Francis braved himself and then went over to the leper, took him in his arms and kissed him. As Francis looked into the face of the leper, he did not see scars and illness: he saw the face of Christ.

Francis was learning the meaning of the words of Jesus: 'As much as you did it to the least of these you did it to me.'

Francis gave up his rich way of life and started to care for the poor, especially those with leprosy. He used churches that had fallen into disrepair as a base for his caring. Some friends and others joined him in this work. By the time he died he had followers all over Europe.

Activity

Play 'Character freeze'. Use as large an area as possible. The leader calls, 'Freeze', and everyone stands still. Then the leader says, 'When I say, "Unfreeze", everyone will be . . .' and name a carer in the community. It could be a doctor, a shop assistant, a nurse, vicar, a fireman; include St Francis. When 'Freeze' is called, everyone remains fixed in the position of the character they were. 'Unfreeze' brings us a new character.

Prayer

God, we thank you for St Francis
and his caring for the poor and the lepers.
May we always be ready to help any who are in need
and to care for the lonely.
Amen.

Song

Give me oil in my lamp

TORCHES

Aim

To encourage the group to see Christ in others.

Teaching

Martin wanted to become a Christian and work within the Church but his father, who was a Roman soldier, was against it. Martin did not have much choice; soon he was in the imperial armour of Rome and he looked splendid. Though he was not yet baptised, Martin lived as a Christian; he gave his money away to help the poor and the needy, and kept only what he needed for the day.

One cold winter's day, when he was 20 years old, Martin was out on duty. The weather was so cold that people were dying of cold. Martin was wearing his uniform and to keep warm he had a great cloak which he could wrap around him and keep out the winter chill. The cloak must have cost a great deal of money. But it served its purpose and kept out the winter chill. Whilst doing his rounds in the city of Amiens, Martin came across a poor man at the city gate. The man had only rags covering him and was suffering greatly from the cold. He was begging for help. Most people passed by without even noticing the man was there. When Martin saw the man he felt for his poverty. But Martin had already given away all that he had to the poor and needy – what could he do? Martin suddenly drew his sword. The poor man now trembled with fear as well as cold because some people had been known to kill the poor and needy. Then Martin took off his cloak and used his sword to cut it in half. He gave half of his cloak to the beggar and wrapped the remaining half around his own body.

Some of the people who saw this started to laugh at Martin because he looked a little foolish in half a cloak. Soldiers were also laughing at him. Some people, though, were feeling a little ashamed because they had more than Martin and could have helped the poor man.

During the night that followed Martin fell in a deep sleep and as he slept he saw a vision of Christ wearing the half a cloak that Martin had given to the beggar. Jesus spoke to Martin quite clearly and said, 'Martin, you might only be learning to be a Christian but you have given me this robe.' Martin then knew that he had met Christ in the beggar. Very soon after this Martin was baptised as a Christian.

Jesus said to his disciples, 'Whoever welcomes one such child in my name welcomes me, and whoever welcomes me welcomes not me but the one who sent me' (Mark 9:37).

Activity

Get the group to read Matthew 25:31-46. It can be read in parts with different people reading 31-34a, 34b-36. Verses 37, 38, 39 can be read by different individuals, each giving emphasis to the question. A narrator can introduce verse 40 and verse 41. Let the rest of 40-43 be read by the same person who read 34b-36. Let the narrator or a new voice read 44-45a. The reader of the two king's speeches should read 45b; this verse should be read with great emphasis. Let the narrator read verse 46. Encourage the group to make this into a mini-drama. Use any time left to discuss the implications of these words.

Prayer

Lord, you have called us to share
in your ministry of love and care.
You reveal yourself to us in the cry
of the poor and the needy.
Help us to be open and generous in our lives
and know that when we care for the least of these
we are showing our love for you, Jesus Christ our Lord.
Amen.

Song

When I needed a neighbour

Proper 21

Sunday between 25 September and 1 October inclusive

Aim

To express the unity of all believers, as there is only 'One Church, one faith, one Lord'.

Preparation

Have a map or diagram showing the other churches and denominations in the area.

Opening activity

Who knows the names of any other churches in our area? Do you know who the minister or priest is, or the leader of the congregation? As each are mentioned, say, 'Let us give thanks for their work and ask God to bless and guide them.' You may like to ask if there are visitors from other churches and welcome them.

Opening prayer

Father, we give thanks for our brothers and sisters in Christ
who work within our area,
seeking to sing your praises
and bringing many to be aware of you and your glory.
Bless them and all who minister to them
that they may show forth your love and your presence.
Amen.

Opening song

Thy hand, O God, has guided

Readings

Esther 7:1-6, 9-10; 9:20-22 or Numbers 11:4-6, 10-16, 24-29
Psalm 124 or Psalm 19:7-14
James 5:13-20
Mark 9:38-50

Thought for the day

Pride and prejudice or a feeling of our own insecurity and uncertainty often make us set ourselves against others. We see people as rivals, when in reality they are seeking the same good that we are. Sadly, the history of the Church is often one of rivalry and bitter factions. We set rules and regulations to say we are special and suggest others are not, especially if they do things in a different way. Many a church is afraid of, or incapable of, change or taking on something new. There seems to be a built-in fear of anything different. This was often the trouble with the Scribes and Pharisees when they met Jesus: they could only accept Jesus on their terms; they could not see that he had anything to offer.

In today's Gospel, John expresses a feeling of being scandalised by an exorcist who was casting out demons in the name of Jesus. In the ancient world there was a universal belief in demons. Everyone believed that physical and mental illness was the work of demons. Anyone who was ill was under a malign influence. The commonest way to exorcise a demon was to find a more powerful spirit and command the demon in that name to come out of the person. The demon could not stand against a more powerful name. John had found a man driving out demons in the name of Jesus and had tried to stop him. The reason he gave was that he was not one of them – that is, the little company of men around Jesus. Jesus said the man should not be stopped. We need to learn that those who are not working against us are for us.

We need to learn there are more ways than we can understand in which God comes to us and we come to God. We should not stop anyone because it is not our way. God is far bigger than our little understanding and works in many ways. We must guard against being exclusive. Heed these words:

He drew a circle that shut me out –
Rebel, heretic, a thing to flout.
But love and I had the wit to win;
We drew a circle that took him in.
Edward Markham (1852-1940)

Let us rejoice in the other churches that are around us and in the work they do.

Question time

Is our church in danger of being exclusive in doctrine or in attitude?

How can we be seen to be more welcoming to newcomers and to members of other churches?

Illustration

Hospitality was of great importance in the ancient world. By being open to others, the great Other, who is God, was given the opportunity to enter into your life. See the example of Abraham and Sarah when visited by the Lord (Genesis 18:1-15). In the story it is hard to decide whether we are dealing with three men, three angels or the three-person God. Ask the congregation who visited Abraham: was it men, angels, God? (Be careful how you phrase the question for it is not an 'either/or'. All visited Abraham at Mamre. The person that replies 'Yes' to the question or says, 'All three' would get top marks!)

There is a Celtic poem which expresses the Other approaching us through others.

I saw a stranger yestere'en
I put food in the eating place,
drink in the drinking place,
music in the listening place
and in the sacred name of the Triune
he blessed myself and my house,
my cattle and my dear ones,
and the lark said in her song
often, often, often,
goes the Christ in a stranger's guise.

Intercessions

Blessed are you, Lord our God,
for you welcome us whenever we turn to you:
you are always ready to hear us and to help us.
We rejoice in your presence
and ask that we may show your love
and your saving power in the world.
Blessed are you, Father, Son and Holy Spirit.

We give thanks for your Church throughout the world.
May the Church be an instrument
of peace and reconciliation
between peoples and nations.
Bless the churches within our area:
may we learn to work together in unity
and in witness to your saving power.
We pray for churches that are struggling to survive
and that are in areas of hostility or apathy.

Silence

Lord, our strength and our redeemer,
hear our prayer.

Father, we give thanks for the peace that you offer us.
We remember in your presence
all who are living in areas of war and violence.
We pray for those who suffer attacks on their communities,
for those who are victims of ethnic cleansing or genocide.
We ask your blessing upon all communities
whose way of life and livelihood are threatened.

Silence

Lord, our strength and our redeemer,
hear our prayer.

Father, we thank you for all our loved ones and friends,
for those who have enriched our lives
through their goodness and example.
We ask you to bless and protect them.
We pray for homes where relationships are breaking down,
especially where there is violence or neglect.
We pray for all who are suffering
through losing a loved one.

Silence

Lord, our strength and our redeemer,
hear our prayer.

Father, we bring to your love
the suffering and sorrow of our world.
We remember in your presence all who are ill
at home or in hospital.
We pray for those involved in accidents
or acts of cruelty and violence this week.
We bring before you all who live in fear
and those who feel they can no longer cope with life.

Silence

Lord, our strength and our redeemer,
hear our prayer.

Father, you created us for yourself and for your love.
As we give our love to you,
we pray for all our loved ones who are departed from us.
May they rejoice in the light of your presence
and in the fullness of eternal life.

Silence

Merciful Father,
accept these prayers
for the sake of your Son,
our Saviour Jesus Christ.
Amen.

Memory verse

Just as you did it to one of the least of these who are members of my family, you did it to me.
Matthew 25:40

Suggested music

We have a gospel to proclaim
Here I am, wholly available
Forth in thy name, O Lord, I go

CANDLES

Aim

To encourage the group to learn to do good for Jesus.

Teaching

Who knows the difference between salt and sugar? They look the same but they are quite different. Both are used at home in cooking. What foods do we put sugar into? What do we put salt into?

Sugar is used for making things sweet. It is used in cakes and in puddings.

Salt is used to help things taste good. It is often sprinkled on food – like chips, potatoes, eggs, or put into the pan when we are cooking things. I have some salt here to show you. (Produce a glass of water with salt dissolved in it.) Who can tell me where the salt is? It is in the water. It is hidden because it has melted, dissolved, in the water. How can we tell if there is salt in the water?

Nearly all cooked meat has salt in it. Sometimes meat that is not cooked has salt in it. Does anyone know why there is salt in it? It is to keep it from going bad; it stops the food spoiling and becoming nasty. Salt is used to keep it good. Salt is used to protect the meat and sometimes it is used to protect people.

Can you tell me where Jesus was born? He was born in a stable at Bethlehem. Fancy, Jesus being born in a stable among the cows and the donkey! (Describe the straw and get them to see it would not be all that clean.) The mother of Jesus would want to make sure Jesus was protected against any dirt and make sure he was kept safe. She would get Joseph to wash him and wrap him in swaddling bands (explain). But before he wrapped Jesus up, Joseph did something else to protect him. He gently rubbed salt on the body of the baby Jesus to keep him good and well and to stop any bad things happening to him. Our mothers and fathers would not use salt; they would use something gentler to protect us. But salt was what Joseph used because there were not so many medicines then. Just think how the little baby Jesus was given salt to keep his body healthy.

Jesus said we have to be like salt and to help to protect the world from bad things. We have to make sure we do not do bad things and upset our mothers or fathers. We should help to keep our rooms and our homes clean – and not expect our mother to do it all. We should not say nasty things or be horrible to anyone. This is not easy but we are to try and do it every day.

Let us see how many more ways we can be like salt and help to make our world a happier place. (Draw out suggestions from the children.)

Activity

'Sprinkled with salt.' Get the children to pretend to be angry or wanting to fight. Let them mime boxing and shaking fists. Then go around them pretending to shake salt on them. As they have salt on them, they are to go around shaking hands and hugging each other. Repeat this two or three times.

Prayer

Jesus, you want us to help you
by being good and caring for your world.
We will try to be helpful in our homes
and to be kind to others.
Amen.

Song

You are the best

LAMPS

Aim

To encourage the children to see they have an active role to play in the community in which they live.

Teaching

Once upon a time there was a rich king who lived in India. He had three beautiful daughters and he asked them how much they loved him. What would you say if your father or mother asked you how much you love them?

The first daughter said, 'I love you more than gold and silver.' The king was very pleased.

The second daughter said, 'I love you more than rubies and jewels.' Again the king was delighted.

The third daughter said, 'I love you more than salt.' At this the king was sad and puzzled. But the third daughter persuaded the cook not to use salt in the meals, and the food did not taste as good. She persuaded the servants not to add salt to the new meat to protect it, and the meat started to go bad. Without salt, things were tasteless and other things were going bad. The king was suddenly aware of what his daughter meant. She had been both clever and thoughtful and he was really delighted.

In the ancient world, salt was greatly valued. The Romans said, 'There is nothing more useful than salt and sun.' Salt does some very important things. Can you tell me any? (List any suggested.)

Salt is used to give flavour. Some things, like potato chips or crisps, are all better for a little salt. Salt is added to bread and to meat to bring out the flavour.

Salt is used to preserve things. Salt is used to stop meat from going bad. Before we had fridges and freezers it was very difficult to stop meat and fish from going off, from smelling and rotting. Salt is used to protect meat and stop it getting germs. People used to think that all sorts of things were waiting to invade their meat and only salt could protect it from evil.

Jesus said his followers had to be like salt. What do you think he meant? (Discuss.) I am sure he meant us to bring happiness and enjoyment to life. We should show people that the world is a wonderful place and life is a joy to live. We should not be saying we are bored, for there are always exciting things around us. As followers of Jesus, we should be attractive by the way we enjoy life.

Salt preserves and protects. Jesus wants us to share in his battle against evil and wickedness. When we can, he wants us to stop any bad things that are happening around us. We are part of Jesus' team to keep the world clean. We can start this in small ways by not dropping litter and by keeping our own room tidy. We can make sure bad words are not used by us and our friends. We can be sure not to do wicked things and anything that would upset our parents or be against God. We need to be kind and friendly as often as we can. (Seek practical suggestions from the group.)

Activity

Can you find the salt? There are two lots of salt 'hidden' in the room. Can you find them both? Have a set of saucers with various powders on them for tasting: sugar, icing sugar, flour, powdered milk, powdered coffee, cocoa, salt, pepper. You may like to get the group to guess every powder and to discover the salt. Near these have a glass of salty water and a glass of plain water – see if anyone discovers the hidden salt.

Prayer

God, thank you for this wonderful world
and for our marvellous lives.
Help us to help keep your world clean and free from evil
and to enjoy living and working for you.
Amen.

Song

There are hundreds of sparrows

TORCHES

Aim

To encourage the group to see they are responsible for their life and what is around them.

Teaching

All who listened to Jesus knew the value and the importance of salt. The high temperatures around Galilee made it difficult to keep food fresh. Fishermen had trouble keeping their fish fresh. Meat would go bad very quickly without the use of salt. People salted their meat, fish and butter to stop them going bad. The air was full of microbes and salt was a protection against them. Salt was in all offerings that were offered to God so that they would be pure and good (Leviticus 2:13).

When Jesus called his followers 'the salt of the earth', they knew what he meant. Life is full of influences that can turn life bad. It is too easy to let impurities creep into life or to let evil sneak in. The task of the Christian is to keep the world and their own life wholesome. We are to fight evil and low standards and to set an example by the way we live. As salt defended things against corruption and rottenness, so must the Christian protect the society and area in which they live. (Discuss how we can do this in our area and lives.)

Salt is also used to give flavour to vegetables, to potatoes, to eggs, to meat. An egg without salt seems to have only half of its flavour. The world into which Jesus came was bored with much of life. Jesus came that we might have life in all its fullness (John 10:10). We, as followers of Jesus, are called to give some zest and taste to life. We are to show that Christians love this world that God has made and that we enjoy living in it. Let people see that because of Jesus we get more out of life and that life is an exciting adventure. (Discuss.)

The Greeks valued salt so much that they called it 'divine' (theion); they believed there was something of the gods about it. Salt was proclaimed as the purest thing in the world because it came from two pure things: sun and sea. We need to know that God seeks to dwell in us and make his home with us. God asks of us an offering that is as pure as we can offer. How can we seek to do this? (Discuss.)

Activity

Can you name the ingredients? Have a set of saucers with various powders on them for tasting: sugar, icing sugar, flour, powdered milk, cocoa, salt. Can they guess what is likely to be made with these as the main ingredients?

Prayer

Lord, we thank you that you have called us
to be the salt of the earth.
Help us to work to improve our lives
and the area in which we live.
May we show that it is a joy
to be alive and to know you.
Amen.

Song

The ink is black

Proper 22

Sunday between 2 and 8 October inclusive

Aim

To show that our relationships are important.

Preparation

Display photos of endangered species and photos of litter, rubbish and pollution. Beside the photos have a notice asking, 'How responsible are we?'

Opening activity

Mini-drama

Voice 1 Look, there's a rare butterfly.
Voice 2 Wait a minute, I am on my mobile.
Voice 3 Have you seen the sunset?
Voice 2 No, I am watching the television.
Voice 1 Did you meet Richard when he called?
Voice 2 No, I had a game on my computer.
Voice 3 How about going out into the countryside?
Voice 2 No thanks, there's a programme I want to see. (*Pause*)
Voice 2 I wonder why I have no real friends. I am so bored and I am lonely.
Voice 1 Well, every time someone approached you they found you occupied.

Opening prayer

Lord God, you made us for yourself
and for relationships with each other.
Teach us to be open and generous in our dealings,
that we may give attention and care to all we meet.
Let us love the world
with the love that you have for the world.
Amen.

Opening song

When God made the garden of creation

Readings

Job 1:1; 2:1-10 or Genesis 2:18-24
Psalm 26 or Psalm 8
Hebrews 1:1-4; 2:5-12
Mark 10:2-16

Thought for the day

In Genesis we hear that it is not good for a human to be alone. The Three Persons God values relationships and love. Human beings are to have a relationship with the world around them. We are put in charge of a world and we are accountable to the Creator for it. God created all out of his love and wants us to love it also. We are to express our relationship with God through our relationship with his creation. We have a responsibility to God for our use of and our sharing in creation. The human cannot survive alone and needs a helper and a partner. We are responsible for and to our partner in all our dealings. Through the love and understanding we share, with each other, we will grow in our love and understanding of God. Our relationship with God is expressed through our relationship with each other. If we do not treat each other with respect and the world with respect, it is not likely that we will respect God. In the same way, if we betray our God, we are as likely to betray each other! When our relationships break down it is bound to affect our relationship with God who loves us equally.

In Job we see a wife who feels deeply for her husband and his suffering. She suggests he should curse the Creator for what has happened to him. Obviously she underestimates his relationship of trust with God. Job understands that life in this world is not all sunshine and roses.

We disturb the relationship with creation when we act through selfishness and greed; by doing so we act irresponsibly. The destruction of so many creatures and plants in the name of so-called progress is a good example. What is happening to the rain forests and what is happening to the poor of our world are reflections of our relationships. There is a danger we just use people and creatures for our own gain, regardless of the results.

The most testing relationships are those we live with. It is said of a home that it is where we are treated the best and react the worst. Do not let that be true of us.

Relationships must be worked at, must be maintained. We must never take each other for granted, or deal with each other as if we had a servant or a slave. Relationships are meant always to reflect love. When our hearts are hardened we are already beginning a divorce, a break in our relationships. This is as true of neglecting our prayers as of taking each other for granted.

The disciples did not want to be bothered by the children or those who were bringing them. Jesus saw a desire for a relationship with himself and with the Father.

Question time

Is our church involved in Fair Trade and justice for the oppressed of the world?

Do we see that our relationships with each other and the world reflect our relationship with God?

Illustration

Once a bird flying high overhead saw how our world was becoming polluted. The bird saw the rubbish dumped into the sea and fish struggling to survive, great tracts of land being robbed of trees, the ice-caps slowly melting. So it decided that it must tell the humans about what was happening. The first group would not listen – well, who would believe a bird! The next group were making good profits and did not want anything to be disturbed. A third group said they would happily talk about it for years. No one wanted to do anything. Yet the bird knew that all things were linked together. If the humans destroyed the environment, all the birds and all the animals would also suffer. Why were the humans so insensitive to their surroundings and to each other? The bird learnt that the humans had lost a sense of awe and wonder because they had broken their relationship with the Creator God. If they would not listen to the cries of creation, if they would not listen to the voice of God, they were not likely to hear a bird.

Intercessions

Blessed are you, Lord our God,
for you have created the world and all that is in it
out of your love and for your love.
You offer us a relationship with you
through your creation and through each other.
Teach us to care for your world and to respect all peoples.
Blessed are you, Father, Son and Holy Spirit.

We give you thanks and praise for the beauty of the earth
and the wonders of each creature.
Lord, help us to have a reverence and awe
for all that you have made.
May your Church encourage a sense of wonder
in all our dealings.
We remember the Church working among
oppressed peoples
and all who are treated as unimportant or dispensable.
Let us all learn good stewardship
of the gifts and the world you have given to us.

Silence

God our Creator,
in your love, hear us.

We praise you for the diversity of life on our planet,
for the balance of nature and the goodness of the earth.
We ask your blessing on areas and creatures
that are endangered.
We pray for the people of the rain forests
and for primitive tribes that are being robbed of their land.
Lord, guide the decisions of all who influence
the future of the earth.
We pray for multinational companies
and for all who wield power.

Silence

God our Creator,
in your love, hear us.

We give you thanks
for all who have shown us love and care.
We remember before you our families and friends
and all our loved ones.
We ask your blessing on all who feel lonely,
all who are neglected
and all whose relationships are breaking down.
We pray for any who have lost a loved one this week
or who have been deserted by a loved one.

Silence

God our Creator,
in your love, hear us.

As we rejoice in life
we pray for all who are doing genetic research
and all who probe into the mystery of life.
May your blessing be upon all who make discoveries
that deeply influence our lives.
We remember all who are struggling.
We pray for those who have lost any sense of wonder or joy,
the depressed and the disillusioned.
Lord, comfort all who are ill
and all who are finding life difficult.

Silence

God our Creator,
in your love, hear us.

We give thanks for the mystery of our own life
and that you are with us always.
We ask your blessing on all who have departed from us
and pray that they may rejoice
in the glory of your presence in your kingdom.

Silence

Merciful Father,
accept these prayers
for the sake of your Son,
our Saviour Jesus Christ.
Amen.

Memory verse

O Lord our governor, how exalted is your name in all the world!
Psalm 8:1

Suggested music

For the beauty of the earth
All creatures of our God and King
O Lord, my God (How great thou art)

CANDLES

Aim

To show that God wants us to share in the care of his creation and to love one another.

Teaching

God made the world out of his love. When he made the human being he did not want him to be lonely, so God filled the world with wonderful creatures so that the man could look after them. God made all the animals on the earth, all the fish in the sea and all the birds of the air. God then brought them to the man so that he could give all the things a name and so that he could look after them. The man enjoyed giving names to cattle and to animals and birds. Let us see if we can name some of the animals God has made. (Look at the activity suggestion below.)

There were lots of wonderful things in the world but the man was still lonely, he needed a partner to share in looking after the world. He needed someone to love. So God made a partner for the man. Now the man not only had to care for the world, he also had to learn to love. He was not lonely any more. God made it so that we should all have people who love us and whom we love. Tell me who loves you and whom you love.

God wants us to look after his world and all that is in it. He wants us to show care for all the birds, the fish and the animals because he also cares for them. He wants us to care for the earth and the sea. He wants us to love him because he loves us.

How can we show we care for God's world? (Get ideas from the children. These could include tidying up and not throwing litter, being kind to animals, feeding the birds.)

And how do we show we love our mothers and fathers? (See if they can express a care for their homes, helping to tidy as well as doing what they are told.)

Activity

Have pictures of animals for the children to recognise. Include pets. See if they can name them. Then let the children choose a picture without telling anyone and make the sound of the creature. The rest of the group have to guess what it is. When it is guessed we all say, 'Thank God for . . .' and name the creature. On the activity sheet draw your favourite animal.

Prayer

Thank you, God, for a wonderful world,
for all the animals, birds and fish.
Thank your for our mothers and fathers
and thank you for making me.
Amen.

Song

God who made the earth

LAMPS

Aim

To look at our responsibility towards the earth and towards each other.

Teaching

When God made the human he did not want him to be lonely. God created a most wonderful and balanced world for us to enjoy. He gave us power over the birds of the air, the fish of the sea, all animals and all growing things. To be responsible is also to be accountable to God. It is not our world. God created it out of his love. God continues to love it and he wants us to love it. He wants us to treat his creation with respect and awe. We are not to use it to selfish purposes or with disregard for others. It would be very sad if we allowed some creatures to disappear from the earth just because of our greed. At the moment there are many creatures in danger and, because one often depends on another, if one disappears, soon another will follow. If we destroy the food source of an animal, we endanger its future. (Show examples from the groups listed in the Activity for today.) The children might like to 'adopt' an animal and help to save it. If there is a local scheme to care for something needing attention, all the better.

To teach us love, God made sure we were not alone: God created people to love one another. If a person learnt to love and care for their husband or wife, for their children, then they would learn about God's love for his world. We all need to be loved and we need to love others. We need to express our love and respect for each other in our homes. Let us make a card that says 'Thank you' to our parents for loving us.

If there is time, the group could discuss how to care for the area in which they live. They could make sure they do not drop litter or throw things away as they walk about. They need to take a stand against graffiti or disfiguring buildings through damage or stone throwing. They may like to plant bulbs that will grow next spring or a tree that will benefit people in the future.

Activity

Look at endangered species from home and abroad. Use material from the Worldwide Fund for Nature (formerly World Wildlife Fund), the Royal Society for the Protection of Birds, Friends of the Earth. Get the group to see it is our impact on the world that is endangering many species.

Let's play 'Animal freeze'. When I call, 'Freeze', everyone must stand still, caught in the action they are doing. When I say, 'Unfreeze. Everyone will be a . . .' you must then become the animal I mention.

Prayer

God, we thank you for a wonderful and beautiful world.
We thank you for the love and care of our parents.
Help us to care for the world
and make sure that we do not spoil it for others.
Amen.

Song

Who put the colours in the rainbow

TORCHES

Aim

To show that our attitudes and relationships with the world and each other make us what we are.

Teaching

The world is made up of wonderful relationships. We may think we can stand alone but we are dependent on many other parts of creation and they are often held in a wonderful balance. We need the sun, the rain, the healthiness of the soil, the quality of the air, not only to live comfortably but to survive.

By reading the passage from Genesis we see how the human was placed in a position of responsibility. By the God-given powers the human is to look after and care for the world. God did not create humans and then made a church for them to worship in; he gave them a world through which they could express their love for its creator and where they could meet him in and through each piece of creation. Insensitivity towards creation shows insensitivity towards the Creator. It does matter what we do to the world and what is in it. Our responses to every bit of creation do matter.

Notice that for the human the peak of relationships is our relationship with each other. Genesis sees life-long relationships between couples as God's way of teaching us love and care. It is only when we learn to love that we learn what deep relationships are about.

Now look at today's Gospel, where Jesus is talking about divorce. The difficulty with divorce is that it is a breakdown in relationships, and that often means the complex relationships of family and friends, not just two people. In an ideal world divorce would not happen, but we do not live in an ideal world. If divorce is made too easy, we cheapen what we believe about relationships. Relationships are not an option and they are not disposable. Divorce becomes necessary because we are not ideal people and we do make mistakes and we do make wrong decisions.

Marriage is not to be entered into lightly or on an impulse. We need to give thought to our lives together and our future together. Yet marriage should be the great adventure where we learn more and more of love, of giving and of sharing. We should see marriage as a wonderful relationship that will change and grow throughout life. Above all, marriage is where we learn the deepness of relationships. We learn of love and in learning of love we begin to know the love of God.

Activity

Look at the marriage vows and see them as an adventure in love. Ask the young people to talk about the taking of the vows. Do they see that God is involved in all relationships and that God enriches our relationships by his presence?

Prayer

God our Creator, we thank you for the wonder of creation
and that all things are related.
We pray that we may use the resources of the world
to the benefit of each other
and in the care of our planet.
Make us sensitive and caring
in our dealings with each other,
that we may learn through each other of your great love.
Amen.

Song

Dance and sing

Proper 23

Sunday between 9 and 15 October inclusive

Aim

To show that God wants all of us and not just gifts and prayers.

Preparation

Have a poster in the entrance saying, 'God wants you'. (You may like to have a pointing hand as part of the poster.)

Opening activity

Voices

Voice 1 Here is my collection. Sorry, I cannot come today – we're off to the zoo.

Voice 2 Lord, I would pray every day – if I were not so busy. I might manage once a week.

Voice 1 I would spend time with you, Lord – but I have a job to do. I will give something to the church.

Voice 2 I have brought some flowers for church – but I am part of a fitness club and we meet on a Sunday.

Voice 3 (*With arms outstretched in cross shape*)
Lord, today and every day,
I give myself to you –
in sickness and in health,
in success and in failure,
in joy and in sorrow,
in time and for eternity.

Opening prayer

Lord, you made us for yourself.
We come to offer you our whole life,
to give you our love.
Amen.

Opening song

Be thou my vision

Readings

Job 23:1-9, 16-17 or Amos 5:6-7, 10-15
Psalm 22:1-15 or Psalm 90:12-17
Hebrews 4:12-16
Mark 10:17-31

Thought for the day

It seems some people have everything going for them. Today we hear of a rich man coming to Jesus. St Matthew tells us the man is young (19:20). St Luke tells us he is a ruler (18:18): he is a rich young ruler – obviously God has blessed him. We also learn that he keeps the commandments. Now he comes asking what he should do to gain eternal life. He comes running to Jesus and throws himself at his feet. Surely here is a chance of a useful disciple. There is something startling about this situation when this rich young man of authority throws himself at the feet of a penniless wanderer from Nazareth.

Jesus seems to be hard on this man. Maybe it was the way the question was phrased. First, there is a bit of flattery – 'Good Master' – and then 'what must I do to gain . . .' It would seem this man was in the business of making a profit. He did not come to give of himself but to gain for himself. He already had many blessings but he wanted more. No doubt he was willing to give something for it. But Jesus replies that the man cannot pay the price. God does not want things instead of ourselves; he does not even want prayers or sacrifices unless we can give ourselves to him. Obedience to commandments is good but God wants more: he wants our love.

There is always the danger of being possessed by things. Instead of owning things, they begin to own us and we become possessed by our possessions – or some of us are possessed by the lack of them! We spend much of our lives seeking to gain, to get, to have, and we can be in danger of losing sight of loving and giving of ourselves. Money can be a good reflection of this. Some people's pockets are as hard to touch as their hearts.

Here was a man given a glorious opportunity; the same one that was offered to Matthew when he was at the tax desk: 'Leave it all and follow me.' Jesus invited this man to a great adventure, offered him the way to eternal life. But he went away grieving, and it is possible he would grieve for ever. Why did he grieve? Because 'he had many possessions'. He could not enter into the fullness of life because of the things that were around him. This is surely one of the most tragic stories of the Gospels and a warning to all of us.

Question time

Are we sure we give ourselves to God and not just gifts and a bit of us?

Is the church in danger of being possessed by possessions? Are we?

Illustration

Imagine a table. I want you to put on it all the things you want to give to God: your time, talents, money; your home, your friends, your loved ones; your job, your plans, your future.

You are going to need a great big table. We raise up the things we want to give to God and say, 'All things come from you, O God, and of your own do we give you.'

But wait, one thing that God wants is still missing. Who knows what it is?

GOD WANTS YOU.

More than any gift, more than gold or silver, God wants you.

God wants you to give yourself to him.

God wants you to give your love.

God wants you more than anything.

St Paul said, 'If I give away all my possessions . . . but do not have love, I gain nothing' (1 Corinthians 13:3).

Intercessions

Blessed are you, Lord God of all creation.
Through your goodness
we live in a rich and wonderful world.
You have given us the stewardship of your creation.
Lord, help us to work together
for the benefit of your whole world
and to reveal your glory within it.
May we strive for the protection and care
of all you have given into our charge.
Blessed are you, Father, Son and Holy Spirit.

God our creator, we give you thanks
for the mystery of life and the beauty of the earth.
We remember in your presence
all who strive to reveal your glory.
We pray for churches throughout the world that seek
to help in the care and protection of the environment.
We ask your blessing on church groups
that work in areas of deprivation
and with people that are counted as of little importance.
We pray for all relief organisations
and those working with the world's poor.

Silence

Lord, in your love and goodness,
hear our prayer.

We give thanks for artists and craft workers,
for musicians and all who enrich our lives
by their talent and care.
We ask you to bless all who influence our future
by the decisions they make in governments
or in multinational companies.
We pray for the work of all who are involved
in conservation and in Fair Trade.
We remember the unemployed
and all who are denied human rights.
We ask your blessing
upon all oppressed and homeless people.

Silence

Lord, in your love and goodness,
hear our prayer.

We give thanks for our homes, our talents
and all that you have given to us.
May we use our resources for the benefit of those in need
and for the improvement of the world around us.
Bless our homes, that they may reflect your love
and be where your peace and your presence
are known to abide.

Silence

Lord, in your love and goodness,
hear our prayer.

Lord God, giver of life and health,
we come in our weakness to your strength,
in our troubles to your peace.
We ask your blessing upon all who are suffering,
all who are ill at home or in hospital.
We give thanks for the talent and attention of doctors,
nurses and all in the caring professions.
We pray especially for all who feel lonely or neglected
and all who have no one to care for them.

Silence

Lord, in your love and goodness,
hear our prayer.

Holy and merciful God, we rejoice in your saving power
and that you give us life that is eternal.
We ask your blessing upon all the saints
who have revealed your glory by their lives.
We remember also all who have enriched us
by their goodness and care,
and we pray for all our loved ones and friends
who are departed from us.

Silence

Merciful Father,
accept these prayers
for the sake of your Son,
our Saviour Jesus Christ.
Amen.

Memory verse

For God all things are possible.
Mark 10:27b

Suggested music

Will you come and follow me
Take my life and let it be
O for a closer walk with God

CANDLES

Aim

To show that Jesus wants all of us, not just our money or our prayers.

Teaching

Once there was a little boy who lived with a very rich mother and father. He could have anything he wanted. He just had to ask and it was bought for him. He had all the toys he wanted and lots of nice clothes. When it came to his birthday he looked forward to having a party. Friends were invited and they had servants to look after them. Most of the children enjoyed themselves but the little boy was very sad. He had lots of friends and lots of presents but he felt lonely because his mother and father had gone away without him. What he wanted most was his mother and father, but they were always too busy and paid someone else to look after him. He wanted something more than presents; he wanted his parents to show they loved him . . .

Once a man came running to Jesus. The man was very rich and would have bought Jesus anything that he asked for. The man threw himself down at the feet of Jesus and asked how he might be given eternal life. The man would have bought eternal life, but Jesus knew you cannot buy it because it is a free gift from God. God does not want our money or gifts. Like the little boy in the story, God wants us to give ourselves to him; he wants us more than our gifts. When we give ourselves to God, God gives himself to us and gives us eternal life. When we come to church God wants us to give ourselves more than our collection, even more than our prayers – God wants all of us.

Activity

Let us look at the song 'Jesus wants all of me'. Say the words of the first verse and get the children to repeat them after you before you sing them.

Go through the second verse, getting them to point at each part of the body. Let them wave their hands, jump with their feet, swing their arms, shake their legs, wiggle their toes and knock their knees together. Go through the actions a few times before they attempt it to music.

End with shouting, 'What does Jesus want?' and let them reply loudly, 'Jesus wants all of me.'

Prayer

God, you give yourself to us.
We come to give ourselves to you.
As you love us, help us to love you.
Amen.

Song

Jesus wants all of me

LAMPS

Aim

To show that God wants us to trust in him and not in our own wealth or strength.

Teaching

Most cities used to have a wall around them to protect them from enemies. During the day the gates of the city were wide open and people would go in and out. Traders would come with foods and cloth. They would bring them in on camels or on horses. The biggest animal most of them ever knew was a camel. Has anyone ever sat on a camel? It makes you feel very high off the ground. Very often camels would come into the city bearing heavy loads. When night came, the main gates to the city were closed but often beside the main gate was a little gate that was low and narrow. It was hard for a man to get through this gate without having to bend. Sometimes this gate was called the 'eye of the needle'. People had to thread their way through. Occasionally, when someone came late, you could see them trying to get in with their goods and even with a camel – but the gate was too small and the camel found it impossible.

Jesus said, 'It is easier for a camel to go through the eye of a needle than for someone who is rich to enter the kingdom of God.' What do you think Jesus meant by this? (Get the children to talk about it.)

Having things tend to occupy all our time. We get possessed by possessions. (See if you can get the children to understand this.) Riches tend to make people think they can buy anything. They think they do not need the help of God. Riches can make people selfish and even more possessive.

Yet there were rich men who came to Jesus. Matthew was rich. Zacchaeus was one of the richest men in Jericho. Joseph of Arimathaea was a rich man. Possessions need not stop us coming to God, but they can. How often do we neglect our prayers because we are on our PlayStation, watching television, or listening to our CD?

There is a sad story in the Gospel of St Mark about a good man whom Jesus loved, but this man could not follow Jesus because he had too many possessions. Would someone like to read it? (Encourage them to find Mark 10:17-22). Talk over how many Gospel books there are and how Mark comes after Matthew.)

Activity

Act out the idea of the camel trying to get through the eye of the needle.

Have an obstacle race. The children have to carry two balloons, or two books and a jacket, and they have to crawl under a rope held at a suitable height above the ground. Put the children into teams. When the children get to the end they can run back to their team and the next person takes the goods and sets off. Once a team has won, you may like to let the children have a try without having to hold things and see how much easier it is.

Prayer

God, we thank you for all that you have given us.
May we be generous to others
and care for any who are in need.
Amen.

Song

Two little fishes, five loaves of bread

TORCHES

Aim

To show how God wants us more than any gift we can offer.

Teaching

Act out the story of the rich young ruler.

Narrator	Once when Jesus was on a journey a rich man ran up and knelt before him.
Chorus	A rich man, a rich man.
Man	Good Teacher, what must I do to get eternal life?
Chorus	Eternal life, eternal life.
Jesus	Do not call me good; only God is good.
Chorus	God is good, God is good.
Jesus	Keep the commandments.
Chorus	Keep the commandments, keep the commandments.
Man	I have kept them all, every one.
Chorus	Kept every one, every one.
Jesus	One thing more: go and sell all that you have and give your money to the poor.
Chorus	To the poor, to the poor.

Narrator The rich man went away sad, because he had many possessions.
Chorus Poor rich man, poor rich man.

Talk about the text, 'It is easier for a camel to go through the eye of a needle than for someone who is rich to enter into the kingdom of God.' Explain that often there was a small low gate in a city wall – sometimes called the 'eye of the needle' – which was the only way to enter the city at night when the main gates were closed. Goods were carried into a city on camels and there was no way that a camel – especially a heavily laden one – would get in. Many adventure films about lost treasures show at least some of the people over-burdened with wealth and therefore unable to escape. Only if they get rid of the 'treasure' will they survive. (The group may be able to give examples.)

You may like to discuss some of the dangers of riches.

- A person will be judged by how they got their money and how they use it.
- There is the danger that being rich makes you think you can buy anything. (Money can't buy you love.)
- Riches can make people selfish. The more you have, the more you want.
- Riches give you a false feeling of independence. But you cannot buy health or friends.
- Riches tend to make you concentrate your life on them. You can become possessed by your possessions.

Activity

Stand the group in a circle. One person is given two heavy bags. They must walk around the outside of the circle and drop a heavy bag at the feet of someone. The second person picks the bag up and runs around the circle and back to their place before the first person with the other bag goes round in the opposite direction and takes the place. Whoever is left repeats the process.

Prayer

Lord, we thank you for all that you have given to us.
May we use all to your glory
and the benefit of any who are in need.
Lord, give us a generous and loving heart.
Amen.

Song

Fisherman Peter on the sea

Proper 24

Sunday between 16 and 22 October inclusive

Aim

To compare the ambition of James and John and the servant role of Jesus.

Preparation

Have a notice in the porch saying, 'Service Centre'. Have a crown of thorns and crucifix in front of the notice.

Opening activity

Arrange for someone to carry the crucifix to the front of the church and hold it up for people to see.

Voice 1 Look, this is the man you follow.
Voice 2 See how he gave himself in love.
Voice 3 Know that he died for you.
Voice 1 He died that we might live and show his love.
Voice 2 He rose again that we might know him.
Voice 3 As he gave himself for us, let us give ourselves in love to all who are in need.

The three face the crucifix and sing:

Jesus, we adore you,
lay our lives before you.
How we love you!

(Verse 2 of 'Father, we adore you' by Terrye Coelho)

Opening prayer

Lord Jesus, King of kings,
you took upon yourself the role of a servant
and became obedient even to death on the cross.
Help us to show our love for you
in the way we deal with each other
and the world about us.
Amen.

Opening song

Thy kingdom come, O God

Readings

Job 38:1-7 (34-41) or Isaiah 53:4-12
Psalm 104:1-9, 24, 35c or Psalm 91:9-16
Hebrews 5:1-10
Mark 10:35-45

Thought for the day

Jesus is on his way to Jerusalem. He has turned towards the opposition, towards the cross and death. He wants his disciples to understand and be prepared. It must have been so hard for Jesus when they failed to grasp what he was saying.

James and John had just heard Jesus talking about his death and yet they were still thinking in terms of power and rule. They still did not understand what sort of Messiah Jesus is. They could only think in earthly terms. Only after the crucifixion would they see in a different way.

James and John were after position and promotion: they wanted personal gain and power. Their thoughts were on getting not giving, on success rather than sacrifice. The other ten disciples were angry with James and John because they thought they had tried to steal a lead on them. The twelve could only see the rule of Jesus and his kingdom in earthly terms of power and force. The Messiah the Jews hoped for was the Lion of Judah, a king like David who would drive out their enemies.

In today's reading from Isaiah we get a glimpse of a different Messiah: not so much the Lion of Judah but the Lamb of God. We see the portrayal of the Suffering Servant who gives his life for the sins of the world.

Jesus wanted the disciples to understand that he is about to fulfil the role of the Suffering Servant (see Mark 10:32-34). There may be a triumphal entry but soon the road will lead to the cross. Jesus did not come to win by force or to wield power. He came to win by love and to give his life as a ransom for many. Jesus could call on all the power and might that he desired but he chose the way of self-giving and love. Jesus understood you cannot force people into the kingdom, you cannot make people love God; you can only win them by love and grace. It is for this reason he calls his followers to do as he does, to give of themselves and to serve. A Christian can be seen as someone who has come down in the world. We should be able to step off our pedestal, relinquish our hold on power and possessions, and give ourselves in love and service. The question will not be how much you have gained but rather how much you have given of yourself.

The church that wields power and strives for position, that is full of pomp and possessions, is in danger of betraying the Servant King.

Question time

Does our church set out to serve the community in which it is placed, or does it seem to suggest the community should serve us?

How can we make our lives and our church more able to give and to serve?

Illustration

When Toyohiko Kagawa, who lived in Japan, met Christianity he was captured by its call to serve. He prayed, 'O God, make me like Christ.' To become like Christ he went to live in the slums of Tokyo to care for others. He chose to live in a shed that was about two metres square. On the very first night he was asked to share his room and bed with a man with a contagious itch, the first test of his aim to serve. He welcomed the poor man. Then a beggar asked for his shirt and he gave it. The next day the beggar came back for Kagawa's coat and trousers. Kagawa gave them and was left wearing a ragged kimono. At first the slum dwellers laughed at him but they soon came to admire him. Kagawa wrote:

> God dwells in the lowliest of men. He sits on the dust heap among the prison convicts. He stands with the juvenile delinquents. He is there with the beggars. He

is among the sick; he stands with the unemployed. Therefore let him who would meet God visit the prison cell before going to the temple. Before he goes to church let him visit the hospital. Before he reads the Bible let him visit the beggar.

Intercessions

Blessed are you, Lord our God.
You have created us out of your love
and redeemed us by your love.
In the offering of our Lord Jesus on the cross
you have freed us from sin
and opened to us the way to eternal life.
Grant that, as Christ came not to be served but to serve,
we may give our lives in your service
and to the benefit of your world.
Blessed are you, Father, Son and Holy Spirit,
one God now and for ever.

Gracious God, you give us life and love.
Help us to give our life and love to you.
May the Church seek to serve the world
and to give itself for the benefit of the communities
in which it lives.
We ask you to bless all who are working
among the poor and the destitute.
We pray for prison visitors
and those who visit the ill and the lonely.
We remember all who reach out in love
to the outcasts and the neglected.
Bless the work of Christian Aid and all relief organisations.

Silence

Lord, our Saviour and Redeemer,
hear us and save us.

We give thanks for the caring professions
and for all who give their lives in the service of others.
We pray for doctors and nurses.
We remember the social services and care workers.
We ask your blessing upon all children who are in homes
or who are in need of protection.
We pray for the Children's Society
and all who work looking after children.

Silence

Lord, our Saviour and Redeemer,
hear us and save us.

Lord, we thank you for those
who have given us of themselves in love and care.
We pray for our parents and our families.
We ask you to bless all who have enriched us
by their goodness and their sacrifice for us.
Lord, teach us to be generous in our dealings
and sensitive to the needs of others.

Silence

Lord, our Saviour and Redeemer,
hear us and save us.

As we rejoice in your saving power,
we remember before you
all who work in the rescue services.
We pray for firefighters and ambulance workers,
for the lifeboat teams and the air and sea rescue crews.
We pray for all who have been involved in accidents
this week,
remembering the injured and the bereaved.
We ask your blessing upon all who are ill
at home or in hospital.

Silence

Lord, our Saviour and Redeemer,
hear us and save us.

Lord, we give thanks
that through the death and resurrection of Jesus
you have opened for us the way to life eternal.
We pray for all who have served you faithfully
here on earth
and are now in the fullness of your kingdom.
We remember our friends, benefactors and loved ones
who are departed from us:
may they be at peace with you.

Silence

Merciful Father,
accept these prayers
for the sake of your Son,
our Saviour Jesus Christ.
Amen.

Memory verse

The Son of Man came not to be served but to serve, and to give his life as ransom for many.
Mark 10:45

Suggested music

Meekness and majesty
Brother, sister, let me serve you
Strengthen for service, Lord

CANDLES

Aim

To compare a king's life and the life of Jesus. (Use this as revision of what they know of Jesus.)

Teaching

Who knows what a king is? A king is a ruler of people and in Bible times he usually made them do what he wanted.

Where does a king live? He is usually born in a palace or a castle and that is where he lives.

Jesus is our King and he was born in a king's town. Where? Bethlehem. But he was not born in a castle. Where was he born? He was born in a stable among the cows and the donkeys. His mother's name was Mary. What do you call the day when Jesus was born? (Encourage all the children to say, 'Christmas Day'.) Jesus did not live in a palace; he lived in an ordinary house and worked in a carpenter's shop. (Make sure they know what a carpenter is.) Jesus would help to work with wood.

When Jesus grew up and left home he did not have lots of money or a rich house. He often slept outside in the countryside. He did not spend his time ordering people about, but he helped people and made ill people well again. All his life he cared for people.

A king sits on a throne and commands people, but Jesus was put on a cross (show a crucifix).

Who knows the name of the day when Jesus died? It is called Good Friday. (Encourage all the children to say, 'Good Friday'.) Jesus was given a crown but it did not have jewels in it and it was not made of gold. Who knows what it was made of? Encourage the children to talk about how painful it would be. Jesus came to give his life and his love for all people. He came as a king but a different king because he came to serve and to look after people. He wanted people to know that God loved them. A king would have called his army to fight but Jesus did not want to hurt or force people, so he died on the cross.

Jesus died, but after three days what happened? Yes, he was alive again. He rose from the dead. Does anyone know what we call the day when Jesus rose again? It is called Easter Day. (Get all the children to say, 'Easter Day'.) Because Jesus is alive he wants us to work with him and help him. He wants us to look after others. Let us think of things we can do for Jesus.

Spend the rest of the lesson making a list of suggestions of things that the children think they can do. Ask them to try and do at least one of them today.

Activity

Play 'The king says' version of 'Simon says'. Whoever is made king (or queen) commands people. When he says, 'The king says do this', he then does an action that the children must do. If the king gives an order without saying, 'The King says', no one should do what he does. Anyone who does is out and is relegated to the dungeons. The last one out becomes the next leader.

Prayer

Jesus, we thank you that you came to give your life for us.
Help us to give our life to you
and to care for others.
Amen.

Song

Jesus' hands were kind hands

LAMPS

Aim

To show that the Servant King calls his followers to serve.

Teaching

James and John thought that because Jesus was going to Jerusalem he would soon show that he was the Chosen One of God (Messiah) and his kingdom would begin. 'When Jesus is king,' they thought, 'it would be good if he put us in charge. We could rule others and tell them what to do. We could have power. He could make us important people and give us thrones.' They went to Jesus and asked if they could sit at his right and left in his kingdom.

This made the other disciples angry. They thought, 'Why should it be James and John? We could do it.' They were only angry because they thought they too would like to have a position of power. It would be nice to be a prince and have a throne.

All of this made Jesus rather sad. It seemed the disciples did not understand him at all. He did not want to rule like a king and make people do things. He wanted to give himself to people and show his love for them. He had spent day after day caring for people and yet the disciples did not really understand. He did not want people to be forced into his kingdom; he wanted to love them in.

Jesus had told them how he was to die but they still did not understand. It would only make sense to them after the crucifixion. Who knows the name of the day when Jesus died? (Good Friday.) So Jesus had to tell them again, 'The Son of Man came not to be served but to serve, and to give his life as ransom for many'(Mark 10:45). Jesus was to be the strangest of kings because he was to be the Servant King. He was to work for others and to give his life for others. Because he came to serve, he wants his followers also to be servants and slaves of others. Remember, Jesus will not force us; he wants us to do it because he loves us and so that we can show our love for him.

Activity

Play 'Character freeze'. The leader calls, 'Freeze', and everyone must stand still. She then calls, 'Unfreeze and everyone will be . . .' and she names a carer or a person serving others.(Examples: a mother looking after a baby, a fireman, a doctor, a road sweeper, someone tidying a room or picking up litter.) When 'Freeze' is called again, everyone has to be frozen in the action they were doing. There is no need to eliminate anyone in this game. Get the children to extend their actions as much as possible.

Spend the rest of the session discussing how we can serve others. Perhaps the group can take on a small project.

Prayer

Jesus, you are the Servant King.
Help us to care for others
and spend time looking after them.
Amen.

Song

Jesus, you are my king

TORCHES

Aim

To show that Jesus came to serve and save.

Teaching

Jesus chose his disciples so that they could continue his work. Already he had sent them out to tell the Good

News of God and to share in healing. They began to believe that he was the Messiah, the Chosen One of God, who would bring in the kingdom of God. They could only think of earthly kings who were concerned with power and position, with privilege, promotion and possessions. (Get the group to see how these five words beginning with 'P' are what still drives nearly everyone.) James and John thought in these terms and if Jesus were soon to be king they would like a good position. They could wield power if they were at his right hand and left. To sit whilst others stood would show their power. That they asked Jesus this only made the other disciples angry – because they too wanted an important place. They wanted to know what they would get for being his disciples.

The disciples made Jesus sad because they still had not learnt what sort of king he would be. Nor did they understand how he would give his life for others. Jesus saw himself as the Servant King and even more as the Servant willing to give his life for others. Let us read Isaiah 53:4-12. This is a passage that tells us what sort of Messiah Jesus was to be. Rulers command and force people – Jesus wanted to win them by love and by the giving of himself. Where the world was concerned with getting and gaining, Jesus was ready for giving and losing his life.

How can we, as followers of Jesus, learn to serve the community and world in which we live? Let the group put up ideas for action and see if we can take some of them on board.

Activity

On the worksheet there are attitudes towards power, position, privilege, promotion and possessions. Get the group to see how the life of Jesus does not give these high priority.

Prayer

Teach us, Good Lord,
to serve you as you deserve,
to give and not to count the cost,
to fight and not to heed the wounds,
to toil and not to seek for rest,
to labour and not to ask for any reward,
save that of knowing that we do your will.
Ignatius Loyola (1491–1556)

Song

Make me a channel of your peace

Proper 25

Sunday between 23 and 29 October inclusive

Aim

To show that Jesus opens our eyes to the reality of the world.

Preparation

Have posters from Sight Savers International (Grosvenor Hall, Bolnore Road, Haywards Heath, West Sussex RH16 4BX) or some other organisation that helps to restore sight. It would be good to have a few accounts of how people have benefited by having their sight restored.

Opening activity

Voice 1 I do not see the need to keep the speed limit.
Voice 2 I cannot see why I cannot drink and drive.
Voice 3 I do not see any need to worship.
Voice 4 I cannot see why I should care for others.
Voice 5 I do not see why I should not throw litter.

Let all these be loud voices coming from around the church.

Let someone come down the aisle using a white stick. If you have a blind person in the congregation use them as this final voice:

Voice 6 Lord, there are so many people blind to your presence; people who cannot see their responsibilities. LORD, OPEN THEIR EYES.

Opening prayer

Lord, open our eyes to see the beauty of the world.
Help us to see your love and power
revealed in all that is around us
and to behold your presence in the poor and needy.
Lord, give us a vision of the world
as you would have it be.
Amen.

Opening song

Praise, my soul, the King of heaven

Readings

Job 42:1-6, 10-17 or Jeremiah 31:7-9
Psalm 34:1-8, 19-22 or Psalm126
Hebrews 7:23-28
Mark 10:46-52

Thought for the day

Jericho is the lowest town in the world at about 700 feet below sea level. Here Jesus meets two people who were counted among the lowest of the low – a blind beggar and Zacchaeus, an inspector of taxes.

Jesus is on his way to Jerusalem, which is 17 miles from Jericho. This last journey is uphill nearly all the way. The Son of David is coming to the city of David and neither will be the same again from this encounter. In just over a week Jesus of Nazareth will be crucified. But at the moment Jesus is passing by.

Bartimaeus sees this as a once-in-a-lifetime opportunity not to be missed. The people had come out to see the miracle worker, the Rabbi, the wandering preacher. Here is a man more perceptive than them all. He can see his own need and he can see an opportunity when it presents itself. With both eyes closed he can see what the crowds do not. Here among them is the Messiah, the Son of David. The crowds are blind to this fact and try to keep the blind man quiet. But the man knows his urgency and cries out, 'Jesus, Son of David, have mercy on me.'

Jesus stands still and says, 'Call him here.'

When he is called the man throws off his cloak; not to be hindered, he springs up and comes to Jesus.

Jesus asks, 'What do you want me to do for you?' We all feel the answer is obvious – but not Jesus. He does not offer a cure without the man pointing out his need: there is no prescription without talking to the patient. The Saviour meets each need personally.

The man's sight is restored and he then follows Jesus in the way. He did not just come to get what he wanted and leave; he became a follower of Jesus.

One of the signs of the Messiah and the coming of God's kingdom would be the opening of the eyes of the blind (Isaiah 29:18; 35:5). Those who are saved will see properly (Isaiah 52:10). Sadly there is a blindness of those who do not see God (Isaiah 43:8; 56:10; 59:9-10). Vision is about how we see the world and how we perceive our God. Without vision, people and nations perish (Proverbs 29:18).

One of the great moments of our life is when our eyes are suddenly opened and we see as if for the first time. We see a world that is full of wonder and mystery, and we see a world that is God-filled and not empty. Let us make these word of Origen ours: 'May the Lord touch our eyes, as he did those of the blind. Then we shall see in the visible things those that are invisible.'

Question time

Do we see the church as a place that extends our vision of the world and of our God?

How can we increase our vision and see a more wonderful and God-filled world?

Illustration

The comic character Mr Magoo is funny because he is short-sighted, though in real life he would be a tragic person. He walks across crocodiles thinking they are logs. He steps out of a window in high-rise flats just as a window cleaner's hoist reaches the window. He steps off the side of a pier as a boat pulls level alongside. He does not come to harm but he often leaves a trail of chaos and disaster behind him.

Can we see what is happening around us, to our communities and the way we are shaping the future? Or are we content to leave it in the hands of those who are blind to many of the finer things of life? If we allow the blind to lead us, will we not both fall into the ditch?

It is of extreme importance that we make sure we are led by men and women of vision. It is no use having a quick fix or a laugh now if we are destroying our future. Pray for vision for yourself and your leaders.

Intercessions

Blessed are you, Lord God.
You created light out of darkness
and gave us eyes to see the beauty and wonders
of your creation.
Lord, through the visible things of this world
lead us to see the invisible;
extend our vision beyond our eyes
that we may see with our hearts also.
Blessed are you, Father, Son and Holy Spirit.

We give thanks for the beauty and colour of our world,
for the gift of sight.
We ask your blessing upon men and women
who help us to see beyond the obvious,
upon all who are prophets and visionaries.
We pray for all who study your word
and who celebrate your sacraments.
We remember those training for ministry
and ask your blessing upon theological colleges
and all who teach Religious Education.

Silence

Lord, open our eyes
to see the invisible.

We give thanks for explorers, discoverers and inventors;
for all who have enriched the world by their wisdom
or by extending themselves.
We ask your blessing upon the leaders of nations,
upon governments and ruling bodies.
We pray for the United Nations
and all peacekeeping forces.
We remember today all writers and broadcasters,
artists and craft workers,
and all who influence our lives by their actions.

Silence

Lord, open our eyes
to see the invisible.

We rejoice in the protection and the peace of our homes.
We thank you for our families and friends
and ask your blessing upon them.
We pray for families who have become bored with life
and with each other,
for couples who have lost the spirit of exploration
and adventure.
We ask your blessing upon all who influence
the minds of the young and the vulnerable.

Silence

Lord, open our eyes
to see the invisible.

Lord we give thanks for all who have guided us
into the ways of goodness and love,
all who have enriched our lives by their wisdom.
We remember before you
all who have lost their way in life.
We pray for the confused, the disillusioned
and the despairing.
We remember all who are ill at home or in hospital.
We pray especially for all who suffer from blindness
or partial vision.

Silence

Lord, open our eyes
to see the invisible.

Lord, open our eyes to your kingdom
that is growing among us;
let us see your presence and love at work.
We give thanks for your saints
and for all our loved ones who have departed this life.
May they rejoice where faith has vanished into sight
in the glory of eternal life.

Silence

Merciful Father,
accept these prayers
for the sake of your Son,
our Saviour Jesus Christ.
Amen.

Memory verse

Jesus, Son of David, have mercy on me.
Mark 10:47

Suggested music

Amazing grace
Be thou my vision
How sweet the name of Jesus sounds

CANDLES

Aim

To show Jesus giving sight to Bartimaeus.

Teaching

Jericho was a very busy city. People were coming and going through its gates on the way to Jerusalem. There was a poor blind man called Bartimaeus. Can you say his name? That's right, Bartimaeus. Let us say it together once more.

Poor Bartimaeus, he was blind. His eyes could not see. He was always in the dark. (Touch your eyes and close them and shake your head.) He could not go around without bumping into things. Sometimes he held on to walls to know where he was going. Sometimes friends led him by the hand to take him to where he wanted to be. Most days his friends took him to the gate through which the main road went. There he sat with a bowl, begging. When he heard people passing by he cried out, 'Please help me! For the love of God, give me something!' (Act this out for the children to see.)

Because he was blind, Bartimaeus used his ears to listen more carefully. He listened to the noise of feet and to voices. He listened to friends who talked about Jesus and what he had been doing. He heard that Jesus made people well again and was speaking about God. Bartimaeus wondered if Jesus was the special One God had sent to bring peace and love to the world. Could Jesus be the Son of David who would put all wrong things right?

One day when he was sitting by the roadside he heard a great crowd coming and there seemed to be a lot of talking. Bartimaeus asked, 'Who is passing by?' They told him, 'Jesus is passing by.' Bartimaeus did not want to miss Jesus. He began to wave his arms and shout, 'Jesus, Son of David, please help me.' The people around him tried to make him be quiet. He waved his arms and shouted out again and again, 'Son of David, help me.' Let us wave our hands and shout like Bartimaeus, 'Son of David help me.'

Jesus heard Bartimaeus and stopped walking. He said, 'Let him come to me.' The people told Bartimaeus, 'Jesus is calling you.' He jumped up from his seat. He threw off his cloak in case it got in his way and with the help of the people he hurried to Jesus. Suddenly all was quiet and Bartimaeus heard Jesus saying in a very kind voice, 'What would you like me to do?'

What do you think Bartimaeus wanted most of all? Yes, he wanted to be able to see, so he said, 'Lord, make me see.' Then he hear the voice again, saying, 'Your faith has made you well.' Bartimaeus' eyes opened. He blinked in the sunlight. He could see Jesus in front of him. Bartimaeus could see. He could see people, he could see houses, he could see the road. He could see everything. He knew that Jesus must really be God's special One and he followed Jesus on the way.

Wasn't that wonderful? Jesus made the blind man see. Bartimaeus was lucky to meet Jesus and to know Jesus was God's Chosen One. Jesus is so kind and so clever he even makes the blind to see.

Activity

Have everyone stand in a circle. One person is blindfolded and placed in the middle. Turn them round a few times. They have to call 'Jesus'. A second person in the circle pretends to be Jesus and replies 'Timothy'. The blind person needs to keep calling until they find Jesus. Jesus must reply to each call.

Now let two more do the same.

Act out the story. Have a child for Jesus, a good few for the crowd (some can put money into the hands of Bartimaeus and others can tell him to be quiet), a child for Bartimaeus, two to help him to his place, and a child to say Jesus is passing by.

Prayer

For eyes to see, we thank you, God.
For colours and patterns, we thank you, God.
For the beautiful world and all its animals,
we thank you, God.
For books to read and pretty pictures,
we thank you, God.
For kind faces and good people, we thank you, God.
Amen.

Song

Two little eyes

LAMPS

Aim

To explore the restrictions of being blind and the freedom of sight.

Teaching

One of the most common illnesses in the time of Jesus was blindness. To be blind was very sad because it meant not only that you could not see but that you could not go around by yourself, you could not run, you could not work. If you had a family and you became blind, you would not be able to care for them. (Let the group discuss the problems of being blind. Encourage them to close their eyes and to be led around the room by another.)

Bartimaeus was blind and each day he was taken to sit at the gate into the city. He sat there because there were many people coming and going. He could catch rich merchants and pilgrims and hope for a gift. Wrapped in his cloak, he held out his hands or a bowl and asked for help: 'In the name of God, help me. Spare a coin for a blind man.' Some days were good and others were not. Because he did not see he trained his ears to listen very carefully. He could tell when a camel train was passing or a large crowd. He also listened to stories about what was happening and about God. He believed that one day God would send his Chosen One who had King David among his ancestors. He heard stories of what Jesus was doing and began to wonder if he was the Son of David, God's Chosen One.

One day he was begging at the gate when he heard a crowd. He listened to the sound of their feet on the dusty road. They were quieter than usual, as if they were listening to someone as they walked. Bartimaeus asked, 'Who is it that is passing?' They told him that it was Jesus who was passing by. Jesus the healer and teacher – he could not miss this! An opportunity like this comes only once. Bartimaeus began to shout, 'Jesus, Son of David, have mercy on me.' People tried to make him be quiet but he would not stop shouting, 'Jesus, Son of David, have mercy on me.'

Jesus stopped quite close to him and said, 'Bring him to me.' The people near to Bartimaeus told him he could now be quiet because Jesus was calling for him. Bartimaeus threw off his cloak so that it would not get in his way. He jumped up and with the help of people stood in front of Jesus. Bartimaeus could not see him but he heard a kindly voice saying, 'What would you like me to do?' Bartimaeus was in no doubt. What he wanted more than anything was to see, and he believed Jesus could cure him: 'Lord, that I might receive my sight.' Then he heard the voice again, saying, 'Go, your faith has made you well.' Bartimaeus was aware of a brightness that made him blink. He was aware of a kindly face looking at him. He could see. He had received his sight; it would give him a wonderful new freedom. He was really grateful to Jesus and from that moment followed him.

Activity

Have teams where one person in each team is blindfolded. Make a small obstacle course for each team – say, four chairs that they must weave in and out of. Each member of his/her team then leads the blind person around the course. If they knock things over they must stop and replace them and then start again. The first team to finish is the winner.

Let the group act out the story of Bartimaeus.

Prayer

God, we give you thanks for our eyes.
We are grateful that we can see,
we can read,
we can enjoy colour and light.
We pray for all who suffer from blindness
or whose lives are darkened by poor sight.
Amen.

Song

He made the eyes of the blind man see

TORCHES

Aim

To show there is more to seeing than just using your eyes.

Teaching

The Gospels always hint that there is more to sight than seeing and that blindness is not just about having eyes that do not see. People can be blind to the truth or to the reality that is about them. After the Parable of the Sower, Jesus talks about those who look but do not perceive: 'They have shut their eyes so that they might not look with their eyes' (Matthew 13:15; Mark 4:12). Jesus talks about the eye as the lamp of the body (Matthew 6:22-23). For those who could see what Jesus was talking about Jesus says, 'Blessed are the eyes which see what you see.' Seeing is about vision and how we perceive our world.

Blindness has always been one of the most common problems of the East. It is caused partly by ophthalmia and partly by the constant glare of the sun, and it is aggravated by the fact that flies carry the disease from one person to another. To see people with closed eyes that are encrusted with matter is quite common. But there is another blindness and that is blindness to the love and the presence of God.

In today's Gospel, Bartimaeus sees an opportunity and sees Jesus as the Son of David, but most of the crowd are blind to this. (At this stage read and then act out the story. Then in the Bible study which follows get the group to use their Bibles.)

One of the signs of the Messiah and the coming of God's kingdom would be the opening of the eyes of the blind (Isaiah 29:18; 35:5). Those who are saved will see properly (Isaiah 52:10).

Sadly there is a blindness of those who do not see God (Isaiah 6:9-10; 43:8; 56:10; 59:9-10). Vision is about how we see the world and how we perceive our God. Without vision people and nations perish (Proverbs 29:18). The things that make the most demands for our attention, the fads and fashions of the day, often blind us. The danger is that the spiritually blind is leading us. Jesus paints a sad picture of the blind leading the blind and the danger of them both falling into the ditch. (Luke 6:39) We need to make sure we are following people who have vision.

Many of us live in a world of blurred vision. When Jesus comes into our lives we suddenly have our eyes opened and we see the world in a different way as we learn to walk in the light of Christ. Spend the rest of the session looking at the words of John Newton:

> Amazing grace! How sweet he sound
> that saved a wretch like me.
> I once was lost, but now am found,
> was blind but now I see.

Activity

Play 'Minefield'. Set up a course with obstacles that are mines. The whole area is a minefield. Have teams and blindfold one person from each team. They have to cross the minefield without touching any mines. The other members of their team can help them by calling out directions. If they touch a mine, they have to stop while their team counts to ten. When they reach the end of the minefield, they take off their blindfolds and run back to their team. The next player is blindfolded and sets off. The first team to finish sits down quietly.

Prayer

Lord Jesus, you opened the eyes of the blind
and touched the hearts of many people.
Continue this work in us:
open our eyes
that we may perceive your presence and power.
Touch our hearts
that we may warm to your love.
Amen.

Song

The Spirit lives to set us free (Walk in the light)

All Saints' Day

1 November
or Sunday between 30 October and 5 November inclusive

Aim

To rejoice in God's saints.

Preparation

Prepare a quiz as outlined below. Provide candles for all who would like to light one in thanksgiving for the life of a holy person.

This is a good day for a procession with the children carrying banners or flags and playing musical instruments.

Opening activity

Quiz

Who is the patron saint of our church?
Name the four Patron Saints of the British Isles. (George, Andrew, David, Patrick)
Which one of these saints was an Apostle? (Andrew)
Who is the patron saint of animals and birds? (Francis)
Who is the patron saint of musicians? (Cecilia)
Who is the patron saint of shoemakers? (Crispin and Crispinian)
Who is the patron saint of mothers? (The Blessed Virgin Mary)
Who is the patron saint of carpenters? (St Joseph)

You could extend this quiz and ask about the symbols for the Evangelists or various saints.

Opening prayer

God, you have called us
to share in the fellowship of all your saints.
Help us to do what you would have us do
and to become the people that you would have us be,
that we may live to reveal
your love and your presence in the world,
through Jesus Christ our Lord
who lives and reigns with you and the Holy Spirit,
one God now and for ever.
Amen.

Opening song

Rejoice in God's saints

Readings

Wisdom 3:1-9 or Isaiah 25:6-9
Psalm 24:1-6
Revelation 21:1-6a
John 11:32-44

Thought for the day

When a child was asked what is a saint, she replied, 'Someone who lets light in.' She was probably thinking of a stained-glass window. But in a sense she was absolutely right. Saints are like bright lights in a dark world. Through them the light of the Gospel and the glory of the presence of God is revealed. As we look at the lives of the saints we get glimpses of how life ought to be. The saints challenge us in our way of living: they invite us to risk and adventure. The saints challenge our way of looking at the world, our attitude to life and our priorities. Through them we get a glimpse of how we can live to the full and serve God. The saints are not people who diminish their lives but who show us the glorious freedom of the children of God. The saints live their lives to the full to the glory of God. They challenge us to do the same now: to live for God now and to reveal his glory now.

If we make our heroes from the world of sport and the film industry or the fictional characters of the soaps, we may find we are not getting good examples of how to live. To be a good footballer does not guarantee the wisdom to lead a good life. We need men and women of deep and courageous faith to be our guides. We need to know how the saints have lived. We need also to know that there are many people now who are saints revealing God to the world.

Because God wants us to live our lives to the full we often see God choosing people who were far from perfect but had a zest for living. St Francis was called from being a carefree partygoer to show how we can enjoy living for God. Augustine of Hippo was called from living a passionate life with a mistress and a son born out of marriage to show us how to use our passion for God. To be a saint means to have a great appetite for living life to the full.

The saints reveal the love and glory of the Trinity. They share a common union with Father, Son and Holy Spirit and in so doing are part of the Communion of Saints. We are called to be part of that communion. The saints we remember today are not just the great and well-known but those who have no memorials but who lived their lives revealing God's glory and their love for their fellow beings. We rejoice that the souls of the righteous are in the hands of God.

Question time

How can we learn to reveal God's love and glory in the world around us?

You are called to be a saint. What difference should that make to the way you live?

Illustration

The Lantern Saints were a group of early Methodists who lived on the North Yorkshire Moors. They had a meeting place on one of the highest points of the moor at Trough House at the head of Fryup Dale. And people came from outlying farms and hamlets, from the dales of Westerdale, Danby Dale, Farndale, Glaisdale, Rosedale and Great and Little Fryup. It made Trough House look like the centre of a web that spread out into each moorland valley. Often in the winter they struggled up to the moorland height and met in a shuttered room. As each family entered they would light their lantern (a good symbol of receiving the light of the Gospel and the Light of Christ). Once the service was over they would set off in every direction. You could see the light they had received and carried with them travelling to each dale, to farms and homes. From that light they would see in the dark and light other lights. This light was a symbol of how they sought to live by the Light of Christ. These ordinary folk were rightly known locally as the 'Lantern Saints'.

Intercessions

Blessed are you, Lord our God,
for you have called us out of darkness
into your own most marvellous light.
You call us to know and to love you.
Grant that our lives may help to reveal
your love and glory in the world.
As you have called each of us to be saints
may we be worthy of our calling.
Blessed be Father, Son and Holy Spirit.

O Lord God, we rejoice in the fellowship of all your saints
and we give thanks for all who have enriched
our world and our lives by their examples.
We thank you for (*N*), our patron saint
and for this church in his/her name.
Bless all who are striving to live godly and holy lives.
We remember in your presence
all who are growing in the faith,
those in Sunday schools, study groups
and confirmation classes.
We pray for all who feel called to be priests, deacons
or teachers of the faith.
Lord, we ask your blessing on our lives
that we may be the people you want us to be
and do what you want us to do.

Silence

Lord, make us to be numbered with your saints
in glory everlasting.

We give thanks for all who have served the world
in their vocation.
We pray for kings and queens, princes and rulers.
We remember Elizabeth our queen.
We ask your blessing and guidance
on all who hold positions of authority
or who influence the lives of others.
We pray for all who quietly give themselves
in the service of the community in which they live.
Bless all who are carers
and those who are an example for us to follow.

Silence

Lord, make us to be numbered with your saints
in glory everlasting.

As we give thanks for our homes and loved ones,
make us aware of the quiet sacrifice and love
that is often given unheeded.
We thank you for all that our parents have done for us
and for any who have been benefactors in our lives.
We ask your blessing upon all who suffer
from violence or neglect in their homes,
all who are discouraged and disheartened
by their surroundings
and any who lack a good example to follow.

Silence

Lord, make us to be numbered with your saints
in glory everlasting.

We give thanks
for the saints who have triumphed through suffering
and have revealed your glory
despite persecution and pain.
We ask your blessing upon all who are struggling
at this time.
We remember those caught up in vice, drugs or crime
and who cannot find a way out.
We pray for victims of terrorism or war,
remembering stateless and homeless people.
We bring before you friends and loved ones who are ill
and all who fear the future.

Silence

Lord, make us to be numbered with your saints
in glory everlasting.

We give thanks for all who have served you on earth
and now are at rest in your kingdom.
We pray for friends and loved ones
who are departed from us,
asking that as they shared their love with us on earth
they may know your love in eternal life.
We rejoice in the fellowship of all your saints
and pray that we may share with them
in your eternal kingdom.

Silence

Merciful Father,
accept these prayers
for the sake of your Son,
our Saviour Jesus Christ.
Amen.

Memory verse

The souls of the righteous are in the hand of God, and no torment will ever touch them.
Wisdom of Solomon 3:1

Suggested music

For all the saints
Captains of the saintly band
Give thanks for those whose faith

CANDLES

Aim

To tell the story of St Francis and the Wolf.

Teaching

At the beginning of the session play 'What time is it, Mr Wolf?' Encourage the wolf to growl as it chases the children. Then settle the children down.

Once upon a time in Italy there was a big bad wolf. Most of the time it lived in the forest near a place called Gubbio. (Let us all say 'Gubbio'.) The people who lived in Gubbio could not leave their hens or ducks or lambs out at night because of the wolf. If they did not shut their animals up, the wolf would come and steal them and eat them up. He was a big fierce wolf and he frightened the children and a lot of the grown-ups. If they saw him, they shouted at him and threw stones or sticks at him. They showed that they did not like him. They shouted loudly at him, and in turn he growled back at them. They were afraid to go into the wood at night in case they met the wolf. Some nights they could hear him howling but they were just as afraid when it was quiet because they did not know where he was. Before it got dark they used to shut their doors and put shutters on their windows so that the wolf could not get them. The people of Gubbio did not get on with the wolf at all.

Early one morning there came a man dressed in a brown robe. He looked very poor. For a belt he had a piece of rope. He was called Francis. (Let us say Francis.) Francis loved animals. He spoke to the birds and once preached a sermon to them (explain). Francis noticed a lot of the houses had their doors locked and their windows blocked out. He wondered what the people were afraid of. He had no money and he begged for some food. Often people gave him crusts or the food they were going to throw away. Whilst he was eating some bread, he asked what the people were frightened of. They told him about the wolf of Gubbio. They told him how it growled and how they threw sticks and stones at it. They often shouted at it to scare it away. Francis said he would go into the forest and try to find it and make friends with it. The people said it was very dangerous but Francis set off.

He had to look for a long time in the forest. He went right into where it was dark. Suddenly Francis heard a big growl. (Let us make a big growl. No, it was bigger and fiercer than that. Let us do it again.) The wolf thought it would frighten Francis but he spoke to it in a quiet voice and offered it a little of the food he was given. At first the wolf would not come. So Francis put some food down for it and moved away. The wolf could not understand because no one had ever been kind to it. Francis spoke to it gently with a friendly voice. He did not shout at it. He got it to eat some food from his hands. He stroked it and made friends with it.

As it was beginning to get dark, the people of Gubbio thought that perhaps the wolf had eaten Francis. Suddenly someone saw him coming out of the forest and following him like a dog was the big bad wolf. At first people were frightened but Francis persuaded them to care for the wolf, to feed it and not to shout at it. Because they did this the wolf of Gubbio became friendly and did not steal chickens, ducks or lambs. Everyone thought that Francis was brave and wise; that he was a man of God. They said Francis was a saint.

Activity

On the worksheet there is a stained-glass window with Francis and the wolf for colouring.

Prayer

God, we are happy that Francis was kind
to the birds and the wolf.
Help us to be kind to the birds and to all animals.
May we not do anything to hurt them.
Amen.

Song

Come on and shine

LAMPS

Aim

To tell the story of St Cuthbert and the ravens.

Teaching

Once, a long time ago, there was a very holy man called Cuthbert. (Let us say 'Cuthbert' together.) What do you call a holy person? A saint. But usually they are not called saints until after they died. Do you know the names of any saints? (Talk about any saints they know the names of, especially the patron saint of the church.)

Cuthbert had lived on a very busy little island called Lindisfarne. From there he went out to teach about God and then came back to look after the brothers in the monastery where he lived (explain).

After about 12 years Cuthbert wanted to spend more time alone with God. He got permission to go to a very small island called Farne where he could live by himself. Some of the brothers took him in a boat and left him. Cuthbert planted his own crops, built his own house, and talked to the eider ducks that lived on the island. He spent a lot of time praying and speaking to God.

On the island there had been a pair of ravens for a long time. (Explain how they are large black birds.) When they saw the straw that Cuthbert had used to make a roof over his house, they thought it was wonderful. It was just what they were looking for to repair their nest. Cuthbert saw them come and take some of the straw from his roof and then some more, and he was not amused. He tried to wave them away but they would not go. He shouted, 'Shoo, shoo', but they ignored him and pulled at the straw. Cuthbert then shouted, 'In the name of Jesus Christ, go away and do not stay in this place you are damaging.' They immediately flew away. But as they left, it made Cuthbert sad. He had been greedy and was not willing to share. Really he could have spared a bit of straw for the birds. He wished he could get them back. Three days later one raven returned whilst Cuthbert was digging. Its wings drooped and it croaked in a strange way. Cuthbert thought it wanted to be friends and to return to the island. Cuthbert was kind to it and shared with it. After a while it flew off and Cuthbert felt sad. About two hours later it returned with its mate. They had come back to stay. The second bird was flying slowly because it was carrying a large piece of pig's fat that it dropped at Cuthbert's feet. Whenever Cuthbert told anyone this story he produced a large piece of pig's fat and offered to grease the visitors' shoes for them. Cuthbert also showed them the ravens' nest but asked them not to disturb the birds.

Activity

Act out the story of Cuthbert and the ravens, with two children being the ravens.

There is also a chance to design a Cuthbert window.

On the worksheet there are various names of saints to be found in a wordsearch, and there is a sentence to discover that runs around the border.

Prayer

God, you called Cuthbert to be a holy man
and to care for the birds of Farne Island.
Help us to care for the birds and for all creatures.
May we learn to give ourselves to you.
Amen.

Song

Be holy, be holy

TORCHES

Aim

To look at the symbols of the saints and to see why they are used.

Teaching

Who knows the names of a saint?

Explore what the young people know about the saints and what stories they know.

All sorts of different people have been saints – rich and poor, young and old, scholars and quite simple or ordinary people. What they all had in common was that they loved God and wanted to serve him. Some left their homes and all that they had; others served God in their homes and in the ordinary things they were doing. St Paul says we are all called to be saints – that is, we are to show that we belong to God and that God is with us and works through us. To be a saint we have to try and do what God wants us to and to seek to be the person God made us to be. We can copy the example of saints but God wants us to be ourselves and to give ourselves to him. (Discuss how we can serve God better.)

Because saints are different from each other, when they are drawn or depicted in stained glass they each have certain symbols to show who they are. We shall look at some of these symbols (they are on the worksheet).

Crossed keys are used for the sign of St Peter. The crossed keys are used because Jesus said to Peter, 'I will give you the keys of the kingdom of heaven, and whatever you bind on earth will be bound in heaven, and whatever you loose on earth will be loosed in heaven' (Matthew 16:19).

St Andrew has a cross shaped like an X. It is believed that this was the way he died on a cross.

St James has a scallop shell. This is a symbol for pilgrims and James is the Patron saint of pilgrims.

The Evangelists (Gospel writers) each have their own symbol. Matthew has a man usually writing at a desk with an angel in the background; Mark has a lion; Luke has a bull; John has an eagle. These symbols can be found in Revelation 4:7: 'The first living creature was like a lion, the second living creature like an ox, the third living creature with a face like a human face, and the fourth living creature like a flying eagle.'

St Francis is shown in a brown robe with a white rope belt, and usually has birds, animals and flowers around him.

St Nicholas is shown with three bags of gold that he had given away to three poor young women. Sometimes they are made to look like three golden balls and are used as a sign of pawnbrokers (explain).

St Catherine was shown with a wheel or on a wheel, as a wheel was used to kill her.

Bishops are shown with mitres on their heads. Founders of churches or monasteries are shown with the building in one of their hands. Kings, queens, princes and princesses are shown with crowns on their heads. Writers were often shown with a quill pen.

As each saint showed their own individuality, God wants us to give our gifts and talents to him. Above all, God wants us to give ourselves to him as he gives himself to us.

Activity

If your church has stained-glass windows it would be good to spend some time looking at them and looking for various symbols. If this is not possible, look at some postcards or pictures of stained glass and pick out the symbolism.

There is an opportunity to create a stained-glass window on the worksheet.

Prayer

Father, we rejoice in the saints
and the examples they have put before us.
Help us to learn of your love
and to give our love to you this day and always.
Amen.

Song

O when the saints go marching in

Fourth Sunday before Advent

Sunday between 30 October and 5 November inclusive
For use if the Feast of All Saints was celebrated on 1 November and alternative propers are needed

Aim

To encourage love of God and of each other.

Preparation

Print the summary of the law for everyone to be able to sing (as below).

Opening activity

To the tune 'London's burning' sing the summary of the law as a round.

> You shall love the Lord your God with
> all your heart and all your mind and
> with all your strength! All your strength!
> And love your neighbour, and love your neighbour.

Opening prayer

Lord, you love us with an everlasting love.
We come to give our love to you.
We seek to love you with all our heart, our mind,
our souls and our strength:
to give our whole life to you as you give yourself to us.
Through Jesus Christ your Son who died for us
and rose again to reign with you and the Holy Spirit,
One God for ever.
Amen.

Opening song

Love divine, all loves excelling

Readings

Deuteronomy 6:1-9
Psalm 119:1-8
Hebrews 9:11-14
Mark 12:28-34

Thought for the day

The opening scene is a typical one: religious authorities disputing with one another. So often the Church is seen in dispute with itself, talking about God rather than talking to him.

One of the scribes comes and asks Jesus which is the greatest commandment. The answer Jesus gives is the traditional Jewish answer: 'Hear, O Israel: the Lord your God is one; you shall love the Lord your God with all your heart, and with all your soul, and with all your mind, and with all your strength.' The emphasis is that there is only one God and that God asks us for our love. There is no conflict here: this is a Jewish student bringing a question to a teacher and receiving an answer. Jesus is quoting from Deuteronomy 6:4-5. This is known as the Shema, which is the imperative Hebrew word for 'hear' or 'listen'. So the whole gets its name from the first word. This hearing demands attention and obedience, two things we can often be weak on. It is with this sentence (Deuteronomy 6:4-5) that the service in the synagogue begins every day. 'You shall love the Lord your God' is part of the daily prayers for every Jew.

In this account by Mark, the words 'with all your mind' have been added to the original. As Mark's community contained many Gentiles, it was obviously felt important to offer the mind along with the rest of us. In fact, God wants us to offer our whole self to him in love.

These words were also contained in little leather boxes called phylacteries (Matthew 23:5), which the devout Jew strapped to his hand and his forehead when he was at prayer (Deuteronomy 6:8). In the same way the words were put into a little cylindrical box called the mezzuzah and fixed to every door of a Jewish house. It was to remind them that God was ever with them in their going out and coming in (Deuteronomy 6:9). These were words that they were to keep in their heart, recite to their children and talk about. It would do us well to know them and to practise what they say.

To this first commandment Jesus added another commandment: 'You shall love your neighbour as yourself.' This is a quotation from Leviticus (19:18b). The Jews were to love fellow Jews and allowed to hate Gentiles. Here with Jesus this love is to be all-inclusive and applies to everyone.

Jesus was the first to put these two commandments together and show how they were dependent on each other. St John will say:

> Whoever does not love does not know God, for God is love (1 John 4:8).
>
> God is love and those who abide in love abide in God and God abides in them (1 John 4:16b).
>
> Those who say, 'I love God', and hate their brothers or sisters, are liars; for those who do not love a brother or sister whom they have seen, cannot love God whom they have not seen (1 John 4:20).

Jesus makes these two commandments into one and shows how we cannot love God if we hate any of his creation, and we cannot truly learn to love our neighbours if we do not love God. Very often in this world the love of another human is the way to reveal to us the love of God.

Question time

How can we express our love of God in dealing with the people we meet?

Do we devote our energies, our heart, our soul, our mind and our strength to God? Does God get as much attention as our favourite pastime?

Illustration

My Dearest,

I love you with all my heart.

I think of you every minute of the day.

I would do anything for you. I would swim shark-infested rivers to get to you. I would climb the steepest of mountains. I would travel the whole earth to be with you. I would brave fire and frost, wind and hail to be at your side.

But I cannot see you this week. I was coming tonight but it is too cold and damp for me to bother. Tomorrow I have fitness training and I am out with the lads the day after. I have a new computer game I want to try out on Wednesday, and a match to go to on Thursday. Friday as ever is swimming, and on Saturday the finals are on the television. I would do anything for you but it is a busy week. Sorry.

Keep in touch,
Yours always.

Not what I would call a promising relationship but is this the way we often deal with God and our prayers? Do we really love the Lord with all our heart?

(Extra illustrations can be found in Proper 20.)

Intercessions

Blessed are you, Father, Son and Holy Spirit,
the one and only God:
to you be praise and glory for ever.
We love you, O God, with all our heart, with all our soul,
with all our mind and with all our strength.
We come to give ourselves to you
as you give yourself to us.
Blessed be God for ever.

Father, we give thanks for all who have loved you deeply
and revealed your love to us.
We pray for all who teach from the Scriptures
and for all who preach.
We remember the young in the faith
and pray for their enthusiasm.
We remember also all who have served you
for a long time;
may they still have warm hearts and a living faith.
We ask you to bless all who minister in your name.
May the Church reveal your love and your glory
in the world.
We pray for all who seek to dedicate themselves to you
through baptism, confirmation and ordination.

Silence

God of love and mercy,
hear us as we call to you.

We give thanks for all who have used their minds
to improve and care for our world.
We ask you to guide the work of scientists,
inventors and explorers.
We pray for all who seek to expand our knowledge
and who work on the boundaries of science.
We ask you to give wisdom to all who deal with
genetic engineering in humans and in plants.
We pray for musicians and artists,
for craftspeople and all who enrich our world.

Silence

God of love and mercy,
hear us as we call to you.

We give thanks for our homes
and all places where we have learnt of love.
We ask your blessing upon our families and friends.
We pray for all who feel unloved and unwanted,
for the neglected
and all who suffer from violence or cruelty.

Silence

God of love and mercy,
hear us as we call to you.

We give thanks for our talents and abilities
and we remember before you
all whose powers are waning
or who feel that they cannot cope with life.
We pray for all who are weakened
by illness or circumstance,
all who are deeply in debt.
We ask your blessing upon those who feel unfulfilled
or thwarted in leading a meaningful and joyful life.

Silence

God of love and mercy,
hear us as we call to you.

We give thanks that you love us with an everlasting love.
When we forget you, you do not forget us.
We rejoice in the promise of life eternal
and remember in your presence
the saints who gave themselves fully to you.
We pray for all our loved ones who are departed from us.

Silence

Merciful Father,
accept these prayers
for the sake of your Son,
our Saviour Jesus Christ.
Amen.

Memory verse

You shall love the Lord your God with all your heart, and with all your soul, and with all your mind, and with all your strength.
Mark 12:30

Suggested music

Father, we love you
A new commandment
Father, Lord of all creation

CANDLES

Aim

To encourage the children to show their love to God and to their parents.

Teaching

Once upon a time there were two pretty kittens and they were given to a brother and sister. The girl's kitten was forever saying 'thank you' and showing its love. If she fed it, it sang to her. What is the sound it would make? It would purr. Let us all make the sound together.

(Purr.) If she stroked it, again it would purr. (Get the children to make the sound.) If she cuddled it, it would make a lovely sound. (Purr.)

The other kitten did not think it was necessary to purr. The boy ought to feed me. He ought to stroke me. He should be giving me a cuddle. The boy did all these things but the kitten did not purr. It did not make a sound. After a long time of caring for the silent kitten, he started to cuddle his sister's kitten. Immediately it purred. He stroked it and it purred. He liked being with his sister's kitten because it showed you when it was happy and it sang 'thank you' when it was fed. He knew this kitten loved them but he was not sure of his own little kitten. He wanted to love it but he did not know if it loved him. It was lucky that the kitten soon realised what was wrong. It had failed to say 'thank you' or to appreciate that it was loved and cared for. It listened to the other kitten and it learnt to sing. It sang when it got its supper, it sang when it was cuddled, it sang when it was stroked. You could hear a wonderful sound all through the house, a sound that made the boy very happy. Let us make that sound.

Now, it is good to remember that our mothers and fathers look after us and love us. We must learn to say 'thank you' to them. To say 'thank you' for our meals and for their love and care. We do not want to be like the selfish kitten. We should tell our parents we love them and say 'thank you' for what they do for us.

God gave us a wonderful world to live in. He loves our parents and us. He wants us to show we love him. How can we do that? We could purr! But God made kittens to purr; he wants us to show we love him by coming to him in our prayers and by caring for his world and other people. Let us say together, 'Thank you, God, for loving us.'

We are not to live like the selfish kitten, so let us make a reminder to take home. It says on one side, 'Love God', and on the other, 'Love each other'. Let us say, 'Love God' together. Again. Now let us say, 'Love each other.' Again. Good, now let us say them one after the other: 'Love God. Love each other.'

Activity

There is a tag to make. The words are in outline. Let the children colour the words and then decorate the heart with glitter or with sticky stars (obtainable from most stationers).

Play musical statues. The children are to run around knowing God loves them. When the music stops they are to stand absolutely still; anyone who moves is pointed at and says, 'God loves me'. If they can say it, they stay in. (The youngest members may need to be encouraged to say it.) This is not an elimination game but one to help them to know and verbally express the love of God.

Prayer

God our Father,
we thank you for loving us.
We give you our love with all our heart.
Amen.

Song

Father, we adore you

LAMPS

Aim

To learn the text of Deuteronomy 6:4-5 by singing it.

Teaching

In a Jewish home every boy and girl learnt a bit of the Scripture off by heart and they learnt to say it every day. The same words were in little cylinders on every door of their house and on their gates. Whenever they went into the house or left it they would touch the little cylinder called a mezzuzah and remember the words. We will make our own mezzuzah and take it home to help us remember the words. These are the words: 'Hear, O Israel: the Lord is our God, the Lord alone. You shall love the Lord your God with all your heart, and with all your soul and with all your might.'

We will write the words out and then roll them up. To help us to remember them we will sing them. We will sing them as they were said by Jesus in St Mark 12:30. You may notice an addition to the words. We are to love God with our mind, and that means thinking about what we are doing and saying. Let us read together the words. Now we will listen to the tune and then sing them. We could try and sing it as a round. Now we can put some actions to it.

Love the Lord your God
(Make the shape of a heart using both your hands starting from above your head, almost touching the top of your head)
with all your heart,
(Place both hands on your heart)
with all your mind.
(Point fingers with both hands and touch your head)
Love the Lord your God
(Make the shape of a heart)
with all your strength.
(Do strong person act by flexing muscles)
Love the Lord
(Make the shape of a heart)
with all your heart.
(Place both hands on your heart)
Love the Lord
(Make the shape of a heart)
with all your strength.
(Flex muscles)

Let us see who can say these words. If we look at the words Jesus said in Mark 12:30 there is something missing from the song. We are to love God with our soul. We are to love him with our whole being – body, mind and spirit.

Activity

Make a mezzuzah to put up at home.

Prayer

Lord our God, you are the only God
and we love you with all our heart,
with all our mind and with all our strength
today and every day.
Amen.

Song

Love the Lord your God

TORCHES

Aim

To explore giving our whole being to God.

Teaching

We cannot love to command. If you are told you will love such and such, you would not be able to do it to order. But you can learn to love. In the summary of the law we are meant to discover that our relationship with God and our relationship with each other is not about rule-keeping but about love. This is a relationship not of force but of the desire and longing of our whole being. Like most things in life, if we are to become experts in loving, we have to practise each day. The summary of the law is a good place to start. 'You shall love the Lord your God with all your heart, and with all your soul, and with all your mind, and with all your strength. You shall love your neighbour as yourself. There is no other commandment greater than these' (Mark 12:30-31).

Love is learning to give our whole self to God and to each other. So often both God and the people we meet do not get our undivided attention. (Ask the group to give examples.)

Where our heart is, there will our attention be. Do we seek to give our self to God each day in love? The heart is about obedience as much as loving. It is about not doing anything that would harm or distress our beloved. We need to keep our hearts true to our loved ones.

To love God with our soul is to give our whole being to him. God does not just seek prayers. He does not only look for obedience: he looks for our love as expressed in how we live and react.

Sadly some people never seem to grow in the faith. They have beliefs that are acceptable for little children but not for grown people. We should see that all our learning and experience helps us to know and love our God better. The mind, like the heart, is easily distracted and we need to centre it each day on the presence of our God and his love.

Sometimes people give the impression that God is not interested in the world or our physical being. That is to deny that God made us and loves us. God made the world, God made us. God is deeply involved in the material that makes up our world. God does not just want our spirits; he wants all of us to be offered to him in love, including our bodies and our strengths, our talents and our energies. If we do not use our strengths to express our love for God, it is likely they will lead us away from God.

If we exclude our heart, our mind, our soul (whole being), our strength from our love and adoration, then we have become divided in our worship. There is always the danger that worship is limited to the mind or the emotions: true worship must be greater and include our whole being.

In learning to love God with our whole being, we begin to know that our whole being is loveable. It is only when we are able to love ourselves that we can truly love others! (Discuss.)

Activity

Split the group into twos and ask them to give each other their undivided attention for a minute. In that time ask one to talk about something they like doing. Then get the listener to speak and the first speaker to listen for a minute. Let them be honest about wandering attention. There is a worksheet to be filled in about how we express our love to God.

Prayer

God, we rejoice in your love for us.
We seek to love you with our whole being:
with our heart, our mind, our soul and our strength.
As you love each of us
help us to learn to love you better
and to love each other.
Amen.

Song

God is love: his the care

Third Sunday before Advent

Aim

To show that God calls each of us and we all have an opportunity to answer that call.

Preparation

Make a notice for the entrance saying: 'The church needs Andrews to get it moving.' Posters concerning vocations would be useful.

Opening activity

Voice 1 Jesus chose fishermen and shepherds.
Voice 2 So that he could get people into the kingdom by hook or by crook.
Voice 3 Jesus chose fishermen who were used to seeking out and landing their catch.
Voice 4 So that they could seek out the lost and the straying and bring them to Jesus.
Voice 1 Andrew spent much time bringing people to Jesus, and so the kingdom grew.
Voice 2 When did you last bring someone to Jesus?
Voice 3 How can the church grow without your help?
Voice 4 Bring someone to church with you next week.

Opening prayer

God, as you have called us,
make us worthy of our calling.
May we be the people you want us to be
and do the things that you want us to do.
Help us to reach out in love to others
and so bring them to be aware of you and your love.
Amen.

Opening song

I, the Lord of sea and sky (Here I am, Lord)

Readings

Jonah 3:1-5, 10
Psalm 62:5-12
Hebrews 9:24-28
Mark 1:14-20

Thought for the day

The Sea of Galilee is 13 miles long by 8 miles across at its widest from east to west. St Luke never calls it a sea but only a lake. The Sea of Galilee lies in the rift of the Jordan valley and is 680 feet below sea level. The Jordan flows into it in the north and out in the south going towards the Dead Sea. In the days of Jesus, Josephus, who was governor of Galilee for a while, tells us that there were about 330 fishing boats that sailed Galilee. Galilee had at least nine populous towns. Bethsaida, the home of Andrew, Peter, James and John, meant 'the house of nets'; another had the name of Tarichaea, the place of salt fish. People ate little meat and fish was their staple diet. Fish was salted to keep it fresh and it was exported from Galilee to Jerusalem and Rome.

There were three modes of fishing. The first used line, hook and bait. The second was with a drag net that had ropes at the four corners and was dragged behind a boat, or, more often, behind two boats. The third method was a casting net which was circular and up to about nine feet across. This net was skilfully cast from the shore or from a boat in shallow waters. It was a casting net that Simon and Andrew were using as Jesus passed along the shore.

Mark gives the impression of a call from out of nowhere, but if we read John 1:35-40 we discover Jesus had contact with the fishermen before today.

Jesus had talked to them. They had listened. What Jesus wanted now was not discussion but reaction. At this moment it was time for the talking to stop and for them to answer his call. Very often when God or Jesus calls, man stalls. See the story of Jonah. The first time God called Jonah and asked him to go east towards Iraq, Jonah set off in the opposite direction and went west towards Spain. If we turn a deaf ear to the call, it does get harder to hear, yet God still calls each of us. Vocation is not for some people only; God has a calling for everyone.

Fish must have often escaped and slipped through the net of the disciples. They often went out and caught nothing. Sometimes they must have seen great storms and thought, like the Breton fishermen, 'Lord, the sea is so large and our boat is so small.' Jesus wanted men who had learnt patience and perseverance, who were courageous and who knew the right time to 'fish'. Jesus wanted them to use their expertise and their talents in his service. The word Mark likes using, and he uses it about the reaction of Simon, Andrew, James and John, is 'immediately' . . . they followed him. If we put off following Jesus, it gets harder to do it later. There are times when we must be aware of the immediacy of the call.

Question time

Are we aware that God calls each of us? TEAM-work means **T**o **E**ach **A** **M**inistry. Are you fulfilling yours?

What prevents us from hearing God's call and obeying it?

Illustration

The need to react to God's call is caught well in Shakespeare's *Julius Caesar*, Act IV:

> There is a tide in the affairs of men,
> Which, taken at the flood leads on to fortune;
> Omitted, all the voyage of their life
> Is bound in shallows and in miseries.
> On such a full sea we are now afloat,
> And we must take the current when it serves,
> Or lose our ventures.

Fortunately, our God will call us again and again. There is a time when we have to stop talking about Christ and set out to follow him.

Jesus calls us, whoever we are.

There was once a very ordinary man (if there is such a being) called Aeshines, who came to Socrates and said, 'I am a poor man. I have nothing to give you but myself.'

Socrates replied, 'Do you not see that you are giving me the most precious thing of all?'

Jesus wants the gift of ourselves far more than talk and theory. Will we truly seek to follow him?

Intercessions

Blessed are you, Lord our God,
for you have called us out of darkness
into your most glorious light.
In calling us, you give our lives direction and purpose:
you offer us the opportunity
to reveal your love and your presence to the world.
Blessed are you, Father, Son and Holy Spirit,
one God now and for ever.

Lord, we give thanks that you have called us
to know you and love you.
Keep our ears open to your call
and our hearts open to your love.
Bless, O Lord, each in their vocation,
that every life may be filled
with purpose and meaning through you.
We remember all who have never heard or known you,
all who feel that life is empty or without purpose.
We ask you to guide all who preach
and teach of your presence.
We pray for all who feel thwarted in their vocations
by circumstance or illness;
may they know that God still calls them where they are.
We pray for the Mission to Seafarers
and all who care for those who work on the sea.

Silence

Lord you have called us:
help us to fulfil our calling.

We give thanks for all who are called
to govern and guide the nations of the world.
We ask your blessing on Elizabeth our queen
and on all in authority.
We pray for all who are called
to bring peace and maintain peace throughout the world,
especially any who are risking their lives for others.
We pray for the work of the United Nations.
We remember before you all who work upon the sea,
fishermen and merchant seamen,
all who are crewing lifeboats and who are coastguards.

Silence

Lord you have called us:
help us to fulfil our calling.

We give thanks for those who have taught us
of you and your love,
for those who have guided us in awareness of you.
We ask your blessing upon our homes,
our families and friends.
May we reveal your glory in our lives.
We remember all who are called to be parents
and ask your blessing upon them and their children.
We pray for any who feel unable to cope
with their families or with relationships.

Silence

Lord you have called us:
help us to fulfil our calling.

Holy and strong One, we remember before you
all who suffer from weakness or illness,
all who suffer from being handicapped
or restricted in their lives.
May they know that you love them
and continue to call them.
We ask your blessing on all who are called to work
in hospitals, surgeries and health centres.
We pray for friends and loved ones who are ill.

Silence

Lord you have called us:
help us to fulfil our calling.

Lord, you call us to yourself and to life eternal.
May we learn to enjoy you and our calling
this day and for ever.
We rejoice in the fellowship of all your saints.
We pray for our friends and loved ones
who are departed from us.
May we with them have a share in your eternal kingdom.

Silence

Merciful Father,
accept these prayers
for the sake of your Son,
our Saviour Jesus Christ.
Amen.

Memory verse

Follow me and I will make you fish for people.
Mark 1:17

Suggested music

Will you come and follow me
Jesus calls us: o'er the tumult
Jesus calls us here to meet him

CANDLES

Aim

To know that Jesus called the disciples and he calls us too.

Teaching

Jesus wanted people to help him to tell about God and his love. He needed people who would not give up, even when it was hard; people who were not afraid to work. He thought of some of the fishermen who worked on the Sea of Galilee. They were used to trying to catch fish, they did not give up, they worked hard and they were often very patient. They were not scholars or book men, they were not priests or holy men, but they were ordinary working men. Jesus thought it would be good if they would follow him.

Jesus went down to the seaside. It was in the morning and the fishermen were still busy. Andrew and Simon were still trying to catch fish. (Let us say their names: Andrew and Simon.) They had a net and they were throwing it into the sea and pulling it in. They were hoping to catch more fish, for they did not easily give up. They looked up and saw Jesus. He knew them and said to them, 'Follow me, and I will make you fish for people.'

Immediately, without asking any questions, they left their nets and followed Jesus. Now Jesus had two helpers. What were they called? (Andrew and Simon.)

A little further down the beach there was a group of fishermen with a large boat. There was a man called Zebedee. (Let us say it together: Zebedee.) He had two sons working with him and at this moment they were mending the nets. They had a special needle and some rope and were repairing the large hole in their net. There was also some men who worked with Zebedee. Jesus called to the ones he knew, James and John. (Let us say these names: James and John.) 'James and John, come and follow me.' Immediately they left their father Zebedee and the workmen and followed Jesus. Now he had four followers Andrew and Simon, James and John. (Let us say their names together: Andrew and Simon, James and John.) They were the first followers of Jesus.

Jesus still needs people to help him. He needs young people and old people. He wants them to bring others to him and show them how he loves them. He needs people who know him to follow him and tell others about him. We know the names of four disciples. Can we add our name to the followers of Jesus?

Activity

Cut fish out of card and put a paper clip on each fish. Cut a few people out of card and put a paper clip on their head. Divide the group into teams and give them a fishing rod that has a magnet on the end or a hook made from a paper clip. The idea is to transfer a fish from one end of the room to another and then to bring back a card person. (Each team will need at least two fish and two card people – and a monitor who continuously transfers the fish and people to the right end of the room.) The winning team is declared 'Champion Fishers of People'.

Prayer

Lord Jesus, I want to follow you.
I want to be a fisher of people.
I want to tell others that you love us all.
Amen.

Song

Fisherman Peter on the sea,
drop your net, boy, and follow me.

You may like to add the following verses:

Andrew, his brother plain to see,
leave your net, lad, and follow me.

James and John, sons of Zebedee,
stop your mending and follow me.

LAMPS

Aim

To know Jesus calls disciples to help him in his work.

Teaching

Have you ever had a hard job to do that you cannot do alone? What do you do then? Yes, you would get friends to help you. Sometimes we need the help of friends (Let the group offer examples.) There are lots of games you cannot play by yourself: you need a team of people and you have to be part of the team (Again, get examples).

Jesus wanted the whole world to know about the love of God. But he could not do it on his own. He needed friends who would get to know him and tell other people about him. He needed some followers. He could go to the temple and look for priests but he wanted to show that God called ordinary people and that he wanted people in ordinary jobs to know him and speak of him. Jesus thought of some of the people who had come to listen to him and to talk to him. He thought about some of the fishermen from the Sea of Galilee and thought if they would follow him it would be great. They would make good strong members of his team.

Jesus went down to the seashore and the first people he saw were Andrew and his brother Simon. Jesus would later give Simon a nickname. Jesus called him Peter, which means 'Rocky'. Let us call him Peter. Andrew and Peter were still fishing. They were using a casting net, throwing it out into the shallow waters and hoping to catch fish. Suddenly they were aware of Jesus watching them. When they looked at him he said, 'Follow me and I make you fishers of people.' How wonderful that Jesus wanted them to help him. They left their net and followed Jesus. They were the first of the followers.

A little further down the beach was a family of fishermen with their workmen. It was Zebedee and his sons James and John. The two young men were mending their nets. Jesus went up to them and invited them to follow him. Immediately James and John left their father and the boat and followed Jesus. Now Jesus had four followers, four disciples. Let us say their names together – A is for Andrew, P is for Peter, J and J is for James and John.

Jesus would choose more disciples. How many were there to start with? Twelve. Do you know their names?

Wouldn't it be great if you were one of the disciples? Well, you are! Jesus has called you to know him and to tell other people about him. Perhaps next week you could bring someone to our group. Just think how the group would grow if we all brought someone. Will you be a fisher of people?

Activity

Make some fish and some people out of newspaper. Then give each team two fish and two people. Give them a magazine to use as a fan. The idea is to place a fish on the floor and waft it over a fixed distance. At the end there is a 'paper person'. Once the person is reached pick up the fish and waft the person back to your team. The next one picks up the person and wafts the fish to the end of the course, picks up the fish and wafts the person back to the team. Everyone in the team takes a turn to waft first the fish and then the person. The first team to finish are the champions.

Prayer

Lord God, open our ears to your call.
May we be ready to work for you,
to bring others to you,
and to show your love to the world.
Lord, help us to be your disciples.

Song

Fisherman Peter on the sea

TORCHES

Aim

To encourage everyone to be part of an active team working for Jesus.

Teaching

Once upon a time there was a group who called themselves fishermen. The waters around them teemed with fish. In fact, the streams, the rivers, the lakes and the seas had fish in abundance. Week by week the fishermen met and talked about different ways of fishing, about their calling to fish, about the abundance of fish in the sea and how they should catch them. They could name the good areas for fishing, they could tell you the gear to use, but they did not go out and use it. They were not really fishermen; they were talkers.

It is no use talking about mission unless we are going to reach out. It is no use talking about discipleship unless we are preparing to follow Jesus.

Jesus had met Andrew and Simon before; most likely he had also already met James and John. Now as he walked along the beach he saw them at work. Jesus was passing by – as he often does – and as he passes he calls, 'Follow me.' Andrew and Simon (whom Jesus called Peter) were casting their nets in the hope of a catch. These were men of action, just what Jesus wanted. They could use their talent to catch *people* from now on. Jesus said to them, 'Follow me and I will make you fish for people.' We are told that 'immediately they left their nets and followed him'. They could not just let Jesus pass by for they had an opportunity of working with him. He would be their teacher and they would be his disciples.

A little further along the shore there were two more fishermen, James and John, friends of Andrew and Simon. They were sitting in their boat mending their nets. Jesus called them by name and they left their father and the hired men in the boat and followed Jesus.

All four fishermen had probably talked about Jesus, even talked to Jesus; now they were leaving everything and following him. We need to stop being talkers and become disciples, workers with Jesus.

Wilfrid Grenfell was a medical student in a London hospital. He was a keen boxer and a rugby player. His ambition was to get a comfortable practice (explain) and then work in Harley Street. One night he went to a circus tent and found it was a religious meeting and the speaker was Moody, the American evangelist seeking to win men for Christ. Grenfell went again the next night and the speaker was the cricketer J. E. Studd. Studd asked all who wanted to follow Christ to stand up. A lad from a training ship stood up. Then Grenfell offered to work for Jesus. He promised to follow Jesus but where would he lead? Grenfell soon became a Sunday school teacher. He also gave boxing lessons. When he was about ready to take on a good practice as a doctor, he heard about the fishermen on the Dogger Bank. He spent the next three years in a mission boat that cared for them. On its wheel was carved, 'Follow me and I will make you fishers of men'. He made his boat a floating hospital, library, rest room and church. Then he heard the call again, this time to Labrador, an ice-bound land that had no church or doctor. He went there to be a fisher of people.

Jesus calls us to be more than listeners: he wants us to be part of his team. Remember if one member of the team is weak it weakens the whole team.

Activity

Let us explore how we can be part of a team that fishes with Jesus. Team = **T**o **E**ach **A** **M**inistry. (Explore this as a reality for the group.) Remember all members of a team need to be active.

On the sheet there are examples of how God calls and people try to stall. There is an invitation to offer ourselves to God.

Prayer

God, we thank you that you have called us
to know you and to love you.
By our example may we bring others
to see your love and give themselves to you.
Amen.

Song

I will always follow Jesus

Second Sunday before Advent

Aim

To know that whatever happens in this world or to us, God is always with us and promises us the victory through Jesus Christ our Lord.

Preparation

Have forecasts of world disasters, pictures of war, flood and famine. Put these up in the entrance to the church. With them, in large letters, have the words, 'Do not be afraid'.

Opening activity

Voice 1 Hi, folks, I am misery Jim. The world will end when a meteorite hits it.
Voice 2 Hi, I am Christian. God says, 'Do not fear, for I have redeemed you.'
Voice 1 Another ice age will destroy all life.
Voice 2 'When you pass through the waters, I will be with you. They will not overwhelm you.'
Voice 1 A massive volcano will cause all life to disappear.
Voice 2 'When you walk through fire you shall not be burned.'
Voice 1 Something awful is bound to happen.
Voice 2 'Do not fear for I am with you.' Victory is ours through him who loves us. Alleluia!

Opening prayer

Though the dawn breaks cheerless on this Isle today,
my spirit walks in a path of light.
For I know my greatness.
Thou hast built me a throne within thy heart.
I dwell safely within the circle of thy care.
I cannot for a moment fall out of thine everlasting arms.
I am on my way to thy glory.

Alistair Maclean, Hebridean Altars

Opening song

All my hope on God is founded

Readings

Daniel 12:1-3
Psalm 16
Hebrews 10:11-14 (15-18) 19-25
Mark 13:1-8

Thought for the day

The dark cold days are about here. It is as if darkness is triumphing over light. It is a time when people easily despair. So often the news of world events or what is happening nearer home does nothing to uplift us. We need to hear the Good News, we need to know that Christ is risen, that God is in control and that life is eternal.

Today's Gospel hardly sounds like Good News. As Jesus came out of the temple, the disciples admired the solidity and largeness of the stones and building. Surely the temple was a symbol of endeavour and lasting achievements. The temple, which Herod built, was one of the wonders of the world. It was begun in about 20 BC and was not completed when Jesus was alive. Josephus tells us that some of the stones were 40 feet long by 12 feet high and 18 feet wide. It was these stones that suggested strength and solidity to the disciples. Jesus, however, saw that they were not 'for ever'; in fact, he prophesied that the stones would all be thrown down and the temple destroyed. Salvation was not found in the temple.

In AD 70 Jerusalem fell after being under siege: over a million people died of starvation and the temple was destroyed. When the Gospel was written, Mark could have known this fact. This does not detract from the conversation of Jesus on the Mount of Olives; if anything, it enhances his prophecy.

It is too easy to trust in things we think will last when only God is eternal. All sorts will lead us astray promising us youth, fitness, peace, life: yet all these are dependent on God alone. False Christs abound, promising quick deliverance – beware. The world is in the grip of the evil one. There will be wars and rumours of wars, there will be famines. There will be all sorts of pain and suffering. You cannot escape them in this world. But these are only the beginning of the birth pangs of the new age, the new kingdom that is dawning. We may feel we are losing battle after battle (and this sadly can be true) but the final victory is assured us in Christ Jesus our Lord. Think again on the words from the hymn 'All my hope on God is founded':

> Human pride and earthly glory,
> sword and crown betray his trust;
> what with care and toil he buildeth,
> tower and temple fall to dust.
> But God's power, hour by hour,
> is my temple and my tower.

Our trust is not to be in any man-made thing, not even in the Church or prayer; our trust is to be in God alone. In the words of Julian of Norwich, 'He did not say, "You shall not be tempest-tossed, you shall not travail; you shall not be distressed." But he said, "You shall not be overcome."' It is this trust in God that made Julian to understand these words the Lord spoke to her:

> I shall make all things well.
> I may make all things well,
> and I can make all things well;
> and you shall see yourself that all things shall be well.

No matter how dark the days, the Light of Christ is with us: we are never alone or left in the dark. Victory is ours through him who loves us.

Question time

What are some of the false Christs that we are tempted to follow?

Do we understand that salvation is in God alone and in him victory is assured?

Illustration

When you go to an airport there are two places with frightening names. There is the 'departure lounge' and the 'terminal'. One is for those who are departing from us and the other is where it all ends! Well, you could look at it that way. Sometimes the departure lounge is a sad place because we are seeing people off whom we might not see again for a long time. But usually it is full of excited people who are going on holiday or going somewhere special. When we come to the terminal, it is not that we are going to stop there. It can be where all traffic is halted but we are going on to a better place. We are not going to stop at the terminal.

I tell you this because Jesus was talking about the end of the world, as we know it. He was pointing out that there are certain signs that point us towards what seems to be the end. But for us it is the beginning of something new. All the troubles are but the birth pangs of the coming of the kingdom. It is easy to quake with fear when we do not know what lies ahead. But we do know who is waiting to meet us. We may fear that we are losing round after round of the battle but in Christ Jesus we are assured the victory will be ours. The terminal will be where we move on to a better kingdom.

Intercessions

Blessed are you, Lord our God.
You never leave us or forsake us.
You have promised us the victory
through our Lord Jesus Christ.
Lord, help us to know you and to trust in you always.
Let us know that in you is the gift of life eternal
and that through you we have the power
to survive whatever happens to us or to the world.
Blessed are you, God Almighty,
Father, Son and Holy Spirit.

We give thanks for those who have taught us the faith
and brought us to know you, O God.
We ask your blessing on preachers
and teachers of the Word,
upon theological colleges and their students.
We remember any who are struggling with their faith
at this time,
all who are tempted to despair and to give up.
We pray especially for all who are sorely troubled
by circumstances or relationships.

Silence

Lord, in our darkness,
let your light shine.

As we give thanks for the world and its beauty,
we remember before you all areas of conflict and disaster.
We ask your blessing upon all who are suffering
from natural disasters such as flood or famine,
all who are driven off their land by war or tyranny.
We pray for all who are denied minimum rights and wages
and those who live as slaves.
We ask your blessing on all who work
for the good of the world and humankind.

Silence

Lord, in our darkness,
let your light shine.

We give thanks for our homes and our loved ones.
We pray for all families who are suffering
from a breakdown in relationships,
where there is tension and discord,
where there is violence or neglect.
We ask your blessing upon all who are seeking
to improve the neighbourhood in which they live.
We pray for counsellors and carers.

Silence

Lord, in our darkness,
let your light shine.

We rejoice in your love and care for us at all times.
We remember before you
all who have faced trouble or disaster this week.
We ask your blessing upon those who are ill
and whose illness finds no cure;
on all who have been injured in accidents
or who have suffered at the hands of others.
We pray especially for those whose future looks bleak
and who live in fear.

Silence

Lord, in our darkness,
let your light shine.

We give thanks for your everlasting love.
We rejoice in the saints who have witnessed to you
and to their faith in life eternal.
We remember friends and loved ones
who have departed from us
and pray that they may rejoice
in the fullness of your love
and their presence in your kingdom.

Silence

Merciful Father,
accept these prayers
for the sake of your Son,
our Saviour Jesus Christ.
Amen.

Memory verse

You show me the path of life; in your presence there is fullness of joy, and in your right hand are pleasures for evermore.
Psalm 16:11

Suggested music

Do not be afraid
God moves in a mysterious way
Lord, the light of your love (Shine, Jesus, shine)

CANDLES

Aim

To show that whatever happens God is with us and loves us.

Teaching

Where have all the leaves gone off the trees? Where have all the flowers gone? Some have blown away, some have become fruit and some have been burnt on the bonfire. If you went to a firework display, what did you like the best? Some fireworks went right into the sky with sparkles and sounds. What were they called? Rockets. Then some made big bangs and threw flames in the air before they went out. None of them lasted for hours. Some things do not last long at all, like pocket money or chocolates. Can you tell me some other things that do not last?

Some things seem to last a very long time. Perhaps you have travelled a long way in a train, a car, a boat or an aeroplane. Some journeys seem to go on for ever but they do come to an end. Everything has an end – well, nearly everything. (You might like to spend some time with this. Children are not usually bothered about endings, not even life's end.) Sometimes we get warnings that things are coming to an end. The smoke alarm peeps when its batteries are running low. There is a road sign that says the road comes to an end.

Jesus said that when the world was coming to an end we would see signs. Bad things could be happening, like wars, famines and floods. People could be doing wicked things. But Jesus said we are not to worry because we are not coming to the end. This is when we are going to go somewhere better because God loves us and Jesus invites us to be with him in his kingdom. God and Jesus go on for ever; they do not come to an end. They love us and their love will not come to an end. They will love us always and for ever. So we know that love will not end, and we know that, because God loves us, we will not come to the end. Let us say together; 'God is with us and loves us for ever.' Let us say it again and say, 'Alleluia' after we say it. 'God is with us and loves us for ever. Alleluia.'

Activity

At the beginning of the session play 'Jenga' or use dominoes to build as high as possible without it falling down. Then gently remove certain dominoes near the bottom without it toppling. The one who causes it to topple is out.

Prayer

God, we thank you that you are always with us,
that you love us and care for us.
We give our love to you.
Amen.

Song

Jesus' love is very wonderful

LAMPS

Aim

To affirm that whatever happens our God is with us and cares for us.

Teaching

Begin by looking at the signs on the worksheet. Talk about warning signs, such as on a bottle of poison or a packet of cigarettes. Why are the signs there? They are for our benefit and the safety of us all. Signs are to tell us of danger and to help us to escape from running into trouble. Signs are about what lies ahead but at the moment they may be hidden from us – like the sign for a dangerous bend in the road or for bumps in the road.

When Jesus was with his disciples in Jerusalem they looked at the large stones of the temple and thought they would last for ever. Jesus warned them that the temple would not last for ever and that the stones would all be pulled down. He then told them of all sorts of troubles that were coming. There would be wars and rumours of wars, there would be famine and earthquakes, and many of the disciples would face persecution and rejection. It sounded very sad and dangerous. But Jesus wanted them to know that this was not the end, not even signs of the end; they were signs of a new beginning. Terrible things might happen but the disciples were not to be frightened because God still cared and God was still in control. Maybe evil was trying to win because all the powers of evil knew that they would finally be defeated by the love and power of God.

Jesus said that all the pain and troubles were only the signs that God's kingdom was being born. When a woman gives birth to a baby, the birth usually causes her much pain, but the pain is a sign that the baby is being born and she puts up with the pain for the joy of the birth that is happening. She is willing to suffer so that she might enjoy the fact that she has a child. Jesus said we should realise that the pains and troubles of the world are signs of a new birth and the coming of the kingdom of God.

Activity

Look at the various warning signs on the worksheet and create a new warning sign about something you are concerned about.

Prayer

God, we thank you for your love and protection.
Whatever happens in this world
you still love us and care for us.
Help us to know your power
and to be aware of your presence.
Amen.

Song

We are marching along in the power of God

TORCHES

Aim

To show that God is our maker, friend and protector.

Teaching

Julian of Norwich was born in the fourteenth century. It was a time of war with France. The Black Death was killing lots of people. It was a time of trouble and fear for many. When she was 30 years old and very ill she had a series of visions about the love of God. These visions helped her to realise that whatever happened God is in control and that God loves us. Julian lived until she was about 74 and saw four different kings on the throne of England. This is part of one of her visions:

> He showed me a little thing, the size of a hazelnut, in the palm of my hand, and it was as round as a ball. I looked at it with my mind's eye and I thought, 'What can this be?' And the answer came, 'It is all that is made.' I marvelled that it could last, for I thought it might have crumbled to nothing, it was so small. And the answer came into my mind, 'It lasts and ever shall because God loves it.' And all things have their being through the love of God.
>
> In this I saw three truths. The first is that God made it. The second is that God loves it. The third is that God looks after it.
>
> From *Enfolded in Love: Daily Readings with Julian of Norwich*, edited by Robert Llewelyn

Explore the ideas of this vision with the group. If possible, have a hazelnut and use it as the words are said. Get the group to explore the truths of God as creator of all things, as loving all things and as the protector of all things. Make sure they learn he made each of them, loves them and cares for them. It is good for every member of the group to say, 'God made me. God loves me. God cares for me.'

In today's Gospel, Jesus warns the disciples of coming troubles. Even the beautiful temple in Jerusalem will be destroyed. There would be wars and rumours of wars, there would be earthquakes and famines. But the disciples were not to be over-alarmed, as all of this was just the beginning of the new age, the beginning of God's kingdom coming. Jesus wanted them to know that whatever happened God was with them and loved them. Though we may not know what lies ahead, we know who is with us and cares for us.

Activity

On the sheet there is an opportunity for each one to make signs to show that God is our creator, our friend and our protector. In this there should be some opportunity to show that life is eternal through Christ our Lord.

Prayer

Lord our God, we thank you
that you have made the world and all that is in it.
We rejoice in your love and protection.
Help us to trust in you
and to know you are with us always.
Amen.

Song

We are marching in the light of God

Christ the King

Aim

To show that Christ is King and seeks to rule in our hearts.

Preparation

In the entrance have a golden crown and a crown of thorns. You may like to add the words: 'The head that once was crowned with thorns is crowned with glory now.'

Opening activity

Play the 'Hallelujah Chorus' from Handel's *Messiah*. You could ask the congregation to stand for this and clap when it is finished. You may like to announce, 'In a world that seems out of control, where evil appears to win, Christ is our King and triumphs over all.' This is a good day to sing the Te Deum (in procession with the children waving flags and playing instruments, perhaps): at least sing the verses that begin, 'You, Christ, are the King of Glory, the eternal Son of the Father.'

Opening prayer

God our Father, you created the world out of your love
and redeemed the world
through the love of Christ our King.
Give us grace to welcome Christ into our lives
and allow him to reign in our hearts,
that we may be one with him in his glorious kingdom.
We look forward to the time
when the kingdoms of the world
will become the kingdom of Christ our Lord.
Through Jesus Christ our Lord
who lives and reigns with you and the Holy Spirit,
one God for ever and ever.
Amen.

Opening song

Jesus is Lord

Readings

Daniel 7:9-10, 13-14
Psalm 93
Revelation 1:4b-8
John 18:33-37

Thought for the day

Jesus is brought before Pilate on charges of sedition, but Jesus does not look like a leader of a serious revolution. (How wrong Pilate was!) Jesus looks far more like a peasant. As yet the charge had not been made, so Pilate questions the prisoner: 'Are you the King of the Jews?' The question is asked with a tone of derision, implying that he surely could not be. Pilate cannot accept the idea. Jesus replies by asking how Pilate has come to ask this, as this was not the charge against him. Who had suggested this to him? 'Do you ask this on your own, or did others tell you about me?'

Pilate shows contempt for the Jews: he is not one of this despised race but a Roman, whereas Jesus is a Jew and his own people have brought him to this. He can hardly be their leader. 'What have you done?'

In reply Jesus talks of his kingdom that is not of this world. Not of this world's way of thinking or acting. If it were, his disciples would surely be fighting to rescue him. But a kingdom of love cannot use force to gain its ends. It is love that will keep Jesus on this track and on the cross, not weakness or lack of power. The kingdom of Jesus is the one that captures hearts and wills.

Pilate does not understand this talk of other-worldly kingdom and asks, 'So you are a king?' To this Jesus cannot answer because of Pilate's limited idea of kingship, which involves power used to force people and to control people. Jesus has changed the whole idea of kingship by becoming the Servant King, and the Suffering Servant at that. Our terms are too limited when it comes to describing the majesty of Jesus. A sad comment comes from the chief priests when they say, 'We have no king but the emperor.' Only too true, for they, like Pilate, have found it impossible to accept Jesus as their king and lord.

Have we allowed Christ to be our King? Do we seek to let him rule in our hearts and wills, or do we let other powers and events control our lives? Let us pray earnestly, 'Your kingdom come, your will be done in us as it is in heaven.'

Question time

Do we allow the rule of Christ to enter our lives by regularly seeking to do his will?

How does the rule of Christ differ from the rule of an earthly king or governor?

Illustration

The school bus is at the top of a steep hill when the driver slumps at the wheel. The bus starts to swerve all over the road and is picking up speed. There is general panic on the bus for it is out of control. Two lads rush forward and move the driver off the seat. A girl grabs the steering wheel and gently applies the brakes. She has never driven before but knows what to do. One minute everything was out of control and the next the busload of children was rescued by the quick thinking and acting of three young people.

The world seems to have a tendency to run out of control; wars and rumours of wars, famine and earthquakes, violence and force seem to take over. Last week's Gospel warned us that these things would happen but that we should see them as the birth pangs of the new age, the coming of God's kingdom. We should celebrate that God is in control, that Christ is our Redeemer and King.

Intercessions

Blessed are you, Lord our God, King of the Universe.
All things are in your control and in your power
for you are almighty.
In the troubles and darkness of our world
help us to know your presence and your love.

May we know that though we are beset by many troubles
we cannot for a moment fall out of the everlasting arms
and that we are on our way to everlasting life
in the fullness of your kingdom.
Blessed are you, almighty and ever loving God,
Father, Son and Holy Spirit.

We rejoice this day that Jesus is the King of kings
and Lord of lords.
We give thanks that through him
we have the victory and triumph
over all that would seek to defeat us.
We pray that your Church may walk with confidence,
trusting in you and your love.
May we reveal your loving care
for the whole of your creation.
We remember Christians who are struggling
to bring peace and love to areas of hatred and strife.
Lord, may each of us seek to do your will.

Silence

Lord, your kingdom come.
Your will be done.

We look forward to the time
when the kingdoms of the world
will become the kingdom of Christ the King.
We remember this day all who are suffering
from tyranny or despotic rulers,
all who suffer through famine or flood.
We pray for any who feel that life is beyond their control
and all who feel utterly helpless.
Lord, bless all who strive to bring freedom and prosperity
to the peoples of the world.

Silence

Lord, your kingdom come.
Your will be done.

We give thanks that you are our guide and helper
in all of life.
We ask your blessing on our homes and our loved ones.
May your kingdom be revealed and your will be done
in all that we do and say.
We pray for families who are suffering at this time
from debt and poverty,
from difficulties in relationships and
from watching a loved one who is ill.

Silence

Lord, your kingdom come.
Your will be done.

We rejoice, O Lord, in your saving power.
We remember before you all who are ill
at home or in hospital,
all who struggle to survive
and all who are oppressed in any way.
We ask your blessing upon all who will find this
a difficult week,
those who will have to face hard decisions
and those who feel they have little or no freedom.

Silence

Lord, your kingdom come.
Your will be done.

We put our trust in you, O God,
and in the promise of the fullness of your kingdom.
We remember before you
all who have departed from this world
and are now at peace with you.
We pray for loved ones and friends who have died.
We rejoice in the fellowship of all the saints
and pray that we may share with them
in your eternal kingdom.

Silence

Merciful Father,
accept these prayers
for the sake of your Son,
our Saviour Jesus Christ.
Amen.

Memory verse

The Lord is king.
Psalm 93:1

Suggested music

O worship the King
Crown him with many crowns
The King of love my shepherd is

CANDLES

Aim

To enjoy the reality of Christ as our King. To use this as a time of checking on what the children know of Jesus.

Teaching

Who knows who is our queen? Where does she usually live? Kings and queens live in palaces and have lots of servants. What else do you know about kings and queens? They have crowns, usually made of gold and jewels. They are usually very rich and tell other people what they must do. Kings and queens are powerful people and make others do what they command.

We have a King who is very different from most kings. He is more powerful but he does not make us do things. He wants us to do things because we love him. Our King was not born in a palace, not even in a house. Who can tell us our King's name? Where was he born? In a stable. And what was the name of the place? Bethlehem. Do you know who came to see Jesus our King when he was a baby? The shepherds and the wise men. When Jesus was a boy, he did not live in a palace but he lived with his mother Mary and with Joseph. Do you know where it was and what Joseph did? It was at Nazareth and Joseph was a carpenter (explain). Jesus grew up in an ordinary home, like you and me.

When Jesus grew up he asked some men to help him. Do you know how many? There were twelve special helpers and they were called disciples. Lots of other people wanted to help because Jesus was so good and loving. The disciples thought if Jesus was powerful they might become very important. Jesus showed them he was a different sort of king. He wanted to serve people. He took a towel and washed the disciples' feet. He wanted them to know he loved them all and wanted them to love others rather than trying to be powerful over them. Jesus was a different sort of king because he was a Servant King. He was always giving himself for others and working for others. If any came to him he did not turn them away; he welcomed them and cared for them. He is the King of love.

Our King had to fight against evil but he did not want to use force; he wanted to win by showing his love. The evil people put him to death. Who knows how Jesus died? He died on a cross and he had a crown on his head but it was not a crown of gold; it was a crown of thorns (explain). After Jesus died he was buried in a cave, but on the third day what happened? Jesus rose again. He was alive and his disciples saw him. Jesus the King had won the battle against evil and death and is alive for ever.

Jesus is our King. He loves us and wants us to be his friend. Jesus wants us to speak to him each day. He wants us to be children of the King and to love him as he loves us.

Activity

Make crowns out of gold paper and add jewels to them. Play 'Pass the crown'. Let it go from head to head. When the music stops, whoever is wearing the crown must say, 'We are children of the King.' Everyone else says, 'Alleluia' and waves their hands. The music starts again and the game continues.

Prayer

Jesus, you are our King.
Help us to love you
and to do what you want us to do.
We know that you love us and care for us.
Amen.

Song

We're the kids of the King

LAMPS

Aim

To accept Christ as our King and to be part of his kingdom.

Teaching

If you live in a kingdom, or a country, you have to live by its rules. If you live in Britain, you drive on the left side of the road. If you cross to France and drive on the left side of the road, you will cause an accident or soon be stopped by the police. In our country, everyone who can must pay taxes to keep the country running properly. There are laws and unless we keep them we will be in trouble. (Ask the children for examples.) A kingdom only continues if people keep its rules. If the rules are broken, the kingdom uses force to keep them or it will break up and not exist.

When Jesus was born there were hints that he was to be a king. The wise men came to Herod and asked, 'Where is he that is born king of the Jews?' Because of this Herod tried to find the baby Jesus to kill him. Herod did not understand that Jesus would be a different kind of king and was not after worldly power. The rule of Jesus was to be one of love.

When Jesus rode into Jerusalem the people wanted to make him king. Because they thought in terms of power and force, Jesus rode in on a donkey and not a war-horse. Jesus did not want to win a kingdom by force but by love. Jesus would not force people to accept him. He wanted them to accept him because they loved him. If there were to be rules, they were about loving God and loving each other.

Jesus could have escaped the cross and the crown of thorns, but he chose out of love to allow this to happen. The cross shows the deep love of Jesus for us all. As the King of love, Jesus was still in control. He was giving himself in love for the whole world.

Jesus rose again to offer us all eternal life. In love he rescued us from death and wants us to share in his kingdom. Even now he wants us to be part of his kingdom of love. Every time we try to love and seek to do what Jesus wants, we are part of his kingdom. Jesus is with us. He is alive and is our King; let us give our love to him. Let us keep a time of quiet and say, 'Jesus my King, I you adore, O make me love you more and more.' (Keep a time of silence and repeat these words two or three times.)

Activity

On the worksheet there is the opportunity to make a card that rejoices in Jesus as King.

Prayer

Jesus, you are our King and our God.
We want to love you and serve you always.
Help us to do your will
and so be part of your kingdom.
Amen.

Song

King of kings

TORCHES

Aim

To rejoice in Christ as King of kings and Lord of lords.

Teaching

Use a concordance and get the group to look up all references to Jesus as king.

St Matthew begins his Gospel by saying Jesus is the Messiah and the son of David, and so tells that Jesus is of royal lineage (Matthew 1:1).

In Matthew 2:2, 'Wise men from the east came to Jerusalem, asking, "Where is the child who has been born king of the Jews?"' Sadly this will cause Herod to seek to kill Jesus, as he does not understand what sort of king Jesus will be. Perhaps the wise men did not understand it very well either, as they were looking in the capital city and in a royal palace. Jesus would be a very different sort of king, as his birth in a stable helps to show. Kings rule by power and force; Jesus would seek to win people by love. Kings are rich and live in palaces; Jesus owns nothing and lives wherever he can lay his head.

Matthew tells of a king again in 21:5: 'Tell the daughter of Zion, look, your king is coming to you, humble and mounted on a donkey.' Kings ride chariots and war-horses; Jesus rides a donkey. Kings come in pomp and power; Jesus comes humbly. Kings force people to do their will; Jesus seeks people to come to him in love.

Pilate asks Jesus, 'Are you the king of the Jews?' (John 18:33; compare Matthew 27:11.) How can Jesus answer when Pilate only understands kings who rule by force and are earthly kings? Pilate is unable to understand when Jesus tells him that his kingdom is not of this world (John 18:36-37). Pilate cannot accept that Jesus is really a king, but he will put over the cross 'This is Jesus, King of the Jews' (Matthew 27:37). Sadly the chief priests' comment is, 'We have no king but the emperor' (John 19:15).

It would seem that love was defeated on the cross and that it was the end for Jesus, but we know he rose again. Listen to how Jesus is described in the book of Revelation 1:5-6: 'Jesus Christ, the faithful witness, the firstborn of the dead, and the ruler of the kings of the earth. To him who loves us and freed us from our sins by his blood, and made us to be a kingdom, priests serving his God and Father, to him be glory and dominion for ever and ever. Amen.' There is no doubt in the writer's mind that Jesus is alive and is King of kings and Lord of lords. Jesus seeks to draw us into his kingdom by his love. Jesus is alive and wants us to work with him and for us to let him work through us. Whatever happens in this world, the promise is that 'Victory is ours through him that loves us' (Romans 8:37, *Good News Bible*). Our God is in control and Christ is King.

Activity

Use a concordance to explore the texts of Jesus as king. If time allows, use the concordance to look at what Jesus says about the 'kingdom of heaven' or 'the kingdom of God'. Get the group to explore ideas of why Jesus is different from earthly rulers.

Prayer

Jesus, we welcome you as our King and Saviour.
Take our hearts and fill them with your love.
Take our minds and work through them.
Take our wills and act through them.
Take our lives and make them yours.
As you give yourself to us, we give ourselves to you,
Christ our King and our God.
Amen.

Song

The King is among us

Acknowledgements

The publishers wish to thank all those who have given their permission to reproduce copyright material in this publication.

Main resource book (Proper 21)
He drew a circle that shut me out –
Rebel, heretic, a thing to flout.
But love and I had the wit to win;
We drew a circle that took him him.
(Edward Markham)

Main resource book (Proper 24)
Second verse of 'Father, we adore you' by Terry Coelho © 1972 CCCM Music/Marantha Music/Administered by Copycare, PO Box 77, Hailsham, BN27 3EF, UK. E-mail: music@copycare.com

Main resource book (Second Sunday before Advent)
Though the dawn breaks cheerless on this Isle today,
my spirit walks in a path of light.
For I know my greatness.
Thou hast built me a throne within Thy heart.
I dwell safely within the circle of thy care.
I cannot for a moment fall out of thine everlasting arms.
I am on my way to thy glory.
(Alistair Maclean, Hebridean Altars, Hodder & Stoughton)

Torches worksheet (Second Sunday of Easter)
First verse of 'Spirit of the living God' by Daniel Iverson.